To John,

, ~eS.

Mallin~

June 2001

German Anglophobia and the Great War, 1914–1918

This is the first major study of German attitudes towards England during the Great War, 1914–18, continuing the story of Anglo-German antagonism where previous studies have ended. In particular it focuses on the extremity of anti-English feeling in Germany in the early years of the war, and on the attempt by writers, propagandists and cartoonists to redefine Britain as the chief enemy of the German people and their cultural heritage.

New material is also offered concerning the development of an extreme rightist network in Munich and Berlin during the war years, which used anti-English feeling as a focus for attacking the supposedly defeatist government of Chancellor Bethmann Hollweg. Such views formed the background to the disastrous decision to begin unrestricted submarine warfare against England in January 1917; and they also contributed to the ideological polarisation of German politics at a crucial juncture in European and world history.

MATTHEW STIBBE is Lecturer in History, Liverpool Hope University College

Studies in the Social and Cultural History of Modern Warfare

General Editor
Jay Winter   *Pembroke College, Cambridge*

Advisory Editors
Paul Kennedy   *Yale University*
Antoine Prost   *Université de Paris-Sorbonne*
Emmanuel Sivan   *The Hebrew University of Jerusalem*

In recent years the field of modern history has been enriched by the exploration of two parallel histories. These are the social and cultural history of armed conflict, and the impact of military events on social and cultural history.

Studies in the Social and Cultural History of Modern Warfare presents the fruits of this growing area of research, reflecting both the colonisation of military history by cultural historians and the reciprocal interest of military historians in social and cultural history, to the benefit of both. The series offers the latest scholarship in European and non-European events from the 1850s to the present day.

For a list of titles in the series, please see end of book

German Anglophobia and the Great War, 1914–1918

MATTHEW STIBBE

Liverpool Hope University College

CAMBRIDGE
UNIVERSITY PRESS

PUBLISHED BY THE PRESS SYNDICATE OF THE UNIVERSITY OF CAMBRIDGE
The Pitt Building, Trumpington Street, Cambridge, United Kingdom

CAMBRIDGE UNIVERSITY PRESS
The Edinburgh Building, Cambridge CB2 2RU, UK
40 West 20th Street, New York, NY 10011-4211, USA
10 Stamford Road, Oakleigh, VIC 3166, Australia
Ruiz de Alarcón 13, 28014 Madrid, Spain
Dock House, The Waterfront, Cape Town 8001, South Africa

http://www.cambridge.org

First published 2001

Printed in the United Kingdom at the University Press, Cambridge

Typeface Adobe Palatino and Frutiger 10/12pt   *System* QuarkXPress™   [SE]

A catalogue record for this book is available from the British Library

ISBN 0 521 78296 1 hardback

Contents

Contents

For Judith

Illustrations

Cartoons 1, 2, 3, 4, 5, 8 and 9 are also reproduced in William A. Coupe, *German Political Satires from the Reformation to the Second World War*, Part II, 1849–1918 (New York, 1987).

Acknowledgements

This book is based on my original D.Phil. thesis, 'Vampire of the Continent. German Anglophobia during the First World War, 1914–1918', which I submitted to the University of Sussex in the autumn of 1997. It is now a great pleasure and a privilege to be able to acknowledge the many sources of assistance I have received while researching it and rewriting it for publication.

First and foremost I would like to thank Professor John Röhl, my supervisor at Sussex, for his constructive criticism, moral support and enthusiasm for my project. The following people at different times and in different places have also helped with their friendly advice and encouragement: Karl-Ludwig Ay, Stefan Berger, Christopher Clark, William Coupe, William Davies, Elizabeth Harvey, Janet Hollinshead, Paul Hoser, Rod Kedward, Mark Mazower, Manfred Messerschmidt, Ingo Materna, Annika Mombauer, Raffael Scheck, Matthew Seligmann, Jim Simpson, Duncan Tanner, Jeffrey Verhey, Jay Winter and Hartmut Zelinsky.

I would also like to express my gratitude to the staff and directors of the many libraries and archives which I have worked in over the past few years. These include the university libraries at Sussex, Bangor and Liverpool Hope, the British Library and the Newspaper Library (Colindale), the German Historical Institute, London, the Institute of Historical Research, London, and the Wiener Library, London. During a twelve-month stay in Germany in 1995/6 I was able to make extensive use of the Staatsbibliothek I in Berlin (Unter den Linden) and in particular its extremely useful Weltkriegssammlung or collection of pamphlets written during the First World War. In addition I was granted permission to use the following archives: the Bundesarchiv-Militärarchiv in Freiburg, the Bundesarchiv in Koblenz, the Politisches Archiv des Auswärtigen Amtes in Bonn, the Bayerisches Hauptstaatsarchiv in Munich, the Bundesarchiv, Abteilung Potsdam (now in Berlin-Lichterfelde), the Geheimes Staatsarchiv in Berlin-Dahlem and the Archiv der Berlin-Brandenburgischen Akademie der Wissenschaften in Berlin-Mitte.

Financial sponsorship and assistance with travel expenses came from a wide variety of sources: the British Academy, the Graduate Research Centre in the Humanities at the University of Sussex, the Erasmus-Socrates scheme and (since 1997) the research committees of the University of Wales, Bangor, and of Liverpool Hope University College. In this respect I would also like to thank the Göttingen-based British Centre for Historical Research in Germany and its director, Joe Canning, for their hospitality during a six-week stay in the summer of 1998.

Finally, I would like to thank all those people who have assisted me in more indirect ways. I include in this respect my father Paul and step-mother Hazel, my six sisters and brothers, my two nieces Elin-Judith and Eva, and the many friends who have helped towards the success-ful completion of this book. Simon, Katherine, Noah and Harriet deserve special mention for their endless hospitality and Simon in par-ticular for his ability to lose gracefully at backgammon. Last, but by no means least, I am deeply grateful for the love, support and patience of my partner, Samantha, who has contributed so much to the happiness in my life over the past five years.

I dedicate this book to the memory of my mother, Dr Judith Dimock.

MATTHEW STIBBE
Manchester, March 2000

Abbreviations

AA   Auswärtiges Amt (German Foreign Office)
ABBAW   Archiv der Berlin-Brandenburgischen Akademie der
    Wissenschaften (Archive of the Berlin-Brandenburg Academy
    of Sciences, formerly the Prussian Academy of Sciences)
BA Koblenz   Bundesarchiv, Koblenz (German Federal Archives)
BA Potsdam   Bundesarchiv, Abteilung Potsdam (German Federal
    Archives, now in Berlin-Lichterfelde)
BA-MA Freiburg   Bundesarchiv-Militärarchiv, Freiburg im Breisgau
    (German Federal Military Archives)
BHStA Munich   Bayerisches Hauptstaatsarchiv, Munich (Bavarian
    State Archives)
GStA Berlin-Dahlem   Geheimes Staatsarchiv Preußischer
    Kulturbesitz (Prussian Secret State Archives)
OHL   Oberste Heeresleitung (German Army Supreme Command)
PA-AA Bonn   Politisches Archiv des Auswärtigen Amtes, Bonn
    (Political Archive of the German Foreign Office)
SPD   Sozialdemokratische Partei Deutschlands (German Social
    Democratic Party)
Sten. Ber./Pr. Abg. Haus   Stenographische Berichte der
    Verhandlungen des Preußischen Hauses der Abgeordneten
    (Proceedings of the Prussian House of Deputies)
Sten. Ber./Reichstag   Stenographische Berichte der Verhandlungen
    des deutschen Reichstages (Proceedings of the German
    Reichstag)
USPD   Unabhängige Sozialdemokratische Partei Deutschlands
    (Independent Social Democratic Party, founded in April 1917)

Introduction

We need look no further, for anti-Semitism betrays an inner weakness in the internal dynamics of a nation, just like that unjustifiable and aggressive imperialism which recently led Germany into such a disastrous war. Even before 1914 England was hated by many Germans, exactly in the same way as the Jews are hated today, for they too are believed to have denied Germany its rightful place in the sun.[1]

The novelist and social critic Heinrich Mann, who wrote these words in Paris in June 1933, was to pay a heavy price for his opposition to the Nazis and his alleged 'defeatist' attitude during the First World War. In May 1933 his books, and those of many other left-wing German writers, were publicly burnt in a carefully stage-managed protest on the *Opernplatz* in Berlin. This was an act of symbolic revenge by a regime which claimed to speak for the 'front generation' and which was expressly dedicated to reviving the lost 'spirit of 1914' among the population at large. A few weeks earlier, in February 1933, Mann had been the first prominent writer to flee Germany in the aftermath of Hitler's rise to power. He was also among the first to be formally debarred from German citizenship in August 1933.[2] Like his younger brother, Thomas Mann, he was forced to live the rest of his life as an exile and refugee, eventually leaving Europe for the United States where he died in Santa Monica, California, in 1950. In a very real sense he was a victim of the kinds of militarism and nationalist hatreds he had spent his whole life trying to oppose, albeit one who was fortunate enough to have got out before it was too late.

Like many other bourgeois anti-fascists, Mann was a Marxist sympathiser who had called for a united front of the German left in 1933 and believed that only fundamental changes in the relations of production – the abolition of private property – could bring an end to war and violence in society. For this reason too he was an early (although somewhat critical) supporter of the German Democratic Republic and its efforts to create a new and better Germany based on anti-fascist and anti-imperialist principles.[3] That experiment is now over, and today, after the collapse of communism and the end of the cold war, Europe is faced with new challenges in the never-ending quest for peace and security.

Mann's views are also interesting in another respect, however, for they offer a critical insight into an important, if often overlooked, aspect of modern German history, namely the problem of the growth of anti-English feeling among the educated middle classes and its close connection with the emerging ideologies of imperialism and anti-Semitism. Anti-English sentiments had already been evident, for instance, in the writings of the nationalist historian Heinrich von Treitschke in the 1880s and became more intense as a result of imperial conflicts in South Africa and elsewhere at the turn of the century.[4] But, as Mann tries to convince us, the social construction of *Englandhass* had far deeper causes than the Boer war itself, causes that were more closely related to established social structures and cultural norms than to the literary outpourings of a handful of pro-Boer idealists. And this, too, is the real meaning of his devastating critique of the militarism of the Wilhelmine period and of the 'ordinariness' of National Socialism. As a result of the First World War, hatred for the enemy – whether internal or external – had become so ingrained in middle-class German society that it was almost taken for granted as part of everyday life. Or, as Mann himself wrote in a continuation of the above-mentioned essay:

After the lost war the Germans at first had no opportunity to practise their false feelings of superiority against foreign powers. They had to seek the object of their revenge at home, and found the Jews, who allegedly did not belong [in Germany] and could not be assimilated . . . But this had nothing at all to do with the truth, rather it was an excuse to get rid of their guilty consciences and also a means of undertaking domestic annexations, the only ones which could now be carried out.[5]

This study too is interested in exploring the underlying continuities in German history between 1914 and 1933. Its main aim is to rethink the impact of the First World War on the course of German nationalism and on the subsequent politics of the Weimar and Nazi eras, with particular reference to anti-English attitudes in the period 1914–18. In so doing it also raises the important question of whether it is still appropriate to talk of 'peculiarities' or 'separate pathways' in German history, leading ultimately to the racist and genocidal policies of the Third Reich.[6] Before we can proceed further, however, it is first necessary to take a closer look at the broader historical and historiographical framework surrounding this issue. This in turn should provide us with an understanding of the context in which previous debates on Germany's role in the First World War have taken place.

1914 and 1933 in German historiography

In the historiography of twentieth-century Europe the question of Anglo-German relations has naturally and quite correctly assumed a position of great importance.[7] This was the case even before the publication in 1961 of Fritz Fischer's groundbreaking study of German war aims during the First World War; and since then the task of identifying the root causes of Germany's alienation from Britain (and vice versa) has continued unabated.[8] The formal and theoretical aspects of *Englandhass*, for instance, have been closely analysed by experts on the cultural and intellectual history of the war. But hitherto its place in the politics and diplomacy of the period has received surprisingly little attention.[9] Rather, the debate has centred on different ideological interpretations of the imperial period *before 1914*, ranging from the Marxist–Leninist emphasis on the role of monopoly capitalism;[10] via the western critique of the survival of pre-industrial, neo-feudal traditions and structures in Wilhelmine society;[11] to the alternative, neo-Marxist position that actually stresses the bourgeois nature of late nineteenth-century Germany and its similarities with Victorian and Edwardian Britain.[12] Historians of international relations, by contrast, have usually rejected theory in favour of asking more obvious questions: 'What went wrong in Anglo-German relations?' and 'When exactly did it go wrong?'. Or, in other words, why did Britain and Germany, two countries with fundamentally compatible foreign policy interests and no direct conflicts over territories or borders, find themselves on opposing sides in 1914? And why – if we are to look at similar studies of the inter-war period – did they fail to resolve their differences in time to prevent the even greater tragedy of the Second World War in 1939?[13]

The most comprehensive account to date is Paul Kennedy's *The Rise of Anglo-German Antagonism, 1860–1914* (1980), which has had a substantial impact on all subsequent studies of German (and English) imperialism in the half century before the First World War. It therefore deserves closer analysis, as a result of the depth and breadth of its approach and because of its broader methodological implications for all scholars working in the same area.[14]

As far as the present study is concerned, Kennedy's work is significant in two major respects. Firstly, it has helped to break down the artificial and increasingly outdated distinction between domestic and external motives in determining the foreign policy decisions of the major imperial powers. Rather, a wide variety of strategic, diplomatic, economic and cultural factors were at play, each helping to promote the Anglo-German antagonism into a genuine clash of opposing interests. This is perhaps obvious, but nonetheless worth stating in view of recent attempts by revisionist historians to downplay the role of the German challenge to British naval supremacy as one of the fundamental causes of the First World War.[15]

Secondly, Kennedy's work has much to say about the relationship between national phobias and imperialism at the turn of the century and in the run-up to war. In particular, he shows how aggressive anti-British and anti-German stereotypes were able to migrate from one crisis period to the next, without losing any of their intensity during intervening periods of relative calm. This can be seen, for instance, at the time of the Jameson raid in 1895, or later, during the Second Moroccan crisis of 1911.[16] It can also be seen in the failure of the all-important Haldane mission in February 1912 and the subsequent reactions on both sides of the Channel.[17] The main deficiency in Kennedy's study, however, is the absence of a serious consideration of the historical development of German attitudes towards England *after* the outbreak of war in 1914 and *before* its end in 1918. This in turn creates a significant gap in our understanding of the relationship between the aggressive anti-English policies of the Wilhelmine period and those of the Nazi era. The present study will aim to fill this gap.

The first chapter will look at the remarkable upsurge of a violent anglophobia in German society in the first weeks and months of the war, paying particular attention to the role played by the press, the military and censorship authorities, and propagandists of various political persuasions. In order to provide an element of contrast, aspects of German attitudes towards its other main enemies, Russia and France, will also be touched upon. The key question to be asked, however, is why England, which before 1914 had been one of several potential enemies, suddenly moved to being seen as Germany's enemy number one (the *Hauptfeind*), and why its defeat and overthrow became the most longed-for outcome of the conflict. The answer, so it seems, is that the language of anglophobia fitted in most easily with the official interpretation of the war's origins, which was used to disguise and deny Germany's own responsibility for the outbreak of armed conflict in July 1914. Britain's failure to restrain its allies, it was now argued, was not just a 'mistake' or the result of errors in diplomacy, but a deliberate act of betrayal designed to unleash a world war with the ultimate aim of destroying its most feared commercial rival.

Having established that anglophobia provided a dominant part of the initial public discourse on the meaning of the war, the second chapter will go on to explore how leading German intellectuals were able to incorporate their own critique of English society and English ideals into the so-called 'cultural war', which was to be waged alongside the 'military war' at the front. Four main 'types' of argumentation against England and its involvement in the war will be analysed: the racist, the geo-political, the economic and the cultural arguments, all of which served as an intellectual or political basis for anti-English views. The economic motivation for anglophobia seems to me to be particularly interesting, not only because it ties in with the immediate resentments caused by the Allied blockade of Germany, but also because it helps to reveal more general anti-capitalist undercurrents in the thinking of the German right. This can be seen most famously, of course, in Werner Sombart's book *Händler und Helden*, first published in 1915, which identified the German war effort as a battle against the English 'commercial spirit'.[18] By contrast, the more extreme versions of the racist critique of England – such as the alleged identity of interest between Anglo-American foreign policy and Jewish world finance – assumed a much greater importance only during the latter part of the war and in the immediate post-war era.[19]

Chapters 3, 4 and 5, the core part of the book, explore the impact of anglophobia on German domestic politics, in particular the brutal and bitter controversies which raged over such issues as German war aims and submarine warfare. Especially relevant here is the attempt by the extreme right, including those circles around the ousted Naval Secretary Alfred von Tirpitz, to use anglophobia as an ideological weapon in the propaganda battle for control over the home front.[20] Their main target was the Chancellor, Theobald von Bethmann Hollweg, who throughout the war was accused of harbouring secret pro-English tendencies which threatened the attainment of a German victory. Eventually, in September 1916, elements of the anti-Bethmann *fronde* came together to form a Committee for the Rapid Overthrow of England, which was the forerunner to the German Fatherland Party founded a year later. The story of the rise and fall of the Volksausschuß für die rasche Niederkämpfung Englands is an extremely important aspect of the political atmosphere in Germany (and especially Munich) during the war, and is told here in depth for the first time.[21]

Another important aspect of the impact of anglophobia on German domestic politics in the year 1916 is the growing evidence of a link between anti-English propaganda on the one hand and revival of anti-Semitic feelings on the other. It is very significant, for instance, that the high point of agitation in favour of unrestricted submarine warfare against Britain also coincided with the high point of agitation against Jewish 'war profiteers' and 'shirkers', as witnessed by the notorious 'Jew count' ordered by the Prussian Ministry of War in October 1916.[22] But in the area of symbolic meaning, too, the war was increasingly seen as being a battle against the 'enemy within', against the agents of foreign (English, French or American) political ideas and traditions which were allegedly damaging to German national identity. Berlin, as the centre of a vibrant pre-war cosmopolitan spirit and as the home to a large number of Jewish-owned newspapers, was often a target of such nationalist suspicions. It is also here, in the right-wing agitation of 1916, that we can see the origins of the post-war stab-in-the-back myth which played such an important role in undermining the legitimacy of the new republican regime in the 1920s.[23]

Chapter 6 goes on to explore some of the new themes which emerged in German anglophobia during the last year and a half of the war, from April 1917 to November 1918. This period is significant for two reasons: firstly because for many right-wing Germans the entry of the United States into the war tended to confirm existing fears of an Anglo-Saxon capitalist world conspiracy to destroy the German empire and over-throw its dynasty, and secondly because mounting internal tensions also reinforced the notion that Germany was fighting the war on two separate fronts, both abroad and at home. The comments of the Kaiser are particularly interesting here, for he now shared the view that England, although a monarchy itself, was at the head of a coalition determined to overthrow the Christian monarchical principle in Europe and replace it with the rule of Satan and an atheistic Mammonism. In this way he was able to anticipate much of the conspiracist thinking which characterised German anti-Semitism and right-wing extremism at the end of the war and in the early years of the Weimar Republic.[24]

Another important theme which emerged in the final phase of the war was the link between anti-English rhetoric and shifting definitions of the role that propaganda itself was to play in modern warfare. This in turn was a result of the growing power of the military authorities in Germany to intervene in civilian affairs and even to redefine the very notion of 'citizenship' itself. It was also a reflection of Ludendorff's adherence to the idea that victory would come only through the collective will of the nation, defined in practical terms as the spiritual and moral mobilisation of all manpower resources deemed necessary by him to defeat the enemy.[25] In reality, though, it had to be admitted by the summer of 1918 that the German propaganda effort had failed and, perhaps more importantly, that England had won the 'battle for minds' as well as the battle at the front. The lessons to be learnt from this were later channelled into a complex discourse on propaganda and public opinion in the 1920s which has been recently unravelled by the historian Jeffrey Verhey.[26] They were also experiences which Adolf Hitler was to take to heart when he made his own assessment of the causes of Germany's defeat in his famous autobiography, *Mein Kampf.*[27]

Finally, at the end of the book, a short epilogue discusses the more general impact of the First World War on German politics after 1918, and in particular its relationship to the rise and fall of the Third Reich. It should be said here that the aim is not a full-scale study of Nazi ideology itself, but rather to look at the way in which hatred of England came to form a significant part of the National Socialist agenda in Europe, especially from the late 1930s onwards. The fact that Hitler personally had favoured an alliance with Britain does not make him an outside party to all this. Rather, such collaboration was demanded primarily on the assumption made in *Mein Kampf* that England was still a world power of enormous strengths and resources, and that it could do much damage to Germany's prospects of victory in the inevitable wars of the future. Indeed, as one prominent historian has noted, once it had become clear to Hitler that the British government could not be won over to an Anglo-German alliance, Britain moved again from being one of several potential enemies to being regarded as the chief opponent of Germany's expansionist ambitions on the continent.[28] This held true particularly after the failure of Hitler's final attempts to woo Britain in the summer of 1940, and continued in spite of the launching of the Nazis' war-cum-crusade against 'Judeo-Bolshevism' a year later, since the final overthrow of England (and with it world Jewry) was now seen as a necessary precondition for the permanent acquisition of *Lebensraum* in the east.[29]

It would be wrong, of course, to claim that all that went wrong in Germany after 1933 can be traced back to the years 1914–18, at least not without severe qualification and differentiation. Anti-Semitism, for instance, had a number of different manifestations in Germany, of which hostility towards England and English 'commercialism' was only one, albeit an important one.[30] Likewise, German imperialism before 1914 was subject to a diverse range of pressures and influences, including the anti-French stance of Rhineland industralists such as Gustav Krupp von Bohlen and August Thyssen and the anti-Polish stance of land-hungry German aristocrats living in the border regions of East and West Prussia.[31] Anglophobia existed alongside these other, more traditional forms of national animus and overlapped with them on a great many issues; but it also developed an important set of assumptions of its own about the true meaning and significance of German national identity and Germany's mission in the world. The key point here is to place such views within their broader political and cultural context and to identify their importance in relation to the totality of German war aims in the First World War.

Some notice, too, must be taken of the boundaries of this book. The evidence offered here is by and large confined to organised politics and the economic and intellectual elites, that is to those individuals and groups who have left a substantial trail of sources regarding their views of England. At the level of historical record, such a focus is necessary in order to identify those aspects of German anglophobia that had a decisive impact on the political decision-making process of the period under review. It also enables us to locate the hard core of anti-English feeling which continued regardless of changes in Germany's military fortunes and which intensified once the goal of a separate peace with Russia had been realised in 1918. Even within this relatively narrow section of German society, however, there were important elements who either disapproved of or – as was the case with the anti-war USPD (Independent Social Democratic Party) and the radical-left Spartacists – actively resisted the arguments put forward by the anglophobe extremists. This means that anglophobia, although quite clearly a national issue in 1914, also became, later on, a sectional if not a class issue, one that contributed directly to the ideological polarisation of German politics as a whole in the final years of the war.

If anglophobia cannot be separated from the underlying class antagonisms in German society, however, then nor should it be treated in isolation from the equally violent Germanophobia that took hold of British society during the same period.[32] Indeed, looking beyond the Nazi era, German anglophobia can hardly be seen as being any better or any worse than some of the other manifestations of national and ethnic hatreds which characterise modern warfare in the age of mass communications. Such hatreds may lie dormant for several decades, only to be revived by fresh political upheavals or group conflicts. At other times the memories of such conflicts are deliberately exploited by specific groups and individuals with an axe to grind. It is somewhat ironic, for instance, that many of the anti-English slogans employed by Germany in both world wars were derived from formulas originally used during the French revolution and Napoleonic period.[33] To this the Germans added slogans of their own, arising from the political and economic frustrations of the 'generation of 1848' or the arguments of a later generation of nationalists in favour of the development of a powerful German navy.[34]

Finally, the alert reader might legitimately ask why I speak of 'anglophobia' as opposed to 'Britannophobia'. In part this is merely a matter of linguistic usage: the German language has traditionally employed the word 'England' to cover all areas of the British Isles, even in circumstances where 'Großbritannien' is clearly the intended meaning, and in deference to that tradition I have done the same throughout this book. Notwithstanding the linguistic issue, the failure to distinguish accurately and at all times between two very different entities – England and Britain – also reflected a more immediate and striking set of assumptions about the all-important role of the state in shaping national character. Indeed, as Eckart Kehr first argued back in the 1920s, the chief weakness of German historiography had always been its tendency to confuse the state-idea with its current political form, a practice which also encourages identification with history's winners as opposed to its losers.[35] This was no less the case with narrative constructions of English history than it was with constructions of German history itself.

Thus it was quite possible for German historians, before and after 1914, to conceive of Englishness as if it were a uniform characteristic of all of those different national groups and individuals who had contributed to the growth of 'English' state power since the sixteenth century, and to leave out consideration of those who had opposed it.[36] Furthermore, it was also possible to define 'British' imperialism as if it were merely an outgrowth of 'English' Puritanism, an ethical system which was seen to encourage aggressiveness and worldly success at the expense of genuine philosophical contemplation.[37] In fact, as we shall see in chapter 2, it was in only a very small number of instances that attempts were made by German historians and other propagandists to include or exclude the Celtic fringes (Scotland, Wales, Cornwall) in their cultural construction of England as an enemy. The one clear-cut exception to this rule was Ireland, which was conveniently defined, alongside India, Egypt and the former Boer Republics, as an object of 'British' imperialism rather than as an integral part of the 'English' or (later) 'Anglo-Saxon' war effort.[38]

If anglophobia was a more problematic and more volatile aspect of German wartime politics than it might at first seem, however, and also a less easy concept to define, this does not mean that its effects should be trivialised or made harmless as a result. On the contrary, it is one of the central theses of this book that the German preoccupation with 'enemies all around', with competition for world power and with the search for a 'place in the sun' took on a new and more brutal form after the outbreak of war in 1914. Although my main subject is German attitudes towards England, I have found myself devoting a considerable amount of attention to wartime developments within the German Conservative party, the various nationalist leagues and the radical right more generally. In so doing I have also tried to address the issue of which individuals and organisations were responsible for laying the political foundations of the extreme nationalism and anti-Semitism of the post-war era, which even before 1923 had claimed the lives of a number of prominent liberal and left-wing statesmen. Why this was allowed to happen, why the hatred and violence directed outwards between 1914 and 1918 were later applied with full force against the 'internal enemy' is indeed the most disturbing question to arise from the study of German anglophobia during the First World War.

1 *Unser gehasstester Feind.* German anglophobia and the 'spirit of 1914'

The outbreak of the First World War saw Germany temporarily united by an outburst of patriotic solidarity that bridged the divisions inherent in the Wilhelmine structure of society. Under the *Burgfriede*, or domestic political truce, proclaimed by the Kaiser on 1 August 1914, previously outcast minorities such as the Social Democrats and the Jews were now to be readmitted to the national community. The Reichstag – in accordance with the wishes of the government – also voted unanimously for war credits when it met on 4 August. The few warning voices raised in opposition (and they were at first very few in number) could not make themselves heard or were easily suppressed. It was only in the 1920s that pacifist organisations in Germany felt confident enough openly to declare a 'war on war'.[1]

Even so, the war had not come wholly without warning and to more critical observers it was obvious that diplomatic and military preparations had been laid well in advance. From the turn of the century, for instance, and especially in the immediate pre-war years, Germany's armed forces had been considerably strengthened and its armaments subject to technological improvements.[2] In addition to military rearmament, there had also been a 'rousing of minds', as the popularity of books such as Friedrich von Bernhardi's *Deutschland und der nächste Krieg* (1912) clearly illustrates. War was consciously viewed by many of Germany's rulers as an 'escape forwards', a solution to the countless political, social and economic problems inherent in German society.[3] In this they were urged on by the propagandist agitation of the so-called 'new right', the nationalist associations such as the Pan-German League and the Navy League.[4] And in 1914 even oppositional movements such as the German Social Democratic Party came to see in the war an opportunity to overcome stagnation within its own ranks, while individual mavericks such as the Marxist Paul Lensch proclaimed the 'German war' as the start of the 'world revolution'.[5]

The outbreak of war also saw a transformation of the mood and activities of historians and other members of the academic profession. Through a wave of patriotic publications – poems, war lectures and sermons, 'academic' treatises, novels and art periodicals – they were able to reach a wider audience and thereby to play a leading role in defining and giving voice to what later became known as the 'spirit of 1914'. This included the idea that the collective experience of mobilisation for war and the popular perception of war itself should serve as a model for the future order of German society, one in which technological progress would be harmonised with traditional Germanic values and the idea of a German *Sonderweg*.[6] And for the time being, at least, it seemed as if the apparently spontaneous coming together of the nation would finally bring an end to the old divisions between different classes and religions which had paralysed the political system before 1914. This, at any rate, was the impression given by the *Bayerische Staatszeitung* on 9 August 1914 when it spoke proudly of Germany's 'war of liberation' against the threat of foreign invasion.[7]

In previous literature, much emphasis has been placed on the additional nourishment this mythical war fever received from hate-filled stereotypes of the 'Erbfeind France' and of 'Slavic hordes', negative images with a long tradition in Germany.[8] The French were hated not only as the embodiment of the revolutionary spirit of 1789, but also as the heirs to the decadence of the Roman Empire. The Russians, on the other hand, were both hated and feared as the 'barbarians of the east', the protectors of the 250 million Slavs who threatened to overwhelm the culturally and racially superior German minority in eastern Europe through sheer force of numbers. It is thus significant that the German Chancellor, Theobald von Bethmann Hollweg, should lay the greater emphasis in his speech to the Reichstag on 4 August 1914 on the Russian menace, even if this speech was designed primarily to persuade the SPD to vote for war credits.[9]

By the end of August, however, many German statesmen had come to regard England, and not Russia, as the *Hauptfeind*, the chief obstacle to the achievement of Germany's continental and world power aspirations. This new attitude was shared not only by hardened anglophobes such as the Kaiser, Erich von Falkenhayn and Admiral von Tirpitz, who had perceived British policy in this light before the war and continued to do so, but also by many who had previously been inclined to look upon England more favourably: men such as the foreign policy expert Kurt Riezler, the industrialist Walther Rathenau and the shipping magnate Albert Ballin.[10] Disappointment at Britain's behaviour soon turned to anger, bitterness and in some cases a sense of personal betrayal once Britain began to increase its naval and military contribution to the war and made public its renunciation of separate peace deals in the London agreement of 5 September 1914. By this time even Bethmann Hollweg, who throughout the war was accused by extreme nationalists of harbouring secret anglophile tendencies, was beginning to make statements to the effect that 'England's determination to wage war *à outrance* against Germany' would eventually force Germany to respond in kind.[11]

What most impressed contemporary observers about the situation after August 1914, however, was the apparently spontaneous and irrational nature of the outbreak of hatred towards England, which had little, if anything, to do with the realities of Germany's new external position. According to Werner Sombart, for instance, a sociologist at the University of Berlin and author of the highly influential work, *Händler und Helden* (1915), there was something elementary and instinctive at work here, a phenomenon that could not be explained by rational thought processes:

On the contrary, it seems to me that the spontaneous and elementary hatred against England is anchored in the deepest core of our being, there where 'rational considerations' no longer exist, where the 'irrational', the instinctive, has sole jurisdiction. We hate in the English a principle which is alien to our innermost and highest being. And it is proper that we should become fully conscious of this, because in so doing we also reveal the ultimate purpose of the struggle which we are now waging.[12]

Similar views were held by Julius Schiller, a Protestant pastor from Nuremberg, who spoke of a process of change, of rethinking and relearning, which had accompanied the outbreak of war with England:

Previously we used to think it immoral to hate. Whoever sought to undermine this principle, we would have it no other way than that we have a right to hate, that we must hate. Lissauer's Hymn of Hatred against England is in full keeping with our current mood, with the depths of the German national soul. All remonstrations against this [mood] fall on deaf ears, all objections are cast aside ... We Germans hate in a different manner to the sons of Albion. Our hate is honest, based on just principles. England's hate is dishonest, driven by envy, malice and jealousy. It was high time that we finally saw England in its true contours.[13]

In the pages below we will seek to examine more closely the reasons for this sudden outburst of hatred of England.

From russophobia to anglophobia

The entry of Great Britain into the war on 4 August 1914, following the German violation of Belgian neutrality, was received throughout Germany with a mixture of dismay and outrage. Kaiser Wilhelm II, in his own typical fashion, had decided even before the outbreak of war that responsibility for the diplomatic intrigues against his person lay in London. In the margins of a report on Russian mobilisation sent by Friedrich von Pourtalès, the German ambassador in St Petersburg, on the night of 30 July 1914 he noted:

So the famous *'encirclement'* of Germany has finally become a complete fact, despite every effort of our politicians and diplomats to prevent it. The net has been suddenly thrown over our head, and England sneeringly reaps the most brilliant successes of its persistently prosecuted *purely anti-German world policy* against which we have proved ourselves hopeless whilst it twists the noose of our political and economic destruction out of our fidelity to Austria, as we squirm *isolated* in the net. A great achievement, which arouses the admiration even of him who is to be destroyed as its result.[14]

The initial press reactions to the English declaration of war were, however, of a more sober nature, indicative of the widespread view that it was Russian aggression that presented the greatest threat to Germany in the future. This was certainly the chief concern of nationalist newspapers such as the *Kölnische Zeitung*, which had warned as early as March 1914 that the Russians were 'arming for war against Germany' and would be ready to attack in a few years' time.[15] Critics of the *Kölnische Zeitung*, such as the Social Democratic *Vorwärts* and the liberal *Frankfurter Zeitung*, strongly suspected that the army and its industrial allies were behind the new anti-Russian campaign in order to gain public support for further increases in military spending.[16] Yet anti-Russian feeling was also typical of many left-wing papers, including *Vorwärts* itself, which on 29 June had called for an alliance with France and Britain against the 'east European danger', as well as liberal newspapers such as the *Frankfurter Zeitung* and the *Vossische Zeitung*, which continued to welcome any signs of a worsening of Anglo-Russian relations in the months after March 1914. The liberal–pacifist *Welt am Montag* even continued to express these views right up until 3 August 1914, when it carried a direct appeal to England not to join the war on Russia's side.

We Germans should have stood on the side of the western powers a long time ago, and they on ours. England now has the task of serving this, the only possible goal for the future. This is the proper and natural European state system and this system alone offers England the chance to prolong its own power. If Germany and Austria should sink in the dust, then England will surely be next in line.[17]

This was also essentially the stance taken by the *Frankfurter Zeitung* in an article published in the evening edition on 4 August 1914, just a few hours before the deadline for the English ultimatum expired. Here, however, the *Frankfurter Zeitung* could not resist making an indirect reference to the British government's acceptance of secret Anglo-Russian naval talks, news of which had broken in Germany at the end of May 1914.[18]

England is still not involved [in the current crisis]. It is difficult to believe that it could ever join forces with the Dual Entente. But short-sighted envy and promises, which have been kept secret from the House of Commons [*Volksvertretung*], have led the government to falter. We cannot understand this, since a victory for Russia would make it the master of the world, and England's rich possessions in Asia and India, in Persia and Arabia, would be placed in jeopardy. England cannot imagine that it can stand up to the Russian colossus alone. Its world empire and its culture are just as much at stake as Germany's culture and national existence. Mr Asquith and Sir Edward Grey are on the verge of making a fateful decision, for the world and for England.[19]

Once the war with England had broken out, however, it was the right-wing and nationalist press which took a much more hostile line on what was seen as England's 'perverse alliance' with Russia. The *Alldeutsche Blätter*, organ of the Pan-German League, for instance, betrayed its bitterness and anger on 8 August towards what it saw as England's alliance with the 'Slav and Latin defenders of the Serbian assassins'. This was all the more significant, since only a few days earlier the same journal had been speaking of the 'common blood' and 'common codes of honour' of the Germans and the English. England, it now argued on 8 August, was a 'betrayer of its own race' (*Verräter am eigenen Stammestum*).[20]

For others, England's declaration of war was a disaster not only for Germany, but for the entire civilised world. Matthias Erzberger, a leading figure in the Catholic Centre Party and confidant of the Chancellor, made this point in an article published in *Der Tag* on 9 August under the revealing title 'England for regicides and Tsarism'. And, in a report appearing on the same day, the Berlin organ of the Centre Party, *Germania*, wrote:

That England has sided with the Russians in the *Kulturkampf* against Russian expansionism in the west, and that it has helped to break the German and Austrian resistance to this [Russian] onslaught with its minor naval contribution, will never be forgotten by the German people. It has become a matter of common belief that the English declaration of war is the result of a policy of encirclement, whose origins lie in the fear of Germany's economic development and whose ultimate goal is to keep Germany weak. For this reason a feeling of relief is evident in all conversations and all newspaper commentaries concerning the English declaration of war, [relief] that finally the true aims of English policy have been revealed for all to see.[21]

Over the next few weeks and months, the idea that it was England, and not Russia, that had started the war was enthusiastically developed by the right-wing press, and even received some support from official sources. On 8 August, for instance, Count Ernst zu Reventlow, an ex-naval officer and foreign affairs editor of the *Deutsche Tageszeitung*, the organ of the Agrarian League, launched a vicious attack on the former German ambassador in London, Prince Lichnowsky, accusing him of consistently failing to understand the real motives behind British foreign policy and of having allowed himself to be duped by Sir Edward Grey.[22] Reventlow was known as a long-standing critic of official German foreign policy, and it was obvious that his censure of Lichnowsky was intended as a criticism of the entire diplomatic establishment. However, when Lichnowsky wrote to the Foreign Secretary Jagow requesting an official rebuttal of Reventlow's attacks, he received a reply which he most likely did not expect. Jagow informed Lichnowsky that Reventlow had been justifiably upset about some pro-English speeches the prince had made before his departure from London, and continued: 'We often wrote to you about this, but you did not want to believe us. R[eventlow] has apparently or actually been proved right with his constant mistrust towards England; no wonder he is now trying to make an issue out of this.' At the end of the letter Jagow agreed to enquire whether any official action might be possible, but stated that he personally would not be engaging in any polemics with Reventlow and therefore left the impression that the prince now stood on his own.[23]

Jagow's response is all the more surprising given that Reventlow was well known as a critic of official German foreign policy and his articles contained thinly disguised attacks on the German diplomatic establishment in general as well as on Lichnowsky personally. His highly publicised views on the corrupt and plutocratic elite alleged to be in control of British foreign policy were now enthusiastically taken up by the rest of the right-wing press, only to reappear twenty-five years later in National Socialist propaganda. The *Tägliche Rundschau*, for instance, published in August 1914 a collection of hate-filled quotations alleged to have been made by Napoleon I against England, while failing to mention that Prussia itself had forged alliances with 'perfidious Albion' against the French emperor.[24] Similarly, the Stuttgart-based *Süddeutsche Zeitung* published an article on 16 September by the well-known Baltic-German historian Johannes Haller under the title 'Britannia delenda!' in which he spoke of the 'cold calculation' underlying British policy, a matter made all the worse by the fact that for the English 'war is fundamentally a matter of enriching oneself' (*wesentlich Sache des Geldbeutels ist*).[25] And on 29 September the nationalist *Kölnische Zeitung* called for a 'war against England's attempts to bamboozle the world' (*Krieg gegen die englische Weltknebelung*) and vowed that Germany would not make peace until 'we can re-sheathe the sword, which we have been forced to unsheathe, in full confidence that the world will be safe from English aggression for decades to come'.[26]

Even more significant was the fact, as noted by Lothar Wieland, that none of the more respectable and knowledgeable papers, such as the *Vossische Zeitung* or the *Frankfurter Zeitung*, were able to provide correctives to the more extreme forms of anglophobia.[27] Instead, both papers now agreed that improvements in Anglo-German relations since 1912 had been overrated and that 'primitive self-interest' and 'commercial jealousy' were the key factors involved in Britain's decision for war on 4 August 1914; the German violation of Belgian neutrality merely served as a pretext so as not to let the opportunity pass 'for driving back the German rival'.[28] On 6 September the *Vossische Zeitung* even published an article by Alois Brandl, professor of English at the University of Berlin, which blamed the English democratic party system and its corrupt press for the outbreak of war.

In our country we have scarcely any idea how the political parties are funded in England [i.e. by multi-millionaires] . . . These multi-millionaires, on whom there are plenty of statistics, are the uncrowned kings of Great Britain, thanks to the semblance of democratic government . . . They control public opinion, which sometimes demands peace and sometimes war, according to their own requirements. This is how it has been for centuries; Cromwell not only had the king executed, but with him the only genuine form of monarchy which can truly protect the people [from exploitation]. Then he passed the Navigation Acts, the ruthless ban on imports and exports carried by non-English ships, by which means the wealth of the English moneyed caste first began to rise.[29]

Indeed, by the middle of September 1914, barely six weeks into the war, the dominant tone of the German press had switched from russophobia to anglophobia, while some newspapers, such as the National Liberal *Leipziger Neueste Nachrichten*, even designated the destruction of England as the *only* German war aim:

Here, and here alone, lies the goal of the war. We must first break France, Belgium and Russia, so as to be able to get at the swollen body of England, this gigantic snake, which swallows [other nations] bite by bite and is now also greedily demanding the fruits of German labour. Russia, France and Belgium must be defeated so that they no longer stand in the way of our great historical reckoning with the Britons . . . Down with England! – this alone is the goal of the war. And so may enmity exist between this people and our own until England has finally atoned for its thousand-fold guilt with its own destruction. Hypocrites, thieves and liars is how Frederick the Great once described them. And therefore we say: 'No treaties, no surrender!'[30]

Gott strafe England!

In contrast to this bellicose attitude towards England, Germany's traditional enemies, Russia and France, were extended a kind of 'benevolent sympathy' for the duration of the war, as the left-wing pacifist Hellmut von Gerlach later put it.[31] The French in particular were often admired as patriots fighting to defend themselves against inevitable decline as a great power. More often than not they were depicted as the mercenaries of England and only very rarely as the instigators of the war.[32] This opinion was so widespread that even the *Straßburger Post*, traditionally one of the most francophobe German newspapers, carried an article on 1 January 1915 in which it admitted:

There is a surprising calm and lack of hot-headedness towards France, and no trace this time of the deep stirring of the German national soul which occurred in the year 1870; all the anger, resentment and hatred which is currently astir in Germany has been diverted onto the English . . . the English have become the most hated of all our enemies. This is instead of the French; they have borne the brunt of the war so far, whilst the English have borne the brunt of the hatred . . . Germany will ultimately come to terms with France [and] with Russia again, but never with England. Therefore there is only one method to be applied against our island neighbour: to render it as harmless as possible and to protect ourselves from it in every possible way.[33]

The same impression was confirmed in the reports on public opinion sent by the Berlin Police President Traugott von Jagow to his superior, Gustav von Kessel, the Commander-in-Chief in the Marches. As early as 5 October 1914 Jagow spoke of a 'general demand for an attack against the English on *England's* soil' and added that this was a reflection of widespread confidence in the strength of the German army and navy.[34] On 2 November 1914 he reported that the news of the internment of German civilians in England had provoked widespread bitterness and the demand for German reprisals.[35] And a week later, on 9 November, he underlined this in a report stating that:

For the vast majority [of Berliners] the war which we are currently waging has only one passionately desired end, the reckoning with England. In this respect the internment of all English males living in Germany, the bombardment of the English coast by the German fleet and the naval victory off the coast of Chile have been greeted with great joy, the latter even with wild displays of jubilation.[36]

In keeping with this new mood, the English rapidly replaced the Russians and the French as the arch-enemy of the German Reich, not only in the press, but also in middle-class opinion as a whole. The bourgeois women's movement, for instance, which had declared itself ready for war service on the home front as early as the end of July 1914, soon adopted the new anti-English slogans of the day. As a sign of the times, the main periodical of the Deutsche Vereinigung für Frauenstimmrecht carried an article by the wife of Captain Boy-Ed, propaganda chief in the Reich Naval Office, in which she not only declared that she felt a 'startling, horrendous hatred' for the English, but also exhorted German women in general to share this 'venerable hatred' and urged the German navy 'to be hard, even against women and children, when they belong to English men'.[37]

An important role in the orchestration of hatred against England was also played by the adoption of the popular greeting 'Gott strafe England' and the reply 'Er strafe es!', which, according to Police President von Jagow, was in wide use among Berlin schoolchildren by January 1915.[38] The shops were full of articles – mugs, handkerchiefs, pocket knives, buttons and badges – printed with this same phrase, which even became an accepted opening to telephone conversations. It was also rubber-stamped onto letters, printed on millions of postcards and engraved on scarf-pins, cufflinks, brooches and wedding rings.[39] At one point the Swiss authorities were even forced to intervene and issue a warning that any letters from Germany bearing the imprint 'Gott strafe England' would no longer be handled by the Swiss post office![40]

German clergy often gave active encouragement to these sentiments when they compared England in their sermons to Judas Iscariot, the man who betrayed the Son of God to His enemies. Others were more concerned that Britain, by attacking Germany in concert with 'Asiatic Russia', had somehow betrayed European culture and Christian civilisation. According to the Berlin theologian Adolf von Harnack, Britain was now responsible for efforts to break down the barriers which protected western Europe from the Asiatic *Unkultur* (non-culture) of Russia. As a result, the Germans must now take up the struggle invoked by the Kaiser's famous painting: 'Peoples of Europe, protect your most holy possessions!' If England should succeed in destroying Germany, he warned, then it would bear the major responsibility for the collapse of western civilisation: 'The day that Great Britain broke the dam will never be forgotten in world history.'[41]

German cartoonists, on the other hand, tended to play much more on the cowardly and treacherous nature of the British, who were seen to have no sense of honour and instead sought to profit from the misfortunes of other nations. Typical in this respect was a cartoon which first appeared in *Simplicissimus*, the famous Munich-based satirical magazine, on 17 August 1914 and was later reproduced for the collection *Gott Strafe England!* (fig. 1). Here the British foreign secretary Sir Edward Grey is given the ironic epithet of 'guardian of international law' as he presides not over the 'rights of smaller nations' but over the commercial and trading interests of 'Albion & Co.' Meanwhile, all around him are piled up the bloody skulls of the dead from previous wars and battles, among them Frenchmen, Belgians and Germans. The caption reads: 'War is a business like any other.'[42]

In a second cartoon, this time taken from the left-wing *Wahre Jacob* in September 1914 (fig. 2), German troops are seen on the mountain tops preparing to defend their towns and villages against a fiery, culture-destroying dragon ridden by the demonic-looking figure of John Bull. Behind John Bull sits a Japanese Samurai warrior holding a flag which

1 'The guardian of international law', from *Simplicissimus*, 17 August 1914

2 'Profits are what is important', from *Der Wahre Jacob*, 4 September 1914

is a hybrid version of the Union Jack and the Rising Sun. The reference, quite clearly, is to the Japanese declaration of war on Germany on 23 August 1914, an event which was attributed to English intrigues. Once again, the imagery is also intended to conjure up memories of Wilhelm II's painting 'Peoples of Europe, protect your most holy possessions', only this time it was all the more powerful for associating Britain explicitly with the appearance of the 'Yellow Peril' at the very gates of European civilisation. The caption reads:

> That you begrudge the German everything is not unknown,
> Business is Business for you John Bull!
> But that you should set upon us your ally
> the Yellow Dragon – John Bull – that
> is something prompted by your close friend -
> the devil!

Foreign observers also noted the changed mood in Germany. On 19 November 1914, for instance, the liberal Viennese paper *Neue Freie Presse* carried a report on a visit one of its journalists had made to Hindenburg's headquarters on the eastern front. Hindenburg and his entourage allegedly spoke with admiration of the Russians, who were waging their war fairly and squarely, and of the French. There was no trace of hatred for these two countries. But with regard to the attitude towards England the Austrian journalist noted with apparent alarm:

The same hatred towards the English exists here as it does in the whole of Germany. Herr v[on] Hindenburg says the Bavarian Crown Prince, with his outstanding field orders branding the English as the most hated enemy, has expressed his own sentiments exactly [*habe ihm ganz aus der Seele gesprochen*].[43]

The field orders of the Bavarian Crown Prince Rupprecht, which Hindenburg appeared to have endorsed, were also given much publicity in the German and foreign press. In one of these orders, issued at the end of October, Rupprecht declared:

Soldiers of the Sixth Army! We now have the pleasure of also facing the English before us, the front-line soldiers of that nation whose envy has for years been hard at work in order to encircle us with a ring of enemies, in order to strangle us. It is above all [to England] that we owe this bloody, terrible war. Therefore, now that we are facing this enemy, let us seek retribution for such hostile cunning, for the many heavy casualties! Show them that the Germans are not so easy to eliminate from world history, show them this through German blows of a special kind. Here is the enemy which more than any other stands in the way of the restoration of peace. So let's waste not a moment more![44]

Hindenburg's endorsement of Rupprecht's views is significant, because his own popularity was based on his claim to embody the opinion of the average German. In another field order, Rupprecht is also said to have ordered copies of Ernst Lissauer's famous 'Hymn of Hatred' against England to be issued to all units in the Bavarian army.

> French and Russian they matter not,
> A blow for a blow and a shot for a shot;
> We love them not, we hate them not,
> We hold the Weichsel and the Vosges gate,
>
> We have but one and only hate,
> We love as one, we hate as one,
> We have one foe and one alone:
> England![45]

In the meantime, the hate campaign against England did little to help the German war effort other than to convince opinion abroad that the Germans really did hate England, as Lissauer said. It was thus no more useful than the so-called Amerikanisches Aufklärungskomitee ('American Truth Society'), a propaganda organisation set up in Munich in October 1914 by a group of anti-English Americans,[46] or the Zeppelin raids on England in the early part of 1915, which, according to Hellmut von Gerlach, merely made the introduction of conscription in England easier for the government there to justify.[47]

The militarisation of public opinion

During the July crisis and the weeks that followed the government pursued a systematic policy of misinformation, so that even usually well-informed individuals such as the journalist Theodor Wolff at first remained unclear about the true nature of the diplomatic and military preparations for war taken after the Sarajevo assassination. On 27 July 1914 Admiral von Müller, the head of the Kaiser's naval cabinet, noted in his diary that the tendency of German policy was 'to keep quiet, letting Russia put herself in the wrong, but then not shying away from war'.[48] And three days later, on 1 August, he recorded triumphantly: 'The mood is brilliant. The government has succeeded very well in making us appear as the attacked.'[49]

The origins of this state of affairs, which have been described as representing 'the militarisation of German diplomacy',[50] go back to 8 December 1912, when the Kaiser called together his chief military and naval advisers for the so-called 'war council'. Opening this meeting personally, the Kaiser envisaged a scenario strikingly similar to the one that actually occurred eighteen months later, in July 1914: Austria would attack Serbia, Russia would intervene on Serbia's behalf and Germany would find itself at war with Russia, France and Britain. According to the account left in von Müller's diary, Army Chief of Staff Helmuth von Moltke's demand for 'war the sooner the better', made during the course of the council, was delayed only by the need to prepare public opinion and by Admiral von Tirpitz's insistence that the Kiel canal must first be completed, which it was by June 1914. The most important passage in Müller's account, which was left out of the original published version of the diaries, reads as follows:

> The Chief of General Staff says: War the sooner the better, but he does not draw the logical conclusion from this, which is: To present Russia and France with an ultimatum which would unleash the war with right on our side.[51]

Shortly thereafter Müller also wrote to Bethmann Hollweg instructing him of the Kaiser's wishes that the press be used to prepare public opinion for the possibility of a major conflict.[52]

The situation facing Germany after 4 August 1914, however, and in particular the failure to win a quick victory over France at the Battle of the Marne, also made it necessary for German diplomats to present the violation of Belgian neutrality as a 'military necessity', to use a phrase later adopted by Bethmann Hollweg. To this end the German Foreign Office itself published selected documents it discovered in the Belgian government archives in Brussels concerning secret military conversations between the British and Belgian military alleged to have taken place in 1906. This in turn allowed the German propagandists to claim that Belgium had already forsaken its claim to neutrality well before August 1914, and that responsibility for the plight of the Belgian people lay with Britain and the Belgian government itself, not with Germany.[53]

Significantly, even the Social Democrat *Vorwärts*, which had at first recognised Belgian neutrality as a factor in British policy after 4 August, had apparently changed its mind by 17 September, when it decided to carry an article containing a declaration by the Independent Labour Party in England against Sir Edward Grey.

> It was not the Serbian question or the Belgian question which drew our country into the fearsome struggle. Great Britain is not waging war on behalf of oppressed nations or because of Belgian neutrality. Even if Germany had not illegally violated Belgian neutrality, we would still have been drawn into the war.[54]

Similarly, the left-liberal *Berliner Tageblatt* argued on 13 October 1914 that the discoveries in the Belgian archives had proved that 'the German General Staff correctly judged the issue of Belgian neutrality when it planned the march into France through Belgium. Belgium had ceased to be a neutral state long before the war and instead had become an active member of the anti-German coalition.'[55]

A second means of influencing public opinion was the broadening of the government's control over the press as a whole, based in part on the informal truce it had negotiated with the SPD but also backed up by the ultimate sanction of military censorship and stiff penalties for those journalists who refused to toe the line. Indeed, the proclamation of the state of siege following the German declaration of war on Russia allowed the wholesale suspension of many basic civil liberties guaranteed by the Imperial Constitution, with the military authorities given sweeping new powers to bully and censor newspaper editors, to confiscate pamphlets, to read private mail, to ban public meetings and to order the imprisonment of political suspects.[56] Not surprisingly, these powers were mainly used against left-wing opponents of the war, especially those connected to the international labour movement. As the radical Social Democratic women's paper, *Die Gleichheit*, noted with a certain degree of resignation on 4 September 1914:

> The martial law which is in force makes it quite impossible for us to seek a conscientious answer to the question: Did it have to be? It prevents us from showing up plainly the social forces whose inexorable rule has dashed the hopes and desires of the millions in all countries who have been dragged into the tornado of the war.[57]

Similarly, on 20 September the radical leftists Karl Liebknecht, Franz Mehring, Rosa Luxemburg and Klara Zetkin issued an illegal declaration to the socialist parties in Sweden, Italy and Switzerland in which they denounced the behaviour of the pro-war faction within the SPD and went on to claim that:

> . . . we and indeed many other German Social Democrats regard the war, its character as well as the role played by [German] Social Democracy . . . from a standpoint which differs from that of the comrades Südekum and Fischer. For the time being the state of siege makes it impossible for us to make these views known in public.[58]

The new powers given to the military authorities under the state of siege made it difficult even for moderate opponents of the war to criticise the official line, especially with regard to sensitive issues such as the Belgian question. This can be seen quite clearly from the diaries of Theodor Wolff, editor-in-chief of the *Berliner Tageblatt* and a well-respected figure in government and journalistic circles. As early as 12 October 1914 Wolff described how an article written in a 'very guarded and moderate form' was cut by the military censor and robbed of its actual meaning. And a few days later he recorded details of a conversation with the industrialist Walther Rathenau, in which the latter had asked 'in a foolish way . . . why I "went along with" it [the war]. As if the [Berliner] Tageblatt could write against the war under the censor.'[59]

The use of censorship, however, does not explain why other papers, such as the *Vossische Zeitung*, which before 1914 had been a broadly *freisinnig* paper that backed Bethmann Hollweg's pro-English orientation, should suddenly do a U-turn in September 1914 and argue – in an article written by Dr Friedrich Freund (a director in the Prussian Interior Ministry) – for a post-war continental alliance against England on the grounds that England's intention was not only to destroy Germany 'but to weaken its friends Russia and France and to build its claim to absolute power over Europe upon the ruins of the three most powerful European empires'.[60] In his post-war publication, *Die Kriegspolitik der Vossischen Zeitung* (1919), the paper's editor, Georg Bernhard, even claimed to have supported a pro-Russian policy from the outset of the war. An alliance of Germany with Russia and Japan was the only practical means of opposing an Anglo-Saxon world imperium, and renunciation of large-scale annexations in the east would have made peace with Russia possible by 1916. Such an orientation, Bernhard argued in 1919, would have made Germany into a world power after the war.[61]

Indeed, the views of Georg Bernhard provide a useful insight into the mentality of those sections of the German bourgeoisie that came out against any policy of courting an alliance with Britain after August 1914. The attitude of the *Vossische Zeitung* in branding England as the main warmonger in September 1914 also reminds one of the marginal comments made by Wilhelm II on a telegram which Jagow received from Lichnowsky shortly before the outbreak of the war, which included a serious warning from Sir Edward Grey not to speculate on the possibility of British neutrality in the event of war:

[Sir Edward Grey's] words to Lichnowsky are the outcome of a guilty conscience, because he feels that he has deceived us. At that, it is as a matter of fact a threat combined with bluff, in order to separate us from Austria and to prevent us from mobilising, and to shift responsibility for the war. He knows perfectly well that, if he were to utter one single, serious, sharp and warning word at Paris or St. Petersburg, and were to warn them to remain neutral, both would become quiet at once. But he takes care not to say the word and threatens us instead. England *alone* bears the responsibility for peace and war, not we any longer [*sic!*]. That must also be made clear to the world.[62]

Opposition to a pro-English orientation also came from within the government, not only from Tirpitz and the economic interests allied to him, but from conservatives such as the Prussian Interior Minister Friedrich Wilhelm von Loebell, who was opposed to the government's 'new orientation' towards the SPD and was clearly behind the publication of Freund's article in the *Vossische Zeitung*. In a report sent to the Reich Chancellor's office in Berlin at the end of September 1914, Loebell noted with satisfaction that the press – and in particular the *Vossische Zeitung* – had given way to public opinion, which, in spite of the atrocities committed by the Russians in East Prussia, had swung full circle towards an unbridled hatred of England. The general feeling now was that 'Russia is the immediate enemy of Austria and only incidentally an enemy of Germany, whilst the western powers direct their entire war effort against Germany'. By contrast, the propaganda of the SPD press for a war of revenge against Tsarism had, according to Loebell, lost ground.[63]

In November 1914 Loebell put these views even more forcefully in a secret memorandum entitled 'Gedanken über den Friedensschluß'. Here he argued that Germany's best interests lay in a separate peace with Russia, from whom 'we . . . require little or nothing at all'. He concluded by appealing for a continuation of the war against England as the only means of securing Germany's future as a world power.

This war, behind which England is the driving force, was forced upon us as we moved along the path of world politics towards the [goal of] a Greater Germany. Its gains are to be sought less on the continent and more in the field of world politics, and it is precisely these gains which will also best meet our future requirements. Large and enclosed colonial areas, predominantly in Africa, creating an empire from the Atlantic to the Pacific Ocean, are the most sought-after prizes to be won.[64]

Similar views were held by Gustav von Kessel, the Commander-in-Chief in the Marches and a former Adjutant-General to Wilhelm II, who had full authority over the police in Berlin and the province of Brandenburg for the duration of the state of siege. On 3 December 1914 Kessel wrote a personal report to the Kaiser, based in turn on information gathered by his deputy, Police President von Jagow, which warned that public opinion would adamantly oppose any premature peace settlement with England.

The populace of the capital and residential city of Berlin and indeed of the entire Fatherland retains complete confidence in our victory in the struggle for life and death which has been forced upon us first and foremost by England . . .

Your Majesty can scarcely imagine how deeply the will to victory, the burning desire for a reckoning with the enemies who want to throttle us, above all with England, and the belief in the final victory, has become firmly rooted in our entire people. The strength and the spirit of sacrifice of our people rests on the steadfastness of our national and political will, which stands behind our military organisation, and on the excellent quality of our armies and their leaders. A peace which fails to provide guarantees of our complete security in the future would not be understood by public opinion in Berlin, and indeed in the whole Reich, and the Foreign Office would naturally be held responsible.

Like Loebell and like his deputy Jagow, Kessel noted that the mood of the workers in Berlin was giving no cause for concern: 'The behaviour of Liebknecht on the occasion of the last sitting of the [Prussian] House of Deputies has even aroused ill-feeling among the workers of Berlin. In fact, the organised workers think much more intelligently in this respect than their irresponsible leaders.' By contrast, he argued: 'Every bit of news concerning Turkish victories and the precarious position of the English in Egypt and South Africa is greeted with increasing satisfaction.'[65]

In fact, as a number of previous studies have emphasised, the main beneficiaries of the state of siege were the Pan-German League and its supporters on the radical right. Heinrich Claß's famous memorandum on war aims, which the government tried unsuccessfully to suppress, was followed by countless petitions sent to the Reich and state authorities containing bitter criticism of the government's prosecution of the war abroad as well as angry denunciations of those politicians who propagated the idea of a 'new orientation' towards the SPD and the removal of existing conflicts between classes and religions at home.[66] What also seems significant, however, is the extent to which the views of the extreme right – and in particular the views of those taking on an anti-English, pro-Russian orientation – were shared by government ministers and the very people responsible for overseeing press censorship. This is a point which we shall return to in later chapters of this book.

Propaganda initiatives

In addition to the officially tolerated press campaign against England between August and December 1914, countless pamphlets and brochures also sought to 'enlighten' public opinion with regard to the causes of the war and the role played by England. Although individual propagandists often differed in emphasis regarding the precise motives behind British policy, they were unanimous in agreeing that England must bear a large portion of responsibility for the Entente's 'unprovoked' attack on Germany.

According to Count Ernst zu Reventlow, the main motive force behind British policy had always been fear of the consequences of Germany's growth as an economic power and trading nation: 'The envy, which was directed against little Prussia in 1857, arose in a more gigantic and expanded form against the healthy German Reich in 1897, as it conquered for itself an ever greater share of the world market and world trade.'[67] It was from motives of economic greed that England had also begun its 'war of destruction' against Germany in 1914 and had encouraged its allies to do the same.

Neither Russia nor France would have seen the peaceful development of the German Reich and people as a cause for war, had this not been the fundamental view of British policy. Only after both these powers had recognised that commercial rivalry against Germany was in fact the *Leitmotiv* of British policy – only then did France gain the confidence and reach the decision to launch itself into a struggle for existence in pursuit of revenge for 1870 and in order to recapture

Alsace-Lorraine; only then did Russia begin purposefully arming itself for a war of conquest, in order to smash Austria-Hungary and weaken Germany, in order to gain control over the Balkans and lay its hands on Constantinople. Neither one of the two continental powers regarded the war as a matter of survival in the present or the future. Both of them could have continued to live in harmony with the German Reich, growing in power and stature. It was Great Britain, and Great Britain alone whose persistent, skilful and business-like policy provided the Russian empire and the French republic with the will and the motivation to wage a war of destruction [*Vernichtungskrieg*] against the German Reich. That is the central feature of European politics in the long years of unrest which have now drawn to a close with the outbreak of war.[68]

Another important piece of anti-English propaganda, from which Reventlow himself drew many of his ideas, was a book by the Austrian Pan-German Alexander von Peez, *England und der Kontinent*, which first appeared in 1908 and was reprinted in its eighth edition in the middle of the war, despite its overtly anti-Semitic character.[69] In this book, which was written against the background of the Bosnian crisis of 1908/9 and accused Britain of waging a behind-the-scenes war against Austrian interests in the Balkans, Peez borrowed quotes from Kant and Napoleon I to illustrate the well-worn thesis that British policy had always been to stir up wars on the continent in order to ensure its continued domination of the seas and boost its profits from trade and world commerce. Continental wars, he argued, were 'harvest time' for England, and at the centre of its current intrigues stood the Jewish 'money princes' of the City of London.[70] He also quoted approvingly from a book written by the French racist Emil Flouren, *La France Conquise* (1904), to back his own theory that a secret Anglo-Jewish alliance, with the help of King Edward VII and the freemasons, was aiming at world domination. British policy had taken on a distinctly 'oriental character' and even cabinet ministers were 'only officials directed by the City' (*nur geleitete Beamte der City*).[71]

In popular cartoons Edward VII himself was often pictured sitting like a spider spinning his web of intrigues at the centre of world affairs, while Germany, represented by 'der deutsche Michel', appeared as a fly sitting in Berlin (fig. 3). Sir Edward Grey and Winston Churchill were also portrayed in German propaganda as the only ministers who counted in the Asquith cabinet, the 'executors of the last will and testament' of King Edward, as the economist and Progressive Reichstag deputy Gerhard von Schulze-Gaevernitz put it.[72] In other cartoons, such as the one taken from an issue of *Der Wahre Jacob* in April 1916 (fig. 4), Grey himself is seen to have inherited Edward VII's position as the nation-devouring spider, trapping his helpless victims in his web. The caption reads:

Das Spinnennetz.

3 'The spider's web', from *Ulk*, 26 June 1908

> My hunger seeks its nourishment throughout the whole wide world.
> Who full of trust falls in my web, woe shall that man betide.

By contrast, far less attention was given in the German press to those English ministers who had favoured a policy of salvaging peace in 1914, including pacifists such as Lord Morley and John Burns, who had resigned from Asquith's government rather than support the cabinet's decision for war.[73]

Another pamphletist, Ernst Haeckel, Professor of Zoology at Jena University and the founder of the German Monistenbund in 1906, was surprisingly candid in revealing the true motives behind German anti-English propaganda. In an article which first appeared under the title 'Englands Blutschuld am Kriege' in the *Jenaer Volksblatt* on 12 August 1914 and which received wide publicity in the national press, Haeckel

4 'The world cross (or garden) spider', from *Der Wahre Jacob*, 28 April 1916

was one of the first to point the finger at England as the instigator of the war and at Edward VII, 'that cursed prince of German blood', as the author of Germany's diplomatic encirclement. The individual responsible for the decision for war, he argued, was not the 'weak' Russian Tsar Nicholas II, or the 'ambitious' President of the French Republic Poincaré, but 'solely and purely the scheming English minister Sir Edward Grey, who for years has woven the great iron web intended to encircle Germany and strangle it'. Nevertheless, Haeckel also emphasised that England's decision for war was a disaster not only for Germany, but for the cultural world as a whole, which was relying on a German victory over its continental enemies.

When Russia declared war on Germany and Austria at the beginning of August [*sic!*], we were confronted only with the burden of a continental war on two fronts, in the east and the west. Even if this war had been fearsome, we could still have hoped to win it, supported by our tried and trusty sword and in the knowledge of the justice of our cause and our clear consciences. But after England declared war on us on 4 August the political and strategic position was completely transformed. Now we are confronted with a hard struggle for life and death, [a struggle] on three fronts, against two powerful land armies in the east and the west, and against the greatest sea power in the world, which threatens our fleet, our naval forces [and] our overseas colonies with destruction. Only now – as a result of England's actions – has the dreaded 'European war' been transformed into a universal war of unprecedented magnitude![74]

Haeckel had enjoyed extensive academic contacts with colleagues in England since his first visit to London in 1866. During the 1870s he had worked in Glasgow with Sir Wyville Thomson and Sir John Murray on the Challenger Project on deep sea life. On 18 August 1914, a few days after the first appearance of his article, Haeckel and a colleague from Jena, the philosopher Rudolf Eucken, became the first German academics publicly to renounce their honorary degrees and other academic distinctions awarded by British universities. At the same time they issued a joint statement denouncing the 'national egoism' of the English who 'above all bear the moral responsibility for the *Völkerbrand'*.[75]

Other academics offered a more moderate view of the motives behind English policy, arguing that England had indeed planned for war, but had not deliberately brought it about. In an essay published in the September 1914 issue of the highbrow *Süddeutsche Monatshefte*, and written in the last week of August, Hermann Oncken, Professor of History at the University of Heidelberg, came much closer to the truth surrounding the events of 4 August when he wrote: 'Belgium is only the outer shell, and the nucleus which it disguises is that well-known dogma of the English imperialists, to which even moderate groups subscribe: France must under no circumstances be weakened.'[76] Nonetheless, Oncken also went on to argue that in this particular case

Germany had offered England sufficient guarantees with regard to the integrity of French territory, and had further promised not to attack the French north coast and French shipping. The real villains of English policy were in his view Grey and Churchill (the 'bellicose authors of the Anglo-German war'[77]), who had sought to hide the truth from the English public. On the other hand, Oncken also had many good things to say of Lord Haldane ('he does not carry with him the narrow-minded insularity of Sir Edward Grey, but fits in with the cosmopolitan world of culture, so that one can relate to him as if he were one of our own'[78]) and also mentioned the radicals – Morley, Burns, Trevelyan – who resigned from the cabinet in protest against the war.

Like Haeckel, Oncken had enjoyed extensive pre-war contacts with England, especially with Lord Morley and the National Liberal Club, as well as with Lord Haldane. In conclusion he wrote:

And this we also know: that only victory on our part can bring forth the better England, the leading intellectual figures, the honest and peace-loving radicals, the mass of the workers, English idealism, all of that which we love on the other side of the Channel and which is now divided from us by a separate world. Only our victory, and nothing else on Earth, will bring us back together in joint efforts towards the betterment of mankind.[79]

Oncken sent a copy of the article to Bethmann on 9 September 1914 and received a reply on 13 September in which the Chancellor particularly praised 'the fine manner in which you deal with Haldane'.[80] An article which appeared in the government paper, the *Norddeutsche Allgemeine Zeitung*, on 5 September reflected similar views, holding England only indirectly responsible, in that it bound itself too closely to Russia, the main aggressor, and put maintenance of the Triple Entente above maintenance of peace with Germany.

There is no doubt that during the years 1912 and 1913 the English government strove in all seriousness and with a dogged perseverance for the maintenance of world peace. There is also no doubt that an Anglo-German agreement was pursued after a fashion by the English government. They did everything in their power to steer German policy in this direction. But it is also clearly evident that English policy directed its main efforts to ensuring that in the event of world war the political and military parameters were so positioned as to ensure the destruction of Austria and the overthrow of Germany. This was the core of English policy since Edward VII, so that all other factors were pushed into the background.[81]

These more moderate attempts to provide an academic foundation for Germany's case against England should not, however, lead us to the conclusion that the government or Bethmann Hollweg personally were willing to do a separate peace deal with England in September 1914. The Chancellor's own change in outlook after 4 August was clearly demonstrated in instructions he sent to Arthur Zimmermann, the Under Secretary of State in the German Foreign Office, on 12 September for his official answer to an American offer of mediation.

We did not want the war; it was forced upon us. Even if we defeat France, Russia and England will still be in the field against us . . . If we now accepted an offer of mediation from America, this would be interpreted by our enemies only as a sign of weakness, and not understood by our people. For the people, who have made such sacrifices, want guarantees for our security and tranquillity.[82]

Nor was Bethmann ever able – even in retrospect – to come to a full understanding of the underlying motives behind British policy in 1914. In his speech to the Reichstag on 2 December 1914 he expressed his personal feelings of anger and bitterness at what he saw as Britain's two-faced behaviour during the July crisis in the following words:

Right into the summer English statesmen continued to assure their parliament: no treaty, no agreement restricts England's right to determine its own course of action in case of war. Great Britain was apparently free to decide whether it took part in the war or not. And so, *Meine Herren*, it was not alliance obligations or pressures, it was not even a threat to their own country which caused English statesmen to allow a war to break out and then immediately to enter into it. There remains only one possible explanation, that the London cabinet allowed this world war, this terrible world war, to break out because England saw in it an opportunity, with the help of its allies, to destroy the vital nerve of her greatest European competitor on the world market.[83]

'Perfidious Albion': anglophobia in poetry and prose

One of the most striking aspects of the hate campaign waged against England in the first months of the war was the considerable interest shown in the history of anti-English slogans, particularly those which were non-German in origin and which could therefore be presented as having a universal significance. German propagandists, for instance, were well aware of the fact that France had traditionally viewed the English as habitual traitors, an idea summed up in the age-old concept of 'la perfide Albion' or 'perfidious Albion'.[84] In some cases, this awareness of the existence of a continuous tradition of anti-English feeling amounted to little more than the assertion that England was waging a 'war of assassins' or that it would fight 'until the last Frenchman' or 'until the last Belgian'. The aim here was quite clearly to revive the idea of England as an unreliable ally in order to undermine the basis of the wartime coalition against the Central Powers. In other cases, however, the idea of the 'perfidious English' took on a more sophisticated and literary form, giving added impetus to the adoption of the slogan within Germany itself.

A good example of this is the play *John Bull*, written by the theologian Johannes Lepsius in the first weeks of the war and published in the right-wing journal *Der Panther* in April 1915.[85] The play takes place against the background of the War of the Spanish Succession (1702–13). It is set in London in April 1711, at the time of the death of the Habsburg Emperor Joseph I and the succession of his brother, Charles VI. This marked the turning point of the war when Bolingbroke, the Tory leader, treacherously opened peace negotiations with the French behind the backs of Britain's former allies, Holland, Austria and the German states (Brandenburg, Saxony, Hanover and Hesse-Cassel). Under the subsequent Treaty of Utrecht (1713) Britain also gained Gibraltar and Minorca, and thus potential mastery of the Mediterranean, whereas the Dutch, bullied and then deserted by the British, completely lost their commercial predominance in the Spanish empire and therewith their status as a world power. The clear-cut anti-English bias of the play is all the more significant given that after 1918 Lepsius himself played a prominent role in the campaign to revise the war-guilt clause of the Treaty of Versailles. In particular, he was one of the co-editors of the multi-volume *Große Politik der Europäischen Kabinette* (1922–27), an important collection of official documents relating to European diplomatic relations in the run-up to the First World War.

Although *John Bull* was set in 1711, there could be little doubt that it was written with the events of 1914 in mind. In the first act, for instance, a three-way conversation takes place between John Bull, a prominent Whig member of parliament, the Duke of Marlborough, who has returned to London in order to thwart Bolingbroke's plans and gain further subsidies for his armies in Europe, and the Dean of Westminster Abbey. When Marlborough asks Bull how much the war has cost him in terms of lost business, the following dialogue takes place:

Bull: Let's try and understand each other, Your Excellency . . . Even an experienced horseman makes a blunder sometimes . . . Do you really believe that I voted for the war and gained nothing from it? Do you seriously believe that I have voted for war for ten years and become poorer as a result?

Duke [of Marlborough]: It is on the basis of such rumours that Bolingbroke has won the Queen's ear, that the Tories are now beating the drum of peace.

Bull: Are there really so many idiots in England? . . . Let me think for a minute . . . You are so to speak our commercial representative on the continent. When one has been in business for a long time, one has to take stock of things from time to time, to establish what is going on in the market out there . . . Let's go over this again . . . One must have a reason for starting a war . . . that's obvious . . . but it's often quite difficult . . . I don't like putting a strain on my memory . . . We doubtless had a very good reason for our cause.[86]

When the Dean of Westminster Abbey interrupts Bull to remind him of the importance of England's 'sacred cause' and the role of the English as God's chosen people, called upon to set an example of piety and humanity to other peoples and to uphold the inviolability of international law, Bull replies:

If an English statesman should ever dare to plunge the United Kingdom into a war simply because he wanted to play the nightwatchman of Europe . . . I would string him up . . . with my own hands . . . in Westminster Abbey . . . as a permanent warning . . . Are there chickens who could believe such rubbish? (To the Duke): I only want you to tell me . . . how things are looking for our trade out there in Europe . . . They call you the Duke of Marlborough . . . I like the way it sounds . . . victor of Blenheim, Oudenaarde, Malplaquet . . . it sounds good when after every victory your name is called out in the streets, as if it were a brand of boot-polish or gravy . . . But when I imagine that you run around with your twenty pound cannons and flirt with death and the Devil . . .[87]

This dialogue was obviously intended to demonstrate the mercenary and utilitarian spirit of the English, as well as their hypocritical religiosity. In the rest of the play, John Bull, who as chief whip for the Whigs has a controlling majority of one vote in Parliament, is gradually won over to vote with Bolingbroke against the extension of subsidies for Marlborough's armies. His price for abandoning Marlborough and cooperating with Bolingbroke's efforts towards peace with France is the promise of the latter's own help in promoting Bull's efforts to gain the exclusive right to sell 5,000 Negro slaves annually to the Spanish Indies. At the same time, we see how the English Parliament itself is controlled by a corrupt clique of politicians and journalists, gathered together by Bull at the Phaeton club, who have the final say over war or peace. At a meeting before the crucial vote on Marlborough's subsidies, Bull tells his fellow Whigs that they must consider three main points when deciding on how to vote on a particular bill: firstly, whether the bill is in the interests of the kingdom, secondly, whether it is to the advantage of the traders of the City of London, and, thirdly, whether it is honourable in the eyes of God:

As far as point one is concerned, it has always been our unaminous view that every war which is fought on the soil of our island is detrimental and to be condemned, but that every war which is fought on the continent for the benefit of our kingdom is beneficial and should be welcomed (widespread agreement). As for point two, nobody in our midst has ever doubted that the Phaeton club is the barometer which tells us what kind of world pressures are currently being exerted on London traders (murmurs of approval) . . . Concerning point three, the honour of God, I am of the opinion that we can best leave God to sort his own problems out (agreement).[88]

Although the queen's personal preference is for Bolingbroke, she too can do nothing unless he enjoys a parliamentary majority. Similarly, Marlborough admits to the queen: 'Your pen and my sword are both beholden to Parliament, since we can only remain silently respectful in the face of the sovereign will of our [politically] mature people.' Everything, including questions of war and peace, therefore depends on the arbitrary balance of power between different parties and factions, an obvious indictment of the British parliamentary system. (By way of a joke, the speaker of Parliament himself is called 'Servatius Gleichgewicht'.)

In the meantime, the only figure who comes out well from the whole episode is Marlborough, portrayed as the honest soldier, who cares little for politics and enjoys war for its own sake.[89] At one point he confesses to Bolingbroke that he is considering giving the whole game up, and retiring to his estates: 'To be perfectly frank . . . I am sick and tired of it all. In hundreds of battles I have looked death in the face, and now I have to go begging for subsidies from these shopkeepers. It's a disgrace.'[90] This is then contrasted with the unmanly attitude of Marlborough's own supporters among the Whigs, i.e. the financial backers of the war, who have names such as 'Armbruster' and 'Spinnefeind':

Armbruster: We are already carrying out shooting practice on the coast of Dover. But our cannon balls do not reach as far as Calais.
Spinnefeind: Couldn't we cross over and start shooting from there?
Armbruster: We might just as well fill up the Channel itself. There's enough idiots out there on the continent to do the fighting. English blood is too good for all that.[91]

In pamphlets and political songs, too, the term 'perfidious Albion' was applied to denounce England's alleged treachery and its callous attitude towards its own allies, the French and the Belgians. Walter Unus, for instance, noted ironically in his brochure *England als Henker Frankreichs* (1915): 'It is of course a total absurdity that "Perfidious Albion" – as France used to call it – can today be seen loyally fighting on France's side.'[92] This same point was made even more forcefully by the historian Eduard Meyer when he wrote in his *Nordamerika und Deutschland* (1915): 'As for the rest, England has so far been waging war in its customary manner. It gets its allies to fight for it using all their strength, while it itself can take part with only a relatively minor force [of soldiers] which it aims to spare wherever possible.[93]

A sense of the great moral outrage which many patriotic Germans felt or were told they must feel towards England can also be seen in Friedrich Weidig's poem, *An Albion!*, which was printed as a fly sheet in

Munich in November 1914 and contained all the usual accusations of cowardice and disloyalty.

> Beware England, beware, for waves of fire are closing in on you,
> The sea is surging at your shores,
> The sea which you basely abuse
> To commit crimes and robberies in all corners of the earth.
>
> Woe to you England, a day of judgement awaits you,
> It will crush you, destroy your bloody empire,
> Which you so treacherously created –
> From the life and property, the possessions of murdered nations![94]

Another example would be the work of the satirist Otto Ernst, whose anti-English poems and songs appeared under the title *Deutschland an England* in 1914, and were later reproduced in a pocket-size edition for soldiers at the front, with the new title *Gewittersegen*.[95] In the poem 'Deutschland an England', for instance, Ernst speculated on the gender identity of Britannia, the 'band of murderers' or 'Judas', who betrayed Germanic blood for thirty pieces of silver, and concluded, in the final two verses, that England is neither male nor female – in fact it is not human at all:

> You are neither a man nor a woman, a Jackal are you,
> Who will not fight alone but hunts in packs,
> Who slyly creeps and comes to steal
> After the lion has dared to leap and fight.
>
> Beware: the curse of millions of downtrodden
> will be fulfilled in these sobering times!
> Already the Frenchie feels my hand around his throat,
> And from Calais to Dover is not so far![96]

And in his song 'Romanze zum Preise Englands', we once again find a contrast between the 'noble' attributes of the ordinary French and Russian soldiers, fighting to defend their national honour and past historical greatness, and the cowardly, profit-oriented English, whose last and only genuine military hero was Richard the Lionheart back in the twelfth century. The last verse and the chorus went as follows:

> In spite of Kluck and Hindenburg
> You talk a brave war indeed
> And will hold out until
> The very last Frenchman and Russian are dead!
> You push them bravely out in front
> And cry 'My country, right or wrong!'
> But were your hero Lionheart
> To rise up from his tomb:

> Doubt not, England, in your pride,
> He'd spit right in your face,
> Your Richard, your Richard,
> The brave Lionheart![97]

Even more violent attacks on the aims and methods of England's military intervention were meanwhile made by Nanny Lambrecht in *Die Eiserne Freude* (1914) and *Die Fahne der Wallonen* (1915), and by Otto Ernst in *Hermannsland* (1915). In these novels, which were widely distributed in the early part of the war, the French and particularly the Belgians were accused of all manner of barbarities committed against German soldiers, while the English were represented as scheming villains who had duped the unfortunate Belgians into resisting the peaceful passage of the German army through its territory.[98] At the same time, by justifying the German invasion of Belgium, these war novelists reinforced annexationist demands and supplied important arguments of their own against the restoration of Belgian independence. Indeed, as we shall see in a later chapter, the alleged 'perfidy' of the Belgians persuaded even moderate and anglophile groups that some sort of measures had to be taken to prevent Belgium from allying itself with Britain and France in the future.

England and France as the 'betrayers' of the white race

One final aspect of the wave of popular anti-western sentiment which swept across Germany in the first months of the war was the attempt to cast England and France in the role of 'betrayers' of the white race, a charge which was intended to demonstrate the alleged 'racial treason' of the Anglo-Saxon and Romance peoples. This aspect of German anti-western propaganda is also of interest because of its obvious links with racism and anti-Semitism as a whole and with later National Socialist ideology in particular.

None other than Chancellor Bethmann Hollweg told representatives of the American press in Berlin on 2 September 1914:

England is already beginning to realise that it has made a big mistake and that Germany will triumph over its enemies. So it is trying, as far as circumstances allow and using the pettiest of means, to harm German trade and German colonial interests. Unconcerned at the damage it has done to the cultural unity of the white race, it has incited the Japanese to undertake a raid against Kiautschau, encouraged the Negroes in Africa to wage war against Germans in the colonies, and, having cut off the German news service from the rest of the world, has opened up a campaign of lies against us. Thus, it tells its own people that German soldiers have burned down Belgian villages and towns, but doesn't tell them that Belgian girls have been gouging out the eyes of wounded men on the battlefield.[99]

And, in his Reichstag speech of 2 December 1914, he further fanned the flames of nationalist hatred when he declared:

Now that all the details of the Anglo-Belgian war plan have been brought to light, the policy pursued by English statesmen can be identified for all time . . . But English diplomacy itself has committed yet another crime. On its orders Japan has seized heroic Kiautschau from us and thereby violated Chinese neutrality . . . Has England intervened against this breach of neutrality? . . . Has it shown, in this instance, its scrupulous concern for [the rights of] neutral states?[100]

Englands Blutschuld gegen die weiße Rasse was also the title of a pamphlet written by the pan-German propagandist Woldemar Schütze in the first weeks of the war and published at the end of 1914.[101] In his foreword, Schütze made quite clear his view that England was a 'foreign body' in the community of nations, which must be destroyed in the interests of humanity.

If a foreign body enters the organism of the human body and manages to disturb the functioning of one or all the organs, the doctor will insist, in the interests of maintaining human life, on the ruthless extermination of that foreign body . . . If I succeed in convincing the reader that England is just such a foreign body, which, motivated solely by its own selfish interests, has committed an unforgivable crime against humanity, then the purpose of this book will have been fulfilled.[102]

England, he went on, had always opposed the healthy economic development of other white nations, as its destruction of the Boer republics in South Africa at the turn of the century had shown. The current war of 1914, 'for which England is to blame, which England alone could have prevented if it had wanted to', was no exception to this rule.

There can be no doubt that Germany would have agreed to any English proposal to limit the war to Europe with the greatest of pleasure. The active extension of the theatre of war beyond the borders of Europe is the dubious handiwork of England, which first of all attacked the defenceless German colony [of] Togoland on Africa's west coast and thereby scored a cheap victory.[103]

England's attack on Togoland meant in turn that the Germans had been forced to defend their other possessions in Africa, in spite of the fact that future control of these and other colonies in Africa should and would by right be decided by events on the European continent. At the same time, England was destroying the image of solidarity of the white race in Africa, just as it had done at the turn of the century by encouraging the 'lowest instincts' of black South Africans against the Boers.

In this way the English have burdened themselves with a terrible guilt, not only towards Germany and Austria-Hungary, but also towards the entire white race, including their own allies . . . [They] have transformed the struggle between nations of one and the same race into a struggle between races, and the European war into a world war.[104]

England's behaviour in the Far East, where its fear of rival European competitors had turned it into the 'champion of the yellow race', was, in Schütze's view, even more ignominious. England had deliberately encouraged its ally Japan to attack the Russians in 1904–5, in order to reduce pressure on itself in central Asia and India, and had further bribed Japan with 100 million yen to declare war on Germany and attack the German-leased territory of Kiaochou in September 1914. All this in spite of the fact that England

... must know that sooner or later Japan will free itself from British tutelage and emerge as its enemy; it must understand that, as was the case with the North Americans one and a half centuries ago, the great colonies Canada, South Africa, Australia and New Zealand will renounce their ties with the motherland as soon as their colonial interests are no longer compatible with those of the island empire; finally, it must face the fact that as a consequence of advances in civilisation even the savage and semi-savage peoples of Africa and Asia will attempt to free themselves from British rule.[105]

In view of all these threats facing the British empire, Germany should have been England's natural ally and helper in the world, 'even from a purely egotistical standpoint'. But, argued Schütze, the English lacked the national character required to adopt such a far-sighted policy and would rather dig the grave of their own empire than grant equality to their most hated commercial rival.

In the Boer war England openly set aside the fundamental precept of national and international economics – that lasting and healthy economic development requires peace – and thereby revealed the core aims of its world policy. At the same time, of course, it also channelled a large amount of the world's gold reserves into its own coffers and thus acquired the means of engaging in further acts of aggression overseas. But whether in the long run it will be able to claim success through its ruthless disregard of all the rules of economics is quite another story. *Die Weltgeschichte ist das Weltgericht* – world history will make the final judgement.[106]

Schütze's pamphlet later appeared on a recommended reading list for members of Dietrich Schäfer's Independent Committee for a German Peace in 1916 along with books containing similar ideas, such as Alexander von Peez's *England und der Kontinent* (1915) and several works by Count Ernst zu Reventlow, including his notorious *Vampir des Festlandes* (1915).[107]

German cartoonists, too, were quick to exploit the presence of black colonial troops on the western front, partly, it must be said, in order to counter Allied atrocity stories about invading 'Huns' raping Belgian women and slaughtering Belgian babies. In a cartoon which appeared in the Berlin-based satirical journal *Kladderadatsch* in June 1915 (fig. 5),

5 'John Bull as he is today', from *Kladderadatsch*, 20 June 1915

John Bull appears as a fearsome-looking, cannibalistic African tribes-man with thick lips and flattened nose. To indicate his allegiance to the British crown he wears coins bearing the head of George V in his ear lobes and also carries an enormous ring through his nose. The caption reads: 'In view of the colour of the English who face the Germans in Flanders, it would appear to be time to correct the figure of the nation personified.'

The sexual fascination behind such images can also be seen in another cartoon, 'Christmas in England', which appeared in *Simplicissimus* in December 1914 (fig. 6). Here, well-dressed English women are seen dancing in close embrace with black and turban-headed partners. The accompanying text explains: 'Whilst previously the English did not associate with coloureds, their dark-skinned broth-ers-in-arms have now become all the rage in London society. Many of them are allowed to give a blonde young lady the traditional Christmas kiss under the mistletoe branch.'

Similar accusations were made against the English with regard to the Japanese declaration of war on Germany at the end of August 1914 and the subsequent capture of the German-leased territory of Kiaochou by Japanese troops, an event widely attributed to English intrigues. In a cartoon that appeared in *Simplicissimus* in September 1914 under the title 'The Englishman and his Japanese friend' (fig. 7), Germany is depicted as an eagle sitting majestically high up in a tree, while below Japan is represented by a circus monkey. The monkey's trainer, a pipe-smoking English imperialist, is saying: 'Now just you climb up the German oak tree and see if you can't pluck a feather from his tail.' Meanwhile, other victims of British imperialism are seen hanging from the tree's branches.

Images such as these became a standard feature of German wartime propaganda, forming part of a broader continuum of anti-western feeling which alleged that Britain and France, far from protecting western Europe from the invading 'Hun', were actually engaged in acts of savagery and cultural vandalism themselves. More than this, they were systematically betraying the white race to 'inferior', uncivilised breeds, the black and yellow races, whose presence on the battlefields of Europe signalled the final collapse of western civilisation itself. In 1923, at the time of the Franco-Belgian occupation of the Ruhr, ex-Kaiser Wilhelm II returned to this theme when he wrote:

At last I know what the future holds for the German people, what we still have to achieve! . . . We shall be the leaders of the Orient against the Occident! I shall now have to alter my picture 'Völker Europas'. We belong on the other side! Once we have proved to the Germans that the French and the English are not Whites at all but Blacks . . . then they will set upon this rabble.[108]

6 'Christmas in England', from *Simplicissimus*, 22 December 1914

7 'The Englishman and his Japanese friend', from *Simplicissimus*, 1 September 1914

The cartoonists and England

The initial hate campaign against England continued throughout 1914 and was given further impetus in January 1915 following the success of the first Zeppelin raids on the English east coast. As early as the autumn of 1914 Berlin school children had been singing a song which went: 'Fly Zeppelin! Fly to England! England shall be destroyed by fire!', whilst postcards were on sale all over Germany depicting the Zeppelins in action.[109] In November 1914 *Kladderadatsch* even published a cartoon depicting the Zeppelin as a sword of Damocles hanging over the head of a hapless-looking John Bull (fig. 8). And on 21 January 1915 the nationalist *Kölnische Zeitung* went on to celebrate what it saw as a significant turning point in the war:

German genius has at last ended the legend of England's invulnerable insularity . . . It has come to pass that which the English have long feared and repeatedly contemplated with terror . . . the most modern air weapon, a triumph of German inventiveness and the sole possession of the German army has shown itself capable of crossing the sea and carrying the war to the soil of Old England.[110]

In some cases, this German animosity towards England developed much darker and more sinister tones, reflecting a deep-seated, almost pathological loathing which went far beyond mere nationalistic rhetoric or sporadic outbursts of xenophobic violence. In June 1915, for example, a gelatine expert in the Bavarian Ministry of War drew up a detailed programme for the use of biological warfare against England. Among his many suggestions were specific proposals to contaminate the water supply with cholera and to introduce typhoid-infected insects and plague-infested rats into all the major English cities. Moral and humanitarian considerations could quite simply be cast aside since the English themselves had hitherto 'not shied away from using any and all means to destroy Germany'. England, he concluded, was simply the 'most perfidious enemy', against whom anything could be allowed: 'If any nation should go to ruin, then at least let it be England.'[111]

Perhaps more alarming than these individual examples of extreme anglophobia, however, was the one-sided portrayal of the war by previously radical and independent elements in German society, such as the satirical journals *Kladderadatsch*, *Simplicissimus* and *Ulk* mentioned above.[112] In 1915, for instance, both *Simplicissimus* and *Kladderadatsch* issued special albums of their best anti-English cartoons under the titles *Gott strafe England!* (God punish England!) and *Am Pranger!* (In the stockade!), respectively.[113] Later, in 1917, further albums were produced by members of the *Simplicissimus* staff at the request of the German Foreign Office for use as propaganda in neutral countries.[114] This was a far cry from the situation before 1914, when some of the very same

8 'The sword of Damocles', from *Kladderadatsch*, 15 November 1914

caricaturists had found themselves in jail for the crime of *lèse-majesté* (insulting the Kaiser) or the lesser crime of insulting the government. Indeed, as Thomas Theodor Heine, the principal cartoonist for *Simplicissimus*, saw it in August 1914, the Fatherland was now in need of a journal such as his to support the war effort: 'it was very wrong to believe that *Simplicissimus* was obsolete . . . may be its great age was just beginning.'[115]

In all likelihood, men such as Heine (whose own mother was English by birth) experienced the war as an opportunity for social integration and personal enhancement under the guise of 'patriotic duty' rather than as a life and death struggle between nations for survival. In this sense England, France and Russia merely replaced older objects of satire such as the Kaiser, the Prussian military or the Catholic Church. But this does not detract from the shockingly racist nature of the images they produced, images whose effects could still be felt in the 1920s and beyond. One of the most striking examples in this respect was Heine's cartoon for *Simplicissimus* in October 1914, depicting a group of evil-looking English women removing the tips from bullets with a variety of implements, including a set of false teeth (fig. 9). The text beneath reads: 'In England, too, great efforts are being made to help the troops. The ladies are competing with each other in the production of dum-dum bullets.'[116]

Such atrocity propaganda was of course not unique to Germany; equally violent anti-German images featured regularly in the Northcliffe press in England (especially the *Daily Mail* and the *Weekly Dispatch*) and *John Bull*, edited and owned by Horatio Bottomley. They too followed the techniques which the American political scientist Harold Dwight Lasswell identified in 1927 as the key to successful wartime propaganda:

There must be no ambiguity about whom the public is to hate. The war must not be due to a world system of conducting international affairs, nor to the stupidity or malevolence of all governing classes, but to the rapacity of the enemy . . . If the propagandist is to mobilise the hate of the people, he must see to it that everything is circulated which establishes the sole responsibility of the enemy.[117]

The remaining chapters of this book will look more closely at some of the broader implications of this sustained spirit of 'hatred', in particular its importance to the war aims debate in Germany and the campaign in favour of unrestricted submarine warfare. First however, it is necessary to take a closer look at the contribution which German intellectuals made to the cultural war against England and to the civilian war effort more generally. This will form the subject of the next chapter.

9 'A picture of English family life', from *Simplicissimus*, 1 December 1914

2 The cultural war. German intellectuals and England

Enthusiastic support for the war was not, as recent research has revealed, as widespread in Germany in 1914 as previously assumed. Particularly among the working class and those living outside the major urban centres the mood was one of resignation, indifference or passive acceptance of the need to fight rather than aggressive nationalism.[1] The so-called 'August experience', in other words, was largely a middle/upper-middle-class and urban phenomenon which attracted the attention of significant numbers of artists, writers, newspaper editors, politicians and businessmen but had far less impact on the remaining population.[2] This has important implications for our under-standing of the manner in which anti-English feeling was expressed and orchestrated in the first weeks and months of the war.

Indeed, it is sometimes forgotten that the myth of the 'August experience' was created not just by the ill-informed crowds who were photo-graphed taking part in pro-war demonstrations, but more often than not by those who were capable of critical thought – the intellectuals and uni-versity professors. Johann Plenge, for instance, the German philosopher credited with coining the term 'the ideas of 1914', welcomed the war as the 'day of German re-birth' and the 'day of awakening of a new spirit of common social, economic and political action in the service of the fatherland'.[3] Other intellectuals also felt called upon to provide the war with a positive philosophy, one which idealised the power conflict in terms of an alleged spiritual antithesis between German culture and political forms and those of its enemies.[4] On the one hand, the so-called 'cultural war' was used to present an appealing image of Germany as the land of poets and philosophers, fighting to defend Christian values against the barbaric East. On the other hand, it was used to assert the superior virtues of the German sense of duty and spirit of cooperation against the selfishness and excessive individualism bred by the democ-racies of the west. Such ideas were developed by intellectuals from all points on the political spectrum, including Thomas Mann,[5] Friedrich Meinecke,[6] Ernst Troeltsch,[7] Rudolf Eucken,[8] Werner Sombart,[9] Max Scheler,[10] Alfred Weber[11] and the Swedish philosopher Rudolf Kjellén.[12]

At the same time, the 'cultural war' intensified considerably through the sharp polemics traded between English and French academics and their German counterparts after the outbreak of war. The starting point here was the issue of the methods of warfare employed by the German army in its conquest of Belgium and north-eastern France, symbolised to the world by the burning of the ancient library in the Belgian town of Louvain and the destruction of the cathedral of Rheims, as well as massacres of Belgian civilians in Dinant and other places, allegedly in retaliation for acts of sabotage committed by French and Belgian *Franctireurs*.[13] The public protests by English and French academics, and the demand that representatives of culture and science in the German empire should publicly distance themselves from Prussian militarism and German imperialism, produced the exact opposite effect: namely the unconditional identification of large sections of the German academic elite with the German war effort and the policies of the military leadership. Indeed, as early as 4 October 1914 a group of ninety-three of the most distinguished German scholars issued an 'Appeal to the cultural world' in which they resolutely denied all charges of German atrocities in Belgium and violations of international law and went on to declare:

It is not true that the struggle against our so-called militarism is not also a struggle against our civilisation, as our enemies hypocritically pretend it is. Were it not for German militarism, German civilisation would have long since been extirpated from the earth. The former arose from the need to protect the latter in a country which for centuries has been afflicted by predatory invasions. The German army and the German people are one. Today this knowledge unites 70 million Germans regardless of education, class and party [affiliation].[14]

Among the signatories of this manifesto were the writers Richard Dehmel and Gerhart Hauptmann, the painters Max Klinger, Max Liebermann, Hans Thoma and Wilhelm Trübner, the musicians Engelbert Humperdinck, Siegfried Wagner and Felix von Weingartner, the famous theatre director Max Reinhardt, the progressive politician Friedrich Naumann and a number of prominent academics, including the zoologist Ernst Haeckel, the mathematician Fritz Klein, the physicists Philipp Lenard and Max Planck, the theologians Adolf von Harnack and Reinhold Seeberg, the economists Lujo Brentano and Gustav Schmoller, the philologists Karl Voßler and Ulrich von Wilamowitz-Moellendorff, the philosophers Rudolf Eucken, Alois Riehl, Wilhelm Windelband and Wilhelm Wundt and the historians Karl Lamprecht, Max Lenz, Eduard Meyer, Friedrich Meinecke and Martin Spahn. A counter-petition organised by the Berlin doctor and lecturer in medicine Georg Friedrich Nicolai under the heading 'Appeal to the Europeans' attracted just three signatures – his own and those of the physicist Albert Einstein and the biologist Friedrich Wilhelm Foerster.[15]

In addition to defending Germany against accusations that it was fighting for an unjust cause, prominent German academics, including venerable scholars such as Otto von Gierke, Adolf von Harnack, Werner Sombart and Ulrich von Wilamowitz-Moellendorff, also played their part in promoting popular hatred of the enemy, castigating England in particular as the author of 'encirclement' and the foremost of those utilitarian, egotistical and purely mercenary powers allegedly so alien to the German 'heroic' spirit. Even before the publication of the 'Appeal to the cultural world' a group of thirty-one academics led by the medical professor Julius Schwalbe had taken the significant step of renouncing their honorary degrees and other distinctions awarded by British universities. At the same time they issued the following statement which was published in the Berlin press:

Under a flimsy pretext, which fails to stand the test of its own history and which has been exposed in its true form in countless documents, England has declared war upon us.

From motives of vile jealousy towards Germany's economic successes England – to whom we are related by ties of blood and race – has incited the other nations against us and in particular has allied itself with Russia and France in order to destroy our world power and deliver a blow to our culture.

Only because of their confidence in England's support did Russia, France, Belgium and Japan feel able to throw us the boxing glove. England more than any one else bears the moral responsibility for the war, which has brought suffering to millions of people and led to unprecedented sacrifices in terms of lives and material goods. England, through its brutal and national egoism, has burdened itself with irredeemable guilt.[16]

Declarations such as these did not, of course, help Germany to win friends and supporters among neutral countries, a point often noted with dismay by the left-liberal journalist Theodor Wolff in his diaries. Wolff found it 'unbelievable', for instance, that the authors of the 'Appeal to the cultural world' should presume to make statements concerning the origins of the war and Germany's total innocence with such certainty when the true facts were still to emerge. 'The worst thing of all', he noted on 8 October 1914, 'is that this uncompromising attitude is losing us the support of opinion abroad, which perhaps could be won over by a more serious and sensible approach.'[17]

On the other hand, the fact that so few German intellectuals were willing in 1914 openly to oppose the general tide of anti-western and anglophobic sentiment is indicative not only of the problems caused by wartime censorship, but also of the widespread agreement that the war would bring about Germany's rise to world power status, and would thus go down in history as the 'German war'.[18] Wolff himself recognised such attitudes even among his closest friends such as the writer Gerhart Hauptmann, who visited Wolff's offices in a highly agitated state one day in early October 1914. Hauptmann, Wolff recorded, had been 'completely transformed into a world conqueror, wants to swallow up Belgium and half the world and above all to overpower England. Like most people he is already having fantasies about a German Calais, from which the cannons can rain down on England. [This is] currently the general obsession.'[19]

In the meantime, the 'Appeal to the cultural world' was followed up with a wave of speeches, books and further public pronouncements which sought to justify Germany's war policy from an academic viewpoint.[20] A significant role was played here by the Bund deutscher Gelehrte und Künstler, which had its head office in Berlin and by the end of 1914 had recruited 192 members throughout Germany, including leading figures from the literary and artistic world such as the novelist Thomas Mann. In a letter to the Bavarian Prime Minister Count Hertling, the Bund described its main aim as follows: 'to set the record straight regarding false reports about Germany's actions and to shed light on the violations of international law and crimes against humanity committed by our opponents in this war.'[21]

Elsewhere German academics continued to publish articles and pamphlets on themes such as the allied policy of 'encirclement', the military and diplomatic justification for Germany's violation of Belgium, the need for a strong German military establishment in order to provide protection for the Germanic culture of central Europe and the superiority of Germany's authoritarian constitution over the parliamentary regimes of the west. Above all, however, the vaguely formulated claims to German cultural, political and military superiority went hand in hand with a new and comprehensive attack on British ideals, policies and national habits as a prelude to justifying Germany's own war aims.

In what follows I shall examine four different approaches adopted by German academics in order to justify their critique of British power and British involvement in the war. This in turn should enable us to explore the underlying assumptions and patterns behind German anglophobia.

The racist denunciation of England

The racist denunciation of Britain can be traced back to the work of the Frenchman Comte Joseph Arthur de Gobineau (1816–1882), whose doctrines on race had a major impact on nineteenth-century European thought. Although his *Essai sur l'inégalité des races humaines* (1853–5) was not translated into German for forty years, it was in Germany that his ideas on the rise and fall of civilisations and the importance of racial purity received the greatest attention, because they seemed to confirm the superiority of the Germanic race in general and Germans in particular. At the same time his basic idea, that social degeneration was caused by racial deterioration, served as a framework to explain domestic frustrations in post-unification Germany, particularly among those opposed to Jewish or Catholic emancipation.

According to George Mosse, an expert on Germanic ideology, there is no reason to suppose that Gobineau himself was anti-Semitic or indeed anti-Catholic. Rather, the nation he despised most of all was England, which seemed to him to be the most bourgeois of all states in Europe. He did not advocate the use of force to halt racial degeneration, or pan-Germanism, or anti-Semitism. He seemed, in fact, somewhat resigned to the fate of the white race, however sadly and with whatever frustrations.[22]

Nonetheless, during the last years of his life Gobineau did form a close friendship with the anti-Semitic German composer Richard Wagner and through him had a major impact on the thinking of the so-called Bayreuth circle, an influential group of Wagner admirers.[23] Ludwig Schemann, a member of the Bayreuth circle, dedicated his life to popularising and translating Gobineau, and in 1894 founded a Gobineau society. An even bigger impact on the intellectual life of Wilhelmine Germany was made by Houston Stewart Chamberlain, the English-born racist philosopher who married Wagner's daughter in 1908. In his *Foundations of the Nineteenth Century* (1899), which reached its tenth edition by 1912, Chamberlain turned to Gobineau for evidence to back his own claim that the Germanic race was the sole architect of modern European civilisation in the wake of the *Völkerchaos* left behind by the Roman empire. At the same time, he used Gobineau's condemnation of the black and yellow races more specifically against the Jews and the Catholic Church in Germany. The future belonged to Germany, he argued elsewhere, so long as it freed itself from anti-Germanic, above all Jewish influences.[24] If, on the other hand, the Germans failed to assert themselves, they would go under.

Not through conflict and chaotic disunion, but only through a unity of purpose can Germany expect to emerge as the ruler of the world; and if Germany does not rule the world (and here I mean not simply by force, but through its overall superiority and moral influence), then it will disappear from the map. It is a question of either one or the other.[25]

During the First World War, Chamberlain was awarded the Iron Cross by the Kaiser for his propaganda activities on the German side, and was in turn denounced as a 'renegade' and turncoat by the British press.[26] Even before this, his ideas were widely admired in Germany by such diverse readers as Kaiser Wilhelm II, Admiral Tirpitz, Albert Schweitzer, Rudolf Kassner, Adolf von Harnack, Paul Deussen, Hermann Bahr, Hans Vaihinger, Egon Friedell and others.[27] From an early stage in the war, academics such as Professors Erich Marcks, Max

Lenz, Johannes Haller, Otto von Gierke, Max Scheler and Karl Lamprecht also employed similar arguments to advance the demand for a German-led 'continental league' or even for German 'world leadership'.[28] The historian Karl Lamprecht, one of Bethmann Hollweg's advisers, introduced racial ideas into his argument when he wrote in the *Rheinisch-Westfälische Zeitung* on 28 August 1914:

It is subjectively recognised and objectively proven that we are capable of the highest achievements in the world and must therefore be at least considered entitled to share in world rule. That is what has given recent times the imprint of world historical greatness . . . It is not only geographically that the Germanic races under German leadership will become the central people of the old European world.[29]

The reverse side of this racially motivated claim to world power was that the 'Anglo-Saxons', formerly Germany's chief rival on the world stage, had now lost their previous claim to supremacy as a result of racial degeneration. Once again it was Lamprecht who provided a measure of academic respectability for this view when he said in a speech in Leipzig on 23 August 1914:

We are experiencing something unique here – in the realm of German culture the entire people is now dedicating itself to the German cause. We will of course remember how tense the relationship between Switzerland and the German Reich has sometimes been in the past, no less than our relationship with Holland, or Denmark, or Norway. But today all this is mostly forgotten by public opinion, our ties of blood have triumphed . . . Only England remains aloof, but we all know that it is no longer a purely Germanic, but rather a Celtic spirit, which currently controls the central organs of the British empire, and in so far as this spirit is still Germanic, it represents the progressive decay of a formerly rich culture. But it is precisely this standpoint which adds particular force to our [other] observations on the development of Germandom in Europe.[30]

In the same speech Lamprecht lambasted what he described as the typical Englishman's belief in his own innate superiority and chosenness and his equally hypocritical tendency to regard other nations and cultures as second class and inferior.

For the other nations this [English] feeling [of superiority] is completely intolerable, and I dare say that the world cannot return to peace until this feeling has been replaced root and branch by a more modest appraisal.[31]

All this in spite of the fact that for Lamprecht the chief threat to Germany was and remained pan-Slavism, a position that led him to regard the war, 'which at the moment is being waged primarily against France and England, as the final struggle of Germandom and the Latin Slav races against the intrusion of eastern barbarism, [a struggle which is taking place] in line with the general course of European history'.[32]

Similar views were expressed in early September 1914 by Lorenz Morsbach, Professor of English at the University of Göttingen, in an open letter addressed to the 'philologists of Germany and Austria':

England has always placed its own interests above all other considerations . . . Barely a dozen professors from Oxford and Cambridge have forced themselves to make a protest against the war. But we no longer have a Carlyle in this country, which cannot even show firmness in the face of domestic troubles, which cannot deal with either the Suffragettes or the rebellious Ulstermen, which cannot avert strikes and is slipping more and more down the slippery slope towards feminism, so that for years it has been trembling at the thought of a German invasion, this once so proud Albion. That England is standing shoulder to shoulder with France can hardly surprise anyone. Germany and the Germanic character are utterly alien to the English, while they have been forging close links with French culture for many years . . . The English do not even want to be an Anglo-Saxon or Germanic people any more, but a newly refined cross-breed that does not like to be reminded of its German cousins. Even their Shakespeare, who was German through and through, has been more than half rejected by them. In the seventeenth century they sought to turn him into a Frenchman, in the eighteenth century they tried to forget him, until the Germans (above all Lessing) restored him to his former honour and dug up the buried treasures. Only then did the sly Britons reclaim him as their own for their own advantages.[33]

The idea that the 'merry olde England' of Shakespeare's time had fallen victim to Celtic or – as was sometimes argued – to Jewish influences indeed provided a useful answer to the question that puzzled German racists most: if national character was determined by race, and the Germans and English came from similar Nordic or Teutonic stock, why were their policies and interests so opposed? In other words, if the differences between the Germanic, Slav and Latin peoples were becoming greater as a result of innate biological differences, were not the 'Anglo-Saxons' bound to join in the racial struggle on the side of their 'Germanic' cousins? This, after all, was what Lamprecht and others had been confidently predicting as late as April 1914.[34]

The answer that appeared most often in German newspapers in the early months of the war was the same answer Lamprecht had given in August 1914: racial deterioration. On 3 November 1914, for instance, the liberal *Frankfurter Zeitung* carried an article by Dr Matthias Schwann of Cologne under the title 'Our English cousins', in which he argued:

The Germanic strain in England exists. But whilst it was once dominant, now it appears to be completely subdued. This is always the case when an exclusive in-breeding takes place within certain social or national groups. The Germanic element in England is apparently not strong enough to resist the forces of internal decay. Celtic and Roman elements have come to the fore – see the struggle of the government classes and parties against the Ulstermen, see the Celt Grey in a leading position with his romantic tendencies towards slyness and dishonesty, see the boastfulness, the blind self-righteousness and many, many other things which are still never discussed today, since the danger, which has become acute [over] there, is also present in Germany.[35]

In an article which appeared in the Berlin-based *Tag* on 4 November with the same title – 'Our English cousins' – Professor Albrecht Haupt was even less subtle in his views.

The so-called Anglo-Saxons in England are not our cousins at all, [they] are much less closely related to us than the French people of northern and eastern France, the northern Italians [and] even the north-western Spaniards: our blood relationship to them is about the same as [our relationship] to the French of mid, west and southern France. A calm, objective and unprejudiced examination of English history proves this beyond all doubt. It is an age-old myth which suggests that England is chiefly inhabited by Germanic people, by migrants from Germany . . . The ancient residents of Britain are purely Celtic. We may assume that they came at least in part or even mostly from the Gaelic parts of France; but we also know that another part of the ancient population were Celtic Belgians from across the channel, whose modern descendants – the Wallonians of Liège – are currently our most fearsome enemies.[36]

It would only be fair to point out, however, that these more extreme views provoked a great deal of amusement and contempt from German philologists and other experts, who soon poured scorn on the idea of a decisive Celtic influence on the development of English language and culture. Heinrich Spies, Professor of Philology at the University of Greifswald and a pre-war expert on English language and culture, for instance, wrote in 1915:

If we look at the result of approximately one thousand years of inter-racial breeding on English soil we find a predominately Germanic people ('Our German cousins') with a scattering of French racial elements, apart from a few insignificant fragments of other peoples. Self-evident as this fact may appear, it must be reiterated once again in view of the various claims put forward by a number of German newspapers in order to explain the sudden and unexpected feud with England, such as the view that the English are a purely Celtic people; only an inadequate knowledge of historical, linguistic and philological developments since 1400 and of the relevant research [in this field] over the past twenty years could lead to such claims.[37]

The current conflict between 'Germanic' England, represented by the mass of Conservative voters in the anglicised parts of Britain, and the 'Celtic-radical' government, which depended on Celtic support for its majority and included 'Celts' from Scotland and Wales among its leading ministers (Campbell-Bannermann, Asquith, Haldane, Lloyd George), was, according to Spies, merely the result of chance occurrences in domestic politics, in particular the split in the Liberal Party following Gladstone's first Home Rule Bill for Ireland in 1886. As far as foreign policy was concerned, the supposed conflict of interest between 'Saxon' and 'Celt', or Conservative and Liberal, was irrelevant, for Spies believed, as he wrote in his conclusion, 'that the English state and the English people stand as one behind this war'.[38]

A more sophisticated version of the racial argument against England was meanwhile provided by Houston Stewart Chamberlain himself. In his wartime essays, which sold 8,000 copies within days of appearing in Germany[39] and were later translated into English under the title *The Ravings of a Renegade*, he welcomed the war as a return to the heroic German spirit of a bygone age of medieval chivalry. He contrasted this with developments in England, where, in his opinion, these old aristocratic virtues had been rotted away by parliamentarism and trade and the rise of a new culture-hating plutocracy.[40] The distinctive English national character, Chamberlain argued, had been moulded by two key events in English history: the Norman conquest of 1066, which had led to the subjugation of the Anglo-Saxon population under a foreign aristocracy with a different language and culture, and, secondly, a 'turn of fate' in the sixteenth century whereby the agricultural inhabitants of England, 'in spite of their innate dread of the sea, were turned into mariners and merchants'. The latter development – the 'change to a commercial nation' – was particularly disastrous in Chamberlain's view since it had produced a mechanical and materialist civilisation which was opportunistic, destructive and pledged to 'further the interests of money making all over the globe'.[41]

Not a spark of intellectual life has ever sprung from this immense colonial empire. The inhabitants are all only cattle-owners, slave-owners, merchandise accumulators, mine exploiters and everywhere there reigns the absolute licence of brutality which develops everywhere where it is not opposed by intellectual culture. Rudyard Kipling, England's most popular poet, has the front to claim this brutality as the highest power and greatest glory of England.[42]

Politically and culturally, England had never flourished except in Anglo-Saxon times. The current state of English parliamentary life and of its corrupt press were merely indicative of an accelerated racial decline. England was in the hands of a corrupt clique of politicians and newspaper magnates who cleverly manipulated public opinion and enriched themselves through shady financial deals, as the Marconi scandal had shown. Recently, the plutocrats had even managed to remove the right of the House of Lords to veto parliamentary legislation, the last remaining obstacle to their absolute power.[43] As for the English people as a whole, they had long abandoned any interest in religion, art or scholarly pursuits in favour of their well-known mania for sports (*Sportsidiotismus*) and other idle pursuits, and had otherwise allowed their political opinions and tastes to be dictated to them by others.

The last time I was in England I made my friends angry because I could not help exclaiming: 'You are truly a nation of sheep'. It begins with the smallest habits of daily life, and continues up to political opinions, everything on the same pattern. Every man wears the same trousers; every woman the same bonnet; I remember once in the whole of London not a single blue tie was to be had: blue was out of fashion: such a thing is impossible in Berlin, Paris or Vienna. All people of both sexes read the same novels, devour one volume a day, the 'novels of the week'. On the day of the boat race between Oxford and Cambridge one walks through literally empty streets in London; the oldest duchess and the youngest chimney-sweep, all as one seized by the same enthusiasm for this event, of which at best they see but little, and in no case understand the achievement; a special knowledge of all kinds of details – tide, wind etc. is requisite, which is only possessed by expert oarsmen.[44]

Indeed, in the first weeks of the war Chamberlain's hatred of his mother country even came to overshadow his hatred of the Jews. 'Germany's victory', he told his brother Basil on 30 October 1914, 'will not only be England's ruin; quite the contrary; it is the only hope for England's rescue from the total ruin in which she now stands. England's victory would be terrible for the whole world, a catastrophe.'[45] And in 1914 he wrote in one of his wartime essays:

Germany has twenty times as many Jews [as England], where are they now? As if blown away by the mighty storm, as 'Jews' no longer to be found; for they are doing their duty as Germans at the front or at home. Whereas the English Jews, who are the natural brothers and cousins of the German Jews, participate in all the disgraceful actions here, hastily changing their names into English ones and, in the [English] Press, of which they have gained almost complete control, lead the campaign of slander against Germany.[46]

Later in the war, of course, Chamberlain became increasingly bold in equating British and Jewish ideals. As early as 1915, for instance, in his *Politische Ideale*, he argued that the decline of traditional values in British politics had begun much earlier than during the reign of Edward VII and was due in particular to the 'influence of the Jew Disraeli'.[47] Admittedly Chamberlain had been saying similar things in private letters many years before the war started; that he should now come out and say them in public was nonetheless significant for it helped forge a link between anti-Semitic agitation and intellectual rejection of western norms and values, also seen in works such as Werner Sombart's *Händler und Helden* and the Count Ernst zu Reventlow's *Der Vampir des Festlandes*, both of which appeared in the year 1915.

As an outspoken 'renegade', Chamberlain won the admiration of many German patriots as one whose comments seemed to verify their own assertions about British values and conspiratorial designs. Upon receiving a copy of Chamberlain's *Kriegsaufsätze*, for instance, Wilhelm II wrote back to him on 25 November 1914:

This is what I have always believed, and this is what I believe today of my beloved Germany. It is my firm conviction that the country to which God gave Luther, Goethe, Bach, Wagner, Moltke, Bismarck and My Grandfather is still called upon to achieve great things for the benefit of mankind. Through His hard school God has again shown us the path we must follow if we are to achieve a distant solution to the problems we are facing, so that we can reflect upon ourselves and straighten ourselves internally in order to fulfil our role as His instrument for the salvation of mankind . . . To Him we entrust our cause, He will bring it to a good end.[48]

Undoubtedly Chamberlain's brand of racism, which combined empiricism with Kantian idealism and a mystical, intuitive philosophy, would also have appealed to broader sections of the German right than some of the cruder versions of Social Darwinism. What all these groups had in common, in spite of their many differences, was a vision of the war as Germany's 'struggle for existence' against a ring of hostile enemies.[49]

On the other hand, the vast majority of German academics, including those with pan-German leanings, were not yet ready to embrace the more extreme versions of biological determinism, especially since the latter seemed to overlook the cultural and ideological factors which were still held to be the main cause of conflict between different nations.[50] What mattered to them, in other words, was not the relative strengths of Celtic, Anglo-Saxon, Norman or even Jewish influences in Britain, but rather the future role which British power might play in world politics, regardless of its racial future. In the next section I shall examine some of the more mainstream attitudes towards England among German academics in the light of what many then saw as Germany's own struggle for world power.

England and the Great Powers

The philosophical speculations of men such as Chamberlain, with their increasingly radical implications for Germany's own future, achieved much greater importance during the final phase of the war. At first, however, they had to compete with rival concepts of German imperialism which, because they were more directly related to the realities of modern economic development and geo-political factors, fitted more easily into the academic mainstream. Previous works have already noted how in the 1890s an influential school of historians in Germany (Max Lenz, Erich Marcks, Otto Hintze and Hans Delbrück, to name but a few) developed a set of theories and ideas which explained how the old European state system of Ranke's day would soon be replaced by a new system of world states in which the German empire would take its place as an equal.[51] For these historians, the chief aim of German imperialism was to force Britain, the oldest of the established world powers, to surrender its previous supremacy and accept Germany as an equal partner. Although some may have hoped before 1914 that this objective would be achieved without the need for a clash of arms, the British declaration of war on 4 August 1914 led to the adoption of a more openly offensive posture.

The change in attitude can already be seen in the first weeks of the war in a series of public lectures delivered by prominent academics of the University of Berlin, later published as the first volume in the cycle *Deutsche Reden in schwerer Zeit*.[52] Of the twelve contributors, all, without exception, identified England as the chief instigator of the war and urged the Germans to 'hold out' (*durchhalten*), even against this most powerful enemy. According to Ulrich von Wilamowitz-Moellendorff, for instance, in a speech delivered to an audience in the Beethovensaal on 27 August 1914, England was 'the actual brains and demonic spirit, which called forth the war from the depths of hell, from the spirit of envy and the spirit of hypocrisy'.[53]

Do we really want to fall into a state where we too become the vassals of England? - No, of course not. Then we must take action, [we] must fight to the death [*kämpfen bis aufs Blut*].[54]

Similarly, Gustav Roethe, in a speech on 3 September 1914, referred to the English as the 'Romans of the modern world'. He went on:

From the moment that England showed its true face there grew in us the certainty: now we knew with whom we had to reckon. When England cast aside the mask of peace, when we saw it as it really was, this enemy, our actual mortal enemy, in whose hands the others are mere tools that are used against us, then arose in us not only a venerable rage, but also an awareness of our own strength, then we knew that we would go forward; indeed, we must go forward, since it is a question of our national existence, of our entire freedom and development. At the moment of greatest danger it suddenly became clear to us how much we had to give, how important the goal was: then all we felt was deliverance, redemption. We must win, whatever it costs! And we will win.[55]

Even the arch-moderate Hans Delbrück, who was attacked much later in the war by right-wing extremists because of his opposition to German war aims policy, and who later still was hailed as a liberal critic of the policies of Wilhelmine Germany, explicitly identified himself with the 'warlike character' of the German people in his speech of 11 September 1914.

The military instinct in us is borne in the first instance by that caste [i.e. the Prussian Officer Corps] which has made war its profession and thereby raised the warlike qualities of the whole nation to a level where truly great acts of war are made possible . . . This nation is invincible, and it is invincible not only against those enemies in the East, which we cannot recognise as equal before the higher claims of humanity, but also invincible against that island nation, which is sufficiently proud and great, as we willingly recognise, but which does not have to shoulder the massive burden of her own national defence; rather, it thinks it can use mercenaries to defeat a people [i.e. the Germans] which is fighting for itself . . . [These] men of commerce [*Geschäftsmänner*], who merely hand out money, who send out mercenaries and mobilise the barbaric masses and think that they are able to defeat us – it is these [men] who we need to be fighting against, not only with the same bravery and, we hope, with the same success, but also with the certainty of our eternal inner superiority . . . a superiority which by its very nature is capable of ensuring us the final victory.[56]

For others, such as the Hamburg professor Wilhelm Dibelius, England's declaration of war on Germany also came as a bitter personal betrayal after years of close cultural and academic ties between the two nations.

The country, which in the year 1807 – in the midst of peace – seized the Danish fleet, which continues to occupy Egypt and in spite of all past promises refuses to leave, which in the year 1906 conducted negotiations for a joint Anglo-French engagement in Belgium, has no right whatsoever to act as if it were the disinterested protector of the neutral states.[57]

What most upset Dibelius was what he saw as the base motives which had led England to enter the war – the pursuit of economic gain – and the ungallant means by which it waged war, using the international press to spread lies about Germany and pitting hired mercenaries against honest German conscripts. Using arguments which represented not only a complete distortion of the facts, but also a gross underestimation of Britain's capacity and determination to fight a long-term war, he wrote:

In a country which has universal conscription, in which war disturbs all the normal paths of civilian life, the act of engaging in war against the will of the nation is an impossibility. For this reason alone Germany must be the land of peace; on the other hand, an unwise and unnecessary war is quite possible in a country like England, where the great mass of the people can stay quietly at home and war means little more than a severe economic crisis, as occurs from time to time anyway.[58]

In spite of this, Dibelius still spoke enthusiastically of a 'common cultural mission between England and Germany'[59] and even predicted (in October 1914) that a quick German victory on the continent would lead to a 'new Königgrätz', whereby England would accept Germany supremacy over Europe just as the Austrians had accepted Prussian supremacy over Germany in 1866.[60]

Other intellectuals, however, were quick to refute Dibelius's idea of a 'new Königgrätz'[61] and instead demanded more concrete guarantees against any attempt by England to renew its struggle against Germany in the future, either by conventional warfare or by means of economic boycott. If it was now England's intention to reduce Germany to the status of a middle-ranking European power – a status it had long since outgrown – then Germany must use all the means at its disposal to defend its position as a world power. The following lines, written in 1915 by A. Meister, Professor of History at the University of Münster, are typical in this respect.

Our policy today ... must remain a world policy; the goal of the war must therefore be to ensure that the power which holds our world policy in chains, which wants to destroy our entire world trade, is no longer capable of forcing us into an unfavourable position [or] of starting another war [against us].[62]

Security against future British aggression meant first and foremost efforts to guarantee the freedom of the seas, the one war aim on which all German academics, from pan-Germans and other extremists to near-pacifists, were agreed and, incidentally, also the one war aim which the censor permitted people to express in public from the very start of the war.[63] Accordingly, a group of 150 prominent academics and writers, including Friedrich Naumann and Thomas Mann, issued a statement to this effect in early 1915 under the title 'Reply of the Kulturbund to the declaration of the professors of Great Britain': 'Only in the course of the war has it become clear to us that the domination of the seas, which England regards as its ancestral right ... calls into question the existence and further development of [our] national culture. To fight against this is our sacred duty.'[64]

Similar ideas were developed by the Freiburg economist and Progressive Reichstag deputy Gerhard von Schulze-Gaevernitz, in a pamphlet which appeared in 1915 under the title *Freie Meere*! Here Schulze-Gaevernitz spoke openly of Germany's spiritual mission to end England's 'culture-destroying' and 'unworthy' domination of the seas.

Germany is fighting for the freedom of the seas, and hence for mankind – even for France. Germany is not seeking domination of the seas for itself – it is not in its power to do so – but rather desires a maritime balance between several sea powers, in which Germany is recognised as being equal and on a par with the strongest [sea] power.[65]

Britain's position in the world, he argued, relied on the Anglo-Saxon ideal type of the strong 'individual personality' (*Einzelmensch*), which had its roots in British Puritanism and had – through a process of *Entzauberung* – emerged during the nineteenth century as a purely mechanical world view. Britain thus represented an older type of humanity, unable to adapt its hypocritical religiosity to the progressive development of the human mind or *Geist*, whereas the Germans had now come to represent a higher form of culture fighting in the service of human history:

The strong *Einzelmensch* of old England has been surpassed by the new Germany and the greater force of its organised community, which . . . combines both the freedom of its individual parts and the unity of the whole. This can be seen in the army, in the state and in capitalist industry. At the highest stage of his development the Briton is able to enslave the world by way of the strong *Einzelmenschen* and in honour of an unworldly God; at the highest stage of his development the German is able to achieve a humane restructuring of the world [*eine liebevolle Weltgestaltung*] by way of the organised community and in line with the historical development of the eternal ideal. It is an unmistakable fact that the idea of the kingdom of God and its visible manifestation in the Church is thus carried forward for the benefit [of mankind].[66]

By far the most important intellectual contribution to Germany's political case against England, however, was made by the volume *Deutschland und der Weltkrieg* (1915), a work edited and produced by the historians Otto Hintze, Friedrich Meinecke, Hermann Oncken and Hermann Schumacher with the express purpose of counteracting the effects of English propaganda on neutral countries, above all the United States. The initiative came from Schumacher, who also made use of contacts with representatives of the Prussian Ministry of Education and the German Foreign Office.[67] The introduction ('Deutschland und das Weltstaatssystem') and the concluding essay ('Der Sinn des Krieges') were written by the political historian Otto Hintze, whilst the case for seeing the war as a defence of German culture and constitutional forms was dealt with most thoroughly by the theologian Ernst Troeltsch.[68]

The main focus of Hintze's arguments was the emphasis he placed on Germany's uniquely unfavourable geographic position in the centre of Europe, a position which in Frederick the Great's day had necessitated the creation of a large standing army in order to secure recognition as a European power, and now, since the turn of the twentieth century, the building of a fleet to protect its trade and worldwide economic interests. England's rigid opposition to German naval building, he argued, was the chief cause of the war, although he also admitted quite candidly that Germany's drive for economic and maritime power represented the most immediate threat to England's supremacy at sea.

We are fighting for the freedom of the seas and for a humane set of laws for naval warfare, as was formulated in the London declaration of 1909 and as corresponds to the rights of all nations, and not just to the interests of England, which has thwarted the enforcement [of such laws]. We want to supplement the balance of power on land with a balance of power at sea and thereby to create the only lasting and healthy basis for a system of world states.[69]

Such an aim – and here Hintze was in full agreement with the other contributors – could be justified only if Germany avoided following the example set by British imperialism, which was essentially a disruptive force in world politics, and instead set itself upon a course which would lead to the establishment of a new balance of power within a global context. No doubt mindful of the censor and of his potential American audience, Hintze was much more reticent when it came to discussing the impact this new global balance might have on the older balance of powers in Europe, although he was quite open about what he saw as the future goals of German *Weltpolitik*.

The main aim for us is first and foremost to frustrate the plans of our enemies, to fill them with necessary respect for our weapons, to destroy the iron ring which through concentrated pressure has paralysed our world policy for so long, to win and secure for ourselves the right to the free development of our strengths and the uninterrupted pursuit of our life interests.[70]

The idea of a balance of powers in Europe was in his view a 'screening device',[71] a slogan invented by British imperialists and used to further their aim of world domination. By contrast, it was German naval and colonial policy which would be the ultimate guarantor of the rights of individual nations in the long run.

England has already been forced to abandon its claim to complete domination of the seas in that it has largely withdrawn its garrisons in overseas naval stations and instead concentrated its [maritime] forces in home waters. That is the result of German naval building. Other sea-faring powers are already reaping the benefits of [these developments]; the pressure which England previously exerted in foreign parts of the world is already visibly fading [and] even the impressive edifice of the British empire is beginning to fall apart.[72]

Similar ideas were expressed by other contributors such as Hermann Oncken and Erich Marcks, although here there was a less subtle understanding of the true causes of Britain's entry into the war and a greater tendency towards moral condemnation. In an earlier essay, Oncken had gone back as far as Thomas More's *Utopia* in order to establish the point of England's departure from commonly held European norms and values.

It is an inborn characteristic of insular politics to be both relatively immune from attack and at the same time to be more perfidious [than the rest]. Its island status has given England an endless amount of wealth, good fortune and grandeur: security from outside aggression under the protection of the sea, national unity at home, a grand route to the world and a tendency towards world domination. Fate has failed to provide it with only one thing: the need to take responsibility for its own actions with its own forces: [in other words] that which is implicit in all true morality. The potential to get others to do the fighting for it, and while they spill their blood, merely to throw money and calculated cunning into the scales: this is what has given English policy its immoral character.[73]

Likewise, Erich Marcks, in his essay 'Die Machtpolitik Englands', condemned England's past record as 'a history of wars of conquest, of wars of aggression which have enabled it to disguise its growth before the world and to crush every European competitor', and further as 'a history of wars, of aggressive world policy'.[74] His conclusions were also confirmed by Hans Delbrück, who once again ridiculed the notion that 'Prussian militarism' was any more aggressive than 'English militarism'.

The English people have, thanks to their mercenary armies and their gigantic fleet, been able to subject over 350 million people, almost one quarter of the entire inhabitants of the globe, and to enjoy absolute domination over all the seas of the world. This could never have been achieved with a conscript army [*mit einem Volksheer*].[75]

Even Friedrich Meinecke, the most idealistic and least political of German historians, reserved some harsh words for England in his essay 'Kultur, Machtpolitik und Militarismus'. Meinecke's main argument, first developed in his multi-volume work *Weltbürgertum und Nationalstaat* (1907), was the Rankean idea that the *Kultur* and character of the German nation could not be separated from its historical mission as one of the great European powers. For this reason he was also ardently opposed to the argument used by English propagandists that there were two Germanys, the Germany of poets and musicians such as Goethe, Schiller and Beethoven, and the Germany of Prussian militarism, of men such as Treitschke, Nietzsche and General von Bernhardi. Rather, it was his opinion that:

[The] characteristics which have been ascribed to us tally far less with ourselves than with the English. The narrow-minded and arrogant belief in the superiority of one's own culture, which can only teach others but has nothing to learn from them, is far more widespread and entrenched among the English than among ourselves, and if not in theory, at least . . . in practice a scrupulous power politics has been at home in England for centuries. Many portraits painted by subjective painters are in fact self-portraits and this is how we should also respond to the current propaganda against us.[76]

Indeed, Meinecke's reflections on the relationship between *Kultur* and *Machtpolitik* ultimately led him to view the war in ideological terms as a struggle to defend Europe's plurality of nations and cultures against the threat of universal monarchy, which he accused Britain of wishing to establish.

Universal maritime supremacy is only another form of universal monarchy, which cannot be tolerated and must, sooner or later, fail. England is fighting against the spirit of modern development . . . Its significance as a world nation and a world civilisation, which we honour and recognise, will not suffer if the balance of power, which it has tried to restrict artificially within the limits of

Europe, is extended to include the oceans and the world beyond. Only then will every nation have the free breathing spaces it requires.[77]

Of all the contributors to *Deutschland und der Weltkrieg*, Hintze represented the middle position between an overtly defensive and a covertly offensive interpretation of the goals of German foreign policy, while Meinecke, less concerned with the brutal laws of power conflicts than his colleagues, represented a more moderate position, one which gradually leaned towards the idea of a negotiated settlement once it became clear that English sea power could not be destroyed.[78] Indeed, conflicting opinions had already emerged during the preparatory stages of the volume. In private correspondence with Friedrich Schmitt-Ott, ministerial director in the Prussian Ministry of Education, both Schumacher and Meinecke argued that Russia was the chief aggressor in the war, whereas Oncken, supported by Hintze, took the opposite view that England was most to blame.[79]

Nonetheless, it is also clear that, at least in the initial phases, the majority of Germany's pro-establishment historians were in full agreement that the main aim of the war should be to transform the balance of power in Europe and the world and to do so by fighting England and the system it represented. This indeed is how contemporary observers interpreted *Deutschland und der Weltkrieg*, many of whom, were impressed by what Friedrich Thimme saw as the 'unanimity' of the individual contributions.[80]

Economic rivalries and Germany's claim to world power status

The arguments put forward by Hintze, Delbrück and Meinecke represented a more idealised and therefore more respectable version of Germany's case against England – in that they continued to pay lip-service to the idea of a balance of powers and stopped short of demanding the complete destruction of England. However, their views were challenged at an early stage in the war by more openly annexationist writers and speech-makers who saw the economic rivalry between England and Germany as the root cause of the war, regardless of its diplomatic origins. Since from this perspective it was Germany who was challenging Britain's previous position as the world's leading economic power, it was hardly surprising that British statesmen had in turn employed all the means at their disposal to resist this trend, including both diplomatic intrigue and the ultimate weapon, war. Otto von Gierke, to name but one example, openly admitted in a speech in Berlin on 18 September 1914 that the destruction of English economic and maritime power would be one of the main results of a German victory.

For our economic life a victorious peace will mean the unleashing of our world-conquering might [*die Entfesselung welterobernder Kraft*] . . . For our agriculture, our industry and handicrafts, for our technology, our transport and trade an immeasurable field of new opportunities is opening up. Of course it is also vital that our victory is a complete one, and not a half-hearted one. We must destroy the most perfidious and most vicious of our enemies, we must break the tyranny which England exercises over the seas in base egotism and shameless disregard for [international] law. Never will our degenerate cousins voluntarily agree to grant us economic equality, because they know that under free competition we will be superior to them, and because they are not inclined to recognise our hard work and our spiritual togetherness. Only direct force can make them yield in this respect.[81]

A similar perspective on the Anglo-German conflict was also offered by Eduard Meyer, a world-renowned scholar and Professor of Medieval History at the University of Berlin, in his book *England. Seine staatliche und politische Entwicklung und der Krieg gegen Deutschland* (1915). Here Meyer made an open comparison between the war forced upon Germany by its jealous economic competitor and the struggles and battles which ancient Rome had been obliged to wage against the 'pirate nation' Carthage:

The analogy between the Anglo-German war and the Punic wars will impress itself upon all those with an awareness of history and has often been emphasised both at home and abroad. But what took place before in the limited sphere of the Mediterranean world is now seizing hold of the entire globe, and on top of this Hannibal's attempt to bring together all states and nations in a final showdown against Rome met with far less success than England's [current] efforts in the world war against Germany.[82]

Indeed, whereas Otto Hintze had compared the position of Germany in 1914 with that of Prussia on the eve of the Seven Years War (1756–63), academics with pan-German or expansionist leanings preferred to use analogies drawn from the great wars of antiquity or in some cases even compared Imperial Germany with Napoleonic France on the eve of the Third Coalition War (1805). Typical in this respect was Martin Spahn, Professor of History at the University of Straßburg, who had close ties to German industrialists and the Catholic Centre Party. A German-dominated Europe, he argued, would be vulnerable to the same type of coalition wars as Britain had organised and financed against the French empire over 100 years before. It should therefore study the methods used by Napoleon I in his military and economic campaigns against England, first and foremost his establishment of a hegemonial position on the continent as a base for destroying British commerce and launching pre-emptive strikes against British power bases outside Europe.

The more [Germany] seeks to expand its sphere of activities beyond Europe, the more safeguards it needs against its neighbours on the continent. In the related case of France after 1805 Napoleon was forced to bring ever greater parts of the occident into his empire, not out of a crude thirst for conquest, but out of states-man-like reflection; but [those territories] he was unable to annex to France directly, he sought to weaken so that they could no longer cause any damage to his plans . . . The end result was a tyranny which collapsed because of the general antipathy towards it. Our own prospects, since we are waging essen-tially the same struggle, are from the outset much better, our conditions much more favourable. The attempt to frighten the nation through a warning against 'Napoleonic policies', which German writers tried to do as soon as the war had started, was premature.[83]

Of the more prominent Berlin historians it was Otto Hoetzsch, an expert on Russia at the University of Berlin and, from November 1914, Theodor Schiemann's successor as foreign affairs editor of the conservative *Kreuzzeitung*, who was the most forthright in advocating the idea of a war fought exclusively against England, a position which was shared both by the new army Chief-of-Staff Falkenhayn and by conservative government ministers such as Admiral von Tirpitz and Friedrich von Loebell.[84] In a secret memorandum written in early December 1914 Hoetzsch called for a sober recognition of the fact that Germany would always have a long common frontier with Russia and that it could not hope to carry out a war on two fronts indefinitely. Expansion of German territory in the east, he reasoned, could be achieved only by sacrificing expenditure elsewhere, above all on the rebuilding of the German fleet, while at the same time making an eventual reconciliation with Russia all the more difficult. Moreover, England's entry into the war had created a new set of circumstances which required a reorientation in Germany foreign policy and the 'acquisition of a broader base for Germany's future world power position'.

[Germany's] western flank has a far more troublesome and difficult border [to defend], and a coastline which puts it in an unfavourable position with regard to the great sea lanes carrying international traffic and above all makes its over-seas commerce dependent on its relationship with England. Therefore in order to maintain its overseas commerce and to secure its future world position Germany must either get by with a friendly attitude towards England or use force against it . . . Since the attempt to win England over through negotiations has failed, the only solution left remains force if we are to win recognition of our naval power and our world position from it.[85]

Others placed emphasis on the key advantage which Germany would have in any future struggle for world power through its control of channel ports such as Calais, Boulogne, Zeebrugge and Antwerp, any or all of which could be seen to represent a 'dagger' pointing at England's breast. This was the view, for instance, put forward by the

Bonn economist Hermann Schumacher in a confidential memorandum of June 1915, which he circulated to like-minded academics and industrialists. Control of the Flemish coastline – 'whether in Zeebrugge or whether further to the west' – would, according to Schumacher, rob England of the geographical advantages it enjoyed from its island status by exposing its own coastlines to attack from German submarines, torpedoes and air ships, thus providing an alternative 'risk strategy' to that offered by Tirpitz's grand fleet.[86] Similar views were also put forward by the shipping magnate Albert Ballin in an article published in the *Frankfurter Zeitung* early in 1915, in which he called for naval stations in Europe as well as overseas in order to protect German ships and ensure their free passage through the North Sea.

The English have been able to place on us the heavy burden of bringing our overseas trade almost to a standstill only because this area of the North Sea turns out to be easy to blockade. The sea-robber like intimidation which England practises on the neutral Scandinavian countries and on Holland would be impossible had we had a base for our fleet which was equal to the stature and heroic valour of its brave officers and men . . . Therefore we must seek a foothold for our fleet beyond this area of the North Sea [i.e. the 'Wet Triangle' between Heligoland and the mouths of the Elbe and Weser] which in the future will at least secure for us in this part of the world the same opportunities as England [now] possesses and ruthlessly exploits.[87]

An alternative to these views, which have sometimes been referred to as 'liberal imperialist', was provided by leading pan-German professors such as Dietrich Schäfer, founder of the Independent Committee for a German Peace (Unabhängiger Ausschuß für einen deutschen Frieden), who argued that what mattered in any future struggle for world power was not further maritime or colonial expansion, but rather Germany's ability to establish itself as the leading power on the continent, above all at the expense of Russia.[88] This was also the view of the Baltic German Johannes Haller, an outspoken critic of Tirpitz's policy of naval expansion, who very early in the war denounced as a 'Phantasie' the idea that Germany could defeat England by means of sea and air power alone. Rather, the new military situation demanded a complete abandonment of Tirpitz's naval schemes and a return to policies designed to defeat England by means of the older method of forcing a union of continental powers under German leadership. Only in this way, he argued, could Germany exploit the chief weapon open to it: the economic boycott.

Not just in Germany and Austria-Hungary, but everywhere where our victorious armies press forward, English commerce must disappear. We should go one stage further, however; we should also try to mobilise the economies of the neutral powers. England's brutal methods, such as the foolish bluff with the threatened boycott against Sweden, have fortunately played straight into our hands. If England – which seems very likely – refuses to come to its senses, if it decides to continue the war to all extremes and if – as appears less likely – it manages to persuade its allies to hold out as well, then we would have a situation similar to that which Napoleon I tried to bring about with his continental blockade, in other words English commerce would be excluded from the greater, the richer and the more wealthy [*kaufkräftiger*] parts of central Europe. We could exploit this situation to our advantage and thereby acquire additional strengths which England does not have.[89]

A more pessimistic view was taken by Oswald Spengler, later famous as the author of *Der Untergang des Abendlandes* (1918 – 1921). Like many other German intellectuals, Spengler believed that Germany's decision to challenge England for world domination was an epoch-making event, one which necessitated a search for adequate historical analogies rather than (for him) meaningless concepts like 'balance of power'. On 18 December 1914 he wrote to his friend Hans Klöres:

I know of only two epochs as important as the present – the history of Europe between the years 1789 and1815, and classical history from Sulla to the death of Anthony. These epochs left behind them a world changed to its depths. You will observe that the crucial decision in this war lies between Britain and Germany. The other powers are only bottle-holders. The point at issue between Sulla and Marcus, Pompey and Caesar, Octavian and Anthony, was Rome and Alexandria (the Latin and Hellenistic ideas) or – for the pre-formation of culture – the Arabic East and the Germanic West.[90]

Germany, he went on, had a mission which was similar to that of Rome in the fight against the Greek and Punic armies of Hellas and Carthage. Only the Roman legions and Napoleon's Grenadiers had something of the same style and appearance of today's German soldiers in their field grey. In the same letter he even speculated on the possibility that the German army might soon appear in London, an event which would be the 'Zama' for England. 'I know that there is a plan to carry this out. If it is now not practicable, a second war against England will bring the victory which history demands.'[91]

Indeed, Spengler's pessimism did not stem from any lack of confidence in the ability of the German army to win great military victories in the struggle against England. Rather, it stemmed from a much more deep-rooted fear that, even if Germany did succeed in making England submit to its will, this would not of itself provide a cure for the enormous crises of national and cultural identity caused by modernity, crises that were threatening to plunge Germany, as well as its western neighbours, ever further into anarchy and chaos. The reality of economic and technological progress meant that the struggle between England and Germany was no more than a struggle between two different sides of the same occidental culture, between what he later referred to as 'English' liberalism, with its emphasis on individual freedom and self-determination, and 'Prussian' socialism, with its emphasis on order and authority.[92] In an earlier letter to Klöres, dated 25 October 1914, Spengler again predicted an imminent German invasion of England ('I assume that it will take place at the beginning of November'), but also spoke, in the same paragraph, of his fears for the future:

What lies before us is unfortunately equally unconsoling, if one thinks and feels as a man of culture. The ray of inner culture from the time of Goethe, which had lost its brilliance after Sedan, since when the Berliner has represented the north German type, has been completely extinguished by this war. In the Germany which made its world position secure through technical skill, money and an eye for facts, a completely soulless Americanism will rule, and will dissolve art, the nobility, the Church, and world outlook in a materialism such as only once before has been seen – in Rome at the time of the First Empire.[93]

An equally fatalistic attitude was taken by Max von Gruber, Professor of Hygiene at the University of Munich and, later in the war, chairman of the Munich-based Volksausschuß für die rasche Niederkämpfung Englands. Gruber regarded Germany's world policy as the root cause of the war with England, and concluded that this was the inevitable result of Germany's dynamic economic growth and the increase in its population from 41 to 68 million since 1870. It was, he argued, 'of the greatest importance for our future actions that we recognise that this war is not, as our pacifists [*Friedensträumer*] living in cloud cuckoo land would have us believe, merely the result of chance acts by fools and criminals, but that this war was unavoidable and had to come ... And we too are guilty! Not morally guilty in the bourgeois sense, but biologically guilty.'[94] In these circumstances, it was also only natural, in Gruber's view, that England should take counter-measures to protect its former position as the leading world power, including the use of force:

Of course the success of one nation does not necessarily have to be to the disadvantage of another; within a certain time period and up to a certain point it can even have positive effects through the mutual exchange of goods, the expansion of markets, but only up to a certain point. When the registered tonnage of German merchant shipping increases threefold within 25 years, while that of the English only doubles, [and] when German capital assets increase in 18 years from 100 million to 300 million, this in itself without doubt represents an extraordinary threat to a country which lives almost exclusively from its industry, its trade and its commerce, which can afford to feed its growing population only via an exchange of [industrial] goods.[95]

Like Spengler, Gruber predicted a military victory for Germany over its corrupt and plutocratic enemies, but also argued that victory in itself was not enough to guarantee Germany's future as a great power.

Of course victory in itself is no guarantee of a prosperous future. The external gains to be made are nothing if they are not brought to life through work.

Affluence and material possessions can all too easily lead to the decay of a nation if it believes that it can sit back and enjoy these peacefully. For Spain the conquest of America was no blessing; but the Spanish and Dutch [colonial] possessions became, in the hands of the English, the means towards an unprecedented economic, and, we must admit, also a cultural upswing, by means of which [England] has for a long time been ahead of the European nations.[96]

Gruber's answer to this problem was to offer a racial-biological solution to Germany's future development, one which foreshadowed many of the policies later adopted under the Third Reich.

The unconditional requirement is first and foremost a strong increase in our national population. Birth and death command the fate of all living things! Only through reproduction is it possible to defeat death . . . But an increase in the national population is not enough on its own; we can see that in the case of Russia. It is also absolutely vital to maintain and increase the average value of the hereditary stock which is passed from one generation to the next in the process of procreation. It is therefore absolutely vital to encourage the propagation of our best people, of our heroes. The fit must proliferate, the unfit must disappear [*Die Tüchtigen müssen wuchern, die Untüchtigen verschwinden*].[97]

Equally important, however, was that Germany should learn to reject the humanitarian and pacifist values of the west, which Gruber despised as degenerate in comparison with Germanic ideals of heroism and chivalry.

This curtailment in the use of one's strengths, this voluntary renunciation of breeding and multiplying, that is the demand of pacifism, of quietism and neo-Malthusianism. Conflict and resistance to conflict form the only effective protection against the diversion of the human instinct for activity into childish stupidity. The neo-Malthusian idea robs women in particular of their true task in life or at least very seriously curtails their enjoyment of their own separate sphere as mothers and housewives. This alone must have a devastating impact on the *Volk* as a whole.[98]

In September 1914 Gruber had been one of the first German professors to call openly for 'absolute domination' over Europe as one of the key aims which Germany had to realise in the current war.[99] This indeed was an idea that won increasing support during the course of the war: the idea that Germany should first seek to expand and consolidate its position of economic hegemony and indirect control on the continent before it could hope to challenge England on the world stage.

The cultural war and the English national character

Whereas the indictment of England as an economic power can be seen largely as resulting from frustrations caused by England's economic blockade of Germany and the increasingly vulnerable external position of the Reich, the most lasting and profound contribution to German anglophobia was made by those intellectuals and writers who deliberately avoided discussing the Anglo-German conflict in terms of day-to-day politics, and instead focused on what they saw as the deeper spiritual side to the conflict. Houston Stewart Chamberlain was not alone in arguing that Germany's world mission was first and foremost to make moral, rather than territorial, conquests. The historian Karl Lamprecht, for instance, who shared many of Chamberlain's ideas on race, also believed that the war called for a re-think of German cultural policy at home and abroad so as to 'elevate the spiritual position of our nation to the heights of its mission'.[100] Likewise the sociologist Max Weber declared in a speech delivered in Nuremberg in August 1916: 'It would be shameful if we lacked the courage to ensure that neither Russian barbarism, English monotony, nor French grandiloquence rule the world. That is why this war is being fought.'[101]

In spite of this, it is astonishing that so little was done to initiate a coordinated policy to counteract the negative effect which allied war propaganda, particularly in regard to Belgium, was having on Germany's image abroad.[102] Rather, for the most part, cultural propaganda was left to the initiatives of private groups and individuals who were often aware of the dilemmas they faced when seeking to defend Germany's war effort from an academic viewpoint and sometimes even expressed resentment that the government was not giving them enough guidance and support. In a telling letter of 7 October 1914 from the medieval historian Eduard Meyer to Theodor Wiegand, an archaeologist and director of the Antikensammlung on Berlin's Museumsinsel who had been recruited to work for the Press Department of the German Foreign Office, Meyer complained:

In the meantime the 'Appeal to the cultural world', of which you sent me a copy, has also appeared. I cannot believe that it will be of much use, since we make assurances in it about things *we* know absolutely nothing about and can say nothing about, except that *we* believe *our* authorities etc. about the way we are waging the war, about the Anglo-French plan to violate the Belgian neutrality and so on; [but] this will never convince the objective observer. Rather, it was the duty of our official organs, of the military and above all of the Foreign Office, to make and distribute the right declarations, to publish documents etc., and they have entirely neglected this duty and are not even fulfilling it now. It is very naive of them to expect us, who know nothing about such things, to stand in for them![103]

One solution to this dilemma was to avoid discussing the political implications of the war altogether in favour of an approach which sought to justify Germany's actions in terms of the intellectual traditions of German Idealism and Romanticism and of German history itself since the great wars of liberation waged against Napoleon at the beginning of the nineteenth century. Germany's right to wage war was thus given a moral and cultural basis over and above the original diplomatic and military arguments.

The historian Friedrich Meinecke, for instance, presented the war as the latest in a long line of nationalist upsurges (*'Erhebungen'*) in Germany, through which the German people had expressed their desire for an independent state committed to securing individual freedoms for its citizens and strong enough to assert its own power against foreign enemies. The first of these 'upsurges' had occurred in 1812–13, during the national wars of liberation against foreign (Napoleonic) domination; this was followed by the German revolutions of 1848–9 and the Franco-Prussian war of 1870–1. The individual genius of Bismarck was in Meinecke's view only one aspect of a broader historical process which had not ended with the death of the man himself; rather the German nation as a whole 'has a mission from God to organise the divine essence of man in a separate, unique [and] irreplaceable form. It is like a great artist, who, by means of his personal genius, creates something above his own personality, something eternal. Through its achievements for the spirit of mankind a nation justifies all its selfish aspirations and thereby its power struggles and wars.'[104] Only the Germans, he continued, had managed to find the combination of *Innerlichkeit*, individual freedom and willingness to sacrifice selfish interests to the good of the whole that characterised their unique spiritual heritage. The parliamentary regimes of the west, by contrast, had produced a 'uniform, mechanical' type of humanity, which carried with it the danger of a degenerate individualism and unbridled egoism.[105]

Indeed, in spite of later differences over specific war aims, which grew in intensity as the war progressed, there was substantial agreement among German academics and intellectuals during the first phase of the war on the role of Germany as the 'Land und Volk der Mitte',[106] as the protector of the values and culture of central Europe in all their diversity against the combined threat of Russian autocracy on the one hand, and the materialism of the west on the other. The philosopher Adolf Lasson declared in a speech in 1914:

Germany is the land of the centre [*Land der Mitte*], German culture occupies a central position. The whole of European culture, which is surely the only universal form of human culture, has gathered itself together like a focal point on German soil and in the hearts of the German people. It would be quite wrong to express ourselves on this point with modesty and reservation. We Germans represent the last and the highest of all that European culture has ever brought forth; upon this rests the strength and the fullness of our self-esteem.[107]

Similarly, the novelist Thomas Mann spoke in his early wartime essay 'Gedanken im Kriege' of Germany's 'indispensable role as missionary' in defending the unique status of German *Kultur* against the superficial, liberal *Zivilisation* of the western allies.

Kultur means unity, style, form, posture, taste, a certain spiritual organisation of the world, even if this may all seem fantastic, ludicrous, wild, bloody and fearsome. *Kultur* can include oracles, magic, pederasty, vitupery, human sacrifices, orgiastic cults, the Inquisition, autos-da-fé, St. Vitus's dance, witches' trials, the flush of poisoning and the most terrible atrocities. But *Zivilisation* means reason, enlightenment, softness, respectability, scepticism, decomposition – *Geist*. Indeed, *Geist* itself is civil, bourgeois: it is the sworn enemy of instinct, of passions, it is anti-demonic, anti-heroic, and it is only an apparent contradiction when we say that it is also ingenious.[108]

By explicitly defining and identifying 'culture' as the venerated product of the German *Geist*, of the land of philosophy and music and of authoritarian government, and contrasting this with western 'civilisation', which he equated with the ideals of the French revolution and of the modern 'corrupt [*unsauber*] plutocratic bourgeois republic' in France, Mann was inevitably providing arguments in defence of the German – and against the western – position in the war. 'It is not so easy to be a German', he wrote in November 1914.

[It is] not so comfortable as it is to be English, and not at all such a distinct and cheerful thing as it is to live as the French do. This people has difficulty with itself, it finds itself questionable, it suffers from itself to the point of outright disgust; but just as among individuals, so among nations it is those that suffer the most that are of the most worth, and whoever would wish that German manners should disappear from the world in favour of *humanité* and *raison* is committing a sacrilege.[109]

Mann also categorically denied that western-style democracy could ever take hold in Germany.

[T]his most introspective of people, this people of metaphysics, of pedagogy and of music, is not a politically oriented, but a morally oriented people. And thus it has shown itself to be more hesitant and less interested in political progress towards democracy, towards parliamentary forms of government, and especially towards republicanism, than other [peoples] – from which one can but conclude . . . that the Germans are the non-revolutionary people *par excellence* – in fact the most non-revolutionary of them all.[110]

The war, in other words, had brought Mann's own lonely artistic struggle against democratic mass society with its 'moral shilly-shallying' and 'flabby humanitarianism'[111] onto a higher stage, transforming it into a broader struggle against liberal modernity. This was also the theme to which Mann returned in 1918 in his famous polemical essay *Betrachtungen eines Unpolitischen*, since described by one historian as 'the most brilliant and penetrating summation of anti-western and anti-liberal German nationalist sentiment written in the twentieth century'.[112]

Of all the anti-English works which appeared in Germany during the First World War, however, probably the most famous and most widely discussed was the book written by the Berlin economist and former Marxist Werner Sombart with the celebrated title *Händler und Helden* (1915). As the title suggests, this book was an unremitting indictment of the commercial mentality of the British and equally a celebration of German heroism and Prussian militarism. Like a number of other books written during the war, it remained a best-seller during the 1920s and also provided an inspiration for those who sought intellectual backing in the campaign to discredit republican culture and democracy.[113]

For Sombart the war was first and foremost a *Glaubenskrieg*, a fight between two different ideologies and two fundamentally opposed *Weltanschauungen*.[114] In this battle of ideas, England represented the values of modern egalitarian mass culture, with its emphasis on 'comfort' and material success; Germany on the other hand was the land of virtue and heroic idealism, the land which had remained true to the values and traditions of its warrior past. Whereas English culture and English politics could be reduced to one and the same dimension, summed up by the question: 'What can life give to me?', the German warrior approached life with a different question in mind: 'What can I give to life?' Similarly, whereas the English 'trader' spoke only of 'rights', the German 'hero' spoke of the 'duties' he had.[115] In Sombart's view there could never be any compromise between these two ideals; it was a question of either one or the other:

The trader in the bog, which one might call commercialism, Mammonism, materialism, sportism, comfortism . . . or the hero at the pinnacle of idealism. For modern mankind this is the equivalent of God and the Devil, Ornuzd and Ahriman.[116]

From this basic conflict between the English 'trader' and the German 'hero', Sombart was able to derive all the commonly held negative stereotypes about the English national character: the reluctance to wage war unless by 'sly and unheroic' commercial means or the use of mercenaries, the application of the purely commercial or *händlerisch* doctrine of the 'balance of power' to the sphere of international relations, and the ability to equate selfish national interests with the interests of international justice and equality. Finally, there was the tendency to treat war itself as a kind of sport, the point at which Sombart argued the English national character differed most from the idealistic outlook of the German warrior.

When the captured Englishmen marched out of the fortress at Liège they held out their hands to our soldiers in field grey: just like at the end of a [football] match! And they were quite shocked when they received the appropriate response: namely a kick in a certain part of the body.[117]

Sombart dedicated his book to the 'young heroes out there facing the enemy' and warned his readers at home that the struggle against British materialism would have to continue even after the military battles had been won. He even went so far as to condemn pan-German expansionist demands on the grounds that they merely served the materialistic interests of mammonistic industrialists and diverted the need for cultural and spiritual renewal in Germany itself. Only against England – and this in itself is revealing, given the doctrines of the time – did Sombart make specific demands for territorial gains:

> If it is necessary to expand so that our growing people have space to develop, then we shall take as much land as we regard as necessary. We shall also put our foot where we think it essential for strategic reasons to maintain our unassailable strength. Therefore, if it is useful for our power position on earth, we shall establish naval bases in perhaps Dover, Malta and Suez. Nothing more [sic!]. We do not wish to expand at all. For we have more important things to do, we have to develop our own spirit, we have to keep the German soul pure, we have to take precautions against the enemy, the commercial spirit invading our own mentality. The task is tremendous and full of responsibility. For we know what is at stake: Germany is the last dike against the muddy flood of commercialism which threatens to swamp all other people because none of them is armed against this threat by the heroic *Weltanschauung* which alone provides protection and salvation.[118]

Reflecting on this quotation, Sombart's latest biographer, Friedrich Lenger, has spoken recently of the 'modesty' (*Bescheidung*) of Sombart's war aims programme, which, he argues, had little to do with respect for the territorial integrity of other European nations. He nonetheless demonstrates that the programme intended by *Händler und Helden* was 'primarily one of cultural regeneration'.[119] However, although Lenger makes much of Sombart's refusal to take part in nationalist propaganda before the war – apart from a brief involvement in naval agitation – and of the relative unpopularity of his extreme ideas on German militarism, the above quotation can only really be interpreted as an unambiguous declaration in favour of German *Weltpolitik* and the aspirations proclaimed by Admiral von Tirpitz and by the Kaiser himself since 1897.

Indeed, that Sombart in no way stood alone with his extreme views on England and the English national character can also be seen if we compare his ideas with those of his friend, the philosopher Max Scheler. In his book *Der Genius des Krieges und der deutsche Krieg* (1915), which was previewed in *Die Neue Rundschau* in October 1914 and therefore known to many educated Germans even before the appearance of Sombart's *Händler und Helden*, Scheler showed a very similar contempt for England and English commercialism. The English, he argued, tended to confuse 'culture with comfort, the warrior with the robber, thought with calculation, reason with economy, God's eternal order with the interests of England, nobility with wealth, power with necessity [and] community with society'.[120] The rise of Germany, on the other hand, represented the rise of the fourth estate, whose revolutionary ethos of work would expel the bourgeois powers of the west from the stage of world history.[121]

Like Sombart, Scheler argued that the war was 'to the first and last an Anglo-German war' and therefore also a 'war against capitalism and its manifestations everywhere'.[122] Not only did he repeatedly emphasise the alleged superiority of the German war ethic over the cunning business ethic of the English; he also sought to underline this by including at the end of the book a fifty-page appendix on the 'psychology of English cant', which he defined as the 'equivalent of lying with a good conscience'.[123]

The key difference between Sombart and Scheler lay less in a difference of temperament or style, and rather in Scheler's concern that, although the immediate cause of the war lay in the Anglo-German conflict, its deeper meaning was to be sought in what he saw as an irreconcilable conflict of interest between Europe and 'Asiatic' Russia. In the long run he was even prepared to accept England as a junior partner in a coalition led by Germany against 'the entire Russian-Byzantine and Yellow [i.e. Far Eastern] world'[124] – provided that England could be cured of its 'sickness', which he defined as an overvaluation of commerce and money-making, favouring natural sciences above the humanities, and misunderstanding civil liberty.[125]

These differences aside, Scheler was also adamant that Germany should not be tempted to make peace in the west until Britain had been purged of the spirit of capitalism and greed which was threatening to spread to other parts of Europe, including France and Germany itself. Indeed, it is this anti-capitalist critique of England which provides the best clue to the sociological origins of modern German anglophobia – the search for a 'German socialism' or that elusive 'third way' between unfettered laissez-faire capitalism (often referred to as 'Manchesterism') and the Marxists' outright repudiation of private ownership and control of the means of production. This search in turn revealed a profound revulsion at the effects that economic growth and industrial change had had on society and equally a widespread belief – particularly among the educated class in Germany – that the state, and above all the civil service, should intervene to check the materialistic excesses of self-seeking minorities in the interests of the general good.

It is hardly surprising, then, that such attitudes towards England were also popular among certain left-wing critics of capitalism, including some Marxists such as Paul Lensch and Konrad Haenisch,[126] as well as more liberal figures from the Christian Socialist movement such as Gerhard von Schulze-Gaevernitz and Friedrich Naumann. Naumann, for instance, argued in his best-selling work *Mitteleuropa* (1915) that the logic of 'war socialism' was leading Germany and central Europe away from the English model of individual laissez-faire capitalism towards a more rational form of economic planning:

The period of essential individualism, the period of imitation of the already declining English economic system has thus passed, but so too has the period of internationalism which boldly sought to overcome the existing nation-state . . . What we have instead is a certain reconciliation between the national-bourgeois and the socialist conception of economics . . . We are *one* nation and through being encircled by a world of enemies and trapped in an economic prison we have discovered the basic principles of national economics [*Volkswirtschaft*].[127]

And similarly Schulze-Gaevernitz reassured his compatriots in 1915 that they would win the war against England by virtue of their superior talent for economic and military organisation and their sense of discipline and idealism founded on a common awareness of the need for collective action in order to solve the new social, economic and demographic problems of the twentieth century.

This Germany cannot be defeated, nor can it be made to suffer the same fate as Hindustan. For today the *Weltgeist* expresses itself through Germany.[128]

Undoubtedly views such as these – precisely because of their non-rational, emotional appeal – helped to encourage the extreme nationalist sentiments that were to proliferate in Germany as the war went on. Indeed, the spirit of irreconcilability bred by the 'ideas of 1914' and the cultural war against England remained a powerful factor in German politics even after 1918, linking nationalist and anti-capitalist resentments against the 'plutocratic' system erected at Versailles and ensuring that the negative image of English politics and culture remained essentially the same until after 1945.

3 German war aims and propaganda against England

The 'spirit of 1914', which formed the subject of previous chapters, provided the German government and the military authorities with temporary relief from peacetime domestic tensions and – by rousing popular
hostility against England – also helped to divert public attention away
from the true causes of the war. Indeed, the wartime emergency had also
encouraged revisionist elements within the SPD – not only those who
had established contacts with the government such as Eduard David,
Albert Südekum and Max Cohen-Reuß, but also powerful figures in the
party executive such as Philipp Scheidemann and Friedrich Ebert – to
place their faith in a reorientation in domestic affairs, chiefly in the guise
of reform of the Prussian franchise, as a reward for their support of the
war effort.[1] On top of this came a firm conviction, fostered by over two
decades of *Weltpolitik*, that the war was a unique opportunity for
expanding the power of the German Reich at the expense of its 'decadent' enemies in the west, Britain and France.[2]

The unity of classes and parties which the war created, however,
proved to be short lived, not least because the promise of an early military victory failed to materialise. Germany soon divided into hostile
camps which failed to reach agreement on the two most urgent issues
of the day: internal reform and war aims. The Conservatives and
National Liberals, for instance, desired large-scale annexations, both to
enhance military security in future wars and to maintain the internal
status quo, which, they believed, could not survive an unsuccessful war.
Many on the right, including members of the Pan-German League and
other nationalist organisations, also despised Bethmann personally and
disliked his conciliation of the Socialists. The SPD, on the other hand,
both demanded internal reforms and – at least in theory – was opposed
to annexations. As the war went on, the party split into pro-war and
anti-war factions, leading to the formation of the breakaway
Independent Social Democratic Party (USPD) by a small minority of
left-wing pacifists and radicals in April 1917. The Catholic Centre Party
and liberal Progressive People's Party adopted a wait-and-see policy,
favouring annexations so long as the military outlook was good while

being willing to acquiesce in considerable domestic changes after the war.[3]

The existence of these mutually hostile camps should not, however, lead one to underestimate the extent of public support for annexationism, especially in the first two years of the war. This was particularly the case, as the American historian Hans Gatzke pointed out in the 1950s, with regard to Germany's war aims in the west (the *Drang nach Westen*). A close community of interest developed between the Pan-German League and its allies among the heavy industrialists on the one hand, and the so-called War Aims Majority in the Reichstag on the other. In what follows I shall explore four major aspects of this *Drang nach Westen*: the views of Admiral von Tirpitz and the economic interests allied to him; the anti-English agitation of key individuals such as Count Ernst zu Reventlow; the growth of parallel tendencies within the extra-parliamentary war aims movement, and the attitude of the major right-wing political parties and organisations towards England. A final section will then go on to consider the stance taken by the government, and in particular the military authorities, in the light of this shift in emphasis from the war against Russia to the war in the west.

Admiral von Tirpitz and the German navy

Owing to Germany's unique geographical position in the centre of Europe, with potential enemies in both east and west, the build-up of its army had long taken precedence over that of its navy. It was only in the late 1890s that Bismarck's successors, Wilhelm II, Bülow and Tirpitz, chose to launch a programme of sustained naval building with the aim of securing for Germany its rightful 'place in the sun'. Tirpitz in particular saw Britain as the most dangerous opponent at sea, and regarded the navy as an instrument of political power which would eventually force Britain to make important concessions to Germany's world power ambitions. At the same time he deliberately played on the idea of a British naval threat in order to justify the continued existence and expansion of the fleet beyond the control of the Reichstag Budget Committee.[4] In 1914, however, Germany still lacked the overseas naval bases necessary to launch a serious challenge to Britain's worldwide maritime supremacy. This meant that, in the event of war, the German fleet would have to deploy its greatest effort between Heligoland and the Thames, or else avoid action altogether.[5]

In reality, the position of the German navy had been significantly weakened in the final years before the war as a result of changes in German armaments policy.[6] In the budgets of 1912 and 1913 priority was given to the task of building up conventional land forces for the coming war against Russia and France, while the programme of naval building was put on hold to facilitate Bethmann Hollweg's renewed efforts to secure British neutrality. The aim here was to ensure that, when the 'inevitable' clash of arms did come, it would be fought under conditions favourable to Germany by dividing Britain from its allies, Russia and France, and making it look as if they had made the first moves.[7]

Neither Helmuth von Moltke, the Chief of the General Staff, nor Bethmann Hollweg and Jagow had much regard for the navy as an instrument of military policy, still less for Tirpitz personally. Their 'continental' strategy was also supported by Admiral von Müller, the Chief of the Kaiser's Naval Cabinet, who nonetheless urged the Kaiser on 30 July 1914 to consult Tirpitz more closely on questions of naval strategy.[8] In fact, this merely served to underline the point that Tirpitz had hitherto played no part in military planning and as Secretary of State in charge of the Reich Naval Office was not even expected to have strategic ideas of his own (this was the job of the Chief of Admiralty Staff, Admiral Hugo von Pohl, who in theory was the Kaiser's chief adviser on naval affairs but in reality was a pale shadow of his prestigious counterpart, the Chief of the General Staff, Moltke).

Indeed, the official attitude at Imperial Headquarters was already clear in the initial cabinet order presented to the fleet on the same day, 30 July 1914, in which the Kaiser instructed his naval commanders to prepare for the possibility of limited guerrilla warfare against Britain only. Shortly after the outbreak of war, on 6 August, the Kaiser, supported by Bethmann Hollweg, Müller and Pohl, issued further instructions preventing the immediate use of the High Seas Fleet in order to keep it intact for use as a bargaining counter in any future peace talks. This in turn was a reflection of their confident belief that early victories on the continent, coupled with large indemnities to be squeezed from France, would force the British to negotiate, or at least ensure their defeat in a 'Second Punic War'.[9]

Tirpitz, on the other hand, found such orders intolerable, first and foremost because he feared that the decision to hold back the navy would lead to a further decrease in its status, particularly if the army concluded the war on the continent by itself and the government then came under pressure to sue for peace with a Britain undefeated at sea. For this reason too he had tried until the last moment to prevent a German declaration of war against Russia and France, since he realised that Britain would never stay out of such a war, but would side with its ally France.[10] In a letter to his wife, written from Imperial Headquarters in Koblenz on 23 August 1914, he gave vent to these growing feelings of anger and frustration, complaining that 'nobody [here] seems to understand that our greatest danger is still the polo-playing Englishmen'. He also went on:

If we had no fleet, England would have been against us ever since Sedan. If we had made more progress with our fleet, England wouldn't have risked it. If we don't want to be utterly beaten, we must build a fleet; that is the only way by which we can gain an outlet for our exports and industry.[11]

In other words, Tirpitz believed that only a strong German navy would deter Britain from attacking Germany in the future, just as he believed that the past mistakes of German diplomacy, in particular the failure to seek an understanding with Russia rather than with 'perfidious Albion', had provided Britain with the opportunity it had always been looking for to unleash war on the continent. Writing to his wife a day later he continued:

Pray God that the arch-scoundrels may be annihilated, for it is they who have set fire to our cultured Europe, in cold blood, from sheer lust for power and gold. I can do but little, and, despite the glorious victories [of the German army], a great weight oppresses me. You will help me to bear it when the time comes and the finger of scorn is pointed at me. Inwardly I am, of course, absolutely certain that the only thing for Germany was to take up the naval question if our people were not to sink.[12]

And, in a crucial sentence in a letter to Admiral von Lans on 30 August 1914, which was later omitted from the edited version of his political documents, Tirpitz argued that 'we must have a fleet of equal strength to the Royal Navy, although this natural and singular goal could not be articulated during the last two decades'.[13] In this way he also revealed that his long-range objectives had not changed since 1897.

During the first weeks of the war, Tirpitz's position was further undermined by a number of naval setbacks, notably the loss of three light cruisers and a destroyer on 28 August during the first major skirmish with the British navy off Heligoland, and also by widespread criticism of his naval-building programme in government circles. Many opponents of Tirpitz, including Bethmann Hollweg and his foreign policy adviser Kurt Riezler, now believed that Germany should seek to establish its position on the continent as a prelude to the final showdown with England.[14] Such continental strength could be achieved only at the expense of France and Russia, which, along with Belgium and Luxembourg, were to be the chief victims of Bethmann's famous war aims programme of September 1914. In addition, supporters of the Chancellor such as Albert Ballin told Tirpitz that it might even be necessary to come to a temporary agreement with England on the naval question in order to bring about a quick military decision on the continent. This in turn, according to Ballin, would provide Germany with its only certain means of pre-empting British opposition to its projected territorial gains overseas once France and Belgium had been defeated.[15]

More sympathetic to the aspirations of the German navy, at least on the surface, was the Prussian Minister of War, Erich von Falkenhayn, who in autumn 1914 took over from Moltke as Chief of the General Staff. On 31 August 1914, for instance, Falkenhayn informed Admiral von Pohl that he too saw 'the ultimate aim of the war in the defeat of England' and that he regarded 'the holding back of the fleet as correct, but its full engagement as necessary, when the prospects [of victory] are good'. And on the same day, in the presence of the Chancellor, he warned that 'it would be impossible to hold back the fleet if the naval chief [i.e. Pohl] were to advise in favour of its deployment'.[16]

Falkenhayn was also an intermittent campaigner for unrestricted submarine warfare, and in November 1914 joined forces with Tirpitz in order to demand a separate peace with Russia. In a letter to the Under Secretary of State Zimmermann on 19 November 1914, Bethmann Hollweg outlined the logic behind this thinking, in effect paraphrasing what Falkenhayn had said to him during a meeting on the previous day:

If we succeed in what must be our first aim, to get Russia to make peace, then we could so crush France and Britain that we could dictate the peace, even if the Japanese came across the seas to France and if England sent a stream of new reinforcements into the field. It could, however, be safely assumed that, if Russia made peace, France would give up too. Then, if England did not submit to us completely, we could defeat it by using our Belgian bases to blockade it, even if it took months.[17]

In the long run, however, Tirpitz and his naval supporters were bound to find themselves at odds with the majority of Prussia's eastern-oriented and land-oriented generals, many of whom, including of course Falkenhayn's successors Hindenburg and Ludendorff, were far more annexationist than Falkenhayn himself.[18] Moreover, Tirpitz also had to face the continued hostility of the former Chief of Staff, Moltke, who in January 1915 wrote to the Kaiser urging him to re-examine the military options available to Germany in its war against Britain, since '[i]n my opinion our fleet cannot deliver a fatal blow against England'.[19] (Moltke's idea, as he told the Kaiser, was to revive 'the old Napoleonic idea of a strike against England's most vulnerable position, Egypt'. Only in this way, he argued, would Germany find itself in a position to bring about 'a great victory against England *on land*'.[20])

Tirpitz himself rejected the view that the present war was being waged purely to secure Germany's continental position, seeing in it a mere consolation for those, such as the Kaiser or Moltke, who lacked the nerve to take on the full might of the Royal Navy.[21] Nor did he have much time for Falkenhayn's *Mitteleuropa* plan of the summer of 1915, which envisaged the creation of an economic and military bloc out of the Central Powers, Turkey and Bulgaria with the aim of gradually wearing down British opposition to the German war effort.[22] In fact,

Tirpitz had already outlined his views on the best means of winning the war in a letter to the Kaiser on 6 August 1914, in which he argued that the 'decisive battle' (*große Entscheidung*) could come about only through a naval confrontation with Britain in the North Sea: 'If the English fleet tries to approach Heligoland, then we must attack.'[23] Similar ideas were also put forward in a letter to the Kaiser's brother, Prince Heinrich von Preußen, on 10 September 1914. Here Tirpitz wrote:

> We must fight this war against England to the bitter end [*bis ans bittere Ende*], otherwise all our victories on land will have been for nothing . . . Knowing England as I do, I believe no understanding is possible, force is the only solution.[24]

In this way, Tirpitz was already beginning to marshal support for his own view of the war as a 'life and death struggle with England' for future mastery of the seas.[25] This can also be seen, for instance, in his early endeavours on behalf of German war aims, in particular his support for the annexation of Antwerp and the Flanders coastline as the first step towards breaking British maritime supremacy.[26] Significantly, these ideas were very similar to those of Albert Ballin, who, in spite of his earlier caution, continued to act as a spokesman for the expansionist aspirations of the naval officer corps.[27] In addition, Tirpitz desired a separate peace with both Russia and Japan in order to gain a free hand against the western naval powers, i.e. Britain, France and the USA. Germany could then expect to acquire enough naval bases around the world to serve as an adequate foundation for its future *Weltpolitik*.[28]

As previous research has indicated, this basic programme of war aims enjoyed the backing of the majority of naval executive officers, including senior figures such as Admirals von Holtzendorff, Scheer and von Trotha and Captain von Levetzow.[29] Moreover, even 'moderates' such as Admiral von Pohl, who had supported the initial decision to hold back the High Seas Fleet, demonstrated total opposition to the idea of any negotiated peace settlement with Britain. On 6 September 1914, for instance, Pohl wrote to his deputy, Rear Admiral von Behncke, expressing the view that:

> . . . peace can only be made after the overthrow of England, or, as you put it, 'in London'. It will require the greatest efforts on our part to achieve this. Our navy hence has a difficult task ahead. In any case a trump card would be the occupation of the coast as far as Boulogne and Le Havre and the mining of the [English] Channel. Then the preparation for an invasion across the Channel and if necessary its realisation through the engagement of our fleet.[30]

In the same letter he went on to express his confidence that the force of public opinion would ultimately prevail against the 'defeatists' who sought a negotiated peace with Britain. In particular he mentioned Arthur von Gwinner of the Deutsche Bank and other representatives of 'international high finance', whom he singled out as the chief opponents of the German war aims programme.

> Herr v. Gwinner and his chums can go to the Devil if they dare to come before the German people with their peace proposals. I believe that there would then be violent unrest and [the people] would hold the government to account for the policies which have led to this war. Only after the war has been completed with full honours and the expectation of a secure peace lasting for 100 years has been fulfilled will the people forgive and forget. Defeatism is therefore not on the agenda.[31]

Pohl's optimism was based on his assumption that Britain's apparent willingness to fight, coupled with the effects of the London declaration of 5 September, would force the Chancellor to change course and abandon his earlier reluctance to engage in all-out economic and naval warfare against Britain.[32] On top of this he believed, as he told Bethmann on 31 August 1914, that Germany would 'hold out longer than England, which will suffer more than us from the disturbance to her trade and industry'.[33] This was also a view shared by Karl Helfferich, one of Gwinner's co-directors at the Deutsche Bank who later in the war became State Secretary to the Reich Treasury Office and incidentally opposed the use of unrestricted submarine warfare.[34]

Tirpitz, on the other hand, continued to express his profound mistrust of 'the Chancellor and his set', whom he suspected of preparing a sell-out on the naval issue. 'Just as their policy could not prevent the war', he told his wife on 4 September, 'it will bring about a wretched peace.'[35] He also believed that Pohl had joined forces with Admiral von Müller, the Kaiser and Bethmann in order to prevent the fleet from being sent into action, arguing on one occasion that 'I have more in my little finger in this question than Pohl has in his entire skull'.[36] It is nonetheless significant that Tirpitz and Pohl were in fundamental agreement on the main issues, namely that the war against Britain should be fought to the end and that the key battles would take place in the North Sea. In this sense at least, common hatred of Britain and a desire to supplant it as the world's leading naval power were able to transcend differences in personality.[37]

Finally, it is worth noting that the German navy also sought to attract powerful economic interests to its side through its use of propaganda suggesting that Britain was waging a war not only against the German fleet but also against German commercial competition. The implication here was that, without a strong fleet to protect its worldwide commercial interests, Germany would fail to recapture lost markets after the war, even if its armies were victorious on the continent. Such considerations also played a key part in the navy's support for the outright annexation of Belgium, or at least of its coastline and chief seaports. In his memorandum of October 1915, for instance, which focused on Antwerp and the Flanders coast as areas of particular importance to German naval and economic power in the future, Tirpitz wrote:

If Antwerp becomes a German port and if the land corridor leading to it belongs to us, then we can hope to have improved our opportunities for economic expansion to the point where, in time, we can overcome the problems caused by the war and be equal to our powerful Anglo-American competitors. But if England is able to get its way with regard to Belgium, then this successful conclusion of the war for our principal enemy will by no means merely throw us back to the status quo ante. Rather, our whole existence as an economic world power would be directly threatened.[38]

In the same memorandum he drew attention to the 'ruthless manner and way in which German exports are destroyed, especially by England', and added: 'In many cases the German export business, which has been built up with great effort and hard toil over the decades, has been destroyed; everything will have to be re-built from scratch.'[39]

As the war went on Tirpitz became increasingly obsessed with the alleged Anglo-Saxon capitalist 'conspiracy' against Germany, as can be seen in the many speeches he delivered on behalf of the German Fatherland Party in 1917–18.[40] In the meantime, he was also able to attract a great deal of public support as a result of his tough stance towards England, especially among the right-wing political parties and the powerful economic interests associated with them. This personal popularity among right-wingers and German nationalists in turn proved to be a valuable weapon in his long drawn out struggle against Bethmann Hollweg and the so-called 'defeatists' within the Kaiser's entourage.[41]

Annexationist propaganda: the case of Count Ernst zu Reventlow

The question of how far the views of Tirpitz and other admirals also represented the opinion of the majority of Germans is difficult to answer, particularly since the strict censorship introduced at the outset of the war prevented many from expressing their true feelings in public. Contemporary observers were doubtless correct when they located the hard-core of anti-English thinking among extreme annexationist groups such as the Pan-German League and its various subsidiary organisations. The influence exercised by their war aims propaganda was probably greater than one would expect, however, particularly when one takes into account other factors such as the publication of the Belgian documents and the particularly bloody nature of the war in Belgium, which cost the lives of an unexpectedly high number of German soldiers. Moreover, groups such as the Pan-Germans had many sympathisers in high places, including the state bureaucracy, the aristocracy and the military. This gave them a built-in advantage over their opponents on the left when it came to exploiting weaknesses and loopholes in the official censorship policy.

One of the leading annexationist papers was the *Deutsche Tageszeitung*, the Berlin-based organ of the Agrarian League. Its editor was Ernst Georg Oertel, a leading Conservative Reichstag deputy and member of the all-important Budget Committee. Conrad von Wangenheim and Gustav Roesicke, the joint chairmen of the Agrarian League, were also closely involved in the paper's editorial policy. By far the most important contributor, however, was 'E.R.' or Count Ernst zu Reventlow, a former naval officer and leading figure on the radical wing of the Conservatives, who had been recruited by Roesicke before the war to serve as the paper's foreign affairs editor.[42]

Ironically, Reventlow had begun his journalistic career as a columnist for the left-liberal *Berliner Tageblatt* and for Maximilian Harden's *Zukunft*, using his position to mount frequent attacks on the naval policy of the German Reich. In 1908, however, for reasons which remain unclear, he suddenly reversed his earlier position and became both a violent anglophobe and anti-Semite, and an ardent admirer of Admiral von Tirpitz.[43] He severed his relations with his former employers and took over the foreign desk of the *Tägliche Rundschau*, later moving on to the *Deutsche Tageszeitung*. He also served for a short period as head of the Berlin branch of the Pan-German League and as editor of its chief organ, the *Alldeutsche Blätter*. Although he left the League in 1910, again for reasons never satisfactorily explained, he maintained contact and resumed collaboration after 1914.[44]

During the first two years of the war, Reventlow frequently clashed with the government and the censorship authorities, mainly as a result of articles he wrote on German–American relations and the submarine question. He also became involved in a fierce polemical dispute with Theodor Schiemann, long-time foreign affairs editor of the rival conservative paper the *Kreuzzeitung* and a personal friend of the Kaiser. Shortly after the outbreak of the war Schiemann wrote an article which seemed to advocate an early peace agreement with Britain and an Anglo-German alliance against Russia, and was immediately attacked by Reventlow in the *Deutsche Tageszeitung*.[45] Reventlow's response was that such a proposal would only give the impression of German anxiety regarding the possibility of a long war with England. Moreover, he wrote:

This peace would be a rotten peace for us, since the decades which would follow its signature would be permanently dominated by the impending war with

England and the preparations for it. Or else Germany would have to submit to England, which would not be proper for its position and dignity, and live under permanent British coercion.[46]

In the ensuing debate, the editorial board of the *Kreuzzeitung* sided with the conservative critics of Schiemann, whereupon Schiemann resigned his position.[47] He was eventually replaced as foreign affairs editor by Otto Hoetzsch, a former pupil of his, who was chosen because of his pro-Russian, anti-British orientation, and who worked in close collaboration with the Conservative leader Count Westarp.[48] Schiemann's enforced departure from the *Kreuzzeitung* for expressing views that until only a few weeks before had been quite commonplace is hence another example of the changes which had taken place in both public and official opinion since August 1914.

In fact, in the first months of the war Reventlow's impact was so great that even the German-language New York paper *Vorwärts*, which represented the anti-imperialist wing of the SPD, was forced to revise its anti-war propaganda in order to take account of it. In an article of 8 May 1915, for instance, the paper admitted that there were now two types of imperialism in Germany:

Those German imperialists who see the future of the 'Greater Germany' in Asia Minor naturally see Russia as the principal enemy, since in their view it is here that the German plans clash with the expansionist aspirations of Russia . . .

Quite different are those politicians who have no concrete goals, but merely dream indiscriminately of a policy of the strong hand, the haters of England, above all the so-called Pan-Germans with Count Reventlow at their head, for whom England is the enemy. Closely associated with them are also the German agrarians, who see in Russia the bulwark of reaction and want to preserve its power as a counter-weight to England.[49]

Meanwhile, in June 1915 and again in October, articles written by Reventlow attacking the government's handling of relations with America in the wake of the Lusitania and Arabic crises resulted in the imposition of temporary bans on the *Deutsche Tageszeitung*. On both these occasions, however, it was also apparent that Reventlow had sympathisers in high places. In June 1915, for instance, he was backed by Oberleutnant Georg von Klitzing, who addressed the following letter to the Under Secretary in the Reich Chancellor's Office, Arnold von Wahnschaffe:

I believe you cannot afford the luxury of needlessly annoying the entire staff of the *Deutsche Tageszeitung*. We have always been the ones who have defended the state and made great sacrifices. I therefore urge you to act a little less nervously or, at the very least, impartially.[50]

And in October 1915 General von Kessel, the Commander-in-Chief in the Marches, who was responsible for the implementation of military censorship in the Berlin area, confided at a meeting with Oertel and Roesicke that he personally shared the views of the *Deutsche Tageszeitung* and was merely carrying out orders issued on behalf of the Chancellor, Bethmann Hollweg.

He made it clear that he had been obliged to implement the directives of the Reich Chancellor . . . He had found the whole affair distasteful. He had already received a huge pile of letters attacking him. When I pointed out that we had the best intentions he concurred and went on to say that we should indeed show these good intentions. We should send him an advance copy of Reventlow's article, and then the paper would be able to reappear in the evening. We gave our agreement to this.[51]

Shortly before this second ban, Reventlow's activities had even come to the attention of the Kaiser, who reportedly compared him in a moment of anger to the Italian nationalist and rabble-rouser Gabriele D'Annunzio, and demanded strong action against him.[52] This was a result of Reventlow's unscheduled appearance at an important event on 2 October 1915 marking the official unveiling of a colossal wooden statue of Field Marshal Paul von Hindenburg, the 'hero' of Tannenberg, in the middle of Berlin's Königsplatz.[53] The organisers of this event had clearly intended it to be a demonstration of the Berliners' solidarity with the military and civilian leadership of the Reich at a time of renewed strains in German–American relations. Towards the end of the day, however, Reventlow suddenly took the stage and proceeded to give his own 'Hindenburg address', one which attempted to claim the Field Marshal as a fellow anglophobe and supporter of unrestricted submarine warfare.

We should no longer, if peace negotiations come, allow ourselves to be deceived by the polished speeches of the old swindler England, as was the case with Prussia in 1815. Rather, we should be led by the spirit of Hindenburg. Just as the general always knows what he wants and how to achieve it, so must the statesman. The will is everything [*Der Wille ist alles*]. This time Germany should come first, and Germany once again, and only then the others! (Applause.) We must fight our enemies with all the means at our disposal, in the air, on land and under the sea, without pity and without letting up. We must learn from Hindenburg how to will, how to win, how to move forward and how to utilise victories. (Rapturous applause.)[54]

This was Reventlow's most audacious act to date, and there can be little doubt that his speech was intended as a warning to the civilian leadership and a rebuke of its cautious submarine policy in the wake of the Lusitania and Arabic affairs.[55] The Kaiser, for instance, described it in a marginal comment as a 'deliberate incitement, with a clear lunge at My Government. Such speeches might be commonplace in Italy or in Paris, but this does not mean that they should be tolerated by us at home. Otherwise politics will fall into the hands of the street.'[56]

In spite of the Kaiser's personal intervention, however, the authorities seemed powerless to take action against Reventlow, both then and in the future. This was no doubt due in part to the sympathy with which his ideas were received within military and police circles, particularly among senior figures such as von Kessel, who, as we have seen, was less than wholehearted in his support for the Chancellor's policies.[57]

Reventlow was well known not just as a journalist and professional trouble-maker, however, but also as the author of a number of books and pamphlets on England and English history which had an important impact on the war aims question in Germany. The most important of these by far was a book entitled *Der Vampir des Festlandes* (1915), one of the most vicious and sustained attacks on British naval power to appear during the war. Here, Reventlow discussed the various stages of English maritime development in order to demonstrate his argument that the English were the pirate nation *par excellence*:

Not a single Englishman is to be found among the pioneers who prepared the way for the great discoveries of the fifteenth and sixteenth centuries. Neither do we find among the English any record of journeys like those accomplished by the Vikings of old – journeys undertaken for the sole pleasure of adventure and of exploring unknown and distant regions. We find, on the other hand, alike in the English people and its rulers, an extremely shrewd comprehension of the value of gold and silver – a comprehension already developed at that period . . . [The heroic age of the Britons] was an age characterised by organised piracy and highway robbery, which was first tolerated and subsequently sanctioned by the English sovereigns – especially by the Virgin Queen [Elizabeth I], the champion of Protestantism.[58]

British naval power, according to Reventlow, was also associated from an early stage with the rise of Puritanism, a religion which encouraged such vices as greed, envy and a hatred of other nations. In this way, the struggle against Britain's odious domination of the seas could also be seen as the logical continuation of the struggle against similar vices within Germany and German religion itself.

The mainspring of [English] Puritanism was the fanatical belief that the English people constitutes a divinely chosen race, which is destined to reign over all other nations and monopolise the world's commerce. The 'religious fervour' of which it boasted did, in the long run, but serve the ends of egotism . . . The pharisaical creed of a greedy, thieving race which, living in the security of an island fortress, cast, like a pack of vultures, its lustful glances over seas and continents – this hypocritical creed could not possibly recognise the Protestantism of other nations [the Dutch in the seventeenth century and, later, the Germans] to be anything like as pure as its own adherents. A Christian people which should be stupid and criminal enough not to grovel in the dust before the Chosen Nation – which should even push such criminal folly to the extent of competing with the Chosen Nation on the sea; such a people deserves nothing else but annihilation. The God of the English commands it![59]

The underlying anti-Semitism behind such arguments could scarcely have been lost on Reventlow's readers, although he was careful to avoid any direct attacks on Jewish interests. He did, however, make a passing reference to his liberal opponents at home, many of whom, as he was no doubt aware, were Jews:

Even after the outbreak of war, after the great war speeches of Sir Edward Grey and his ministerial colleagues, after the final unmasking of England's intentions towards us . . . the view remained widespread and deeply rooted in Germany [that] it was quite inconceivable that Great Britain would ever get involved in a war against [us]. High-standing representatives of German science, who – unfortunately – had developed a tendency to get involved in politics, declared that the participation of Great Britain could be blamed only on the clique led by Sir Edward Grey. These men only needed to be overthrown, which was quite within the realms of possibility, and the way to an 'understanding' between Great Britain and its close relative, the German people, would be open and smoothed over.[60]

It was indeed as an extreme opponent of liberalism at home, as well as of Britain abroad, that Reventlow sought to establish his reputation as a leading figure on the German right.

Reventlow's relations with the Reich Naval Office and Admiral von Tirpitz were a constant source of speculation during the war, not only among his opponents in the left-liberal and socialist press but also among leading government officials.[61] The similarity of views and aims suggests at the very least some form of informal collusion, although Tirpitz was keen to deny rumours that he had hired Reventlow as a paid agent.[62] Both men considered Britain to be Germany's most dangerous enemy and both demanded the annexation of Belgium and northern France as a base for a powerful German fleet. At the same time, Reventlow was a persistent critic of those annexationists who saw Germany's field of expansion primarily in the east and central Europe, arguing instead that the decision on Germany's future would have to come in the North Sea. In an article for the periodical *Das Größere Deutschland* in February 1916, for instance, he wrote:

It is a complete fantasy when the representatives of the *Mitteleuropa* idea suggest that the building of gigantic railways in Asia and Africa could act as a substitute for our oceanic shipping from the North Sea . . . The freedom of the seas can . . . only be built on the foundations of our own power, German power in the German sense of the word. These foundations can also only be located on German soil, on coastlines which are either German or subject to unshakeable German influence. They cannot be made dependent on alliance systems, public sentiment, [spheres of] influence etc.[63]

Such ideas, as we have seen, were completely in accord with the war aims put forward by Tirpitz and the Reich Naval Office in the secret memorandum of October 1915.

Reventlow himself was not content with the mere aim of replacing Britain as the dominant naval power in the waters of northern Europe; he was also keen to emphasise the wider opportunities which such a move would offer to Germany as the leading world power of the future. In his pamphlet *Indien – Seine Bedeutung für Großbritannien, Deutschland und die Zukunft der Welt* (1917), for instance, he urged the German authorities to exploit the opportunities thrown up by the war and the German–Turkish alliance to bring an end to Britain's rule over its most prized colonial possession. An 'independent' India would not only provide crucial protection to German and Turkish interests in Asia Minor, he argued, but also offer opportunities further to advance those interests through the tried and tested means of '*pénétration pacifique*', leading ultimately to German economic domination of the entire southern and south-east Asian region.

Only after the liberation [*Befreiung*] of India would Germany and its Turkish ally be in a position to expand economically beyond Baghdad-Basra and Kuwait. As long as India remains English, or, rather, as long as Great Britain's fleet rules the seas, as long as the Arabian peninsula remains bordered and surrounded by British naval stations and spheres of influence, forming the glacis of India, then all German–Turkish economic ventures, in so far as they move towards the sea or are themselves dependent on overseas aid, will offer no secure rewards, but will remain a burden. It is no different with the Mediterranean Sea and its connection with the ocean.[64]

Reventlow also emphasised that India should not be allowed to come under Russian influence, still less encouraged to develop fully fledged independence. Rather, in his view the advantages of India's 'liberation' from British rule were so great 'that this consideration alone must encourage us to do all in our power to ensure that India and its northern regions do not come under possible Russian control, and that not only is it prevented from any form of independent development, but also it becomes a closed area [*ein verschlossenes Gebiet*] for German–Turkish economic expansion.'[65]

Finally, he argued that the loss of India would make an important contribution to the defeat of Britain at sea, although he also clung to the belief that the decisive naval battles, and thus the moment of Germany's final rise to world power status over Britain, would still take place 'in the waters of northern Europe', i.e. in the North Sea and the English Channel.[66]

Reventlow no doubt enjoyed his reputation as the most uncompromising critic of Britain and British policies during the war. It would be quite wrong, however, to examine his more extreme views in isolation from mainstream and official German opinion. The elusive concept of 'freedom of the seas', for instance, reappeared continually in German annexationist propaganda, giving rise to demands for extensive coastal areas of Belgium and northern France as well. Thus the Conservative leader Count Westarp wrote to Bethmann Hollweg on 17 April 1915 urging that:

Only complete control over Belgium and its fortified harbours close to England and the [English] Channel will gives us that strong position which we will need for generations to come, [since] the enmity of England and France cannot be overcome through understanding and treaties alone. If Belgium is allowed to fall back into its former state, or into a similar state of false independence and neutrality, then this would mean a fundamental worsening of our position when compared to the situation before the war, since after the war Belgium will be more than ever a bulwark for attacks against us and our exclusion from the sea.[67]

To this, the Chancellor replied in reassuringly positive tones:

If a lasting peace is to be won, Belgium must be rendered harmless. We must gain military, political and economic guarantees that England or France will not be able to use Belgium against us in future political controversies. Such guarantees require at least the military and economic dependence of that country upon Germany.[68]

Leading German industrialists such as Hugo Stinnes also demanded German military domination over the whole of the northern coast of France, both to strengthen Germany's strategic position vis-à-vis Britain and to gain the valuable iron and coal fields of Normandy.[69] Similar views were held by Krupp von Bohlen, who set out his own war aims programme in a memorandum of November 1914. The establishment of German power on the Channel, he argued, would compel Britain to offer Germany its friendship, even if history should have taught otherwise.

Here we should be lying at the very marrow of England's world power, a position – perhaps the only one – which could bring us England's lasting friendship. For only if we are able to hurt England badly at any moment will it really leave us unmolested, perhaps even become our 'friend', in so far as England is capable of friendship at all.[70]

Moreover, we now know from archival sources that German officials were giving active encouragement to nationalist movements in both India and Egypt from an early stage in the war as part of a general programme of promoting revolution in vulnerable parts of the Russian and British empires.[71] In part they were acting on the advice of Middle Eastern 'experts' such as Max von Oppenheim, who shortly after the

outbreak of war called for the unleashing of a pan-Islamic revolt stretch-
ing from French North Africa to the Indian sub-continent.[72] At the same
time, support for these activities came from many ordinary Germans,
who, like Reventlow, saw the alliance with Turkey as an instrumental
link in Germany's bid for world power. Having conquered India and
China with Turkish help, it was argued, Germany could proceed to civ-
ilise and Germanise the world in Britain's place, and German would
become the world language. Theodor Springmann, for instance, a
Westphalian manufacturer, wrote in his book *Deutschland und der Orient*
(1915):

The old colonial empire of England must fall, since it is built upon lies and on
subjugation. We will shout out to the emerging nations of the East: from
England's hand you had the lash, now take from Germany's hand the gift of
golden freedom. Come to us, learn our language, learn our technology. To our
enemies we will shut our universities, the source of our strength. We will open
them to our friends, India, the Islamic world, China. Then the German language, with its unique poetry and literature, will become the world language in
this new world, since none of these nations will have any inclination after the
war to take up an English education or [to learn] the English language.[73]

One figure, Dr Albert Ritter (pseudonym Konrad von Winterstetter),
went even further than either Springmann or Reventlow, arguing that
Germany should gain control over the British empire and thus mastery
of the world by dominating the British Isles themselves. After a successful land invasion, Dover would be permanently occupied by a garrison
of German troops and the British empire reduced to a shadow-like existence. Britain itself would be nominally independent, but in reality a
German possession with the mere appearance of self-government. In
his *Nordkap–Bagdad* (1915), he wrote:

England must be rendered incapable of ever fighting against Germany again . . .
This task can best be realised by making ourselves the military overlords of the
European head of the British world empire. The straits from Gravelotte–Verdun
to Dunkirk–Boulogne can find their continuation in the occupation of the
bridge-head around Dover, a fortress on England's soil. This idea might well
appear fantastic – it is as practicable as a landing on British soil, without which
the war will last for years. Only the conquest of London, which we will live to
see, can create the basis for a peace, and after the conquest of London one peace
condition will be as easily imposed as another. England, in possession of only
part of its fleet, while the greater part falls to us, England, militarily in our grasp
but at the same time remaining the administrator of the whole empire, open to
our free economic activity and devoid of tariffs, this England will be our most
compliant neighbour.[74]

On the other hand, it seems only fair to point out that examples such
as this were comparatively rare; most German propagandists, including extreme annexationists such as Reventlow, do not seem to have

considered a land invasion of Britain as a viable option to secure the realisation of their war aims programme.[75]

Annexationist propaganda: the Pan-German League and its industrial allies

In the period after the German military setbacks of autumn 1914, individual agitation against Britain was supplemented by a number of important public statements and petitions put forward by various economic and industrial organisations in Germany. Although some of their demands for annexations on the continent were kept deliberately vague in order to comply with the censorship regulations, they were all agreed that the main object of the war in the west was the defeat of British commercial supremacy. At the same time, these petitions and public addresses were designed to put pressure on the government not to enter into any premature peace discussions with England.

In November 1914, for instance, Jakob Riesser, the chairman of the Central Association of Banks and president of the Hansabund, delivered an important speech at a meeting of the Bankbeamtenverein, which was praised by a colleague for making a fundamental contribution to the 'enlightenment and reassurance of public opinion with regard to the economic war which England is waging against us'.[76] In the published version of this speech, which appeared shortly afterwards, Riesser made no secret of his expansionist and anglophobe views:

There can . . . be no peace until, at the very least, England's power is so broken that it can no longer rule the world and the seas alone, can no longer tread international law under foot and cannot even attempt to set limits on our ability to expand at sea and on land, as well as economically and financially.[77]

The speech is also significant because the Hansabund had previously come under fire from the extreme right and extreme left as a result of its close links with banking and commercial interests and its apparent opposition to Tirpitz and the Anglo-German arms race.[78]

On 17 February 1915 the Verein Deutscher Eisen- und Stahlindustrieller, one of the leading organisations of German heavy industry, demanded in its war aims manifesto a peace 'which corresponds in its entirety to the immeasurable sacrifices [of the German people]', including specific calls for an 'increase in our sea power' and the 'creation of new settlement opportunities for German colonialists'. In addition, it issued the following open letter to Admiral von Tirpitz, welcoming the navy's announcement of the beginning of an economic blockade against the west coast of the British Isles:

On the eve of the intensification of our war effort against England, the author of the present war, the Verein Deutscher Eisen- und Stahlindustrieller would like to express its great satisfaction that the German fleet will henceforth seek to hit England in its most vulnerable position. England's behaviour shows that it will use every means to destroy German economic life, whose tremendous growth has for a long time aroused its envy. This commercial war [*Geschäftskrieg*], which England began in contempt of all international law, categorically demands the use of the harshest of defensive measures on Germany's part.[79]

Similar views can be found in a number of addresses delivered by industrial leaders, such as Dr Schweighoffer, secretary of the Zentralverband deutscher Industrieller, in Düsseldorf (on 9 December 1914) and Ernst Hirsch, syndic of the Essen Chamber of Commerce, in Essen (on 21 January 1915).[80] Finally, there were the public statements of the Deutschnationaler Handlungsgehilfen Verband, the right-wing, white-collar union of commercial employees, which issued a multi-volume *England und die Völker* (1915–16) through its publishing subsidiary, the Deutschnationale Verlagsanstalt. The aim here was to 'expose' Britain's historic economic exploitation of other nations and to discourage still neutral nations, such as the United States, from developing closer ties with Britain and its allies.[81]

A further step towards the systematisation of annexationist propaganda was effected by the foundation of the Kriegsausschuss der deutschen Industrie, and of its subcommittee, which was charged with discussing various aspects of the war aims question. At the subcommittee's first meeting on 7 November 1914, unanimous agreement was reached on the need to acquire Antwerp, Calais and Ostende, as well as the fortresses on France's north-eastern border. There was also a majority opinion in favour of the outright annexation of Belgium, a demand raised by Alfred Hugenberg, chairman of the Krupp's board of directors in Essen, and backed by other participants such as Geheimrat Paul Wilhelm Vogel of Chemnitz (president of the Saxon Diet and second in command of the National Liberal Party in Saxony) and Geheimrat Müller of the Dresdner Bank. Vogel also demanded the annexation of the Belgian and north French coast 'in order to have England under our gaze and the English coast under German cannons'. Similarly, Geheimrat Müller emphasised the need to extract an indemnity of at least 40 million marks from France in order to pay for increases in the German fleet after the war, as well as to meet the costs of war pensions.[82]

On 8 December 1914, the Chancellor, Bethmann Hollweg, also received two of the most prominent representatives of this Kriegsausschuss in Berlin: Landrat Max Roetger of the Zentralverband deutscher Industrieller and Syndikus Gustav Stresemann of the Bund der Industriellen. They repeated the demands already agreed upon in the meeting of 7 November and added to these extensive annexations in the east, especially in Poland, Courland and Estonia, as well as the removal of French interests from Morocco. Before the meeting broke up, the Chancellor had also 'signified his broad agreement' with these demands, and had promised 'only to conclude a peace which gives us at least 50 years of tranquillity'. A meeting with the State Secretary of the Interior Clemens Delbrück on the same day also revealed a 'substantial measure of agreement', particularly with regard to the planned creation of a customs union between Germany, Austria-Hungary, France, Belgium, Switzerland and the Scandinavian countries.[83]

By far the most significant and effective of the war aims programmes developed by German industry, however, was the so-called 'Petition of the Six Economic Associations', submitted to the Reichstag on 10 March 1915 and repeated, in a slightly altered form, to the Chancellor on 20 May 1915. In addition to the five organisations which had participated in the initial discussions – the Zentralverband deutscher Industrieller, the Bund der Industriellen, the Agrarian League, the Deutscher Bauernbund and the Reichsdeutscher Mittelstandsverband – the commercial *Hansabund* also supported the Reichstag petition, and a sixth organisation, the Christliche Deutsche Bauernvereine, added its signature to the second petition of May 1915. The latter demanded a colonial empire sufficient for all German commercial interests, an 'adequately guaranteed war indemnity' and further, as 'chief aim', territorial expansion to east and west. The total area demanded from western Europe alone amounted to some 50,000 square miles, with a population of around 11 million, and included the whole of Belgium together with the French ore-fields of Longwy-Briey, the coal fields of the *Départements du Nord* and *Pas-de-Calais* and the fortresses of Verdun, Longwy and Belfort. To satisfy agrarian interests, the petition also included a programme of demands in the east 'by annexation of at least parts of the Baltic Provinces and those territories which lie to the south of them'.[84]

The origins of the petition were to be found in the Kriegszielbewegung, a loose alliance between the representatives of German heavy industry and the Pan-German League which had evolved from discussions held between Alfred Hugenberg and Heinrich Claß in August 1914.[85] The first action of the Kriegszielbewegung was a joint meeting of various industrial, commercial and agricultural organisations, which came together on 28 September 1914 to express their unanimous confidence in the successful completion of the war. The list of speakers was impressive. It included Dr Kaempf, a Progressive and president of the Reichstag, Count von Schwerin-Löwitz, president of the Prussian House of Deputies, Max Roetger, head of the Zentralverband deutscher Industrieller, and Wolfgang Kapp, the Prussian civil servant who later became famous as co-founder of the German Fatherland Party and leader of the 1920 *Putsch* in Berlin. Members of the Agrarian League were also invited to attend.[86]

Even before this, Conrad von Wangenheim, the president of the Agrarian League, had met with a group of industrialists, including Roetger, to discuss the unemployment problems thrown up by the war. He was pleasantly surprised by what he discovered to be a broad agreement between the representatives of heavy industry and the Agrarian League as regards the key aims of the war. In particular, as he told his colleague Gustav Roesicke on 9 September 1914, both groups were committed to fighting the war against Britain to the finish.

According to Roetger's comments, [German] industry is entirely in agreement with us that a rotten peace with England would be unacceptable . . . He also fears that the government, acting according to Bethmann's theories and blinded by the current stance adopted by the Social Democrats, will make mischief in the sphere of social policy, and he keenly desires that we should all arm ourselves against such an eventuality. I told him that we are in full agreement with his views and that I am of the opinion, as I said in my recent letter, that we must make our preparations in the strictest secrecy . . . But it can only be good news if industry is intending to go along the same path as us.[87]

In October 1914, the Zentralverband deutscher Industrieller, the Agrarian League and the Conservative Party met, at the suggestion of Wangenheim, to discuss the problems of food supply and also the issues raised at Wangenheim's meeting with Roetger. In November 1914 the Pan-German League also joined in and, although the Conservatives, led by Count Westarp, objected to some of the more far-reaching aims of the Hugenberg–Claß programme, individual members, including Roesicke and Wangenheim, continued to take part in further meetings held in December 1914 and January 1915.[88] Wangenheim himself was so keen on the idea of cooperation between the different economic organisations that he was even prepared to abandon the Agrarian League's long-standing feud with the liberal-commercial Hansabund, although the initiative appears to have come from the latter's president, Jakob Riesser.[89]

Further cooperation between the various annexationist groups was also maintained through the Auskunftstelle Vereinigter Verbände, founded in early 1915 by the industrialist Oskar Poensgen, chairman of the Oberbilk steel works, which was affiliated with the firm of Thyssen.[90] Its directors, besides Poensgen himself, included von Reichenau of the Verein für das Deutschtum im Ausland and Gustav Stresemann, newly re-elected to the Reichstag as a National Liberal. Among its individual members were a number of familiar annexationists from the Kriegszielbewegung – besides Roesicke, Kapp and Hirsch they included Emil Kirdorf, founder of the Rheinisch-Westfälisches

Kohlensyndikat, Axel Ripke, editor of the ultra-annexationist journal *Der Panther*, and Gottfried Traub, a defrocked Protestant pastor and somewhat lone figure among the Progressive deputies in the Prussian House of Deputies.[91] The purpose of the Auskunftstelle was to act as a kind of clearing house to coordinate the various annexationist programmes of the Kriegszielbewegung, and during the war it also produced a number of pamphlets of its own, including some with a specifically anglophobic message.[92]

Finally, in July 1915 Dietrich Schäfer's Independent Committee for a German Peace was formed from a nucleus of academic and economic interest groups which had been responsible for the various war aims petitions of 1914–15. By the time the Committee revealed its identity in June 1916 it had already established local branches in most German cities, including Königsberg, Posen, Breslau, Stettin, Kiel, Hamburg, Magdeburg, Halle, Dresden, Leipzig, Plauen, Hanover, Münster, Bremen, Kassel, Frankfurt am Main, Würzburg, Munich, Stuttgart, Karlsruhe, Cologne, Elberfeld and Dortmund.[93] The secretary of the new organisation was Professor Walther Stahlberg, and individual members included well-known annexationists such as Count Reventlow, Wolfgang Kapp and Gustav Stresemann as well as the Agrarian leaders Roesicke and Wangenheim, Professor Max von Gruber and Reichsrat Franz Buhl (a leading figure in both the National Liberal Party and Bavarian politics).[94] Until the end of the war the Committee stood at the forefront of right-wing annexationist propaganda and was also actively involved in the campaign for unrestricted submarine warfare. An illegal petition organised by Schäfer and delivered to the Reichstag on 15 March 1916, for instance, collected over 90,000 signatures, while 268,650 copies were seized by the police in Berlin alone.[95]

Right-wing political parties and pressure groups

Among the parties represented in the Reichstag and the Prussian House of Deputies it was first and foremost the National Liberals who voiced their irreconcilable hostility towards Britain and made this the major plank in their war aims programme. This reflected both an ideological hatred of Great Britain as the alleged instigator of the war and the chief force behind the economic blockade of Germany, and a more straightforward desire to strengthen Germany's strategic and maritime position through a policy of westward expansion.[96]

Professor Hermann Paasche, for instance, who was also vice-president of the Reichstag, declared in a speech in Kreuznach in April 1915:

We are prevented from discussing war aims, but there is one thing which we must emphasise, that in the heart of every German lies the wish: We will not surrender the foreign lands which have been conquered with so much German blood! We must reach the English Channel, even if we have to start all over again and conquer the old fortresses for a second time. The German people also demand that in the east we secure ourselves against a new onslaught from the Russian hordes – this time the pen must not be allowed to sign away what the sword has achieved.[97]

Similarly, the Prussian deputy Wilhelm Beumer told a public meeting organised by the Bremen Chamber of Commerce on 3 October 1915:

We should allow ourselves to be guided not by hatred towards England, but by anger, even when it comes to peace-making. We should only make a peace which brings Germany increased sea power, new coaling stations, naval bases and new areas for settlement, a peace which is 'made in Germany'.[98]

In mid-August 1915 a split occurred in the party when a minority faction, headed by Eugen Schiffer and Friedberg, attempted to introduce a more moderate programme which precluded open attacks on the Chancellor and the Reich leadership. At the subsequent meeting of the party's Central Committee, however, the vast majority voted in favour of a resolution expressing confidence in the party leader, Ernst Bassermann, and his uncompromising stance on the war aims question.[99] In addition, the official publication of the party, the *Nationalliberale Blätter*, continued to carry frequent articles by Bassermann, Paasche, Gustav Stresemann and others in favour of German westward expansion and attacking what Bassermann had referred to contemptuously as Bethmann's 'policy of surrender'.[100]

In the Prussian House of Deputies the annexationist elements among the National Liberals were represented by, among others, Walter Bacmeister, Paul Fuhrmann and Wilhelm Hirsch. Even the more moderate Carl Röchling (of the Saar industrial family) saw the war first and foremost as an 'economic war' (*Wirtschaftskrieg*) against Britain.[101] Finally, the general war aims programme of the party was reconfirmed in a resolution adopted by the Central Committee on 21 May 1916, at the height of the controversy over unrestricted submarine warfare. The resolution leaves no doubt as to whom the National Liberals regarded as Germany's chief enemy in the war:

The Central Committee of the National Liberal Party expressly repeats its conviction, which it first stated on 15 August 1915 and which has since been confirmed by events, that only an expansion of the land and maritime borders of the German empire in east and west and overseas can provide the German people with the necessary real guarantees of their future military, political and economic security.

The Central Committee regards the attainment of this proper measure of security against England, which can be achieved not merely on the basis of treaties, but also on a real expansion of power, as especially important. It therefore views the main task of German policy as being to ensure the German war leadership the complete freedom to use any military means which will guarantee a decisive victory over this, our arch-enemy.[102]

Further to the right, the two Conservative parties also adopted an essentially annexationist and anti-English line, one which cast Britain in the role of the *Hauptfeind*. The Free Conservatives in particular worked in close collaboration with the Pan-Germans and the National Liberals. The party's leader, Baron Oktavio von Zedlitz und Neukirch, had made known his opposition to a negotiated peace settlement with Britain only a few weeks after the outbreak of the war, calling instead for a peace which would provide Germany with its rightful 'place in the sun'. He reiterated these aims in speeches before the Prussian House of Deputies and in a number of important newspaper articles.[103]

An even more outspoken attitude was adopted by the Free Conservative Adolf Grabowsky, editor of the periodical *Das Neue Deutschland*, who wrote as early as October 1914:

Today nothing is more important than that the will for world power [*Welteroberungswille*] should seize hold of the entire German people. Only then can we raise ourselves from a semi-conscious world power to a self-conscious one . . . Only then can we make any headway against England.[104]

The leaders of the larger and more important Conservative Party, Ernst von Heydebrand und der Lasa and Count Westarp, tended to be more reserved in their public pronouncements. This arrangement was determined mostly by their opposition to large-scale annexations in the east and by their more or less open support for the idea of a separate peace with Russia. An additional factor was the growing influence inside the party of Otto Hoetzsch, whose pro-Russian stance as editor of the *Kreuzzeitung* since November 1914 enjoyed the support of the majority, even if it was bitterly opposed by the minority Baltic German faction. In January 1915 the latter went on to found their own journal, *Das Deutsche Reich*, which supported the Pan-German demand for extensive territorial gains in the east at Russia's expense.[105]

In spite of these ideological divisions, the party still felt able to issue an official statement on its war aims policy in the autumn of 1915, even allowing it to appear in a full and uncensored version in the pages of the *Alldeutsche Blätter* on 9 October. The statement expressed confidence 'that the brilliant successes of our weapons will decisively defeat the massive power of the Russian enemy and provide a lasting guarantee of the security of the German people'. It also called for a 'permanent, honourable peace which lays the foundation for Germany's future', and therefore supported 'all territorial expansion which is necessary to achieve this aim'. The most important aim of the war, however, remained 'the use of all means necessary to bring about the downfall of England, which has provoked this war and will never cease to threaten and cut off our position in the world and our further expansion for all time.'[106]

A year later, in August 1916, the party's determination to conclude a victorious peace with annexations in both east and west was further underlined in a speech by Heydebrand in Frankfurt am Main. Here he called for an extension of Germany's frontier into France and for German military, political and economic domination of Belgium 'in order to hold at the heart of England the pistol it has hitherto held at ours'. Heydebrand also singled out Britain as Germany's main enemy, but spoke of Russia in neutral, almost conciliatory terms:

What we must do about Russia remains a very, very difficult question. In my view it would be unreasonable to allow its borders to remain as they were. We owe at least that much to the border areas of Germany that have suffered so much in this war. I really can't see any other type of arrangement with Russia.[107]

Among the Pan-Germans and their subsidiary and allied organisations it was above all the Army League which raised its voice in favour of annexations during the first months of the war.[108] As early as November 1914, for instance, the League and its chairman, the former ambassador von Pilgrim-Baltazzi, addressed a petition to Bethmann Hollweg demanding the 'complete and permanant subjugation of Belgium . . . in all forms' as the basis of future operations against Britain and France. In particular, the petition emphasised that:

We can and must never abandon our domination over the Belgian north coast, which we have finally recovered, because only here do we have the opportunity to bring an end to England's tyranny over the world seas and thereby to put a final stop to England's world domination, which is anyway close to collapse.[109]

In the same petition, linguistic arguments were used to urge German westward expansion as far as 'Boonen' and 'Kales' (the 'Germanic' names for Boulogne and Calais). Efforts to promote Flemish language and culture against alien French-speaking elements were also suggested as a means of winning back 'the old *Reichslande* of Flanders and Brabant, as well as the principality of Lüttich [Liège] to the Fatherland'. And a few days later the Pan-German Kurt von Strantz, president of the League in the absence of its founder General Keim (who was military governor of the Belgian province of Limburg), published an article suggesting that Germany should play the role of 'international arsonist' (*Brandstifter*) by igniting the forces of nationalist resentment in Ireland, India, Egypt and Canada against British rule.[110]

Similar demands were put forward by the much older Navy League in its list of war aims presented to the Chancellor in June 1916. These included, as might be expected, possession of the Flanders coastline and political and military domination of the rest of Belgium, as well as the maintenance of a strong German fleet and the acquisition of German naval stations around the world 'which [are] capable of protecting our maritime commerce and our colonies'. Such goals could only be achieved, the petition continued,'when our arch-enemy, the author of the world war and the driving force behind our enemies, is so badly defeated that it is no longer in a position to continue fighting. [The German Navy League] regards it as impossible, after all that has happened, to come to an any form of understanding with Great Britain other than one based on fear of our strength.'[111]

In the meantime, Heydebrand's prevaricating stance on the war aims question led to a marked increase in criticism of his leadership from within the ranks of the Conservative Party, most notably from among Pan-Germans and other extremists who envisaged large-scale annexations in the east combined with the settlement of German agricultural labourers on land conquered from Poles, Lithuanians and Russians. As early as 12 December 1914, for instance, the *Alldeutsche Blätter* found it necessary to publish an article criticising what it saw as too one-sided an emphasis on the war against Britain:

For weeks now the newspapers have been saying that Germany has only one enemy, that Germany cherishes only one hatred: England, and the logical consequence of this . . . has been the regular demand for far-reaching sympathy towards our other enemies, especially towards France . . . Three great powers have forced this war upon us, and each one of them has acted on the basis of its own free will, and they are therefore jointly and wholly responsible for the terrible sacrifices of blood which have been demanded of us . . . In the interests of our future security they must all be measured with the same rule, we must demand from each of them, as atonement for our spilt blood and as a guarantee of our future security, a level of reparations that will represent an approximate offsetting of our losses of men and materials.[112]

Similar concerns were expressed by leading figures on the radical wing of the Conservative Party, such as retired Admiral Ferdinand von Grumme-Douglas, a member of the Prussian *Herrenhaus* and former Flügeladjutant to the Kaiser who also sat on the executive committee of the Pan-German League. On 12 December 1914, the same day as the article discussed above was published, Grumme-Douglas wrote to Count Westarp:

If from now on . . . Herr von Heydebrand intends to adopt the standpoint which he took in the confidential discussion we had after the [parliamentary] sitting, then I regret to inform you that I have no sympathy with this. I fear that the

Conservative Party is heading for bad times if it continues to follow this line. The people will not understand how we can possibly represent the view that Belgium should be given up and that the acquisition of new land in the east would be injurious and unwelcome . . . I would very much regret it if Herr von Heydebrand and the party leadership continue to uphold this view, and I fear that the party from which we have most to fear, namely the National Liberals, could end up rallying a large portion of our own supporters under its banner.[113]

Five days later, on 17 December 1914, Westarp also received a letter from the Agrarian leader Gustav Roesicke which specifically warned against any moves towards a premature peace settlement in the east:

If the military situation makes this absolutely necessary, then nobody could say anything against it. But if it is not absolutely necessary, then I would see it as a matter for extraordinary regret if we failed to gain a substantial amount of land from Russia. Germany is too small, it must expand, and expand especially from an agricultural viewpoint. In my own opinion this is the first and the last opportunity we will have to achieve this, since it will not be so easy in the future to wage a war against Russia for the sake of expansion in the east. If we fail to achieve this, then the necessary expansion of Germany will, I fear, also be closed off in the future. Expansion in the west is all very well and has much to offer and tempt us, but it would also upset the balance of healthy development in Germany by strengthening the role of industry [at the expense of agriculture].[114]

In the eyes of right-wing extremists such as the Pan-German Konstantin von Gebsattel, who was also a member of the Conservative Party, the ultimate goal in the east could be summed up in the notorious phrase 'Land ohne Leute', or land emptied of its original non-German inhabitants in order to make way for the settlement of ethnic German farmers. 'Without inner-colonisation', he wrote in early 1915, 'there will be no stop to the decline in our birth-rate and eventual racial death.'[115] Similar views were expressed by the Munich-based Pan-German publisher J.F. Lehmann, a notorious racist and anti-Semite, who saw it as 'a matter of life and death for Germany to win the new lands she needs to became strong and agriculturally and industrially independent from foreign influence'.[116]

On the other hand, it is also important to emphasise that many figures on the radical wing of the Conservative Party combined a commitment to exorbitant territorial demands in the east with an equally determined antagonism towards Britain as the birthplace of liberalism and materialism and the chief instigator of the war. These included both Gebsattel and Lehmann as well as others with Pan-German leanings, such as Wolfgang Kapp, Georg Schiele, Count Reventlow, Ferdinand von Grumme-Douglas, Albrecht von Graefe and Prince Otto von Salm-Horstmar. As early as 3 December 1914, for instance, Gebsattel wrote to Westarp:

If you look at the history of England over the last 350 years, then you will see that this stubborn nation will not rest until it has overthrown first Spain, the Netherlands, France . . . and now Germany, the most powerful state in Europe today, all through a series of coalition [wars]. Only if we weaken it to the point of powerlessness, and also strengthen ourselves correspondingly, can we hope to save ourselves from this danger.[117]

In July 1915 he even confided to a friend that he did not share the Pan-German leader Heinrich Claß's obsession with the Slavic danger in the east. The Russians, he argued, were a 'mixed race of eastern Slavs' (*Mischvolk der Ostslaven*) and were therefore not to be feared as much as the racially purer British, especially 'if we acquire enough land to ensure that our agriculture begins to thrive again and our population growth continues to rise'. France too was a 'dying nation' (*sterbendes Volk*) whose military collapse was all but imminent. But England, 'with its hard-nosed policy, which knows no morality, with its ever strong Germanic strain', represented a qualitatively different kind of threat, one which had to be eliminated before Germany could hope to fulfil its mission in the east.[118]

Similar ideas were expressed by the Agrarian leader Wangenheim in an exchange of letters with his colleague Roesicke in April 1915. Roesicke was clearly concerned to moderate the extreme anti-British stand of the Bund's leading foreign affairs spokesman, Count Reventlow, lest it interfere with the more urgent task of defeating Russia and France. Wangenheim, on the other hand, took a more relaxed view of Reventlow's activities, and even managed to find a kind word or two for the Viennese Jew Ernst Lissauer, the author of the notorious *Hassgesang gegen England*:

Lissauer's Hymn of Hate is of course nothing new and is not at all disagreeable to me. I think it is good thing in these soft-hearted times that once in a while this form of hatred against our very worst enemy gets a hearing.[119]

Finally, in a memorandum for Bethmann Hollweg in May 1915, out-lining once again the Pan-German programme of war aims, Gebsattel managed to combine his fierce opposition to a separate peace with Russia with an equally hostile stance towards Britain.

The future security of the German Reich and the [German] people is without doubt dependent in the first instance on the momentum which the Reich and the people are able to achieve and maintain on the continent. But if the most important war aims are to be sought on the continent, it is also vital that we secure our independence from foreign nations with regard to the most impor-tant raw materials and our free access to commerce overseas . . . We must there-fore also continue the struggle against England with all our strength and resolve, until we have put an end to England's tyranny over the seas and pro-vided guarantees for Germany's security in the future.[120]

This passage in turn provides the strongest illustration yet of the interdependence between the two principal currents of pre-war German imperialism – the older overseas tendency, with its support for *Weltpolitik* and the naval arms race, and the more recent continental stream, which was almost invariably as hostile towards Britain as it was towards Russia.

The annexationist agitation continues

Most of the agitation in favour of expansionist war aims in the year 1915 continued to come from the coordinated efforts of various right-wing groups linked to the Pan-German League, especially from Dietrich Schäfer's Independent Committee for a German Peace. In June 1915, for instance, Schäfer himself helped to organise an annexationist 'Petition of Intellectuals' under the direction of Reinhold Seeberg, a close colleague from the University of Berlin.[121] Significantly, the framers of this petition, while welcoming the recent successes of the German army against Russia, were also anxious to assert that 'this war, in the last analysis, is a war of England against our naval and overseas prestige'. For this reason too they elaborated a series of specific demands in the west, while contenting themselves with only a vague commitment to territorial adjustments in the east. The final point, concerning the question of war damages, was written from the same standpoint:

If we could get into the position of imposing an indemnity upon England . . . no sum would be too large . . . But it will probably be primarily, if not exclusively, France who will be in line for a financial indemnity. We must not hesitate, out of false mercy, to burden her most heavily.[122]

By the time the petition was presented to the Chancellor in July 1915, it had gained the support of 1,347 people, including 352 academics, 252 artists, writers and journalists, and 158 clergymen and teachers. By contrast, a counter-petition organised by the military historian Hans Delbrück and the former Colonial Secretary, Bernhard Dernburg, managed to muster only 141 signatures, most of them university professors with links to the left-liberal parties.[123]

In the meantime, the fierce domestic controversy over war aims was beginning to have a major impact on Germany's external position and helped to destroy any chances of a negotiated peace settlement with the Entente powers. Demands for large-scale annexations on Germany's western borders, for instance, strengthened opposition to German imperialism not only in those countries immediately threatened (i.e. Belgium, France and Britain), but also beyond, in neutral countries such as the United States. In addition, the daily efforts of Pan-German propagandists such as Count Reventlow to present the war as an

Anglo-German struggle for world supremacy caused a considerable amount of alarm among the rulers of Austria-Hungary, who began to ask themselves whether the continuation of such a struggle was really in the best interests of the Dual Monarchy.[124]

In spite of these growing difficulties, however, the military authorities showed little inclination to clamp down on extreme nationalist publications, even those that quite blatantly contravened the official censorship guidelines. Still less were they prepared to back the government in its efforts to uphold the spirit of the *Burgfriede* and prevent a major split between pro- and anti-war factions on the left. In November 1914, for instance, as we have already seen, both Tirpitz and Falkenhayn pushed for a separate peace with Russia, in spite of the implications such a move would have for Germany's alliance with Austria-Hungary and for the *Burgfriede* at home.[125] They also went to some lengths to ensure that their opposton to Bethmann Hollweg's war leadership was made known to prominent figures on the German right. As early as January 1915, for instance, Otto Hoetzsch of the *Kreuzzeitung* had advised the Conservative Party leader in the Reichstag, Count Westarp, that there was now only 'a small group of people' who remained antagonistic towards his idea of a post-war alliance with Russia against England, including, most notably, the Chancellor himself.

Otherwise I have found both within the military and among the politicians [and] in the upper echelons of the government bureaucracy a general and principled agreement with our position, especially at the headquarters of Field Marshal von Hindenburg . . . I do not need to emphasise, of course, that the orientation towards the east, which we represent, corresponds completely with the policies pursued by Bismarck as well as with the conservative tradition [in Prussia].[126]

Within the Kaiser's own entourage too there were a number of influential Conservative figures, such as General Gustav von Kessel, the Commander-in-Chief in the Marches, and General Adjutant Alfred von Löwenfeld, who disliked Bethmann's style of leadership and plotted on Admiral Tirpitz's behalf to remove him from office.[127] Other members of this anti-Bethmann court faction included the Crown Prince Wilhelm and his special adviser, Jaspar Freiherr von Maltzahn, the Empress Augusta Viktoria and her lady-in-waiting, Countess Rantzau, and the influential Minister of the Royal Household, Count August zu Eulenburg.[128] Indeed, until he was finally replaced in July 1917, Bethmann's position depended increasingly on the personal support which the Kaiser gave to 'his' Chancellor, as well as the absence of any obvious successor.[129]

The alliance of those opposed to Bethmann Hollweg was very much a marriage of convenience. It was forged, first and foremost, as a result of grave doubts concerning the Chancellor's commitment to an annexationist peace, doubts which had first begun to emerge in the spring and summer of 1915. An equally important factor, as we shall see in the following chapter, was a common hatred of Great Britain and a desire to see the war prosecuted more vigorously against this enemy in particular. In this respect the Kaiser's decision to accept Tirpitz's resignation in March 1916 was the catalyst for a more determined and aggressive Pan-German campaign against Bethmann in the months that followed.

4 'U-boat Demagogy' and the crisis of Bethmann Hollweg's chancellorship

By the beginning of 1916 a swift victory appeared less and less attainable for either side in the war. The German Schlieffen plan had failed to deliver the expected knock-out blow against France and had ended in military stalemate on the western front with no immediate prospect of a solution. The Anglo-French Dardanelles expedition in 1915 had also met with defeat and humiliation, paving the way for the entry of Bulgaria into the war and the final defeat of Serbia at the end of that year. Meanwhile at Verdun, and later on the Somme, vast numbers of troops perished on both sides, for no significant territorial gain. Even in the east, where conditions generally favoured greater mobility of troops, the Central Powers failed to secure a decisive advantage over Russia until after the overthrow of the Tsar in 1917.

At sea, the outlook seemed as bleak and as pointless as it was on the land, although here the German admirals and their British counterparts were far more reluctant to engage in costly all-out assaults against one another because they had too much to lose. Despite the remarkable Battle of Jutland (31 May 1916), both sides preferred to concentrate on economic and commercial warfare rather than engaging in great naval clashes of a traditional kind.[1] The British, using surface ships, were able to establish a 'distant blockade' of German ports and seriously restrict its trade via neutral countries. The Germans responded in February 1915 by establishing an exclusion zone around Britain and Ireland and threatening to sink any ships which entered these waters. The key problem was that, the more rigorously these blockade measures were enforced, the more likely it became that important neutral powers, such as the United States, would be drawn into the conflict on the opposing side.[2]

In Germany itself, unrestricted submarine warfare – that is, the sinking of unarmed merchant vessels without prior warning or search – was supported by most naval leaders and by roughly the same groups who favoured large-scale annexations on the continent. The most important converts at the beginning of 1916 were Falkenhayn and Adolf Wild von Hohenborn, the Prussian Minister of War, both of whom believed that Germany was in a position to survive a break with America, if it should come to that.[3] Falkenhayn in particular was convinced that time was not on Germany's side and that its allies would not be able to hold out much longer than the autumn of 1916. Later he argued that the success of the Verdun offensive depended on the launching of a ruthless submarine campaign against the British Isles and even suggested to the Kaiser that he would have to call a halt to operations on the western front if the government gave way to American pressure.[4]

Although both Henning von Holtzendorff, the new Chief of the Admiralty Staff, and Capelle, Tirpitz's successor at the Reich Naval Office after March 1916, disapproved of such tactics, they too were beginning to succumb to the technical arguments in favour of unrestricted submarine warfare.[5] In January 1916, for instance, Holtzendorff claimed in an audience with the Kaiser at Schloß Bellevue that submarines would knock Britain out of the war in six to seven months. Submarine warfare against English shipping alone, he argued a few days later, would be futile on account of the British abuse of neutral flags.[6] Holtzendorff's views were shared by Admiral von Müller, the chief of the Kaiser's naval cabinet, who nonetheless believed that the final decision should be taken only 'when the High Command and the political situation call for it',[7] and, to take a more extreme example, by Tirpitz himself, who told Matthias Erzberger on 10 January that the submarine could bring Britain 'to its knees' within a mere six weeks![8]

By contrast, Bethmann Hollweg, and with him a number of important figures such as Jagow, Helfferich and Erzberger, believed (correctly) that the number of submarines available was too limited to justify the admirals' optimism.[9] They also feared that any sudden move in the direction of unrestricted submarine warfare would bring not only the United States but also the smaller European neutrals – Holland, Denmark, possibly even Spain – into the war, with disastrous consequences for the Central Powers. They were confirmed in this view by the American ultimatum of 20 April and by the numerous reports sent to Berlin by the German ambassador in Washington, Count Bernstorff.[10]

It is worth mentioning, however, that the opposition of men such as Erzberger and Helfferich to unrestricted submarine warfare – in contrast to that of the SPD and possibly even the Kaiser – was never based upon humanitarian grounds or considerations of international law. Rather, it was based on a more sober estimate of the likely failure of the submarine to bring about decisive results.[11] Besides which, the Kaiser himself seems to have been won over by the 'logic' of Falkenhayn's arguments, since he too gradually relinquished his opposition to ruthless submarine warfare. On 30 April 1916, for instance, he said in the presence of the Chancellor and Admirals Holtzendorff, Capelle and von Müller: 'We are now faced with a choice: Verdun or the U-boat war.'[12]

In the meantime, the debate on submarine warfare was taking place against the background of increasing discontent at home, based at least in part on the social misery caused by the Allied economic blockade. On 24 March 1916 a split occurred on the left when eighteen anti-war deputies, including Haase, Bernstein and Kautsky, voted against the government's new emergency budget and were promptly expelled from the SPD Reichstag *Fraktion*, eventually reconstituting themselves as the Sozialdemokratische Arbeitsgemeinschaft (Socialist Working Group or SAG) within the framework of the existing party.[13] Simultaneously, the ultra right-wing agitation against Bethmann Hollweg had been stepped up, with demands made in the Prussian House of Deputies that the government grant a free debate on the war aims question and that the Chancellor drop his opposition to unrestricted submarine warfare.[14] In the following months the Conservatives, National Liberals and their allies in the Pan-German League did not hesitate to denounce Bethmann and the left-liberal (or 'Jewish') press for their alleged anglophilia and lack of patriotism, and even received some support from official sources.[15] Indeed, as early as December 1914 the fanatical anti-Semite Franz von Bodelschwingh had already identified what he saw as the combined Jewish and English menace to Germany in a letter sent to the (Jewish-owned) Ullstein press and to General von Kessel, the Commander-in-Chief in the Marches.

It is important to realise that we also have Englishmen at home, that is to say people who give too much priority to [overseas] commerce, so much so that it is by no means certain that in the hour of danger they will have it in them to place national interest above these concerns. Over-valuation of commerce, however much its protection might also be in the national interest . . . carries with it the danger of losing sight of long-term objectives for the sake of avoiding short-term losses. It would be a good thing if this problem was given all due consideration in the coming difficult decisions.[16]

In what follows, we will take a closer look at the continuous nationalist and anti-Semitic campaign being waged by Bodelschwingh, Reventlow and other right-wing opponents of Bethmann's war leadership, a campaign which began in earnest in the summer of 1915 and entered a new and more violent phase following the Kaiser's dismissal of Tirpitz in March 1916. Further sections will go on to examine the response of 'moderate' politicians and of the government itself in the face of mounting pressure to abandon their opposition to unrestricted submarine warfare.

The campaign against Bethmann Hollweg

There had been a number of attacks against Bethmann Hollweg ever since his moderate stand on war aims and the submarine question was suspected back in the summer of 1915;[17] but in the first months of 1916 these attacks increased both in number and in intensity. The South German liberal politician Conrad Haußmann, for instance, recorded in a letter to an unknown recipient on 14 January 1916:

The Conservatives are restless. Yesterday, as I arrived, Westarp declared in the Budget Committee [of the Reichstag] in his own words: 'The statement made by my party colleague Oertel, that we do not want to topple the Reich Chancellor during the war, should not be taken to mean that we have confidence in the Chancellor, as the Under Secretary Zimmermann chose to interpret it. It was merely intended to say: we express neither mistrust nor confidence [in him]. And it is on this basis that we shall make our decisions.' This is blatant and shameless.[18]

More ominous still was the Conservative and right-wing reaction to the dismissal of Admiral von Tirpitz in March 1916, which provided the catalyst for an even more aggressive campaign against the Chancellor in the months that followed. Already on 22 March, for instance, one prominent member of the Agrarian League in Bavaria wrote to a colleague, the Conservative Reichstag deputy Luitpold Weilnböck:

Juda, you have triumphed! [*Juda, du hast gesiegt!*] – that is what we are saying in response to the dismissal of Secretary of State Tirpitz. A cry of outrage is passing through our German people, and the Kaiser should take heed for once of the mood that reaches into the smallest Jura villages, since he will find there the same, if not an even greater, bitterness than at the time when Bismarck was booted out. If the war can be shortened through the [introduction of] unrestricted submarine warfare, and the government prevents this from happening, and if as a result just one more of our men in field-grey are sacrificed, then the man responsible, may he be whoever he claims himself to be, deserves to be shot. A bravo to the Conservative Party for its manly resolution [in this matter]. The important thing now is not to slacken in our efforts, since the entire German people, with the exception of Ballin and his chums, stand behind the party. By this means we shall become a *Volkspartei*, a party of the people. What we need now is a motion to abolish censorship and allow free speech with regard to war aims. This will bring many advantages to the party.[19]

In Berlin, too, Police President von Jagow noted that the mood among the middle and upper classes was becoming ever more hostile towards the government, and that the main focus of their newly aroused hatred was the Chancellor and also the Hamburg shipping magnate Albert Ballin, the latter being widely perceived as the 'evil spirit' behind the government's timid submarine policy. In a highly disturbing report of 18 March Jagow wrote:

The apparent U-turn on the decision to intensify submarine warfare has produced an extremely ugly mood, first and foremost among the educated classes who have grown in confidence since the dismissal of Grand Admiral von Tirpitz and do not shy away from voicing the most vigorous criticism of the Reich leadership. Such circles are of the view that England remains our most dangerous enemy and that it can only be defeated through the ruthless deployment of all the means of war at our disposal, especially the U-boats and the Zeppelins. In moving towards this final goal all consideration of America's likely response and of the potential loss of German commercial shipping must automatically recede into the background. This opinion has found widespread approval, even among the workers . . . Indeed, if the right of public protest were granted today then one would be faced almost immediately with a spontaneous procession of 100,000 patriotic demonstrators towards the Reich Chancellor's palace. If freedom of the press were granted, then only a small number of wholly left-leaning newspapers would stand up for the government.[20]

Jagow's report is also significant in that it reveals quite clearly that the original threat to internal unity and the spirit of the *Burgfriede* came not from the revolutionary left, but from the nationalist and anglophobe right. This was something that many government officials recognised at the time, even if it was conveniently forgotten by most after the war, when the myth arose that the German military had been 'stabbed in the back' by left-wing politicians at home. In the meantime, Jagow concluded his report by urging the government to do more to publicise the benefits of its own more moderate line on the submarine question.

If a means can be found to convince public opinion in the Reich capital of the correctness of the measures currently being undertaken, then I would regard this as the most pressing task of our domestic policy.[21]

The Conservatives eventually agreed to a compromise resolution on the submarine question in a closed session of the Reichstag Budget Committee at the end of March, which was supported by all parties except the anti-war minority within the SPD. However, they left no doubt of their determination to continue the struggle for unrestricted submarine warfare in conjunction with their National Liberal and Pan-German allies. On 29 April, for instance, the Conservative leader, Heydebrand, published an article in the *Kreuzzeitung* calling for a show of strength towards the American government in the 'Sussex' dispute and suggesting that the American note of 20 April had been 'presumptuous'. He also hinted that the Americans had been secretly supporting the Allies, particularly Britain, ever since the outbreak of the war in 1914. The article was banned following the intervention of the German Foreign Office, leading to a clash between the government (represented by Jagow) and the Conservatives (represented by Oertel), which took place in the full glare of publicity during a debate on press censorship in the Reichstag on 25 and 30 May.[22]

Similarly, on 23 April 1916 a renewed attempt was made by the supporters of unrestricted submarine warfare to penetrate the isolation in which the Kaiser was allegedly being kept by the Chancellor and his supporters. This took the form of a letter written by Prince Otto Salm on behalf of the Navy League to Rudolf von Valentini, the head of the Kaiser's civil cabinet, a copy of which eventually came into the hands of Matthias Erzberger. The letter contained, among other things, the following passage: 'If the United States declares war on us, so much the better: since we will gain the freedom of action which unfortunately we have been hitherto denying ourselves.' It went on to claim that the introduction of unrestricted submarine warfare would be greeted by a 'shout of joy' among the German people. But the Kaiser's reply was negative and highly incensed at this 'unsubstantiated interference' in the business of the imperial government.[23]

The role played by Count Zeppelin in fomenting opposition against the Chancellor is less clear, although knowledge of the content of his supposedly confidential letters to Bethmann Hollweg was widespread within annexationist circles.[24] Germany's monopoly of the Zeppelin and its first employment of it against the east coast of England in January 1915 awoke in the German press – as did the submarine – expectations which were often widely exaggerated.[25] In January 1916 Zeppelin told Conrad Haußmann in confidence that he was hoping to organise 'a massive combined air and submarine assault' against England, and that he was also trying to push the Kaiser and Bethmann Hollweg in this direction.[26] On 21 March 1916 he was invited to give a talk on aerial warfare in the Prussian House of Deputies, and seized the opportunity to put forward his own views on the subject in opposition to those of the Kaiser and the OHL.[27] Later that month he told Haußmann, whom he met by accident on a train, 'I am no blind worshipper of Tirpitz and I recognise his weaknesses, but at least he has strength and stamina'. He also insisted that his plans for a combined sea and air assault on England would have been ready by the early summer if only the government had been more enthusiastic, and went on to denounce the 'defeatists' in the government and the Reich Chancellor's office, among whom he included 'Lichnowsky and Ballin and whatever all their names are'.[28]

Apart from this evidence of an organised and coordinated campaign against Bethmann Hollweg, there were also several individual attacks on the Chancellor between the end of 1915 and the middle of 1916, some of which caused a considerable stir within government circles. Previous historians usually emphasise three books in particular: Hans von Liebig's *Die Politik von Bethmann Hollweg*, published in two parts at the end of 1915 and the beginning of 1916, Wolfgang Kapp's *Die nationalen Kreise und der Reichskanzler*, which appeared in May 1916, and finally a pamphlet written by 'Junius Alter' (i.e. Franz Sontag, editor of the *Alldeutsche Blätter*), which first appeared under the title *Das Deutsche Reich auf dem Wege zur geschichtlichen Episode* in June 1916, and was later re-issued as an anonymous piece by 'three Germans', with the slightly altered title *Deutsche Reichspolitik seit 14. Juli 1909*. Significantly, all three books aimed their attacks at Bethmann's pre-war and domestic policy, and contained relatively little with regard to specific war aims. On the other hand, all three emphasised Bethmann's failure to pursue unrestricted submarine warfare and his subsequent 'renunciation of victory over England' (Kapp) as his cardinal sins. Liebig in particular referred to those among the Chancellor's advisers who before 1914 had dreamt of a 'German world policy without war' and who even after 1914 appeared to reject any territorial claims on the continent in favour of an understanding with England to rebuild the lost German empire in Africa. Such a policy, he argued, would benefit only those whose aim was the destruction of the German agriculture, the renunciation of the German fleet and the surrender of the German nation as the 'industrial wage slave of the world', the only form in which it was acceptable to the English and their American allies.[29]

Liebig's book was indeed the most disturbing of the three, particularly as it also illustrated the emphasis which right-wing and Pan-German critics of the Chancellor placed on the Jewish question as the key issue of the war. According to the Conservative leader Count Westarp, for instance, Liebig 'tended to find in everything a connection between Bethmann Hollweg and his dependence on the Jews'.[30] In the second part of his book *Die Politik Bethmann Hollwegs*, Liebig referred quite openly to Bethmann as the 'Chancellor of German Jewry' and went on to depict the struggle for German war aims as nothing less than 'a struggle between the goals of German Jewry and those of the truly germanic German':

The true German [*der Germane*] is fighting for land, land suited to his own way of living; since new land, fertile and rich land, awakens all the fresh productive forces within him . . . [and] provides him with new tasks which can only be met by a true nobleman, regardless of whether he is a peasant or a prince, a hero of technology or a businessman of the old type . . . The Jew [on the other hand] seeks new opportunities for trade and nothing else . . . What suited him best were the narrowly defined borders of the old Reich, where his influence was greatest. For this reason, together with his friends abroad, he is hiding behind notions of a world culture and a world economy in order to bring about a peace which changes as little of the old conditions as possible.[31]

Liebig's book was actually the brainchild of the anti-Semitic Munich publisher J.F. Lehmann, prominent in annexationist and Pan-German circles, whose plan was further developed in correspondence with Heinrich Claß, Freiherr von Gebsattel and others.[32] Liebig, a Professor of Chemistry at the University of Gießen, was then commissioned to write the book and Lehmann published it at his own expense. Through an elaborate system of deception, Lehmann managed to get 3,000 copies distributed to leading public figures, including every member of the Kaiser's entourage, before the censor could intervene. Using similar means, he also succeeded in publishing the 'Junius Alter' pamphlet in June 1916 and an annexationist pamphlet of his own, *Deutschlands Zukunft bei einem guten und einem schlechten Frieden*, which he had distributed to every unit in the army in March 1917.[33]

Privately, Lehmann was even more hostile to Bethmann. 'For our Chancellor, too, the hour of reckoning will come,' he wrote in a letter to Liebig in March 1916. 'We should leave the final judgement to God, although I would not criticise anyone who shot a man who was destroying his people.'[34] And in a letter to the Bavarian Minister of War on 25 August 1916 he described Bethmann as 'the foremost danger to Germany's survival'.[35] A month earlier he had already announced plans for the creation of a new publication, the monthly journal *Deutschlands Erneuerung*, which preached an extreme form of *völkisch* nationalism to the educated classes and included on its editorial board such personalities as Houston Stewart Chamberlain, Heinrich Claß, Wolfgang Kapp and Professor Max von Gruber of the University of Munich.[36]

Another figure involved in agitation against Bethmann, who is perhaps less well-known to historians, although certainly known to the police in his home town of Leipzig in Saxony, was one Dr Heinrich Pudor, described in one police report, written in July 1917, as a 'dyed-in-the-wool anti-Semite who has repeatedly taken up the time of the censorship authorities and the courts since the outbreak of the war'.[37] Pudor's brochures and his journal, *Der eiserne Ring*, were produced under the heading 'Deutscher Volksrat' – an organisation which, as the Leipzig police discovered, did not actually exist – and were frequently adorned with the swastika emblem.[38]

On 3 July 1916 Pudor sent a sixty-eight-page petition to the state prosecutor of Berlin (Erster Staatsanwalt bei dem Kgl. Landgericht) in an attempt to bring about a legal indictment of the Chancellor on the charge of 'betraying state and country' [*Staats- und Landesverrat*]. According to the petition, he also intended to call several prominent figures as witnesses, including: Falkenhayn, Tirpitz, Grand Admiral von Koester, General von Keim (Governor-General of Belgium), Hans von Liebig, Count Reventlow, Dietrich Schäfer, Freiherr von Gebsattel, Wolfgang Kapp, Heinrich Claß, Heydebrand, Count Westarp, Adolf Bartels and Generals von Kluck and von Bülow.

The charge sheet itself included accusations that Bethmann had 'aided and abetted our main enemy England' and shown 'undue clemency towards Belgium and France', and further that he had 'deliberately humiliated the Fatherland in its relations with America, to the obvious advantage of our main enemy England'.[39] Once again, however, the main focus was on the Chancellor's domestic policies, and in particular the alleged preferential treatment given to Jewish war profiteers and to the members of the 'judaised' War Food Office and its subsidiary organisations such as the Central Marketing Board, which had led, in Pudor's words, to an 'internationalisation of the internal food market'. Under points 8–11, he also wrote:

If we have already seen from the above how the Reich Chancellor aids and abets our mortal enemy England and has allowed it to import the foodstuffs necessary for its survival, then we must also emphasise once again that he has also shown favouritism towards the enemy in regard to the organisation of the distribution of foodstuffs, this time towards the internal enemy, the anti-*Volk* and anti-state elements, the Jews and the Social Democrats ... The Reich Chancellor ... has admitted in his own words, if only indirectly, that he is pursuing an unnational, anti-national, internationalist policy, as can be seen in his repeated assurances that in the future the conflicts between the national and anti-national parties will fade away ... The *Kreuzzeitung* was correct when it wrote on the 7.VI.[19]16 that he [Bethmann Hollweg] is undermining the very foundations of our state and social order – which is something we would naturally expect from a traitor to the state and nation, but not from a Reich Chancellor.[40]

In reality, there was nothing in Bethmann's statements or actions to justify any of Pudor's accusations. As we shall see later, his Reichstag speeches of 1915 and 1916 had been among the most far-reaching of any public statements about war aims and had been welcomed as such by most annexationists. The growing opposition to Bethmann Hollweg in the spring and summer of 1916 can therefore be explained only if we first understand how closely related the agitation for submarine warfare was to the question of Germany's domestic political future. Above all, it was related to the fear that a weak peace would hasten the rise of political democracy and parliamentarism in Germany and bring about the destruction of the Prusso-German state. In some cases this internal dimension of the struggle against the west even gained priority over external war aims, although there were, of course, just as many annexationist articles, pamphlets and books produced in 1916 as there were in 1914 and 1915. The well-known anti-Semitic agitator Theodor Fritsch, for instance, wrote in a petition to the Interior Ministries of Bavaria and Saxony on 22 August 1916:

For the past twenty years the government of the German Reich has lacked any kind of higher national or cultural goals. We reject the goal of an economic conquest of the world through trade and industry. That is a goal for traders and shopkeepers, but not one for an honest, heroic people. We must recognise that such a goal can only be achieved through the moral and racial decay of our people. We do not wish to see Germany's racial strength and racial health being squandered in the pursuit of all manner of plundering of the world's resources, so that profits can be piled up high in the hands of the few, whilst a nation of proletarians slowly dies of consumption. We know that as a result of such a development a spirit of wretched Mammonism will rise to the fore which will wipe out the freedom and the integrity of all nations for all time. Witness the example of Rome.[41]

Such views, incidentally, are a further indication of the widespread influence of books such as Werner Sombart's *Händler und Helden* in anti-Semitic circles.

In the meantime, one of the immediate results of these attacks on the government of the Reich was a spirited response from Bethmann Hollweg himself. In his Reichstag speech of 5 June 1916, for instance, he singled out Wolfgang Kapp for particular criticism (Kapp was shortly thereafter to be removed from his civil service post as the leading government official in East Prussia) and went on to declare:

Meine Herren, I know that no party in this House approves of agitation which uses falsehoods or invective. But unfortunately the pirates of public opinion frequently abuse the flag of nationalist parties . . . It is bitter to have to fight the lies of our enemies. Slander and defamation at home are just as shameful.[42]

The mainstream liberal press was also almost unanimously behind the Chancellor, as, for the time being, was the Kaiser himself.[43] Other observers were privately very concerned at the growth of extreme nationalism and the violent attacks directed against the person of the Chancellor. On 4 June 1916, for instance, Theodor Wolff recorded that August Stein (editor of the liberal *Frankfurter Zeitung*) had become 'very upset' during a conversation about Kapp and 'Junius Alter', and had gone on to admit that he feared 'a frightful period of military dictatorship after the war'.[44]

Similarly, the revisionist Social Democrat Eduard David, who was one of Bethmann's most loyal supporters on the left, noted in his diary on 15 August 1916 that the period of the *Burgfriede* was now well and truly over:

Anger at the blind agitation of the Conservative and National Liberal annexationists; Heydebrand, Westarp, Fuhrmann, Gebsattel; the naive belief in the supremacy of violence; and at the same time the miserable failure of progressive demands. The [forces of] reaction believe in all seriousness that their time has come. And the Chancellor and the Kaiser do not dare to take up the struggle against them.[45]

The weakness of the moderate opposition to submarine warfare

Ranged against the annexationists and their campaign in favour of unrestricted submarine warfare were a number of organisations and individuals who were generally attacked because of their moderate attitude towards the war aims question and the question of peace negotiations. By 'moderate' I do not mean the very small minority of middle-class anti-war campaigners in Germany whose protests had little effect on either public opinion or government policy.[46] Rather, I am referring to certain more prominent groups and individuals who generally supported the war effort against England but who, for one reason or another, came to oppose the ultra-annexationists and their extremist propaganda. The weakness of their middle-of-the-road position and their lack of effective organisation in turn were a major factor in the eventual triumph of the submarine campaign in 1916–17. They were also another nail in the coffin for Bethmann Hollweg personally in his struggle against his right-wing critics.

The main aim of the 'moderates' seems to have been the rapid restoration of Germany's cultural, financial and commercial ties with the west and the formation of a west European 'cultural bloc' against Russia.[47] In particular they hoped for an agreement with Britain that would provide Germany with extra colonies in Africa and a more active share in world trade as alternative war aims.[48] In return, Germany would agree to surrender Belgium and otherwise refrain from upsetting the balance of power on the continent. This would allow an early end to the war without the need for unrestricted submarine warfare and without permanantly alienating Germany from its trading partners in the west. It would also allow the government room to continue with its domestic programme of integrating the Social Democrats into the 'national community', providing the basis for a healthier and more balanced post-war political system.

Even so, as we shall see later, many so-called 'moderates' were by no means prepared to abandon all of Germany's territorial gains in Europe for the sake of peace. In private, at least, they developed remarkably similar war aims to the annexationists, as can be seen most famously in Bethmann's own secret memorandum on the subject, written in September 1914 and never substantially modified. Among the Chancellor's own advisers and supporters, for instance, there was almost unanimous agreement on the desirability of territorial gains against Russia. There was also a widespread demand for the annexation of Briey-Longwy and the French iron-ore mines, suggesting a strong continuity with pre-war German imperialism.[49] The only region over which there was substantial disagreement, at least on the surface, was Belgium. But even here most 'moderates' agreed that Germany should maintain some control, direct or indirect, over Belgium's political and economic life. As the *Frankfurter Zeitung*, one of the leading 'moderate' papers, wrote on 28 May 1915:

The question is not annexations or no annexations. The question is, how can Germany best secure the fulfilment of her world tasks? If the annexation of foreign districts is necessary in order to secure our military position or to get closer to our aim, we favour it.[50]

A far greater gulf, of course, separated papers such as the *Frankfurter Zeitung* from the pan-Germans and their industrial and Agrarian allies, whose support for annexations in the west was not merely based on patriotic or nationalistic grounds, but also intimately linked to their reactionary domestic policy. Their programme of internal reform, which was largely directed against the SPD, followed the guidelines set down in Heinrich Claß's pseudonymously published work *Wenn ich der Kaiser wär'* (1912). It included the following main points: outright rejection of the government's proposals to modernise the outdated Prussian three-class franchise; a commitment to the preservation of existing monarchical structures and institutions in all German states; reversal of Jewish emancipation and the right of Jews to work for German newspapers; and, finally, uncompromising support for the continued exclusion of Social Democracy from the reins of power.[51] Not surprisingly, these self-same reactionary interests had long regarded Britain as a kind of modern-day anti-Christ, or more specifically as the symbol and embodiment of parliamentary democracy, the political system that stood at greatest odds with the type of authoritarian government they wished to introduce into Germany. This also explains their persistent calls for unrestricted submarine warfare as the only way of bringing England to its knees.

It was not until the summer of 1915, however, that an organised opposition to Pan-German expansionism began to appear, consisting largely of former and acting German diplomats as well as some 'moderate' intellectuals such as Hans Delbrück and the editors of the two great left-liberal newspapers in Germany, August Stein of the *Frankfurter Zeitung* and Theodor Wolff of the *Berliner Tageblatt*. Stein in particular had strong connections with the Wilhelmstrasse through his attendance at daily strategy meetings held in the rooms of the Foreign Office press chief, Otto Hammann.[52] Similarly, Wolff was in touch with a number of retired German ambassadors, including Lichnowsky, Hatzfeldt, Monts and Hans von Flotow. He also managed to conduct several private interviews with Chancellor Bethmann Hollweg, the Foreign Secretary Gottlieb von Jagow and ex-Chancellor Bernhard von Bülow during the course of 1915.[53]

Count Monts, for instance, the former German ambassador to Rome and a regular contributor to the *Berliner Tageblatt*, believed very strongly that Germany would sooner or later have to come to terms with Britain, particular since both powers had more to fear from the Russian 'colossus' than they did from each other.[54] In a letter to Wolff on 30 April 1915 he reiterated this support for peace negotiations with Britain, arguing for the surrender of Belgium in exchange for both the French and Belgian Congo. He was also privately extremely critical of the role played by Admiral von Tirpitz in promoting annexationist propaganda and popular hatred of Britain, and sceptical about the chances of a decisive military or naval breakthrough in the West:

Tirpitz is now trying to cover up his wretched failure as an organiser and politician through his anti-English agitation. He is pursuing a purely personal agenda, but even if he can momentarily mask the bankruptcy [of his policies] through his campaign of hatred and lies, the truth will nonetheless eventually come to light. In the same way those of us who are calling for peace will, perhaps in the very near future, receive due recognition. The light is shining at the end of the tunnel. But we should not slacken in our efforts. With regard to Tirpitz I fear the same thing as in regard to our entire panic-stricken leadership in the west. He wants to send his ships out into battle for the last voyage, hoping for a magnificent fight to the finish, ad majorem suam gloriam.[55]

Even so, Monts himself hoped to maintain some limited war aims on the continent. In the same letter to Wolff, he suggested that Britain might be persuaded to accept German annexation of the Belgian border town of Liège. Other demands might include the French railways in Turkish Anatolia, a war indemnity, and the iron fields of Briey in exchange for Thann. At the very least, Monts believed, Germany would need to annex Liège and Luxembourg in order to guarantee the future security of the Rhineland industrial area.[56]

Support for the idea of a negotiated peace with Britain came from other sources too, such as the Social Democrat Wolfgang Heine and the Progressive politician Ludwig Haas, both of whom wrote for the *Berliner Tageblatt*, and Prince Hatzfeldt, who agreed to speak out against the annexation of Belgium in a conversation with Wolff at the end of March 1915.[57] Similarly, Freiherr Ferdinand von Stumm-Halberg, the former German ambassador in Madrid, called for an immediate peace without annexations and Flotow likewise told Wolff that he regarded an approach to Britain as the only sensible policy, since in his view, if Germany refused to give up Belgium, the war could go on for several years.[58] Finally, Professor Eberstadt, an economist at Berlin University, argued against the inclusion of Belgium in the German Reich on the grounds that this would further increase the number of Catholics living in Germany and thus threaten the Protestant character of the Prusso-German state.[59]

On 7 July 1915 a group of fifty 'moderates' held a meeting in Berlin under the chairmanship of Prince Hatzfeldt to discuss the Belgian problem and to formulate a response to the annexationist Petition of Intellectuals. The petition had been organised by Reinhold Seeberg,

Dietrich Schäfer and several other Berlin professors and presented to the Chancellor at the beginning of July. After an impressive speech by Hans Delbrück, a smaller committee, consisting of Hatzfeldt, Delbrück, Stein, Wolff, Professor Wilhelm Kahl and former Colonial Secretary Bernhard Dernburg was formed to frame a statement expressing the views of the meeting. Two days later the newly formed committee met at Delbrück's house and approved a declaration largely drafted by Wolff, with additional contributions by Delbrück and Dernburg.[60] This counter-petition, which became known as the Delbrück–Dernburg petition, described the various annexationist proclamations of the previous months as 'political errors with grave consequences'. It also opposed the 'incorporation or annexation of nations that were politically independent or that were accustomed to political independence' especially if this meant 'giving up or altering the leading principles of the foundation of the Reich and destroying the character of the national state'. Finally, the framers of the petition insisted that 'the areas which we intend to evacuate as the conditions for any peace settlement should not become a bulwark for our enemies'.[61]

This declaration, like the Seeberg address, was sent to many public figures but had far fewer signatories (141 compared with Seeberg's 1,347).[62] Aside from the names mentioned above, the largest group of signatories consisted of university professors, such as Gerhard Anschütz, Lujo Brentano, Albert Einstein, Gustav von Schmoller, Ernst Troeltsch and Max Weber, as well as former ambassadors Monts (Italy), von Stumm (Spain) and Wolf-Metternich (England). In addition, most pacifist groups which had made separate declarations during the first year of the war now joined up in favour of Wolff's anti-annexationist petition, including Freiherr von Tepper-Laski of the Bund Neues Vaterland and Professors Quidde and Schücking of the Deutsche Friedensgesellschaft.[63]

The impact of the petition was severely weakened, however, by the refusal of some 'moderates', most notably the Hamburg shipping magnate Albert Ballin, to sign it. Ballin gave as his main reason the omission of colonial aims (specifically the Belgian Congo) and the necessity of a German lease over the Belgian port of Zeebrugge, which he believed the British would eventually accede to:

I take the standpoint, as you know, that we must gain access to the sea if we do not want to live through a repeat version of this terrible war in the near future. We must try and construct a peace which allies us with England and reserves the role of world policeman to England and ourselves. If we are able to reach such an understanding with England, then England will have no reason to object to a [German] lease on the port of Zeebrugge, which anyway is nothing but a cancerous growth for Belgium. After the first important events in this war I did, to be sure, expand my horizons towards Boulogne-sur-mer, which in every respect would of course be better for us. But unfortunately I have had to cut back my demands to a great extent.[64]

Such views were also entirely consistent with a speech made by Ballin before the Verein Hamburger Reeder during the later part of 1915, in which he called for the acquisition by Germany of Antwerp, Boulogne and the Canary Islands, proposing that the latter could be purchased from Spain while France could be compensated by being given part of the Belgian coast.[65]

Even among supporters of Wolff's petition there were some who still favoured limited territorial claims against Belgium, including those who had attended the original meeting in Berlin on 7 July.[66] Wilhelm Kahl, for instance, was against the full-scale annexation of Belgium as a German *Bundesstaat*, but nonetheless believed that Belgium owed some compensation to Germany for breaching its own neutrality and for the atrocities committed by Belgian *Franctireurs* at the beginning of the war. He therefore suggested a limitation of the size of the Belgian army, a joint railway convention and the right, in time of war, for German troops to march through and occupy the Belgian coast. Professor Max Sering, who also attended the 7 July meeting, was against annexation but in favour of a customs union and German occupation of Liège, both to protect the industrial Rhineland and to appease nationalist opinion at home. Similarly, Ernst Troeltsch argued in favour of occupying Belgium as far as the *Maaslinie*, as well as the French mining region of Briey, which had 'only by chance' been returned to France in 1871 because German geologists had failed to realise its true value. He also spoke in favour of a customs union and a high war indemnity. Finally, Gerhard Anschütz, Berlin Professor of Law, argued that Belgium should be kept as a bargaining tool in case the British tried to occupy Constantinople at the end of the war.

By contrast, the two main organisers of the petition, Hans Delbrück and Bernhard Dernburg, were opposed to any annexation of French or Belgian territory and the former also cast doubt on the military value of strategic border changes in the west. Later in the war Delbrück was even less compromising in his rejection of the Pan-German and industrialist *Drang nach Westen*, arguing in the *Preussische Jahrbücher* in January 1917 that 'there is no middle way between the annexation and the renunciation [*Freigabe*] of Belgium'.[67]

The next major step undertaken by the moderates was again a parallel development to the *Kriegszielbewegung*. As a counterweight to Dietrich Schäfer's Independent Committee, the German National Committee (*Deutscher National-Ausschuss*) was founded on 6 June 1916 under the presidency of Prince Carl Wedel, former German *Statthalter* of Alsace-Lorraine.[68] The Committee's goal was to mobilise support for the pressurised government of Bethmann Hollweg and to create the political basis in German public opinion for a peace offensive. In its first nationwide appeal of 20 July 1916 it stated its main task: 'to work together with like-minded individuals in building a common platform as the basis for a German peace' and further 'to oppose the extremists on both sides, who accuse our leading statesmen of pursuing either a rotten peace or annexationist madness before the facts can be fully known'.[69]

Like the Independent Committee, the National Committee counted a number of prominent names among its members. Among its founders were leading figures from the Reich Chancellor's staff and the Foreign Office, including Under Secretary von Wahnschaffe, Ulrich Rauschner, Kurt Riezler and Matthias Erzberger. This suggests that the government itself had developed a strong interest in the project. Also involved were the university professors Adolf von Harnack, Max Weber, Hermann Oncken and Friedrich von Liszt; the Progressive politicians Conrad Haußmann, Friedrich Naumann and Ferdinand von Payer; former ambassador Freiherr von Stumm; Generaldirektor Heineken of the North German Lloyd; Paul von Schwabach of the Disconto-Gesellschaft; and the right-wing Social Democrats Albert Südekum and August Müller. Finally, several leading industrialists were, at least temporarily, members of the National Committee, including August Thyssen, the brothers Röchling, the oil magnate Riedemann of the Deutsch-Amerikanische Petroleum-Gesellschaft and Freiherr von Bodenhausen-Degener, a director of Krupps and member of the Mannesmann board of directors.[70]

Apart from Hans Delbrück, one of the leading intellectual forces behind the moderates was the world-famous sociologist Max Weber, professor at the University of Heidelberg, who detailed his opinions about German war aims in an unpublished newspaper article written in November or early December 1915. Annexationist agitation of the type carried on by the Pan-Germans, he argued, was futile, not only because it demonstrated the fundamental wrong-headedness of Pan-German war aims in the west, but because of the serious long-term effects of such propaganda on public opinion at home. As soon as it became apparent that such fantastic goals could never be achieved, disillusionment would set in and the fighting spirit of the nation would rapidly dissolve. In particular, Weber stressed the impossibility of Germany inheriting Britain's position as leading world power and also the likely consequences of a long drawn out war for the German economy. In the present situation, Germany had but two options: 'World policy or a European and especially a west European expansionist policy. Russian enmity is unavoidable. An expansionist policy in the west would unite all of the western powers against us.'[71]

Weber's well-documented opposition to the Pan-German clamour for unrestricted submarine warfare in the spring of 1916 was shared by many leading figures in the Foreign Office, whose main concern seems to have been the likely effect on public opinion abroad, particularly in neutral countries such as the United States. One example here would be Freiherr von Mumm, the former German ambassador to Tokyo and director of the Zentralstelle für Auslandsdienst, the office in charge of official German propaganda in foreign countries. At the end of August 1915, Mumm wrote to his colleague Otto Hammann, the Foreign Office press chief:

The burning issue at the moment is our relations with America . . . The longer tensions remain between us and America because of the U-boat war, the more difficult it will become to reach a settlement. If we had taken up the suggestion of Monteglas a few months ago, that passenger ships would not be torpedoed, then this whole crisis could have been avoided, a crisis which has surely done us more damage in the world with respect to our position in the war than any advantages we may have gained by sinking the *Lusitania* and the *Arabic*. The decision not to adopt Monteglas's proposal came about, as far as I am aware, because of the opposition of Zimmermann, who feared for the popularity of the Chancellor. The result is simply that the conflict has come to a head now, and in a more serious form, and that the navy has meanwhile had ample time to poison the press further.[72]

According to Hammann, Mumm was 'visibly upset' whenever reports came in concerning Zeppelin raids on English coastal towns, 'because he was convinced that this would bring no important military advantages, would encourage atrocity propaganda and would prolong the war'.[73]

For others, the extreme anglophobia and annexationist mania of groups such as the Pan-German League and their Conservative and industrial allies re-awakened some uncomfortable questions about the very origins of the war itself. On 5 March 1916, for instance, Wilhelm von Schoen, the Prussian envoy to Munich, reported on conversations he had had with the Bavarian Minister-President and future Reich Chancellor, Count Hertling:

Count Hertling misses no opportunity in private conversations to make clear his disavowal of the activities of the Pan-Germans, whom, not without cause, he holds partly responsible for the war, since their behaviour aroused the mistrust of the Entente powers towards us and reinforced their concerns that the Kaiser's government would allow itself to go along with their imperialist policies.[74]

These private concerns were shared by Karl von Eisendecher, the Prussian envoy to Baden, who interestingly had been Bethmann Hollweg's preferred choice as ambassador to London in October 1912, although the Kaiser had insisted on Lichnowsky. In May 1917 Eisendecher wrote to Bethmann in the latter's capacity as Prussian Foreign Minister:

I personally am increasingly convinced that the Pan-Germans are not to be acquitted of a certain responsibility for the outbreak of the war. In particular their publications have provoked [Lord] Northcliffe [of the *Times*] and other sections of the enemy press and everywhere have given rise to a false impression of the state of our public opinion at home. The informative brochure produced by Baumgarten, 'The Echo of the Pan-German Movement in America', is full of striking evidence for this, and can also be linked in particular to the British policy of encirclement.[75]

Even more significant were the views of Count Botho von Wedel, who was a *Vortragender Rat* in the Foreign Office from 1910 until his appointment to succeed Tschirschky as ambassador to Vienna in 1916. In a telling conversation with Theodor Wolff in October 1916, Wedel argued that the only way in which war could have been avoided in the period 1912 to 1914 was through a German alliance with Britain. The efforts of those who had sincerely desired such a move had effectively been thwarted, however, by the Kaiser's unswerving support for Tirpitz and by the willingness of both men to mobilise nationalistic public opinion behind a further round of shipbuilding. This combination of the failure of the Haldane mission and Germany's rapidly deteriorating international position in turn gave a free hand to those militarists inside Germany who favoured more drastic action to alter the world constellation in Germany's favour: war with Russia, leading to world war.[76]

Wedel's interpretation is particularly interesting, not only because it casts light on the disastrous effect of nationalistic and anglophobe opinion on government policy before the war, but also because it explains much of his later thinking as German ambassador to Vienna in the period 1916–18. On 11 May 1917, for instance, he wrote to Bethmann Hollweg:

As I have already had the honour to report on various other occasions, the energetic propaganda of the Pan-Germans, [and] especially of Count Reventlow, is viewed here with disquiet, not only within the leading political circles, but also among broader sections [of the population] . . . The Pan-Germans are destroying our image through their elevation of the conflict into an exclusively Anglo-German one. [The Austrians] are not at all pleased to see themselves hitched up to the German waggon in order to settle the Anglo-German conflict, and, as for the future, [they] want to restore peaceful relations with all other nations as soon as possible. The activities of the Pan-Germans are therefore looked upon with a great deal of concern; at any rate they are unleashing latent feelings of hostility towards us and are in danger of creating complications for future collaboration and for the unity of our alliance.[77]

If we now return to the controversy between the 'moderates' and the 'annexationists' in the summer of 1916, it is important to note that the National Committee also planned a major propaganda offensive on 1 August 1916, to mark the second anniversary of the outbreak of the war, with meetings planned in fifty of the larger towns in Germany. The list of speakers was impressive and included Albert Südekum in Mannheim, August Müller in Bielefeld, Paul Rohrbach in Dortmund, Georg Bernhard of the *Vossische Zeitung* in Bochum, Wilhelm Marx in Munich, Hermann Oncken in Kassel, Ferdinand von Payer in Frankfurt am Main, Friedrich Naumann in Leipzig and Adolf von Harnack in Berlin.

The most striking speech was made by Max Weber in Nuremberg, who defended Bethmann Hollweg as 'the only leader who enjoys the full confidence of the field-greys in the trenches' and severely criticised the campaign for unrestricted submarine warfare.[78] On the other hand, when Conrad Haußmann tried to make a similar speech to an audience in Hamburg it was clear that many members of the annexationist Independent Committee were present, since he was shouted down by cries of: 'Bring out the U-boats! Down with England! How dare anyone come and say such things to Hamburgers!'

The National Committee itself was not opposed to all annexations, but merely to large-scale continental annexations. In fact, the majority of speakers did favour the expansion of German power on the continent, but wanted to achieve this through indirect means and without compromising the national character of the Prusso-German state. Weber, for instance, called for military guarantees in Belgium and Poland and emphasised that Germany was fighting to win recognition as a great power in the centre of Europe. And, on a slightly different note, Georg Bernhard in Bochum spoke of the necessity of war indemnities in order to compensate for German economic losses in relation to Britain:

We must have these indemnities either in cash or in kind, so that we can offset our capital burden, or we must occupy the contested lands which we have conquered in hard battle, so that we can use them in order to compensate for part of our interest payments.

Even more alarming were the views expressed by the well-known liberal publicist Paul Rohrbach, an implacable opponent of the Pan-Germans, who emphasised the oriental question as the key issue at stake in the war. Russia, he argued, could not be allowed to occupy Constantinople and England would have to be expelled from the Suez Canal. Germany would have to carry on the war, he continued, 'until England is fully beaten and prepared to tolerate Germany as an equal partner'.[79]

Similarly, August Müller, the Social Democratic member of the War Food Office, argued that Germany's 'life interests' lay in the Dardanelles and the maintenance of Constantinople in Turkish hands. Perhaps it would be possible, he went on, to reach a temporary understanding with Russia guaranteeing it free access to the Straits. On the other hand, no peace with England was possible 'until [it] can be forced into making such a peace'.

The moderation among Germany's intellectuals and diplomats with regard to England was therefore by no means as great as their Pan-German opponents liked to claim. The same could be said of its commercial and financial interests. Arthur von Gwinner, for instance, senior director of the Deutsche Bank, who was also on friendly terms with Bethmann Hollweg, was sufficiently impressed by Germany's early victories to hope for substantial reparations and possession of the French colonies in Africa as possible German gains.[80] At a meeting of the 'Wednesday Club', an association of leading industrialists, bankers, politicians and figures from the cultural world, on 2 September 1914, Gwinner argued against 'blindly following a policy of annexations'. He pleaded instead for a less direct course of action, namely that of 'establishing Germany's economic domination [over Europe]'.[81] Gwinner's pessimistic views on the prospects for German economic warfare against Britain are also believed to have had a major impact on Bethmann Hollweg and his famous programme of war aims drawn up on 9 September 1914.[82]

Another German businessman who had a major impact on official war aims policy was Walther Rathenau, the director of the Allgemeine Elektrizitäts-Gesellschaft (AEG), Germany's leading electrical company, and a member of more than 100 German and foreign business concerns. At the end of August 1914, Rathenau, who had in the same month been entrusted with the organisation of the department for military raw materials in the War Ministry (Kriegsrohstoffabteilung), submitted to the Chancellor a lengthy memorandum in which he recapitulated plans for a German-dominated customs union in central Europe already proposed by him on a number of occasions between 1912 and the outbreak of war. As he argued it, only a Germany reinforced by such a customs union would be in a position to compete with its main rivals on the world stage – Britain, Russia and the United States – in the constant struggle for markets and raw materials. In August 1914 Rathenau now saw the war itself as an opportunity to bring these *Mitteleuropa* plans to fruition, if necessary by use of military force. His favoured option, however, seemed to be a compromise peace with France on the one hand, and the immediate completion of a customs union between Germany and Austria-Hungary on the other, which could be used as a weapon in the continuing struggle against Britain and Russia.[83]

The anti-British thrust of Rathenau's strategic concept of economic warfare was meanwhile revealed quite clearly in a letter to one of Bethmann's personal assistants, Gerhard von Mutius, on 16 October 1914, in which he discussed quite calmly the possibility of bringing Britain to its knees through the destruction of London and other cities by air.[84] Indeed, although Rathenau, like Gwinner, became considerably more moderate as the war went on, the drastic efficiency which he showed in the creation and administration of the Kriegsrohstoffabteilung, and his consistent support for a central European customs union with both France and Belgium participating, undoubtedly made the achievement of a moderate peace settlement with Britain all the more difficult.[85]

Finally, it is worth examining the views of one of Bethmann Hollweg's most intimate advisers during the war, the Catholic politician Matthias Erzberger. Although Erzberger is best known as the organiser of the Reichstag Peace Resolution in July 1917, his activities during the first two years of the war as a propagandist for the German government reveal him to have been both an extreme annexationist and an ardent anglophobe. In an article published in the *Anklamer Zeitung* in February 1915, for instance, which even his biographer Klaus Epstein describes as 'the most regrettable piece [he] ever wrote', Erzberger argued that: 'It would be more humane, if one had the chance, to destroy the whole of London in one blow, than to allow a single fellow-German to bleed to death on the battlefield.'[86]

Similarly, in a letter to Bethmann of 10 August 1915 Erzberger urged the Chancellor to stop hesitating and throw his weight behind a massive air assault on London, adding that this might also be a way of reconciling Tirpitz, who was on the point of resigning over the government's refusal to allow unrestricted submarine warfare.

A major [air] strike against London would be of the highest political importance. Since I know that consent to such an attack has already been given by Headquarters, but has not, for reasons which have not been made known to me, been carried out, I would recommend Your Excellency to make representations to bring about an attack as early as possible. I regard this as all the more important since reliable sources have informed me that State Secretary von Tirpitz is thinking of resigning over the restrictions placed on submarine warfare even before the Reichstag has reconvened . . . If Your Excellency should now wish to carry out an air strike, then in my opinion the causes of the current political crisis would disappear.[87]

Thus it would seem that real opposition to the anglophobia of Pan-Germans such as Count Reventlow was rare, even among those who considered themselves to be anti-annexationist. Return to the status quo ante bellum seemed desirable only to the SPD, but even here an unbridgeable split soon developed between radical pacifists such as Hasse, Kautsky and Bernstein, who opposed the war from 1915 onwards, and prominent figures on the right of the party, such as Eduard David and Albert Südekum, who stood more or less openly behind the government and the Chancellor on the war aims question.

Meanwhile, the SPD leadership tried to steer a middle path between these two positions, basing its continued support for the war effort on the notion that Bethmann was the only statesman in Germany who could negotiate a swift and satisfactory end to the fighting and at the same time deliver on the promise of internal political reform. On both these counts it was to be sorely disappointed.[88]

The government and the annexationists

In spite of the existence of a 'moderate' opposition to Pan-German war aims, it was primarily towards the German government that most annexationist propaganda was directed, since the government, and not the people, was responsible for the conduct of the war and the negotiation of peace terms. This in turn meant that the success of any 'moderate' pressure to conduct a peace offensive aimed at Britain depended on the stance taken by the Chancellor, Bethmann Hollweg.

At first it seemed as if Bethmann was willing to stand up to the extreme annexationists and anglophobes on these issues. In a private conversation with Theodor Wolff on 9 February 1915, for instance, he said: 'as paradoxical as this might sound, I believe that we will more easily come to terms with England – more easily than with the French.'[89] And on 21 February he had an article published in the official *Norddeutsche Allgemeine Zeitung* which underlined the government's commitment to maintaining the ban on public discussion of war aims and declared that the one and only essential war aim was to achieve military victory. This article was supported by Wolff and other left-liberal journalists, but opposed by the Pan-German and Conservative press and by the annexationist majority in the Prussian House of Deputies, which had passed a resolution at the beginning of February calling for immediate permission to debate the war aims question.[90]

On the other hand, we now know that, in secret, Bethmann Hollweg had committed himself to a policy of continental expansion that in many ways was more extreme than some of the annexationist petitions of the first half of 1915. His so-called 'September programme' of 9 September 1914 defined 'the general aim of the war' as 'security for the German Reich to east and west for all imaginable time'. It included, among other things, the proposal to reduce France to a second-rate power and to break Russia's domination over the non-Russian nationalities of eastern Europe. Germany would annex all of Luxembourg, as well as Liège and possibly Antwerp from Belgium, with a corridor from the latter city to the German frontier. In addition, Germany's economic domination over central Europe would be reinforced by the creation of a 'central European economic association', embracing continental western Europe, Poland, Scandinavia and the Central Powers. Finally, there would be a 'continuous Central African colonial empire', the details of which 'will be considered later, as will [those] of the aims to be realised vis-à-vis Russia'.[91]

Indeed, that the Chancellor's war aims differed from those of his right-wing critics in method only, and not in general tenor, can also be seen in many of his public pronouncements during the first two years of the war. The term 'real guarantees and securities', for instance, which he first used in a speech to the Reichstag on 28 May 1915 to describe German war aims on the continent, did not fool Theodor Wolff, who was thenceforth convinced that the Chancellor had caved in to the industrialists' demands. Two days later, Wolff made it known to Wilhelm von Stumm of the Foreign Office that in his view Bethmann was a 'miserable weakling who allows himself to be bullied by others'.[92]

A month earlier, on 25 April 1915, an article had already been published in the *Norddeutsche Allgemeine Zeitung* officially denying rumours that the government was poised to enter peace talks with the enemy, and especially with Britain. The anglophobe press, notably the *Deutsche Tageszeitung*, was delighted, while only the *Berliner Tageblatt* and *Vorwärts* voiced their concern.[93]

This was also quite consistent with remarks made by the Chancellor in private to a delegation of deputies from the annexationist parties and the Catholic Zentrum on 13 May 1915. The similarity between the views expressed on this occasion and the plans already laid out in the 'September programme' at the beginning of the war is unmistakable. According to Count Westarp's account, Bethmann demanded:

Occupation of the whole [of Belgium] and complete economic domination. His statement did not make it clear whether he was thinking of political independence, i.e. some kind of federal relationship, or of annexation, the latter in any case without conferring any political rights. Economically, the Chancellor is considering a customs union, German influence over [railway?] rates – the acquisition of railways he considers difficult, since 80,000 German employees would have to be moved to Belgium – complete economic domination over the port of Antwerp, introduction of German civil law, legal procedure (doubtful) and social legislation, to ensure to German industry the ability of competing with that of Belgium . . . Imposition of German imperial laws, administration through one or several military governors.[94]

Finally, on 19 August 1915 Bethmann declared openly in the Reichstag that the task of forcing Germany's enemies back would require a fundamental revolution in European and global power relations:

A new order must arise! If Europe is ever to live in peace then this can come about only through the emergence of a strong and invincible Germany . . . The English policy of the balance of power must disappear, for it is, as the English [*sic!*] writer Bernard Shaw recently said, the breeding ground for [new] wars . . .

Meine Herren, Germany must create such a position for itself, must establish and strengthen itself to such an extent that the other powers lose all inclination to repeat their policy of encirclement . . . We must obtain complete freedom of the seas for our own protection and salvation as well as for that of all other nations . . . not in order to monopolise the sea for ourselves, as England does for itself, but in order to guarantee equal rights of usage for all nations.[95]

This speech was called an 'achievement of the very first order' and greeted with 'prolonged and tempestuous applause', and indeed it had been made partly in order to assuage mistrust of the great economic organisations and the war aims majority in the Reichstag.[96] That it was also an expression of very real war aims, however, was demonstrated by Bethmann's negative response to a renewed offer of American mediation at the end of January 1916, made through President Wilson's special envoy, Colonel House. House's primary interest was in a quick settlement between Germany and England as the first step towards a general peace based on the restoration of the status quo in western Europe. To this Bethmann replied that from the day he had become German Chancellor in 1909 he had worked for an understanding with Britain and the United States in order to guarantee world peace; this had always been his long-term objective, compared with which he thought the breach of Belgian neutrality 'a small thing'. A separate peace on British terms, whereby Germany would have to countenance the continued existence of the Anglo-French entente while at the same time surrendering 'vital safeguards' in Belgium and Poland, could offer no such guarantee of lasting world peace. And on this crucial point Bethmann assured House that 'no one and nothing stands between me and the Kaiser'.[97]

Here in a nutshell we can see the crucial continuity between Germany's world power policy inaugurated in the mid-1890s and its war aims policy after 1914. The miscarriage of the Schlieffen plan in September and its final bankruptcy in November 1914 persuaded Bethmann that it might be in Germany's interests to seek a separate peace either with Russia in the east (demanded by both Falkenhayn and Tirpitz) or with France in the west (a move advocated by some liberal politicians such as Gerhard von Schulze-Gaevernitz and also supported by the Under Secretary of State, Arthur Zimmermann).[98] As far as Bethmann himself was concerned, such a policy would be worthwhile only if it led to the break-up of the Entente and the formation of a new German-led constellation of powers, and in this he was backed by the Kaiser and his military advisers. A general peace, however, was only conceivable to German leaders if Britain first recognised the basic aim of German policy since 1897, i.e. both the advancement of its power position on the continent and the assertion of its world power status. It

133

was either this or nothing; and, when House returned to Berlin in February 1916 with concrete proposals from Britain (the Grey–House memorandum), Bethmann informed him that, whereas the restoration of Belgium and Poland would have been possible earlier, the German government could not now consider it.[99]

5 The submarine crisis deepens

In the summer and autumn of 1916 the crisis in Germany entered a new
and more disastrous phase, at a time when anti-English and pro-
submarine agitation was also reaching massive proportions. During the
preceding weeks Germany had suffered a number of significant military reverses. Early in June the Russian Brusilov offensive was launched
on the eastern front, inflicting major damage on Germany's ally,
Austria-Hungary. In the same month the Grand Sheriff of Mecca raised
the Arab revolt in the Hejaz against Turkish rule, and thereby created a
distraction to the Turks which the British and French had hitherto failed
to provide in the Dardanelles and other campaigns. On 1 July the costly
battle of the Somme began on the western front, where simultaneously
the struggle for Verdun continued inconclusively (it was finally called
off in December). Finally, on 27 August Romania entered the war
against the Central Powers, threatening the south-eastern front and the
supply route to Constantinople. It was this latter event which led to
Falkenhayn's replacement as Chief of General Staff at the end of August
and the subsequent rise of the Army Supreme Command (the third
OHL) under Paul von Hindenburg and his First Quartermaster General,
Erich Ludendorff.[1]

On 21 August, shortly before his dismissal, Falkenhayn told
Bethmann Hollweg that Germany was about to reach the limits of its
material and manpower resources: 'Given the terrible pressures upon
us we have no forces to spare. Every redeployment in one direction
leads inevitably to a dangerous weakening in other places, which – if
even the slightest error is made with regard to our assessment of the
enemy's next moves – could mean our destruction.' Only a few weeks
before, on 4 July, Admiral von Scheer, Commander of the High Seas
Fleet, had declared in his report on the famous naval battle in the
Skagerrak (the battle of Jutland, 31 May 1916): 'There can be no doubt
that even the best possible outcome of any [future] sea battle would not
force England to make peace in this war.'[2]

In other words, both the head of the Supreme Army Command and
the Commander of the High Seas Fleet had admitted – albeit in private

– that a victory for Germany was no longer possible using the conventional means of warfare at its disposal. In reality such an admission might well have led to the collapse of Germany there and then, had it not been for the repeated promises made by senior naval officers that unrestricted submarine warfare would lead to the premature starvation of Britain and therefore to the overthrow of the enemy coalition. Scheer himself concluded his report by urging the Kaiser to reconsider his opposition to all-out economic warfare against England:

A victorious end to this war in the foreseeable future can only be brought about through the destruction of England's economic life, in other words through the deployment of submarines against English commerce. Through personal conviction and a sense of duty I must urgently warn Your Majesty against choosing a weakened form [of submarine warfare], not only because it is at variance with the nature of this weapon . . . but also because, in spite of the conscientiousness of the [U-boat] commanders, it is not possible, in English waters, in which American interests are also vital, to avoid incidents which could force us into a humiliating climbdown if we do not proceed with every rigour.[3]

The situation on the home front was equally precarious and gloomy. During the summer months riots and strikes took place throughout the country, largely in reaction to the growing food shortages. At the same time, the ultra-annexationist agitation against Bethmann Hollweg was stepped up, with demands made in Munich and other important provincial centres that the government grant an immediate debate on the submarine question and that the Chancellor be removed from office. The internal tensions which had been building up in the first half of 1916 were thus brought fully into the open and made the rest of the war a succession of internal crises. These crises were in turn intensified by an increasing divergence of views between the civilian and military authorities, beginning with the appointments of Hindenburg and Ludendorff to head the new Supreme Command on 29 August 1916 and ending with Bethmann's final dismissal – at the request of Hindenburg and Ludendorff – in July 1917.

In the following pages I shall go on to explore in greater depth the domestic controversy over submarine warfare in the second half of 1916 and its important role in bringing about the eventual fall of Bethmann Hollweg. In particular, I shall provide a detailed account of the events which gave rise to the formation of the Volksausschuß für die rasche Niederkämpfung Englands, founded in Munich in September 1916 with the self-declared aim of creating a right-wing mass movement in favour of the immediate introduction of unrestricted submarine warfare. I shall also examine some of the broader pressures on the government, coming even from 'moderate' parties such as the Centre Party and the Progressives, to relinquish its stance on the submarine question. The final section of this chapter will explore the more complex set of reasons for the government's decision to give way to these pressures in the early part of 1917.

Munich in the summer of 1916: anglophobia and particularism

Following their failure to make any headway at the meeting of the Foreign Affairs Committee of the Bundesrat on 15 March 1916, the nationalist opponents of Bethmann Hollweg increasingly concentrated their efforts on attempts to win over the federal princes as well as particularist forces on the right who were known to be unhappy with many of the policies pursued by the Reich authorities in Berlin. The most powerful voice represented on this Foreign Affairs Committee was Bavaria's – indeed, the Bavarian monarch had a right, under the Reich constitution, to recall the committee for further debate.[4] Therefore Munich seemed to be the most obvious centre for any renewed agitation in favour of unrestricted submarine warfare. It was here on 27 July 1916 that the Pan-German League held a secret meeting and agreed upon a new policy which would not hesitate 'to stir up particularist sentiment in order to reach our goal'.[5] This was followed by a petition sent to all federal princes on 31 July, in which particularist interests were skilfully brought to the fore and combined with the demand for a 'victorious peace' which would ensure that the Entente powers – and not the individual German states – would meet the full costs of the German war effort.[6]

It was in Munich, too, that strong intellectual opposition to the Chancellor had begun to emerge under the leadership of Professor Max von Gruber, which from July 1916 onwards began to meet in secret on a weekly basis at the offices of a building company on the Schwantalerstraße.[7] Gruber himself had strong connections with members of the Pan-German League in Berlin, including Dietrich Schäfer of the Independent Committee for a German Peace, and Prince Otto Salm, the right-wing president of the Navy League and founder of the Salm-Sammlung.[8] The aim of his organisation, which from September 1916 referred to itself as the Volksausschuß für die rasche Niederkämpfung Englands, was first and foremost to seek an audience with Ludwig III of Bavaria and other south German princes in order to 'enlighten' them on the 'true' facts surrounding Bethmann Hollweg's refusal to allow unrestricted submarine warfare, and to persuade them to intervene with the Kaiser in order to ensure an immediate change in policy. Only after this tactic had been tried and seen to fail did the Volksausschuß decide to go public, this time with the new aim of creating as broadly based a movement as possible in favour of the rapid overthrow of England by submarine.[9]

Supporters of unrestricted submarine warfare were no doubt encouraged in their efforts by the fact that Ludwig III had on several occasions during the early part of the war indicated his support for some of the extreme annexationist demands of the Pan-German League, in particular, as one important figure observed, with regard to 'die Dinge im Westen'.[10] His most important statement came on 7 June 1915, at a dinner given by the Bayerischer Kanalverein in Fürth, at which he demanded, in addition to the annexation of Belgium, a 'direct outlet from the Rhine into the sea'.[11] This led to the immediate intervention of the Foreign Office in Berlin, which feared, quite correctly, that the Bavarian monarch's reference to the mouth of the Rhine might seriously damage Germany's relations with neutral Holland. To cover up the blunder, a new version of the speech was published in the official *Bayerische Staatszeitung*, in which it was made clear that the old king had merely been referring to the need for more favourable links between southern Germany and the sea in the future, and had been unaware that the mouth of the Rhine lay in Dutch territory. When this tactic failed to dampen down public excitement, the Berlin censor resorted to banning further discussion of the speech in the press.[12]

Ludwig's support for Bethmann Hollweg's conciliatory policies towards America in the wake of the Lusitania crisis was also rumoured to be luke-warm at best, or at any rate far less certain than Kaiser Wilhelm's loyalty towards 'his' Chancellor. As early as June 1915, for instance, shortly after Ludwig's famous speech at Fürth, the extreme anglophobe Admiral Hans von Thomsen wrote to his Bavarian friend, the Pan-German and ex-cavalry officer Freiherr von Gebsattel, urging him to send a letter to the king warning him of the dire perils of a separate peace with England.

He [Ludwig] is our last hope with his clear vision and strong will. Perhaps he can and will make these considerations his own. The one and only important thing is that in no circumstances should peace be made with England before Germany has landed a million soldiers in England. If the will of our all-highest master [Wilhelm II] remains unbending – in spite of all the observations and statements to the contrary made by his entourage – then we will really win the war, then Germany will have the opportunity to fulfil the task which has been set out for it by God in heaven.[13]

With Thomsen's approval, Gebsattel sent extracts from this letter to the king's cabinet secretary, Dandl, on 28 June, together with a memorandum written by Thomsen on the subject of the eventual peace settlement. According to Dandl's reply a month later, the contents of the letter had been shown both to Ludwig and to Count Hertling.[14]

In the summer of 1915 there were also rumours that leading Bavarian politicians, among them the Minister-President Count Hertling, favoured a separate peace settlement with Russia.[15] This caused Gebsattel to intervene once again, this time at the request of Dietrich Schäfer, who asked him to pass on a memorandum on war aims in the east to Prince Leopold and other members of the Bavarian royal house. In reply, Gebsattel wrote to Schäfer on 29 August:

> I am of course very willing to pass your memorandum on to members of our royal household and would recommend to you: Crown Prince Rupprecht and Prince Leopold. I assume, at the same time, that the text has already been sent to H.M. the King and the Minister of State Count Hertling. If this is not the case, I will gladly undertake the task of presenting it before these two authorities as well.[16]

As early as June 1915 Ludwig III had personally intervened to prevent Hertling from sending a letter to Bethmann Hollweg advocating a separate peace settlement with the Russians. Although Hertling was able to meet the Chancellor on 6 July, he was able to present his idea only as the expression of a personal opinion, and not as the official view of the Bavarian government. Bethmann himself had been pursuing the idea of a separate deal with Russia since the end of 1914, and there can be little doubt that an official declaration of support from the Bavarian monarch would have encouraged him to further his efforts in this direction.[17]

There were other factors, however, apart from the popularity of Ludwig III in annexationist circles, which made Munich a potentially fruitful area for nationalist and anglophobic agitation in the summer of 1916. The most important among these was the increasing war weariness amongst the Bavarian population itself, which was further exacerbated by the lack of government support for small businesses struggling to keep afloat in the war economy and accusations of a pro-Prussian, sometimes pro-Jewish bias in the Reich agencies sent up to administer the production and supply of food and other essential war items.[18] Added to this was disappointment over the failure of the Verdun offensive in February 1916, and rumours of a growing rift between the Bavarian Crown Prince Rupprecht, who commanded the 6th Army Group in Flanders, and his counterparts among the Prussian generals (Alexander von Kluck, Karl von Bülow, etc.). Finally, the Bavarian economy had begun to suffer in other ways too, with the traditional summer tourist trade being hit particularly hard by the war.[19]

All of these factors were deliberately and systematically exploited by the anglophobe opponents of the Chancellor in the summer of 1916, many of whom travelled down from Berlin and other parts of northern Germany to Bavaria for that very purpose. As a Social Democrat newspaper, the *Münchner Post*, noted ironically in an article on 8 August: 'Two types of invasion have overrun our beloved Bavaria this summer:

an invasion of holiday makers and an invasion of the Pan-German *Englandstöter.*'[20]

The first sign of trouble in Bavaria came on 6 July, when Georg Heim, one of the leaders of the 150,000-strong Bayerische Christliche Bauernvereine, used the occasion of a lecture on 'The Organisation of Food Supplies in Bavaria' to launch a sudden and unexpected attack on Bethmann Hollweg and his supposedly 'weak' stance on the submarine question.[21] The attack was particularly effective since Heim made a direct connection between the Chancellor's refusal to make maximum use of the submarine weapon and the heavy German losses sustained in recent fighting on the western front, losses (it was alleged) which had hit Bavarian regiments particularly hard. Only a few days before, of course, the British and French had launched their long-awaited Somme offensive, which had forced the OHL temporarily to halt their own attack on the French fortress city of Verdun.

Exactly one week after Heim's attack on the Chancellor, on 14 July, Sebastian Schlittenbauer, another prominent figure in the Bayerische Christliche Bauernvereine and a Catholic deputy in the Bavarian Landtag, gave a similar speech before an audience in the Löwenbräukeller in Munich. This event was also attended by members of Gruber's Volksausschuß.[22] Once again, the meeting was used as an occasion to express Bavarian opposition to the Chancellor's 'weak-kneed' policies towards England and his alleged plans for a 'rotten peace in the West'. Moreover, in order to circumvent censorship regulations in Bavaria, the organisers of the meeting sent detailed reports to the north German press, thus giving the somewhat exaggerated impression of a mass movement in favour of a more energetic prosecution of the war against England. On 19 July, for instance, the *Deutsche Tageszeitung* expressed its sympathy with the particularist mood among right-wing Bavarians when it noted, with regard to Schlittenbauer's speech:

In south Germany a self-serving anglophilia will never make any headway, as it has done here in northern Germany. In south Germany they have – thank God – developed a more objective view of the English danger. This also explains why the field orders of Crown Prince Rupprecht found such a large echo in south Germany. Finally, in south Germany there is no pull of financial interests towards the west. May Germany be protected from such political ruination.[23]

The high point of this public agitation in favour of unrestricted submarine warfare meanwhile came with a public rally held in the Tonhalle in Munich on 29 July, which was attended by no fewer than 1,000 people.[24] The rally was introduced by the National Liberal Landtag deputy Anton Löweneck, and had as its main guest speaker the Pan-German Count Reventlow. Like Schlittenbauer on 14 July, both

Löweneck and Reventlow singled out England as Germany's *Hauptfeind* in the war and, despite the tight censorship restrictions imposed by the Bavarian military authorities, were able to turn the rally into another clear-cut demonstration against Bethmann Hollweg and the overall direction of his foreign policy.[25]

This public rally was followed by a closed meeting of a group constituting itself as the Ausschuß für einen dauernden Frieden, in reality a cover-name for Gruber's Volksausschuß and other supporters of an annexationist peace, which took place in Munich on 30 July. In addition to Reventlow, the two other main speakers at this new meeting were Walter Bacmeister and Professor Eduard Meyer, the latter a prominent member of Dietrich Schäfer's Independent Committee who was well known for his forthright views on America and the submarine issue.[26] Reventlow himself led the calls for the immediate introduction of submarine warfare, even if this should lead to open conflict with the United States government. He also attacked both the Chancellor and the Reichstag, accusing the latter of failing to press Bethmann hard enough on the submarine issue. Even the Kaiser himself came in for some pretty harsh criticism: according to Reventlow he had fallen victim to some crazy religious ideas and did nothing all day but engage in solitary prayer for the victory of Germany over its enemies. He was also prevented from gaining a true picture of nationalist opinion in the country at large by what Reventlow contemptuously referred to as the 'verminous members of his entourage'. The Prussian monarchy could therefore no longer be relied upon to intervene against the disastrous policies of the Chancellor, even though these policies were bringing Germany dangerously close to losing the war against England. The only hope for a change in the current political situation, Reventlow concluded, lay in the attitude of the 'two south German kings', i.e. Ludwig III of Bavaria and Wilhelm II of Württemberg.[27]

Reventlow's arguments were backed up by the other two main speakers, and by Admiral von Thomsen, who attended the meeting as an 'expert' on naval and submarine issues. The meeting ended with a proposal to form a delegation of men to approach Ludwig III, and possibly the king of Württemberg too, with a request for their support in the campaign for a more vigorous prosecution of the war against England. It was also intended that this delegation would indicate its strong opposition to the policies of Bethmann Hollweg, and further that it would raise issues concerning the government's abuse of censorship regulations.[28]

The audience with King Ludwig took place on 5 August 1916, and did not produce the hoped-for results. The delegation was headed by Max von Gruber and included prominent *Reichsräte* (i.e. members of the Bavarian Reichsratkammer) such as Count Preysing and Franz von Buhl, thus giving an impression of an official deputation. Other participants included the Landtag deputies Robert Einhäuser (Centre Party), Anton Löweneck (National Liberal) and Karl Hübsch (Progressive), as well as the Bavarian Reichstag deputies Franz Joseph Pfleger (Centre Party) and Luitpold Weilnböck (Conservative). Finally, prominent critics of the Chancellor, such as Oberlandsgerichtsrat Wilhelm Rohrer, Bankdirektor Wilhelm Seitz and Geheimer Kommerzienrat Ernst Fromm, also attended.

Gruber himself read out extracts from a petition which he and the other participants had drafted in advance. The petition called for a 'victorious peace' and contained a strongly worded warning that the Reich's current leaders, by refusing to engage in all-out war against England, were driving Germany towards 'certain ruin . . . and with it our beloved Bavaria and its time-honoured ancestral princely house'. It also mentioned the 'disproportionate actions of the censor' as another cause for concern, whereby 'Social Democratic and left-liberal papers . . . can shamelessly poke fun at those circles who are filled with patriotic fervour, whilst the latter are forbidden to speak out in public or in the press'. Finally, Gruber called on the king to exercise his influence over the Kaiser and the Foreign Affairs Committee of the Bundesrat to bring about an immediate change of policy, which in effect could be achieved only if Ludwig were to add his own weight to the chorus of Pan-German demands for the removal of Bethmann Hollweg from office. The petition thus concluded with the following appeal:

We request and beseech Your Majesty to make use of Your sovereign powers to come to our rescue in the final hour . . . The whole of Germany knows that it is Your Majesty alone, the revered head of the oldest German dynasty, the ruler of the second biggest *Bundesstaat*, who can bring about a rapid change in our fortunes. The whole of Germany rests its hopes on Your Majesty.[29]

Also present at the meeting, however, were the Bavarian Minister-President Count Hertling and the Minister of War, Freiherr Kress von Kressenstein, both of whom remained loyal to Bethmann Hollweg and were anxious that Ludwig should appear to do the same. The official report on the audience, published a day later in the *Bayerische Staatszeitung*, therefore sought to emphasise the king's cool reception of the delegation and his disagreement with many of their arguments.[30] By contrast, unofficial reports written by some of the participants themselves, and containing suggestions of a more friendly reception on the part of the king, were quickly suppressed by the government censor and therefore failed to appear in print. It therefore seems likely that Ludwig's personal sympathies still lay with the annexationists, even if he did end up by having to discourage them from any further action which might lead to a loss of public confidence in the responsible leaders of the Reich.

In the meantime, Hertling pressed on with his plan to call a new meeting of the Foreign Affairs Committee of the Bundesrat, which was eventually arranged to take place on 8 and 9 August. As in March 1916, this was intended to be a carefully stage-managed event which would simply confirm the continued confidence of the member states in the foreign policy of the Reich and thereby deflect attention away from the noisy demonstrations of disloyalty taking place in Munich and elsewhere. As such it was a move which was welcomed by the Reich Chancellor himself, who was determined to quash rumours of a split between members of his government and the Admiralty on the submarine question.[31] At the session on 9 August, the oppositional movement in Munich was discussed at length and its demands dismissed one by one. Carl von Weizsäcker, the Minister-President of Württemberg, informed the committee that his government had received a similar petition to the one handed over to Ludwig III on 5 August. He had, he said, simply chosen to ignore it and it was now filed away somewhere in the official records where it would soon be forgotten. He would also follow this course of action if petitioned by the same or similar groups in the future, and recommended the other member states to do likewise.[32]

The military authorities in Bavaria were also determined to prevent any further public displays of nationalist opposition to the Chancellor, which were deemed to be detrimental both to the war effort and to Germany's image abroad. Thus on 1 August the Minister of War, Kress von Kressenstein, intervened personally to ban another rally from taking place in Munich on 3 August, at which the Protestant Pastor Traub had been due to speak on the subject 'England and us'.[33] And on 5 August he sent a directive to all acting military governors in Bavaria informing them of the current situation with regard to the anti-Bethmann movement in Munich and warning them to be on their guard against renewed attempts to revive this agitation in the provinces.[34] Finally, on 24 August 1916 police raids were organised on a number of different addresses in Munich and large quantities of inflammatory material seized, including copies of the 'Junius Alter' brochure and of Dietrich Schäfer's pamphlet 'Zur Lage', as well as a duplicating machine belonging to a local businessman, Theodor Dietz.[35] For a short time, at least, the submarine campaigners seemed to have suffered a severe setback. But this was not to last for long.

The agitation spreads to other parts of the Reich

News of the failure of the audience with King Ludwig III soon reached the highest levels of the Pan-German League. Heinrich Claß, for instance, who had evidently been well informed about events in Munich, wrote to his comrade Gebsattel on 12 August:

So once again we stand before the grave of a hope, although I must admit that my hopes for Munich were not very strong. What can we do now? . . . In my view we must get used to the idea that in the struggle for the redemption of our people we can expect no help from either our princely rulers or their governments – in other words, that we stand quite alone.[36]

Similarly, Gebsattel himself wrote to Count Preysing, one of the key participants in the audience and a close confidant of Admiral von Tirpitz, on 29 August:

I cannot understand how H.M.[Ludwig III] can come to the view (if he really is of this view) that it is impossible to force England under with the U-boats. I not only have spoken with several admirals, who are of the opposite opinion, but also have had occasion to learn of the contents of a private letter from Admiral Scheer, in which the hero of the Skagerrak writes: 'In my view we cannot beat England with the High Seas Fleet alone, but no doubt we can with the High Seas Fleet and unrestricted submarine warfare, if it is put into action *now*.'[37]

In spite of these apparent setbacks in the campaign for unrestricted submarine warfare, however, and in spite of the stringent efforts now being made by the civilian and military authorities in Bavaria to silence right-wing critics of the Chancellor's policies, the agitation in Munich soon spread outwards to reach other parts of the Reich, including Prussia and other states in northern Germany. As early as 4 August, for instance, Hertling wrote to Count Hugo von Lerchenfeld, the Bavarian envoy in Berlin, warning him of the damaging implications which this agitation might have for the Berlin government's authority unless measures were taken immediately to calm public opinion over the submarine issue. He also mentioned, by way of example, what he had heard and witnessed on a recent royal visit to Wilhelmshaven, where naval officers openly referred to the new secretary of state Capelle as 'Judas Iscariot', presumably because (for the time being) he had fallen in line with the Chancellor's views on unrestricted submarine warfare and was no longer pursuing the matter with the same amount of enthusiasm as his predecessor Tirpitz. The letter to Lerchenfeld then continued:

The government has no idea of the wild passions with which the opponents of the Chancellor are working. They have just one central idea: England is the enemy, England must be destroyed and this can be achieved in a few months, if only the navy is given a free hand to launch unrestricted submarine warfare. But the government refuses to budge, the Kaiser continues his love affair with England [*liebaugelt jetzt wie vor mit England*] and the Chancellor is too weak to oppose him, or at least that is what is said by those who do not harbour even worse suspicions against him. If one points to the dangers of a breach with the neutrals, especially with America, should unrestricted submarine warfare be set in motion, then one must hear in reply that in this instance it is only the commercial interests of the Jews that come into play . . . If one refers to the gigantic efforts being made by our troops in the west and the east and the generally favourable military situation out there, one must hear in reply that it cannot come to a decisive victory there, that all the terrible sacrifices would be unnecessary, if only the government would allow the U-boats to set to work . . . At the same time, quite deliberately, it is claimed that the additional taxes which will have to be raised if England is not destroyed in the war will have a seriously negative impact on the rights of individual states to handle their own fiscal arrangements.[38]

Meanwhile in Hamburg on 6 August the Oberegierungsrat reported to the Chancellor's office that a local newspaper, the *Hamburger Nachrichten*, had been carrying advertisements for the illegal 'Junius Alter' brochure, and that copies of the same brochure were being circulated throughout the city, 'especially among circles of high school teachers . . . and among employees of the "Hamburger Nachrichten"'. The report went on:

The recent agitation for Dietrich Schäfer in Hamburg's *Johanneum* has indeed received widespread publicity. Doubtless these malicious attacks [on the Reich Chancellor] come from relatively small groups of people, but they tend to be extremely active and to work with a wild passion to win new ground. It is therefore all the more necessary to prevent them from gaining a further hearing through the press.[39]

Similarly, in Saxony, where, as we have seen, anti-Semitic agitators such as Theodor Fritsch and Heinrich Pudor were also at work, the Chancellor received notification in August that a new anonymous pamphlet attacking his policies, this one with the title 'Either . . . or', was being distributed by local members of the Pan-German League. The worried informant, the Reichstag deputy Oscar Günther, who was at the same time chairman of the Progressive Party in Saxony, wrote:

Since the populace at large sees an energetic prosecution of the U-boat war as the best means of defeating England, the Pan-German agitators and their pamphlets, even if they do not contain an objective view of the real situation, have been able to instil a strong sense of unease among broad sections of the people.[40]

In Berlin itself, Dietrich Schäfer called a second important meeting of his newly formed Independent Committee on 13 August, at which a new 'appeal to the German people' was drawn up, calling on the whole population to recognise England as the chief antagonist in the war. The appeal was issued ten days later, on 23 August, and ended with the following words:

England's overt plans are threatening to reduce us to political and economic helots. It is now a question of our survival as a people and a state, of our culture and economy. We must therefore ruthlessly employ all the military means at our disposal to defeat this enemy of peace. The struggle is being waged to safeguard the jobs of our fellow countrymen, our freedom to engage in trade, the future development of our industry, and not least the maintenance and improvement of the conditions of the German worker. It should not come to pass what the British are saying, that we will win all the battles, but that England shall win the war. Be strong, German people! You are fighting for your being and your future. Hindenburg has provided you with the slogan: it is not a matter of holding out, it is a matter of winning victory.[41]

On 14 September 1916 Schäfer led a delegation of annexationists and submarine enthusiasts to meet Bethmann Hollweg in person. The discussion dealt mainly with the submarine issue and the English menace to the German war effort, but also touched on other issues, such as the government's continued censorship of Pan-German and annexationist publications.[42] A few days after this private meeting, Schäfer and his colleagues met with two of the leading figures from the anti-Bethmann movement in Bavaria, the Conservative Landtag deputy Ludwig Beckh and the Pan-German Prince Friedrich zu Löwenstein, to draw up a new petition to the Reichstag protesting against the impact of the government's censorship policies on public opinion.[43] This action was followed on 15 October with another large meeting of the Independent Committee in the Prussian House of Deputies, at which Count Reventlow appeared as the main speaker and once again used the opportunity to denounce the supposedly pro-English, pro-American policies of the Chancellor and his deputy, Karl Helfferich.[44]

In other parts of Germany, too, local annexationist groups were coming together in the autumn of 1916 to coordinate propaganda activities in favour of unrestricted submarine warfare. For instance, in Saarbrücken, the capital of the Saar mining region close to the border with eastern France, a meeting of local industrialists and members of the National Liberal Party issued a joint declaration on 17 September calling for 'the final battle against England, the chief enemy of our Fatherland in this world war'. Speakers at the meeting included the party leader Ernst Bassermann and the Prussian Landtag deputy Carl Röchling, a prominent representative of the Saar industrial family. Röchling told his fellow party members:

There can naturally be no question of reaching a separate peace with England. England does not do things by halves. Its war aim is to obliterate Germany from the ranks of the nations, that country which plays a decisive role in world politics and the world economy and therefore claims for itself a share in the leadership of the world, in other words a 'place in the sun', as Prince Bülow often put it.

He also went on to issue a direct challenge to Bethmann Hollweg by expressing his confident belief that the new military leaders, Hindenburg and Ludendorff, would 'find through their patient efforts the means to defeat our most dangerous enemy and that they will not hold back from putting this means into action'.[45]

In Kiel two days earlier an anti-English appeal was launched at a joint meeting attended by representatives of the following organisations in Schleswig-Holstein: the Conservative and Free Conservative parties, the National Liberals, the Centre Party and the local branches of the Agrarian League, the Army League and the Pan-German League. The chief organiser of the event was most probably the notorious *Englandfresser* Admiral von Thomsen, who, as we have seen, had already been involved in the Pan-German agitation in Munich at the end of July and who now appeared at the bottom of the list of those who had signed the new appeal on behalf of the province of Schleswig-Holstein. The appeal itself ran as follows:

The situation is extremely serious. We naturally behold with thanks and pride the unequalled victories which our armies have won in a two-year battle of the nations. But all these victories cannot bring us a German peace if the view does not prevail that Germany's honour and greatness depend on the rapid over-throw of England. One thing has become increasingly clear as the war has pro-gressed: England is our most determined and most dangerous enemy, England threatens our existence and our future! To show clemency towards such an enemy would be a crime against our own people! Therefore our foremost task must be to defeat England with all the military means at our disposal. To con-sider making peace before this would be both foolish and unprincipled.[46]

Finally, in Hamburg a group of 'several hundred bankers and traders' came together and drew up their own petition calling for a more vigorous prosecution of the war against England, which they sent out to a number of different government agencies. According to a report in the *Deutsche Tageszeitung* on 26 September, the Hamburg petition ran as follows:

England has for many years spun its net in order to destroy Germany. England has been prepared to go to war itself and to employ the most dubious economic means in order to destroy Germany, and England is making world-wide plans to continue the economic war into peace in order to ensure the even more com-plete destruction of Germany. England – always consistent and true to its own traditions – will be persuaded to abandon its plan to destroy us only if it is forced to do so by being made aware of its own weaknesses. Therefore there can be only one goal for us: to reach a clear understanding that England is the enemy that we must defeat if our previous sacrifices of life and material are not to have been in vain and the great opportunities for the expansion of German economic power in the world are not to be lost for ever.[47]

For the time being, however, Munich continued to act as the unoffi-cial headquarters of the Pan-German sponsored 'movement' against the incumbent Chancellor, Bethmann Hollweg. Efforts made there to circumvent the new, tighter restrictions imposed by the military author-ities in the wake of the police raids of 24 August were to culminate in the first appearance in public of Max von Gruber's Volksausschuß für die rasche Niederkämpfung Englands. The committee began by issuing an appeal for new members from all over Germany at a mass rally held in the Löwenbräukeller on 18 September 1916.[48]

The Volksausschuß für die rasche Niederkämpfung Englands: membership, aims and tactics

Comparatively little is known about the Volksausschuß für die rasche Niederkämpfung Englands beyond its rather absurd name and a few sparse references to its existence in previous scholarly works.[49] One of the key problems, in fact, is the lack of surviving evidence, since the committee's own records, including an entire chest full of letters and notes taken at its meetings, are now untraceable.[50] All that we are left with is a list of members in all parts of Bavaria except Munich itself, who were organised into 60 different *Ortsgruppen*.[51] This membership list, which was found among the papers of Wolfgang Kapp, confirms the claim made by the Munich historian Karl Alexander von Müller that the Volksausschuß contained 'a strongly educated [*akademisches*] element'; but it disguises the secret links which, according to Müller, the committee had developed with other Pan-German organisations, and with people such as Dietrich Schäfer and Prince Otto Salm in Berlin.[52] What can be said with a large degree of certainty, however, is that the programme of the Volksausschuß expressed the aims and aspirations of the national opposition in both Bavaria and the German Reich as a whole towards Bethmann Hollweg, and that the majority of its members came from the nationally minded liberal middle class, the most anglophobe section of Bavarian and German society.

Indeed, of the twenty-eight prominent citizens of Bavaria who signed the original manifesto of the Volksausschuß in September 1916, nearly all had been closely involved in the Pan-German agitation in Munich in the preceding weeks, and eleven had taken part in the delegation which had approached King Ludwig at the beginning of August. The left-wing opponents of the Pan-German League immediately seized upon this point. Thus the apparently unselfseeking manner in which the committee presented its programme for a 'peace with victory' was ridiculed in an article in *Vorwärts* on 19 September, which pointed out that '[t]he "new action" of the new committee turns out to be nothing more than a simple continuation of the campaign which the Bavarian fronde has been waging with great gusto for the past few months.'[53]

The Volksausschuß was also a very well-funded organisation, given both its size and the fact that it relied exclusively on voluntary donations during a period of great hardship and war. According to Ludwig Wenng, a member of the committee and also the secretary of the Agrarian League in Bavaria, the committee claimed to have received approximately 36,000 Reichsmarks in donations by early January 1917, of which it had already spent 20,000 marks on propaganda and other activities.[54] He also mentioned a total membership of 8,000, which had risen to 20,000 by September 1917, the same month in which the Volksausschuß dissolved itself and became the Bavarian branch of the Deutsche Vaterlandspartei.[55] Admittedly this was a much lower figure than the membership of other right-wing pressure groups at the beginning of the war, such as the Army League (90,000 members) and the Navy League (331,000), but it was still substantial for an organisation that had been in existence for only one year.[56]

In organisational terms, the activities of the Volksausschuß differed little from those of other annexationist organisations during the war. Its press section, headed by Direktor S. Müller of the *Bayerische Kurier*, supplied the right-wing Munich press with suitable news and articles.[57] From its central office on the Schwanthalerstraße in Munich (later the nearby Neuhauserstraße) it produced large quantities of anti-English propaganda and its own official publication – the *Münchener Mitteilungen*.[58] Prominent sympathisers included Paul Nikolaus Cossmann, editor of the prestigious *Süddeutsche Monatshefte*, as well as the racist publisher J.F. Lehmann and the anti-Semitic author Houston Stewart Chamberlain, who was officially awarded German citizenship in August 1916.[59]

In contrast to the Petition of the Intellectuals in July 1915, however, the committee also attracted a number of eminent Bavarian Catholics and agrarian leaders, which may have been partly due to resentment at the heavy-handed British action against the Easter Uprising in Dublin in April 1916.[60] Gustav Heim, for instance, leader of the Bayerische Christliche Bauernvereine, was active in carrying out anti-English and pro-submarine propaganda amongst the war-weary rural population of Upper Bavaria, and in this he was supported by a number of local clergymen and priests.[61] All new members of the committee were now urged to cooperate by enlisting new supporters in their area and distributing pamphlets provided by the committee's central office in Munich. In addition they were encouraged to propagate the committee's aims by holding local rallies and forming local branches of their own.[62]

Finally, the fact that the Volksausschuß intended to recruit speakers and new members from all over Germany, but nonetheless retained its headquarters in the Bavarian capital Munich, is also significant, because it reveals the growing importance of anti-Prussian feeling in the southern kingdoms of Germany as the war progressed.[63] In fact, many figures on the German right, including not only south German patriots but also those who described themselves as 'loyal Prussians', now claimed that the aim of the liberal and left-wing opposition to unrestricted submarine warfare was to create a centralised, unitary republic based on the French model, which would destroy the federal traditions of the

Bismarckian Reich and lead to the imposition of direct parliamentary (or worse still, socialist) rule from Berlin. On top of this, the imperial capital itself was routinely denounced as the bastion of international trading interests which were anti-German and pro-English by inclination, and liable to favour a republic over a monarchy in the not too distant future.[64] Like the National Socialists after 1919, the Volksausschuß therefore aimed to build up a presence in Munich as a means of putting increased pressure on the beleaguered rulers in Berlin, except in this case the intention was the overthrow of the Chancellor, Bethmann Hollweg, in order to save the federal monarchical system. The issues of war aims, submarine warfare and opposition to the Chancellor thus became closely interrelated.

The driving force behind the Volksausschuß, at least until the beginning of 1917, was its chairman, the Munich hygienist Max von Gruber, who until the summer of 1916 had played only a relatively minor role in war aims agitation. Gruber was born into a medical family in Vienna in 1853 and was Professor of Medicine at the universities of Graz and Vienna before being called to Munich in 1902, where he was appointed to the chair of his former tutor, Max von Pettenkofer.[65] Even before the war he had developed an interest in racial hygiene, publishing a book on the subject for the J.F. Lehmann Verlag in 1911.[66] During the war he renewed his contacts with Lehmann and became closely involved with the ultra-annexationist journal *Deutschlands Erneuerung*, to which other racial theorists such as Houston Stewart Chamberlain also contributed regularly.[67] After 1918 he withdrew from politics to concentrate on his academic work, and again rose to prominence as president of the prestigious Bayerische Akadamie der Wissenschaften, a post which he held from 1924 until his death in 1927. His most popular work, *Hygiene des Geschlechtslebens* (1927) sold 325,000 copies in its first edition and later had an important impact on Nazi policies towards marriage and sex education.[68]

Although Gruber did not formally belong to any of the established right-wing political parties in Munich, his academic interests and political views were reflected in his sharp opposition to what he referred to as the 'golden and red internationals' (i.e. the Jews and the Socialists) and in his frequent use of the word 'Lebensraum' to indicate his support for a massive programme of territorial conquest and colonisation in eastern Europe.[69] In Gruber's own case, the demand for more German territory in the east was based on the belief that, within its existing borders, the Reich could not maintain its economic independence and political sovereignty vis-à-vis the Anglo-Saxon powers, nor could it hope to remain the most powerful military force on the continent. Lack of raw materials and a rapidly expanding urban population had already led to a growing reliance on world trade while increasing Germany's vulnerability to economic exploitation by foreign-owned companies, particularly the large trusts in America. The only way to protect the German economy from further infiltration by the Anglo-Saxon powers was to seek a rapid military overthrow of England in the present war, and the only way to achieve this was via the introduction of unrestricted submarine warfare, which would destroy British naval power once and for all. The defeat of England would then be followed by the conquest of 'Lebensraum' in the east, which would enable Germany to solve its demographic and social problems, protect its agriculture from outside competition and significantly decrease its reliance on international trade.

Gruber's insistence on the need for 'Lebensraum' and his fanatical belief in the necessity of agriculture as the basis for Germany's survival as a world power had much in common with Heinrich Claß's earlier programme for a greater German Reich, set forth in the pseudonymously published pamphlet *Wenn ich der Kaiser wär'* (1912). Unlike Claß in 1912, however, Gruber did not seek to deny the fact that the Catholic Centre Party and the revisionist wing of the SPD were also moving to the right, particularly where issues such as submarine warfare and the need to win a 'peace with victory' were concerned. For this reason he was determined that his new organisation should exist 'above parties', i.e that it should seek to recruit members from across the political spectrum and irrespective of previous party affiliation. This could already be seen in the wording of the original manifesto, which stated that the committee had been formed with just one purpose in mind, namely to bring together 'the combined forces of our nation for the achievement of one goal only: [the] rapid, merciless overthrow of England':

It is not domestic political goals, war aims or sectional interests which have brought us men of various political persuasions together. What we want is merely the following: 1. We want to enlighten the people about the dangers which would threaten us from an undefeated England, so that the will to hold out and achieve victory can be strengthened. 2. We want, as from today, to mobilise all the forces and means at our disposal to defend ourselves against the efforts which will be made to throttle us economically after the war.[70]

In other words, the committee would avoid other, more contentious issues, particularly the question of domestic political reform, and instead focus on its propaganda activities in favour of unrestricted submarine warfare and a 'strong peace' which would secure Germany's future as a world power.

In the meantime, Gruber's attempts to create a non-partisan approach to the submarine question were reflected in his correspondence with those chosen to act as guest speakers at his rallies, including the Catholic Professor Martin Spahn of Straßburg and the Protestant

Pastor Gottfried Traub of Düsseldorf, who was a left-liberal member of the Prussian Landtag. Thus, on 9 September 1916 Gruber wrote to Traub, who had been chosen to speak at the committee's first public rally in Munich on 18 September:

We . . . set great value by the fact that, when you speak, a person from the Centre Party will be in the chair, and that likewise, when the Centre Party speaker comes, the deputy Hübsch [a liberal member of the Bavarian Landtag] will be chairing the session. Our strength lies in the fact that members of all the bourgeois parties have set their party differences aside in order to concentrate on the great national goal.[71]

Similarly, on 17 March 1917 Gruber told Spahn, who had offered to come and speak in Munich on the subject of the 'crisis of English world power':

With regard to the *neutrality* of the ground on which the Volksausschuß f[ür] die rasche Niederkämpfung Englands operates you can rest fully assured . . . With our meetings we have adopted the rule that the chairman should belong to a different party from that of the speaker. For instance recently the Reichsrat Pfleger spoke under the chairmanship of Oberregierungsrat Rohrer. We regard this as the correct course of action in order to make clear our position of independence above the parties. But if you were to *insist* that a Centre Party person should be in the chair, then we would be able to make an exception this time.[72]

In the end Gruber himself chaired the rally at which Spahn gave his speech on 28 March 1917. According to newspaper reports the following day he used the opportunity to re-emphasise the importance of overcoming internal political divisions within Germany in order to concentrate all forces on defeating the external enemy.

The Mammonism of the whole world has united in order to crush us. We must steel our will towards victory, since the worst still lies in front of us. We must put behind us all the divisions in our domestic politics and focus solely on the goal of victory.[73]

There is also some evidence to suggest that individual Social Democrats, such as the former Marxist/radical imperialist Paul Lensch and the revisionist Eduard David, were persuaded to become members of the Volksausschuß, although in the case of David in particular this evidence is far from conclusive.[74] Another possible member was the SPD Reichstag deputy Max Cohen-Reuß, who since the outbreak of the war had been a champion of reconciliation with (Tsarist) Russia and an ardent supporter of all-out economic warfare against England.[75] The same applied to Paul Lensch, who contributed articles not only to *Die Glocke* but also to right-wing annexationist newspapers such as *Der Tag*. In an article which appeared in late November 1916, for instance, he wrote:

The facts of geography mean that England, by launching its hunger blockade against us, is also in danger of starving out its own loyal ally Russia, and indeed it is the Russian friend which is being made to suffer more than the German enemy.

Germany, he continued, should draw the appropriate conclusion from the objective clash of interests between Russia and Britain and make peace overtures to the Russians in order to resist the coming 'world domination of the Anglo-Saxons'.[76]

And yet, despite Gruber's extensive efforts to establish his committee on a broad, non-partisan basis, it was clear from the outset that his only long-term reliable support outside of Bavaria would come from the representatives of heavy industry and the established parties of the right – i.e the Conservatives, Free Conservatives and National Liberals. Count Westarp, the Conservative leader, refrained from joining in person so as not to tie the hands of his party; but his friendly attitude and willingness to cooperate were clearly revealed in a letter he wrote to the committee on 19 September 1916:

The [Reichstag] deputy Weilnböck has informed me of your request that I might speak in Munich at a meeting [of the Volksausschuß] to be arranged in October. On Saturday the 23rd of this month, from half past nine in the morning until one o'clock, I shall be stopping off in Munich on my way down to Salzburg. I would very much appreciate it if I were allowed to use this occasion to discuss the matter of my lecture with the gentlemen concerned and I therefore request your cooperation in informing me whether and where I might be able to find Herr Geheimrat von Gruber or the other gentlemen at the time mentioned above.[77]

Similarly, the leader of the Free Conservatives, Freiherr Zedlitz und Neukirch, gave his positive assessment of the aims of the Volksausschuß in a newspaper article on 21 September 1916:

The logical conclusion from this assumption, that the defeat of England is our main goal in this war, is self-evident. . . . [We must] demand the full and ruthless deployment of all our weapons of war against England, in so far as these are necessary for the attainment of victory.[78]

The National Liberals were even more enthusiastic in their response, and several of the party's leaders – including the influential member of the Bavarian Reichsrat Franz von Buhl – were among the founder members of the committee. On 22 October 1916, for instance, Gustav Stresemann gave a ringing endorsement to the propaganda activities of the Volksausschuß in a speech delivered to a meeting of the local National Liberal association in the Palatinate region:

We can only welcome the fact that today an awareness of the significance of the struggle against England prevails on all sides [of the political spectrum]. The instinct of the people has in this respect reached a more accurate and better understanding than any diplomacy. One can say what one will against the Volksausschuß für die rasche Niederkämpfung Englands; all the same it is merely the product of a genuine feeling in the soul of the German people and it must by its very nature appear strange that certain Democrats, who otherwise never miss an opportunity to declare themselves for the people, suddenly find themselves sneering at certain populist trends when these trends seem to go in directions other than that prescribed for them by their patented version of democracy. At any rate we should not doubt for a minute that in this struggle between England and Germany it is not a question of larger or smaller victories, but rather a question of victory or defeat, of grandeur or decline, and that we would become a nation of beggars at England's mercy and the slaves of Europe were we to be completely defeated by England.[79]

Continuing in the same vein, Stresemann went on to illustrate how closely related the issues of war aims, submarine warfare and opposition to Bethmann Hollweg had become both for him and for other members of his party:

Some people have described our position on foreign policy as an avowal of brutal power politics, and have set against this the idea of a policy of mutual understanding [*Verständigungspolitik*], by which they set great store. But the history of the past twenty-five years is a lesson in the complete collapse of a foreign policy based on abandoning our claims to world political expansion in order to earn the sympathies of other nations and thereby to maintain world peace.[80]

A similar enthusiasm for the aims of the Volksausschuß was also evident among members of the Agrarian League. Gustav Roesicke, for instance, who had hitherto repeatedly shied away from adopting an openly anti-English stance for fear that this would divert attention from Germany's territorial ambitions against Russia, now wrote to his parliamentary colleague Count Westarp on 23 September 1916 urging him to take an active part in promoting the new government war loan.

If ever our government finally recognises the need to put up an energetic fight against England . . . then it is also vital that it has sufficient financial resources at its disposal in order to implement and carry out this task. We should not refuse them this, otherwise we too will be responsible for creating the conditions under which such a war can no longer be waged . . . Indeed, things have reached such a point that even the most stupid among us must recognise the need to deploy all the military means available to us against England. Nor can we go on underestimating England's contribution to the war on land, which is worthy of our respect and in some instances is demonstrating a superiority over our own weapons.[81]

And a day later, on 24 September, the Bavarian wing of the Agrarian League itself issued an appeal to its members to sign up for the war loan, in which it accused England of being the 'main instigator of the war against Germany' and of having committed the crime of 'racial desecration' (*Rassenschande*) by setting 'coloured troops against our white army like dogs'. The death of Lord Kitchener, 'this English blood hound', who was drowned at sea in June 1916, was to serve as a preliminary warning to the English people that they could go 'this far and no further' (*bis hierher und nicht weiter*). The appeal was signed on behalf of the Agrarian League by three of the most prominent members of the Volksausschuß für die rasche Niederkämpfung Englands: Ludwig Beckh, Luitpold Weilnböck and Ludwig Wenng.[82]

Apart from this impressive show of right-wing support for the Volksausschuß and its aim of bringing about a 'rapid overthrow' of England via full use of the submarine weapon, there are also signs of occasional disagreements between its more moderate and its more radical members, particularly where questions of broader war aims and of relations with the Bavarian authorities were concerned. In early October 1916, for instance, a dispute occurred between two Progressive members of the committee, the Bavarian Archivrat Dr Fritz Gerlich and the Prussian Pastor Gottfried von Traub, with the latter accusing the former of having expressed support for the idea of returning Alsace-Lorraine to France in exchange for peace. The charge was rigorously denied by Gerlich, who insisted that he had merely tried to demonstrate a point, namely that if the government refused to consider the use of unrestricted submarine warfare, then it would be forced, sooner or later, to seek a separate peace agreement with France as the only means of bringing about an end to the war. He personally was in favour of an 'all-out struggle against England' as he did not share the government's view 'that France is willing to make peace if we show moderation and a willingness to compromise'.[83]

A second, more serious dispute emerged at the beginning of 1917, this time between Gruber and the more radical Prince Friedrich zu Löwenstein, brother of the Bavarian Reichsrat Prince Albert zu Löwenstein. Although the details of this dispute are somewhat unclear, it seems to have involved a complaint which the Volksausschuß had received from the king's personal secretary von Dandl regarding the distribution of false reports (*Streiflichter*) about the royal audience which had taken place in the summer of 1916. Gruber was in favour of a conciliatory response, whereas Löwenstein wished to reject von Dandl's complaint and thereby provoke a final break with the Bavarian government.[84] Other arguments centred on whether the committee should retain or discard its original name and on the question of its future relationship to the established political parties.[85] At about the same time Gruber himself appears to have resigned from the chairmanship of the committee, although he continued to play an active role in right-wing and annexationist politics and later re-emerged as the third chairman (in practice leader) of the German Fatherland Party in Bavaria.[86]

By the beginning of 1917 even some of the committee's most loyal supporters were becoming disillusioned with the internal feuding that was going on. Thus Ludwig Wenng, the head of the Agrarian League's office in Munich, wrote to his colleague, Luitpold Weilnböck, on 11 January expressing his misgivings over a resolution calling on the military authorities to execute all captains of armed British merchant vessels who fell into their hands.

If this decision as it appeared in the form in which it was set out yesterday . . . should be laid before one of our public meetings, then it will doubtless cause a scandal, especially if – in spite of our commitment to openness – the audience is not strictly vetted beforehand.[87]

The letter went on to suggest a private meeting between the two men to discuss the future of the committee, and concluded: 'Do not take it the wrong way if I say that sometimes when I take part in these meetings I have the feeling of being in a madhouse.'[88]

In spite of this evidence of significant internal divisions and of a growing cynicism among its chief members, the Volksausschuß für die rasche Niederkämpfung Englands was at least partially successful in the achievement of its aims. It was the first right-wing pressure group of its kind actively to seek a position 'above parties', an aim which could be traced back to the unsuccessful *Sammlungspolitik* at the turn of the century, but which now involved attempts to recruit Catholics and anti-Prussian Bavarians as well as Protestants and Pan-German extremists into the same, broadly based mass party of the right. It had appealed to emotions of fear and greed, exploiting the war-weariness of large sections of the Bavarian population and the particularist ambitions of the south German states in order to further the struggle for unrestricted submarine warfare and the final overthrow of England. Above all, it had contributed to the polarisation of the war aims debate in Germany and thus helped to create the poisoned political atmosphere which eventually led to the downfall of Bethmann Hollweg in July 1917.

At the same time, the formation of the Volksausschuß and the fierce public debates which it provoked with its opponents led to the final breakdown of what remained of the *Burgfriede*, or political truce between the parties declared at the beginning of the war. In particular, it made it all the more difficult for moderates on the left to continue to argue that Germany was still fighting an essentially defensive war against Tsarism. This fact was immediately seized upon by radical newspapers such as the anti-war *Leipziger Volkszeitung*, which commented on 20 September 1916, the day after the first appearance of the Volksausschuß in public:

We interpret these events to mean that the slogan taken up so enthusiastically by the majority faction of the Social Democrats: Down with Tsarism! no longer has any claim to validity. It has been overtaken by the imperialist Pan-German battle-cry: Down with England![89]

The same paper also quoted from a speech by the prominent party theoretician and anti-war activist Karl Kautsky at the SPD national conference in September 1916:

The time for putting up smoke screens and keeping quiet has passed. Anyone who fails to take a clear and unambiguous stand against the deliberate perversion of our party into the exact opposite of what it has stood for over the past half-century inevitably falls into the role of accomplice, who is looked upon with even more contempt than the criminal himself.[90]

Indeed, the division within the SPD now cut across traditional lines between orthodox Marxists and revisionists, so that the chief opponents in the old 'theological' disputation, Kautsky and Eduard Bernstein, were now at one in calling for an immediate end to Socialist support for the war effort. What brought this opposition together was no longer a particular interpretation of Marxist doctrine, but rather an abhorrence (on ethical grounds) of nationalism and militarism and a common commitment to the ideals of socialism and democracy. Almost alone among the anti-war groups, it was these Independent Socialists who recognised the true dangers of German anglophobia, and they looked on with horror as former comrades were gradually won over to the support of militarism and to types of aggressive nationalism more commonly associated with the right. By contrast, the Majority Socialists, who organised a rally in Munich on 4 September 1916, criticised the submarine campaigners on the grounds only that they threatened the domestic position of the Reich Chancellor and the long-term goal of internal political reforms. In other words, they failed to address the more immediate issue of whether the war itself could still be justified as being in the interests of the German working class or of the nation as a whole. This was, of course, a major weakness in the majority SPD's stance at this time, and helps to explain the growing support for the more radical Independents in the final phases of the war.[91]

For the time being, however, the Volksausschuß and its divided opponents on the left were able to have only an indirect impact on the important political debates which took place in the autumn of 1916 and which formed the final backdrop to the launching of unrestricted submarine warfare at the end of January 1917. In this particular instance it was less the outspoken views of the annexationist right and more the hidden attitudes of the Catholic Centre Party and the Progressive Party which threatened, in the final instance, to undermine the authority of Bethmann Hollweg on the submarine issue.

The final move towards unrestricted submarine warfare

I have already briefly sketched the military situation chiefly responsible for the intensification of anglophobic agitation throughout Germany in the months after February 1916. The tensions which had developed over the question of unrestricted submarine warfare and the government's continued negotiations with the United States over this issue were now brought out into the open and ruthlessly exploited by the chauvinistic and xenophobic opponents of the Chancellor. In this poisoned atmosphere even the Kaiser was suspected of harbouring secret pro-English tendencies, tendencies which threatened not only to undermine the German war effort but also to destroy Germany from within. Among the charges levelled against him, for instance, was the following accusation, contained in an anonymous flysheet circulated by an anti-Semitic group in the summer of 1916:

The Kaiser is completely surrounded by Jews. His most powerful advisers are the Israelites Ballin, Rathenau, v. Mendelssohn, Arnold, James, Simon, v. Bleichröder, Goldschmidt-Rothschild, Carow, Koppel and others, who as members of an international plutocracy take full advantage of the fact that their relatives sit in high places in all the governments of foreign lands. Even the Kaiser's Oberhofmeister, Frhr. v. Reischach, is the son of a Frankfurt Jewess, Bertha Bonn. The Kaiser's first Leibarzt, Dr v. Ilberg, comes from a Jewish family. A pillar of the England Party [*Engländerpartei*] is Countess Maria Esther Waldersee, an American Jewess, née Lee, who works in Waldeck on behalf of the English *Judenmission*. The Kaiser is visibly in close alliance with the Jews, associated with, among others, His Excellency Paul v. Herrmann, the son of a Jewish stockbroker in Berlin. Helfferich, whom the Jews have selected to be the next Reich Chancellor, is himself treated by them as one of their own. The exclusion of Germanic elements is apparent everywhere, and so it is now high time to form a front against the suppression of *Deutschtum* in Germany and against the delivery of the government into the hands of the Jews and the international money powers.[92]

It was against this background of increased anti-Semitic agitation at home that the German army conducted its so-called *Judenzählung* or 'Jew count' in November 1916. This was the order sent out by the Prussian Minister of War, Adolf Wild von Hohenborn, to all German military commanders, instructing them to determine, by means of a census, the number of Jews of conscription age who were currently serving at the front, behind the front or not at all.[93] Since the results of the count were never published, the suspicion that Jews were war profiteers and army shirkers remained. This message was also systematically reinforced by anti-Semitic agitators themselves, who now frequently accused both the Chancellor and the Kaiser of conniving in the expansion of Jewish influence over the war economy, or of being indebted to 'international Jewish finance'.[94]

In the meantime, the moderate opponents of unrestricted submarine warfare continued to argue that the best means of securing an early peace settlement lay in a concentration of military forces against the east, with the aim of knocking Russia out of the war and securing its massive potential in foodstuffs and mineral resources. Only in this way could the government hope to overcome the food shortages caused by the tightening of the Allied naval blockade, which undesirable elements at home had sought to blame on the Jews. The most outspoken proponent of this view was the Baltic German Paul Rohrbach, who circulated a confidential memorandum on the subject to members of the government in the autumn of 1916.

As the situation appears today I am absolutely certain that it is not the ideas of the Chief of the General Staff [i.e. Falkenhayn], but those of Hindenburg on the conduct of the war in the east – the overthrow of Russia through occupation of the Baltic coast, Finland, Petersburg with the Putilov works, the arms stores, the shipyards, government institutions, etc. – that are the most suited to bring about a general turn in the direction of victory. Even today there is no need to doubt the victorious self-assertion of Germany. But it is already less likely that victory will come about through pursuing the alternative methods of the Chief of the General Staff than would be the case if one were to proceed according to the plans laid down by Hindenburg.[95]

The defeat of Imperial Russia would in turn create the necessary conditions for the realisation of plans for a German-dominated European customs union in the shape of Friedrich Naumann's *Mitteleuropa* (1915), and in addition would guarantee German military preponderance in the Balkans and the Near East. From here it would be possible to exert even greater pressure on the English position in Egypt and the Suez Canal, with the aim of forcing England to make substantial concessions in the colonial and commercial spheres. Thus Rohrbach wrote on another occasion towards the end of 1916: 'Only with its [i.e. Turkey's] help will we be in a position to reach the turning point where we can force England to grant us the position in the world economy and world politics which we need.'[96]

Rohrbach's emphasis on the strategic importance of the Suez Canal was shared by Carl Peters, the former colonial governor of German South West Africa, who questioned the effectiveness of the submarine blockade and Zeppelin raids and pointed out that the British empire could always move its capital to Manchester or Liverpool, or even to Cape Town or Sydney: 'That we might, in some circumstances, be able to destroy the British in Europe, and yet not be able to destroy its position in the entire world, is not the view taken by the best experts on England.' Peters therefore concluded that:

England can only be directly defeated from a military point of view on the Suez Canal and in the region of the Nile, as the brilliant strategist Napoleon already had the insight to recognise. It is here that we find the nape of this world empire, the dividing line between its western and its eastern halves. In the final analysis the battle for the Suez Canal is at present being fought out on the Danube, just as it was previously fought out at Gallipoli, in Athens, as well as in Salonika. If a forward move into the land of the pyramids, in conjunction with our allies the Turks, becomes a military possibility for us, then the war of attrition in the west, the U-boats and the Zeppelins will also ultimately bring proud old Albion to its knees. Then the peace, which we all yearn for, will come to war-torn Europe as well as to the overseas world.[97]

These arguments were in turn countered by the admiralty, which continued to press the case for unrestricted submarine warfare on the grounds that England would be brought to its knees within six months, thus ensuring victory for Germany at sea before American intervention could make any decisive contribution to the Entente's war effort. Thus, in an important memorandum on 22 December 1916, Admiral von Holtzendorff, still the Chief of Admiralty Staff, argued that it was now time to brush aside the objections of the neutral powers and to make clear that Germany 'does not lag behind England in terms of its will-power and its physical strength'.

To this end, unrestricted submarine warfare is the only given means at our disposal; it will turn the tables [on England] and carry the economic war into the heart of enemy territory; it will lead to a rapid re-think among the neutrals as to where the true force of mind and action really lies.[98]

Similarly, in a reply to Carl Peters on 9 January 1917, the retired admiral Kirchhoff wrote:

The 'war of attrition' on land and on water, and in the air, is already sufficient to bring England slowly to the point of surrender. It can already foresee the imminence of its bloody demise. It already knows that it cannot keep on waging war on land and at sea for ever, that above all other things it cannot hope to win . . . We will be victorious in all areas, we can defeat England if we want to. And we do want to![99]

Bethmann Hollweg himself had been able to ensure the postponement of unrestricted submarine warfare at the end of August 1916 only by emphasising the direct military dangers which might result from an immediate intervention by European neutrals such as Holland and Denmark, dangers that, for the time being, the OHL was also prepared to take seriously. On 1 October, however, Hindenburg let it be known that the military situation in the Balkans had improved and that a defence against a possible British landing in Denmark and Holland was now assured, thus leading to a new dispute between the civilian and military heads of government similar to the one which had previously taken place between Bethmann and Falkenhayn in the first half of 1916.[100] The Chancellor was left having once again to assert his own responsibility for a decision which was not merely military, but fundamentally political. In a private letter to a Professor Wach in Leipzig on 10 October, he wrote with regard to the submarine question:

... *[I]n principle* I can neither approve nor reject it. The only deciding factor for me is its *practical* effects. If I manage to convince myself that it would bring us closer to a victorious end to the war, then I will go ahead with it, otherwise not.[101]

In these weeks, however, the Chancellor's freedom of movement in the struggle over submarine warfare was still further restricted by two factors. First, as we have seen, representatives of the right-wing associations and their allies in heavy industry were still petitioning the Kaiser and the civilian and military authorities for an early opening of unrestricted submarine warfare. Some of them even went as far as to threaten that the success of the new war loan would depend on ruthless employment of the Zeppelins and submarines, and almost all of them supported a change of leadership at the top. The American journalist C.W. Ackerman, for instance, remembered being invited by the Foreign Office to go with a group of German correspondents in October 1916 to visit the industrial centres of Cologne, Essen and the Rhine valley.

In Essen I met Baron von Bodenhausen and other directors of Krupp's. In Düsseldorf at the *Industrieklub* I dined with the steel magnates of Germany and at Homburg-on-the-Rhine I saw August Thyssen, one of the richest men in Germany and the man who owns one-tenth of Germany's coal and iron fields. The most impressive thing about this journey was what these men said about the necessity for unrestricted submarine warfare. Every man I met was opposed to the Chancellor.[102]

Secondly, the Chancellor lost further ground to the OHL when the Centre Party's chief spokesman in the Main Committee of the Reichstag, Adolf Gröber, put forward a motion on the submarine question which hinted quite clearly at a possible conflict of interest between political and military objectives and called upon the Chancellor to 'make his decisions essentially dependent on those of the Supreme Command'.[103] By adopting such a resolution, the Reichstag in effect denied itself the right to intervene in purely technical matters, and thus put a decision of high policy in the hands of the military. The implication was that Bethmann Hollweg would retain the support of the majority parties in the Reichstag only if he in turn obeyed the orders of the Supreme Command.

On top of this, in early November 1916 another traditionally moderate party, the Progressive People's Party or left-liberals, suddenly issued its own statement disowning the allegedly pro-English line taken by the big left-liberal newspapers, the *Berliner Tageblatt* and *Frankfurter Zeitung* and declaring its support for the principle of unrestricted submarine warfare:

We are pleased . . . to be able to note that with regard to the stance taken by our Reichstag *Fraktion* on the question of unrestricted submarine warfare a complete change has taken place since the spring and that it now fully recognises the suitability of the U-boat war as a means to bring about the defeat of England . . . The counter-arguments against the intensification of the U-boat war are well known to us, and it is not our intention to dismiss them as irrelevant. In particular, we are fully conscious of the fact that the entry of the United States into the war would bring us a great number of disadvantages, and that for this reason not every opportunity to begin the submarine war would be a suitable one.[104]

Although the Progressives distanced themselves from the other non-socialist parties by claiming that it was 'not admissible to leave the choice of timing [for the opening of unrestricted submarine warfare] to the leaders of the field army alone', they also stopped well short of endorsing the Chancellor's own position. On the contrary, the new policy statement continued:

We have – as already mentioned – complete confidence in the leaders of our General Staff and regret only one thing, that these two men were not given the opportunity at an earlier date to establish themselves in their current posts. But we also wish that this confidence be installed to the same degree in our Admiralty Staff, whose views tend to be disregarded in discussions on the U-boat question. We cannot, however, express the same degree of confidence in those officers of the Reich who are responsible for the conduct of economic affairs, and, to our regret, we must also say the same with regard to the conduct of foreign policy as well.[105]

By this time, even the most loyal supporters of the Chancellor were beginning to wonder whether he had not in fact lost control of the public debate over the submarine issue, thus seriously undermining his credibility as a statesman capable of making important political decisions. On 18 September 1916, for instance, Max Weber wrote to his friend Friedrich Naumann: 'I do not understand the Chancellor any more. It seems that he cannot accomplish what he believes is correct. If this is so, then he should go.' And a few weeks later, on 27 October, he told Heinrich Simon, one of the editors of the *Frankfurter Zeitung*: 'Bethmann is a heavy burden for us! This has always been my view. It is only because of the submarine hysteria – and they are hysterical – that I am forced to support him out of sheer necessity. And where is his successor?'[106]

It was against the background of this annexationist agitation that Bethmann Hollweg had to conduct his negotiations with President Wilson for a possible mediated peace, negotiations which at any rate failed completely to bear any fruit. The idea of a separate peace with Russia, which had been seriously considered during 1916, was now in effect ruled out in advance when the Central Powers resurrected the kingdom of Poland on 5 November. On the other hand, the forces which favoured a compromise peace in the west were fatally weakened by the German peace offer of 12 December, which, far from offering a step towards a peace without victors or vanquished, was merely intended to provide a moral and political basis for resuming unrestricted submarine warfare against Britain. As Ludwig Wenng – who, as a member of the Volksausschuß für die rasche Niederkämpfung Englands, was certainly no admirer of Bethmann Hollweg – put it, the 'peace offer' was 'in all circumstances a very clever undertaking, whose purpose, among other things, was to put the enemy in the wrong and to offer proof to our army, as well as the mass of the people – who are undoubtedly suffering from war-weariness – that Germany is not responsible for the continuation of the war'.[107]

The OHL, always somewhat sceptical about the feasibility of a Peace Note, had agreed to it on two conditions: that the military situation, especially in Romania, be favourable at the time of publication, so the 'peace offer' would not be interpreted abroad as a sign of weakness; and that the *Hilfsdienstgesetz*, the new law introducing compulsory labour service for Germans outside the armed forces, be passed by the Reichstag. The fall of Bucharest on 6 December and the acceptance of the *Hilfsdienstgesetz* four days previously fulfilled these conditions, and so both civilian and military authorities agreed that the time had come to publish the German peace offer.[108] After the offer had been rejected by the Entente powers, Bethmann could no longer resist the combined pressure of military and public opinion for the removal of restrictions on submarine warfare.

By the beginning of 1917 the Kaiser himself had also moved away from the moderate position he had previously held on the submarine question, first and foremost because Hindenburg had threatened to resign unless restrictions against sinking unarmed or neutral merchant ships were lifted. On 9 January, at a Crown Council held at Schloss Pless in Silesia, the Kaiser now expressed full support for this type of warfare which all his military and naval advisers had declared would lead to England's 'being forced to its knees' within four to six months. If America declared war then 'so much the better'. With a feeble 'If success beckons, then we must act', Bethmann acquiesced and agreed to the launching of unrestricted submarine warfare from 1 February.[109]

Despite this humiliating defeat and the further embarrassment caused to his government by the publication of the Zimmermann telegram at the beginning of March, Bethmann did not resign. For domestic political reasons he may even have welcomed the decision in favour of unrestricted submarine warfare, because at least now the Pan-Germans would not be able to say that the government had had the means to defeat Britain but had refused to use it. On the other hand, it is also clear that the Chancellor did not expect any major results from the use of the submarine weapon and indeed believed that it would be the ruin of Germany. As he told Admiral von Müller on the evening after the Pless conference in Silesia:

Yes, I had to give way to the military arguments, but as I see the future, we shall make the enemy tire of the war in the end, but not until they have achieved notable successes by pushing us back in France and Belgium to the Maas, with the capture of many guns and the taking of a host of prisoners. Then we shall be forced to sign an exceedingly modest peace.[110]

In the long run, of course, the United States' entry into the war on 6 April – a direct consequence of the decision taken at Pless – was more than enough to tip the balance of economic and military power against Germany and its increasingly exhausted allies. By December 1917 there were already 176,000 American troops in France, and by March 1918 the total had reached 318,000. These were the vanguard of a much larger force of 1.3 million Americans deployed in the Allied offensive of August 1918, which finally forced the German Supreme Command to sue for peace.[111]

6 The Anglo-American powers and the collapse of the German empire

In many ways the beginning of the year 1917 marks the major turning point of the First World War. Two developments now determined not only the course of the war itself, but also subsequent world history: in April 1917 the United States Congress declared war on Germany and in November 1917 the Bolshevik revolution forced Russia out of the conflict. The American action not only helped to tilt the balance of military power in favour of the Allies, but, for many right-wing Germans at least, also served to confirm existing fears and anxieties about the alleged Anglo-American domination of the world. By contrast, the Bolshevik revolution, which occurred only a few months later, offered Germany the chance to realise its most cherished war aim: the defeat of the Entente in its entirety and the creation of a new European order under German leadership. Or, as the Kaiser put it in one of his famous marginal notes:

The victory of the Germans over Russia was the precondition for the revolution, which was the precondition for Lenin, who was the precondition for Brest [Litovsk]! The same applies in the west! First victory in the west and collapse of the Entente, then we shall make conditions which they will have to accept! And they will be framed purely in accord with our interests.[1]

In terms of German domestic politics, 1917 also represented a great watershed, particularly as regards the government's official press policy and the ever-growing power of the military to intervene in civilian affairs. Indeed, one of the first actions taken by Hindenburg and Ludendorff following their appointment in the autumn of 1916 was to dismiss the head of the War Press Office, Major Erhard Deutelmoser, whom they considered to be too strong a supporter of Bethmann Hollweg.[2] This was followed almost immediately by the decision to lift the ban on the public discussion of war aims, which took effect from the end of November.[3] Deutelmoser, who now served as the press secretary to the Foreign Office, was well aware that this move was designed to encourage further attacks on the Chancellor from the annexationist right. With the support of Bethmann Hollweg he made some last-minute calls for moderation, which were simply ignored by the Supreme Command.[4]

On top of this came the overthrow of the Tsar in Russia in March 1917, an event which brought with it a considerable increase in the activities of the German peace movement and the outbreak of the first serious wave of industrial strikes caused by almost three years of continued food shortages. When in April the bread ration was decreased yet again by one quarter, over 200,000 munitions workers in Berlin came out on strike, demanding a fairer distribution of foodstuffs, shorter working hours and higher wages. As an earlier police report warned on 14 March 1917:

The current mood among the broader sections of the populace is extraordinarily depressed. A great war-weariness [has set in] everywhere. The food shortages are continually getting worse. The most basic foodstuffs, such as potatoes, are no longer obtainable, [and] the few turnips are poor and frozen. Cabbages can be acquired only with great difficulties. The prices for normal items of clothing are astronomical and quite beyond the means of the less well off . . . As a result of the food shortages a truly lamentable mood has developed among the munitions workers, and this is being made full use of by radical elements.[5]

Increasingly, too, political demands were being made by strike leaders alongside the usual economic demands: the assumption of immediate peace negotiations, the lifting of the state of siege, the release of political prisoners and the introduction of a democratic franchise in Prussia. In Berlin itself, a majority of Social Democratic workers went over to the new opposition party, the USPD, founded by Hugo Hasse and Georg Lebedour on 22 April 1917. The leaders of the Majority SPD, Ebert and Scheidemann, found support for the war effort increasingly difficult to maintain among the rank-and-file, and faced growing pressure to alter their own stance in order to prevent further mass defections to the anti-war radicals. Reports from police spies also indicated a worrying growth in support for the extreme left Spartakus group, which advocated violent revolution as a means of bringing an end to the war and maintained a powerful presence in Berlin in spite of the earlier arrest of its two main leaders, Rosa Luxemburg and Karl Liebknecht.[6]

The response of the military authorities to this situation was to combine ever greater censorship at home with the belief that the situation in Russia could be exploited to Germany's advantage before American involvement in the war became too great. In fact, even before the Bolsheviks came to power in November, the weak and largely defensive military policy employed by the Lvov and Kerensky governments played into the hands of the German Supreme Command and allowed it to maintain the illusion that it was still winning the war and could even defeat Britain and America in the long run. This can be seen in

Ludendorff's insistence, in a conversation with Kurt von Lersner in early May 1917, that England could not hold out for much longer under the strain of the U-boat war and would be ready to sue for peace 'in two to three *months* at the latest'.[7] It can also be seen in his new-found emphasis on the need to include provisions for the commandeering of enemy merchant shipping in any future peace settlement. In a memorandum on the subject, drafted for the Kaiser on 11 May 1917, he wrote:

Only such an occupation of the enemy tonnage would enable us to enforce the execution of the peace treaties vis-à-vis England and America, a security which we already possess vis-à-vis our other enemies in the form of occupied territories.[8]

A somewhat different attitude was taken by Bethmann Hollweg and the civilian leadership in Berlin. Although Bethmann had given way to Hindenburg and Ludendorff on the question of submarine warfare, he continued to advocate a broadly based 'policy of the diagonal' at home using domestic reform coupled with a moderate stance on the war aims question as the best means of upholding public support for the war effort. In his view, the key to which side would win the war lay in the question: 'Who has the stronger nerves and the better chance of holding out?'[9] For this reason he began to take an increased interest in the internal conditions of the Allied powers and to forge links with oppositional groups in these countries in the hope of splitting the enemy coalition. The decision to allow representatives of the SPD to attend the peace conference in Stockholm in June 1917, a decision taken against the advice of the Supreme Command, was no doubt part of this strategy.[10] But its underlying motives were already revealed by Bethmann in a speech he delivered before the Reichstag Main Committee on 31 January 1917, in which he outlined the political objectives lying behind the decision in favour of unrestricted submarine warfare:

I am convinced that we will increase the food supply problems in England, but most of all in France and indeed in Italy, to such an extent that England, *who is the soul of this war*, will no longer be able to keep its allies in line, and that then we will have the means to achieve a peace.[11]

True, Bethmann also hinted in this speech that he did not consider it possible to starve England into submission by means of the U-boats alone, and that ultimately a diplomatic solution would have to be found. Nonetheless, over the coming months he continued to permit Helfferich and Zimmermann to give highly optimistic assessments of the effects of submarine warfare in reports to the Reichstag Main Committee, no doubt in order to put renewed pressure on the right-wing parties to tone down their annexationist demands by holding out the prospects of a quick German victory on the continent.[12]

By the summer of 1917, however, real power had passed from the civilian leadership into the hands of Hindenburg and Ludendorff. Although never formally established in constitutional terms, the 'silent dictatorship' had already begun to make itself felt in certain key policy areas even before Bethmann Hollweg's fall from office. The key dispute during the first half of 1917 now centred on the handling of public opinion and in particular the correct stance to be taken towards the anti-annexationist propaganda of the SPD and of the left more generally. In May 1917, for instance, Bethmann had managed with considerable difficulty to dissuade the SPD leaders Ebert and Scheidemann from sponsoring a motion in the Reichstag demanding an immediate peace without annexations, only to have his efforts in effect opposed by the support and encouragement which Hindenburg and Ludendorff gave to the pro-annexationist forces of the right. On 9 June he turned in exasperation to the Foreign Office with the following note:

There are too many people who know that the Supreme Command wants to annex Courland and Lithuania. If the view emerges that we passed up the opportunity for peace with Russia because of annexations then we shall experience [domestic] collapse.[13]

In the meantime the OHL had developed its own alternative policy of an authoritarian-style manipulation of public opinion based on a ruthless suppression of all anti-annexationist groups, especially the Socialist left, and the imposition of an enforced national unity 'from above'. Already in March 1917, for instance, the military censors had prevented *Vorwärts* from publishing the Copenhagen peace declaration of the Russian Socialists against the advice of the Foreign Office.[14] Later in April the OHL itself demanded the creation of a joint military–civilian Propaganda Ministry,[15] and used Bethmann's unwillingness to crush the anti-annexationists as an excuse to agitate for his removal from office. Once again Bethmann found himself reliant solely on the continued support of the Kaiser, but in fact this support was not to last much longer, as the events of July 1917 were to show.

In the end, of course, the idea of a military dictatorship based on a complete suppression of Social Democracy and other democratic forces remained an ideal which was never fully realised by the OHL, even though it did finally succeed in persuading the Kaiser to dismiss Bethmann in the aftermath of the Reichstag Peace Resolution. Nonetheless, the different conceptions of how to conduct domestic political propaganda and uphold morale among the war-weary population remained a key area of tension between the civilian and military authorities throughout the years 1917–18. Increasingly, too, the dispute spilled over to the question of how to combat the growing effectiveness of Allied propaganda following the United States' entry into the war in

April 1917 and the rise to power of Lloyd George and the so-called 'press lords' in England. In particular it became necessary, as all branches of the war leadership recognised, to meet the ideological challenge associated with the democratic programme which the Americans and British had proclaimed for the whole world. The alternative was 'German freedom', although precisely what this might mean was the cause of some bitter rows in Germany between moderates and the extreme right in the final months of the war. For the latter, but not for the former, Britain was and remained the ideological *Hauptfeind* whose overthrow was the ultimate goal in the struggle for world hegemony.

German freedom versus Anglo-Saxon tyranny

On 2 April 1917 Woodrow Wilson made his famous speech to Congress justifying the American declaration of war on the grounds that German autocracy and militarism threatened the peace and freedom of the entire world. The response of the German academic community to these charges can best be seen in a series of lectures which were organised by the Bund deutscher Gelehrte und Künstler in May 1917 and later appeared in book form with the title *Die Deutsche Freiheit*.[16] Adolf von Harnack, for instance, the first contributor, described Wilson's address as 'the most shameless, the most arrogant and the most hypocritical declaration which has been addressed by one head of state to another people since the days of Napoleon', and went on to warn against the dangers of a democratic ideology which 'is now demanding the destruction of our state in the name of pacifism'.[17] In fact, argued Harnack, there was no idealism at all behind America's declaration of war on Germany: it had little popular support outside of Congress, and was largely the work of a small group of 'unscrupulous plutocrats [*Geldmänner*], who . . . have the President in the palm of their hands and dominate his government'.[18]

Similarly, Friedrich Meinecke firmly rejected any transition in Germany to a western-style parliamentary system on the grounds that this was incompatible with the German idea of freedom: 'Parliamentarism is the constitution of the bourgeois democratic state, which is designed to ensure that two sides of the same bourgeois society provide each other with mutual support and assure an alternating period in power.'[19] This was a sentiment shared by all the other contributors, especially Max Sering, who set out to prove that the parliamentary system in Britain was far less democratic and far more prone to abuses of power than the unreformed system in Prussia.[20] In fact, it was only Ernst Troeltsch who was prepared to recognise some of the 'objective achievements' of the western political model; but even he felt bound to defend the German form of constitutional monarchy, which in his view was better equipped to meet the demands of 'modern state power', especially in the area of social policy.[21]

The Foreign Office, or rather its Zentralstelle für Auslandsdienst, also took an interest in this publication, originally intending to use it for propaganda purposes in neutral countries such as Norway, Sweden, Denmark, Holland and Switzerland.[22] This may also explain why one of the contributors, Otto Hintze, was so keen to stress the peaceful intentions of German foreign policy and to play down any suggestions that Germany intended to annex Belgium.

At the start of the war we were in no way thinking of a conquest of Belgium, and we would falsify the entire purpose of the war if we were now to declare this as our war aim. In fact none of us is thinking of an annexation of Belgium, not even the so-called Pan-Germans. We are all basically agreed that the only important thing is to prevent Belgium from falling into the domain of English interests and from becoming a deployment zone for hostile armies. We must and shall have real guarantees against this [danger], just as the Reich Chancellor said, and the quarrel between the parties is merely over where such guarantees can be found.[23]

Among Hintze's more specific conditions for peace, however, was the proposal that Germany should retain Belgium as a 'bargaining counter' to be used in any final negotiations.[24] In addition, he went on to demand the restoration of Germany's overseas colonies and the 'strengthening of our fleet' as the only means of insuring against English aggression in the future.[25] It was quite clear – even to German diplomats – that such views would not make it easy for Germany to win moral support among the remaining neutral countries. For this reason only a very limited number of copies were ordered by the Foreign Office and targeted at specifically pro-German audiences.

A far more stringently anti-American line was meanwhile taken by members of Dietrich Schäfer's Independent Committee for a German Peace, which, although welcoming the introduction of unrestricted submarine warfare, continued to wage a campaign of hostility towards Bethmann Hollweg and the 'new course' in domestic politics. The three most important figures in this respect were Eduard Meyer, Karl Alexander von Müller and Count Ernst zu Reventlow, all of whom had, as we have seen, strong ties to the Reich Naval Office and to Tirpitz personally. Meyer, for instance, in an article published in the *Berliner Neueste Nachrichten* in May 1917, even went as far as welcoming the American declaration of war as a final confirmation of the fact 'that America has never been neutral in this war, but has always been on the side of the Entente'.[26] Any disadvantages to the German war effort, he argued, were easily outweighed by the fact 'that we are finally using our most effective weapon to its full extent [and] that we have thereby gained a realistic chance of bringing the war to a victorious conclusion'.[27]

Similarly, Reventlow had always considered an outright breach in relations with the United States as being preferable to and less dangerous than the 'false neutrality' maintained by the American government in the period 1914–16. Wilson, in his view, had played a dirty trick on the Germans by pretending to espouse the cause of a negotiated peace settlement while doing all he could behind the scenes to prevent a German victory. Such a policy could only be explained as part of a deliberate plan 'to keep down and to weaken Germany . . . and to cultivate Anglo-Saxon solidarity'.[28] This, in turn, was an argument which came to be adopted by large sections of the right-wing press in 1917, especially after Wilson's address to the Congress on 2 April.[29] The overall feeling was best summed up by the Agrarian leader Wangenheim, who spoke for many when he argued that 'the United States cannot do us any more harm if they declare war on us than the harm they are already causing us today'.[30]

Finally, in September 1917 the nationalist *Kölnische Zeitung* took issue with the Anglo-American idea of a 'world crusade for democracy', which both Wilson and Lloyd George had claimed in several speeches to be waging against the Kaiser and 'German militarism'. Rather, in the usual definition of the word, neither England nor the United States actually possessed a truly representative form of government, a fact which merely underlined the well-known hypocrisy and mendacity of their leading statesmen:

The state system which Lloyd George represents in England is an aristocratic one. In England only those who pay an annual rent of at least ten pounds sterling or an equivalent amount are eligible to vote . . . In America, however, just like in France, politics is governed by corruption and greed, or – as Scheidemann and David had the courage to declare recently in Stockholm – by a small group of capitalist-imperialist interests, an oligarchy.[31]

By contrast, the article continued, a 'true' democracy, or a 'democracy which truly deserves the name' was to be found only in Germany, the country in which the form of government most closely corresponded to the will of the people itself. There were three main historical reasons for this: 'Compulsory attendance at school, compulsory military service and universal, equal suffrage. These three basic principles have already been realised in Germany.'[32]

Unfortunately, however, it was becoming clearer every day that such arguments in favour of a fight to the finish with the Anglo-Saxon powers were failing to stiffen the nation's resolve. Not only did the spring and summer of 1917 lead to a massive increase in industrial unrest and strikes, but also on 6 July the Catholic politician Matthias

Erzberger, hitherto a firm supporter of the war aims movement, made his famous statement before the Reichstag Main Committee, in which he advised the government to enter into immediate peace negotiations on the grounds that unrestricted submarine warfare had failed to achieve the desired military effect. This in turn set in motion the train of events which led to the Kaiser's dismissal of Bethmann Hollweg and to the Reichstag Peace Resolution, indicating, at least in theory, that a broad inter-party front made up of Social Democrats, Progressives and the Catholic Centre was now willing to contemplate the abandonment of German war aims as the basis for a peace of understanding.[33]

England, Satan, the Antichrist and anti-Semitism

The events of 1917, the February revolution in Russia and the April strikes in Berlin had meanwhile forced the extreme annexationist movement in Germany to focus its attention once more on domestic issues, and to re-establish the alleged link between the fight against Germany's enemies abroad and the need to suppress the 'enemy within'. Already in April, for instance, the right-wing *Deutsche Kurier* had published a vicious attack on the so-called German 'radical' press which, it claimed, had wrongly judged England's intentions towards Germany and continued to do so, in spite of the damage this had done to national interests.

This is England's last hope: that a victorious Germany will not be able to exploit its victories as a result of domestic struggles fought around democratic phrases; that the false British doctrine of parliamentarism will eventually tempt a victorious Germany into the tried and tested swamp of corruption and inner decomposition.[34]

A similarly anti-democratic message was put forward in a cartoon drawn by Thomas Theodor Heine for the Munich-based satirical magazine *Simplicissimus* in July 1917 under the title 'Germany's parliamentarisation' (fig. 10). Here Woodrow Wilson and John Bull are seen urging 'der deutsche Michel' – the unsuspecting, simple-minded German – to introduce democratic political reform at home, while from all directions wild animals – snakes and tigers and bears – are laying siege to his house. The caption underneath reads: 'Now is the time to start rebuilding your house, Michel. The moment seems to us to be especially favourable.' The message of this cartoon was clear: the parliamentarisation of Germany was being pushed for by its enemies abroad in order to weaken it from within. The former radical Heine, previously famed for his bold satirical attacks on the Kaiser and the Prussian military establishment, now appeared as an out-and-out reactionary and opponent of any kind of political reform in Germany.

10 'Germany's parliamentarisation', from *Simplicissimus*, 31 July 1917

The best indication of the impact of the Russian revolution and the April strikes on internal politics in Germany, however, is a memorandum penned by the Verein Deutscher Eisen- und Stahlindustrieller in August 1917 on the subject of labour unrest and the best means of tackling it. The memorandum warned that the concessions made by the ex-Chancellor Bethmann Hollweg to Social Democracy had had a disastrous effect on national unity and the German war effort. The Reichstag Peace Resolution was a portent of worse things to follow, since it had become clear that the reform process itself was a reflection of the forces of inner decay. In particular, it was no longer simply a question of equal suffrage in Prussia, 'but rather a question of the establishment of parliamentary government, the complete democratisation and republicanisation of our monarchical German Reich'.[35] Nor did the

Verein see the solution in the adoption of the British model of industrial relations, but rather explicitly rejected it on the grounds that this would only advance Germany further on the course towards internal collapse and social revolution.

> In England it has been shown quite clearly that social harmony cannot be created through concessions of all kinds, through the use of arbitration boards etc., since England has experienced ever greater social conflict in spite of the existence of arbitration boards. Unfortunately in Germany most people seem to have no idea of the power of the English trade unions and of their negative [*unheilvoll*] effect on industrial development.[36]

Instead, the only solution which the Verein Deutscher Eisen- und Stahlindustrieller could recommend to the problem of industrial unrest in Germany lay in a rigorous policy of internal repression, one which would 'cut off the wild and alien roots which have developed everywhere and plant healthy views in their place'.[37]

This document is significant for two main reasons. First, it established a clear-cut link between the threat of materialism and class conflict represented by England and the threat of Bolshevism and social revolution coming from Russia. Both were seen as being alien to Germany and Germanic traditions and as threatening the existing Christian monarchical order. Both were also connected, in a very literal sense, with the forces behind the Reichstag Peace Resolution – the Marxist SPD in league with 'unpatriotic' Catholics and left-liberal admirers of Anglo-Saxon capitalism. Indeed, the connection made between England, the birthplace of the industrial revolution, and the growth of an 'internal enemy' inside Germany in the form of strikes and social unrest added a new dimension to German anglophobia in the last two years of the war. In this sense anglophobia itself became part of a broader negation of the ideals of free trade and social and liberal reform associated with the pre-war Liberal government in England, and in particular with radical politicians such as Lloyd George. It was now very much a part of the ideology of the radical right and its industrial backers, who had most to fear from a democratisation of Germany.[38]

The second point to note is how closely these ideas corresponded with the attitude adopted by the Kaiser and some of the leading members of his entourage in the final phase of the war. Indeed, following the Allied rejection of the German peace offer at the end of 1916 Wilhelm also appeared to abandon his previous moderation on issues such as submarine warfare and to take a more active interest in propaganda, particularly propaganda directed against the west and the Anglo-Saxon powers. This in turn, he hoped, would provide a necessary corrective against the trend towards internal dissolution at home and even win some of the German workers away from their revolutionary leaders. More importantly, it would also mark the beginning of Germany's battle to stand firm against the threat of a Wilsonian 'rotten peace' should the U-boats fail to do their job properly.

At the beginning of April 1917, for instance, upon hearing of the United States' declaration of war, Wilhelm intervened directly to demand that the following three points be emphasised by the Foreign Office in its briefings to the German and foreign press:

1. England was behind the Russian revolution and the abdication of the Tsar, whom she has also let down personally. England must now be held responsible for guaranteeing the personal safety of the Tsar and his wife.
2. In reality America has only entered the war against Germany because she needs a cover for creating a large standing army which she otherwise would not have been able to do and which she intends to use in order to protect the big capitalists against the proletariat.
3. Wilson claims that the war was started by the German government and dynasty for its own selfish interests, although he must know that in 1914 the entire German people stood behind its leaders. By contrast, the American war effort is being conducted in the interests of a small group of big capitalists. It is contrary to the real interests of the American people and serves merely as a pretext for strengthening the rule of the big capitalists over the proletariat.[39]

A few months earlier, in January 1917, he had already expressed his inner feelings about the true nature of the war in a letter to his friend Houston Stewart Chamberlain:

The war is a struggle between two *Weltanschauungen*, the Teutonic-German for morality, right, loyalty and faith, genuine humanity, truth and real freedom, against the Anglo-Saxon [*Weltanschauung*], the worship of Mammon, the power of money, pleasure, land-hunger, lies, betrayal, deceit and – last but not least – treacherous assassination!

There could be no compromise between the two systems, he continued: 'one must be *victorious*, the other *go under!*'[40] This was followed in May 1917 by a list of thirteen 'minimum demands' which the Kaiser drew up as the 'guiding considerations' behind any German war aims programme. These 'minimum demands' were then forwarded to the Foreign Office with the express instructions to reject any further peace feelers on the part of the enemy. They included the German occupation of Malta, Madeira, the Azores, the Cape Verde Islands and the French and Belgian Congo as well as the division of Belgium into Wallonia and Flanders and a military convention with Flanders which would ensure that the Flanders coast from Ostend to Zeebrugge remained in German hands. England would be forced to return Gibraltar to Spain and relinquish its control over Cyprus, Egypt and Mesopotamia, which would probably be returned to Turkey. In the east the Kaiser envisaged the annexation of Lithuania, Courland and the Ukraine (with the possibility of adding Latvia and Estonia at a later date), as well as trade treaties, military conventions and compulsory transfer of populations to and from the newly acquired territories. Finally, Germany was to collect more than 100 million marks in war reparations, including payments not only from the major Entente powers such as Britain, France, Italy and the USA, but also from China, Japan, Brazil, Bolivia, Cuba and Portugal.[41]

Above all, however, Wilhelm now viewed England as a satanic, antimonarchist state, bent on subverting God and country and destroying the ruling houses of Europe in order to further its goal of world domination. In his above-mentioned letter to Houston Stewart Chamberlain, for instance, he wrote that the leaders of England and France had 'fallen victim to Satan' and thereby had – perhaps without knowing it – transformed the war into a German 'crusade against *evil* – Satan – in the world, waged by us as *instruments* of the Lord'.

We *instruments of God* will do battle until the band of robbers in the service of Mammon crumble and the *enemies of the Kingdom of God* lie in the dust!, whose coming in the world is at any rate made virtually impossible by the Anglo-Saxon world view. God wants this war, we are His instrument, He will lead it, so we need not fear the outcome, we will suffer, fight and win under His banner! Then we will have peace, a *German* peace, a *God-like* peace, in which the entire liberated world will breathe again; liberated from the Anglo-Saxon satanic pursuit of Mammon![42]

This idea that the Anglo-French powers were in league with a literal (and liberal) Satan perhaps also explains why Wilhelm continued to regard England rather than Russia or the United States as the chief menace to the German empire and indeed to his own person. In particular he seems to have feared Lloyd George, the alleged 'evil genius' behind the overthrow of the Tsar in Russia and of the monarchy in Greece, events which seem to have had a profound impact upon him personally. In June 1917 he even left the following instructions to the Foreign Office in the margins of a report on German diplomatic efforts in Sweden: 'Now all dynasties must join forces *with Me against him* [i.e. Lloyd George]. This core idea is to be strongly cultivated by My representatives in all neutral countries.'[43] The report itself revealed that the Swedish Foreign Minister shared similar views and even believed that Lloyd George was preparing to oust the British royal family (now known as the House of Windsor) in order to have himself elected as president of a radical-democratic republic. Subsequent diplomatic enquiries in Sweden and Spain – conducted on the express instructions of the Kaiser – seemed to confirm these rumours. The German ambassador in Stockholm, for instance, was able to report: 'The King [i.e. Gustavus V] shares the same views on Lloyd George as His Majesty the

Kaiser and King, and fears that a prolongation of the war will lead to a strengthening of revolutionary elements in all countries.'[44] The German ambassador in Madrid confirmed that King Alfonso had heard similar news from London itself, 'where a strong mistrust of Lloyd George holds sway at the royal palace'.[45]

On 20 July 1917, the day after the Reichstag Peace Resolution, Wilhelm told Arndt von Holtzendorff, the brother of the Chief of Admiralty Staff and Albert Ballin's Hapag representative in Berlin, that German foreign policy should now aim towards an understanding 'with Russia, Japan and Mexico!! In this way we would construct a sort of pincer and counter-balance against the Anglo-American alliance'.[46] On the other hand, when informed by Admiral Paul von Hintze, the German ambassador in Christiania (Oslo), that the Norwegian Prime Minister favoured a return to the pre-war balance of power rather than a clear-cut military victory by one side, he noted in a moment of fury: 'That is just what *we do not want*! Balance of power must cease! It was the cause of the war!'[47] And in the autumn of 1917 he balked at a suggestion by the new Chancellor Georg Michaelis to abandon non-essential war aims such as the coast of Flanders, on the grounds that possession of this coastline was a crucial precondition for a German victory in the 'second Punic war' against Britain.

No cessation of the U-boat war until George has submitted. England has . . . *not won* and therefore has *lost* the first Punic War; we, however, have *not* been able to defeat it . . . For this reason we must begin immediate preparations for the second Punic War – this time with better alliance provisions and better chances. Since it will happen. Until one of us *alone* is victorious, there can be no peace in the world! *Great Britain* will never agree to a condominium, and so it must be thrown out.[48]

Thus it would seem that in 1917 the Kaiser was still influenced by the general goals he had pursued since 1897, combined with a growing concern for his position personally should Germany come under the influence of the Anglo-Saxon powers in any post-war settlement. Undoubtedly this made it all the more difficult for opponents of extreme anglophobia, such as the new Foreign Secretary, Richard von Kühlmann, to make their voices heard.[49]

The German army and total war

An equally bellicose and uncompromising approach can be seen in the propaganda produced by or on behalf of the army and the Supreme Command in the years 1917–18, such as the introduction of 'patriotic instruction' at the front and the recourse to so-called 'home' propaganda. Indeed, with the removal of the prohibition on the public discussion of war aims in November 1916, which Ludendorff had repeatedly demanded, responsibility for 'official' propaganda was increasing placed in the hands of the military and its regional command centres. In July 1917 steps were also taken by Section IIIb of the OHL (the office formally responsible only for espionage and counter-espionage) to ensure centralised control over the propaganda efforts of all regional military commanders. This in turn was part of a new political offensive designed to counter the supposed negative effects of the Reichstag Peace Resolution on army and home-front morale.[50]

'Propaganda officers' (*Aufklärungsoffiziere*) were now assigned to each of the army groups and regional military commands and were given the task of organising compulsory lectures on a fortnightly basis. Strict guidelines were also issued by the War Press Office on how these lectures were to be conducted.[51] Particular emphasis was to be placed on the origins of the war, the economic consequences of defeat (especially for German workers) and the need for authority and strict discipline on all fronts. Above all, the war was to be shown to be a result of England's clever manipulation of the 'French lust for revenge and the Russian greed for land'.[52] Propaganda officers were therefore instructed to include examples of the 'cool, calculating English hatred . . . from the *Morning Post* to the Northcliffe Press', and to reinforce this impression by using extracts from the anti-German speeches of leading English politicians, above all Lloyd George and Balfour.[53]

The troops were also to be told that Germany's offers of peace were simply interpreted abroad as a sign of its military weakness and that the Entente, above all England and America, had no real desire for peace.[54] If the war was lost, moreover, the Anglo-Saxon powers would seek to destroy German economic competition for at least the next 100 years. This latter point was made in particular in a lecture delivered to a group of propaganda officers at Imperial Headquarters on 10 August 1917. Here, Oberleutnant Schmetzer of the 21st Army Corps told his fellow officers:

A peace seemingly based on equality would provide England with the means of cutting off our [future] development. England has the ability to introduce tariffs, we do not. England sits in Calais, in Gibraltar, Suez, the Straits of Medina. We do not [have this advantage]. England has the means, even under apparently equal terms, to restrict our imports of raw materials, even to make them impossible, [and] to cut off our exports of finished goods. Whilst a factory might now be able to employ 1000 or 500 workers, later they might be able to employ only 500 or 250. The remainder would flood the job market, at first acting to depress wages, and later, because they were unable to find work anyway, they would emigrate. Then we could be exporting not only machines, but also labour. And what kind of jobs could our workers expect to get abroad? Only those which the Americans and the English had rejected, and these would certainly not be the best jobs. It is therefore a question of the fate of the broad mass of our people.[55]

Such examples of 'patriotic instruction' were part and parcel of a broader intensification of the war effort at home aimed at holding out to the bitter end so as to preserve Germany's war aims. Concessions were even made to the trade unions, whose legal position was greatly strengthened by the so-called auxiliary law at the end of 1916.[56] On the other hand, the general political concessions of the spring and summer of 1917 (such as the Kaiser's promise, made in reaction to the February revolution in Russia, to consider reform of the three-class suffrage in Prussia) were vigorously opposed by the army leadership. Finally, following the October revolution in Russia, the Supreme Command was able to impose the annexationist peace of Brest Litovsk on the defeated Russians with almost total disregard of conventional methods of diplomacy and peace-making. Indeed, the treaties of Brest Litovsk and Bucharest reveal how completely the civilian leadership had subordinated its own war aims programme to the demands of the military, despite the fact that it still paid lip-service to the principles underlying the Reichstag Peace Resolution.

In the meantime, the military authorities did everything in their power to encourage right-wing attacks on the so-called 'radical press', in other words those newspapers that continued to propagate the idea of a negotiated peace settlement in the west or that were seen as a threat to the army's own 'enlightenment' activities. Even a scholar of international fame such as Max Weber, who before the war had been an active supporter of German *Weltpolitik* and *Flottenpolitik*, was not immune from such attacks. In June 1917 the Supreme Command itself intervened to demand the confiscation of an issue of the liberal *Frankfurter Zeitung*, which had printed a strongly worded article by Weber attacking Wilhelm II's 'personal rule' and its damaging effects on German foreign policy and calling for constitutional reform. Weber in turn addressed an angry protest to the Vice Chancellor, Friedrich von Payer, also printed in the *Frankfurter Zeitung*, in which he referred to the censorship action as a 'purely partisan measure'. For the past year and a half, he complained, the censor in Berlin (i.e. General von Kessel) had permitted 'agitation against the Reich government and [now it did so] against the Reichstag committee on constitutional reform and the loyal parties that were not conservative'. It was therefore only to be expected that 'counter-arguments would use strong language as well . . . As long as the press in the pay of heavy industry is not muzzled, uncompromising support for the opposite point of view is a moral responsibility.'[57]

A number of examples indeed confirm Weber's accusation that the main beneficiaries of the Ludendorff dictatorship were the

Pan-Germans and their financial backers. On 19 July 1917, for instance – on the same day as the Reichstag voted in favour of Erzberger's Peace Resolution – the right-wing *Deutsche Tageszeitung* published an article in which it drew a direct line between the *Engländermacherei* of pre-war progressive politicians such as Theodor Barth and the current peace efforts of Payer, Haußmann and Scheidemann, the leaders of the new Reichstag majority.

What the German people and what every rational person now thinks about the powers of judgement possessed by the world-wide authority of progressivism, which once called the encirclement of Germany a 'comical idea', can of course no longer be held in doubt. A truly 'comical' idea, however, is the fact that those people who used to swear by Theodor Barth and now wish to take up the thread which Barth has spun are still claiming the right to have a say on the direction of Germany's foreign policy. It seems almost as if the entire world war has become a 'comical idea' for these incorrigible people. It must now be a matter for those in responsible positions to ensure that such comical advisers are held at arms length from the business of conducting our foreign relations – so that the Fatherland may not come to any harm through such nonsense![58]

And similarly, on 10 July Dietrich Schäfer of the Independent Committee for a German Peace was permitted to publish the following declaration against the forthcoming Peace Resolution which appeared in all newspapers presumed to be reliable in the 'national cause':

The German people have a right to be told whether the government and the Reichstag now wish to go down this road; they have a right to demand that they are shown a clear-cut goal. Further uncertainty, new declarations about a preparedness to consider peace, in whatever form they might come, only give encouragement to the enemy and thereby prolong the war. Germany must demand that every member [of the Reichstag] keeps in mind the present situation and does not waver from the clear conclusions which must be drawn from it by paying too much attention to domestic political questions.[59]

The reverse side of the army's campaign against the Reichstag Peace Resolution and left-liberalism was the increased emphasis on the military goal: a victorious or (as it became known) a 'Hindenburg' peace. A poster calling for subscriptions to the seventh war loan in April 1917, for instance, included the slogan: 'Only a German victory can protect us and the whole of Europe from enslavement to England' (fig. 11). Underneath, a series of cartoons illustrated England's intentions should it win the war. In Africa, Negro tribesmen carrying Union Jacks would attack German settlers and destroy the white man's rule, thus fulfilling Lloyd George's promise to 'liberate the German colonies from the German yoke'. Germany itself would – along with Ireland and India – become victims of English imperialism, crippled by enormous debts and forced to work for the benefit of English capitalists. The cartoon in

11 'German loyalty – Hindenburg peace', from *Görlitzer Nachrichten und Anzeiger* [1917]

the bottom left-hand corner of the poster indeed shows John Bull standing beside 'Michel's' grave and has the words 'English peace' at the bottom. Next to this is written: 'An English officer has declared that the only chance left of an English victory is the Reichstag's opposition to submarine warfare.'

Similar ideas were contained in an anonymous leaflet circulated in Bremen in November 1917, which depicted the terrible consequences if England were allowed to regain control over Belgium in any post-war settlement (fig. 12). In particular the defensive line which Germany had built up to protect ports such as Bremen and Hamburg from English attack would vanish, to be replaced by a permanent English military presence on the continent. This was why – the cartoon suggested – there could be no question of a compromise peace with England until the latter had been completely defeated and driven from mainland Europe. Anything less than this would be a defeat for Germany itself.

The aim of this and other forms of anti-English propaganda was to secure the loyalty of the so-called war aims majority in the press and public opinion as a means of bypassing the Reichstag altogether. Significantly, the three main exceptions to this trend among the 'national' newspapers – the Social Democrat *Vorwärts* and the left-liberal *Frankfurter Zeitung* and *Berliner Tageblatt* – were frequently branded by their enemies as anglophile and unpatriotic. The following, for instance, appeared in a pamphlet written by the Pan-German August Eigenbrot in 1917:

The *Berliner Tageblatt* and *Frankfurter Zeitung* belong to left liberalism, and no doubt the *Frankfurter Zeitung* to the resolute and most ruthless democracy, the *Berliner Tageblatt* in a less overt sense to the *Freisinn* . . . Both papers have close links with the financial and trading world; in all probability it is this circumstance which to the most salient degree has determined the stance of both papers.

Both, he went on to claim, had failed to appreciate the English danger before 1914: 'The *Berliner Tageblatt* and *Frankfurter Zeitung* appear to have defended the German *Engländerei* both from their own inclination and also in contact with official persons.'[60]

In private, Dietrich Schäfer of the Independent Committee was even more dismissive of the *Berliner Tageblatt*, referring to it once in a letter to Colonel Max Bauer, Ludendorff's chief adviser on domestic issues, as a 'dirty Jewish rag'.[61] And on 5 February 1918 the Crown Prince sent a telegram to the Kaiser urgently requesting an immediate ban of the *Frankfurter Zeitung*, the *Berliner Tageblatt* and *Vorwärts* on the western front:

The mischief which these three papers have caused in the minds of our troops over recent months is deplorable. For us leaders,the mood in which officers and troops enter into the great decisive battles cannot be a matter of indifference.[62]

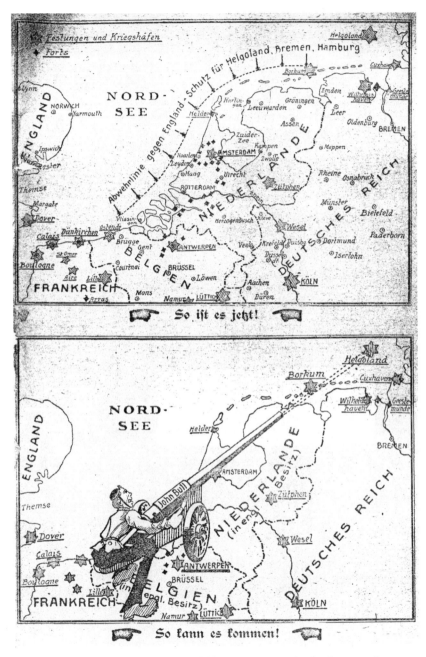

12 'The situation now – and as it could be', anonymous leaflet [1917/18]

The final act in this game came in July 1918, when the Supreme Command forced the Foreign Secretary, Richard von Kühlmann, to resign after the latter had called in the Reichstag for a 'cautious' preparation of German public opinion 'for the possibility of our having to content ourselves with a so-called peace of understanding'.[63] The real reason for the OHL's distrust of Kühlmann, however, was the alleged weakness of his conduct of negotiations at Brest Litovsk and his apparent willingness to accept the idea that the war could no longer be won for Germany by military means alone. This in turn allowed it to maintain that it was the civilian 'loss of nerve', rather than the superiority of the Allies' material and manpower resources, that had caused Germany's defeat in the autumn of that year.

The rise and fall of the German Fatherland Party

Behind the Supreme Command and its campaign against Kühlmann stood the German Fatherland Party (Deutsche Vaterlandspartei), which emerged during the summer of 1917 as a rallying point for those on the nationalistic right who opposed the Reichstag Peace Resolution. Among its leading members were those individuals who had already fought for the overthrow of Bethmann Hollweg in the years 1914–16: Wolfgang Kapp of the Conservative Party, Dietrich Schäfer from the Independent Committee for a German Peace, Heinrich Claß representing the Pan-German League, and in Munich, Max von Gruber, formerly chairman of the Volksausschuß für die rasche Niederkämpfung Englands.[64] This essential line of ideological continuity was confirmed at the founding meeting of the Fatherland Party held in Königsberg (East Prussia) on 2 September 1917, the anniversary of the Battle of Sedan. Here, the newly elected party chairman, Admiral von Tirpitz, declared:

The war has developed into a life and death struggle between two world philosophies: the German and the Anglo-American. The question today is whether we can hold our own against Anglo-Americanism or whether we must sink and become mere manure for others [Völkerdünger] . . . The colossal struggle which Germany is now waging is therefore not one for Germany alone; what is really at issue is the liberty of the continent of Europe and its people against the all-devouring tyranny of Anglo-Americanism. Germany is fighting for a great ideal, and therefore I would cry out to every corner of our Fatherland: 'Germany, awake! Thine hour of destiny has arrived'.[65]

The Fatherland Party now took the lead in producing annexationist and anti-English propaganda on the home front. Tirpitz himself, as well as Kapp, the party's vice-chairman, and various other speakers were constantly on the move, addressing large meetings all over Germany.

Many of these meetings ended in violence after left-wing and anti-war demonstrators attempted to disrupt proceedings. As early as 26 October 1917, Richard Fester, Professor of History at the University of Halle-Wittenberg, told an audience in Halle that an increase in the number of U-boats or an expansion of the German colonial empire would not be enough to avert the danger of a second war with England. Rather, in his own words, 'the only guarantee which we could have of England's future good behaviour is military possession of the Flanders coast'.[66] Similar ideas were contained in a speech delivered by Tirpitz in Munich on 10 November, in which he repeatedly emphasised that 'the central issue of the whole world war is our relationship to England and to Anglo-Americanism', and that therefore 'Germany and not England must hold sway over Belgium'.[67]

And finally, Professor von Heck of Tübingen University, who was chairman of the Württemberg branch of the Fatherland Party, warned in a speech delivered to a public assembly in Stuttgart on 12 December 1917:

If we want a lasting peace then we must ensure a strengthening of German power, for only then will our neighbours accept our [territorial] expansion as unalterable and be glad to find in us an ally against the English danger. Our strength and common interests, those are the best means to ensure reconciliation. We need a protectorate [*Schutzherrschaft*] over Belgium, both because of the Flemish coast and because it would be a disgrace if we were to leave the Flemish people in the lurch.[68]

The Fatherland Party's implacable opposition to the Reichstag's Peace Resolution and to any form of compromise peace with the western powers also came out in almost all its publications. The regional party committee in Saxony, for instance, issued a brochure in 1917 under the title *Los vom 19. Juli!*, in which it argued quite plainly:

Today it is no longer a question of a war just like any other, we cannot simply say that at one minute we are at each other's throats, and the next minute the best of friends. We stand today in a time of world-wide change [*in einer Weltwende*], in which the spiritual forces on our planet are separating. Here the German heroic spirit! There the Anglo-Saxon mercenary spirit! Here Germany, which marches towards death for a moral idea, there England and Mr. Wilson, who send other peoples to their deaths for a sack of gold. Everybody must show their colours, every one of us who today cannot be at the front must take up the struggle at home and fight it through to the end . . . But first and foremost, in order that we can establish a breakthrough: *we must do away with the Peace Resolution of 19 July!*[69]

Earlier, in November 1917, Tirpitz and his followers issued a public appeal to the main political parties in the Reichstag to abandon the Peace Resolution 'as once and for all superseded by recent events', and instead 'to manifest a firm will for the achievement of peace which will assure all the essentials of Germany's existence'.[70] Once again, however, the military authorities refused to take action against this flagrant breach of the *Burgfriede*; on the contrary, such propaganda tactics met with the general approval of the local army commanders and in some cases were deliberately encouraged by individual officers. In Hamburg, for instance, where Tirpitz delivered three important speeches in one day on 14 December 1917, the Fatherland Party was permitted to display its posters on public buildings and in railway stations. One such poster, which appeared on, among other places, the town hall in the centre of Hamburg, carried the following message for passers by to read:

Gegen England:	*Against England*:
Der Brite sucht, im off'nen Kampf geschlagen,	The British seek, after failing in battle,
Bezahlte Zwietracht uns ins Land zu tragen, –	To sow discord amongst us at home, –
So zeigt dem Weltführer es aufs neue:	But we will show this world leader again:
Die stärkste Macht der Welt ist Deutsche Treue.	The strongest force in the world is German loyalty.[71]

Similar sentiments were expressed in a lecture delivered by the historian Karl Alexander von Müller to an audience of war loan subscribers in Munich at the end of 1917. Here Müller accused England of having released an 'unending stream of lies about us throughout the whole world . . . in order to wash away the dams which we have erected':

The two main streams [of lies] which constantly pour down on us are well known to you all: the one about the irreconcilable conflict between Prussia and the rest of Germany and the one about the irreconcilable conflict between the German workers, the lower classes and the German state. Both these streams direct themselves in the first instance against our army – against Prussian, German militarism, which has become the bugbear of the entire world.[72]

The only way to oppose these lies, Müller continued, was for the German people to maintain their faith in themselves and in their military leaders:

To replenish this current which drives everything, without which everything would stand still, to set it in motion, that is at present the most important duty of the home front, the most important demand which our army makes of the *Heimat*, the people at home.[73]

But it was first and foremost with regard to foreign policy and war aims that the Fatherland Party strove hardest to return to the lost 'spirit of 1914'. As early as November 1917, for instance, Johann Albrecht, the

Grand Duke of Mecklenburg, wrote a letter to Tirpitz in which he called for a fresh offensive on the war aims question. In his view it was no longer sufficient to focus solely on the future of Belgium in order to secure Germany from future attack. Rather, the Fatherland Party should concern itself with broader issues too, in particular 'with the liberation of those countries which have been conquered by our enemies against the will of their populations . . . In the first instance I am thinking of Ireland and Egypt.' A liberation of these two countries from the 'English yoke', he continued, would seriously weaken the global position of the Entente powers.[74] In his reply, Tirpitz expressed his private agreement with such aims but nonetheless warned against advertising them in public 'since I fear that the German *Spiessbürger* would become anxious as soon as the words Egypt and Ireland are mentioned, and that we would thereby offer our [domestic] enemies a fresh opportunity to denounce us as rabble-rousers and prolongers of the war'.[75]

Even so, Tirpitz himself was soon making similar demands in the pages of the conservative *Süddeutsche Monatshefte*, penning an article in February 1918 which called for massive increases in the German fleet and a programme of colonial expansion in Africa and elsewhere.[76] In this he was backed up by several senior naval commanders including Captain Levetzow, who as late as September 1918 proposed that Germany should acquire Constantinople as a naval base 'for all future wars', as well as Alexandria to serve as a base from which to threaten the British position in Egypt.[77] He was also further supported by a number of speakers at the second party conference of the Fatherland Party in April 1918, for instance a Dr Gaede from Potsdam, who demanded a peace which would 'break the back of England's world domination' by forcing it to relinquish control over certain key overseas territories. In particular he mentioned Egypt, Malta, Gibraltar, Cyprus and the 'liberation of India'.[78]

Finally, at the same conference, a number of individual members of the Fatherland Party, such as the Württemberg regional party chairman Professor Heck, also tried to raise the question of Morocco as a key German war aim, one which would not only weaken France but also bring Germany a number of important economic advantages vis-à-vis the Anglo-American powers. According to Heck, for instance, a German Morocco would be a 'clear sign of our victory for the entire world'. Likewise Dr Wirth of Munich argued that possession of Morocco could act as a springboard for German firms into the lucrative markets of South Africa and South America. Eventually these efforts led to a resolution adopted at Wirth's suggestion by the executive committee of the Fatherland Party in June 1918, which stated quite simply: 'We must regain southern Morocco!'[79]

Meanwhile the Pan-German League, which supported the

Fatherland Party on many issues, including the Moroccan question, put forward an alternative assessment of Germany's future world power position, namely the continental option of a German-dominated *Mitteleuropa* as the ultimate safeguard against future Anglo-Saxon aggression. In January 1918, for instance, the *Alldeutsche Blätter* published an article by the Bremen lawyer Dr Eggen in which he claimed:

Only a strong *Mitteleuropa* can save us from the threat of destruction . . . From the Flanders coast to the Persian sea, ultimate control must belong to us and our allies. Otherwise we are lost. If the Flanders coastline comes militarily under our control, then our fleet can move out beyond the 'wet triangle' and we can compete with England at sea; only via this means is the 'risk' idea realised, only thus is the freedom of the seas assured. Our border with France must be militarily improved. Areas with metal deposits which are currently in our hands can never be returned. In the east the vast areas [*Bezirke*] where the western Slavs live must be permanently cleared . . . We shall at any rate come to the conclusion that all these goals must be achieved not in a mercenary but in a heroic spirit [*nicht im händlerischen, sondern im heldischen Geist*].[80]

In this sense the objectives of the Pan-German League were remarkably similar to those pursued by Hindenburg and Ludendorff in the occupied territories of the east after March 1918, with the important proviso that the Flanders coastline was seen as a vital counterpart to the generals' plans to incorporate the Baltic states within Prussia. By contrast, German naval leaders had to be content for the time being with gains in the Baltic and Black Sea areas as the only minor (and totally irrelevant) improvement in their strategic position against England. The goal of gaining overseas bases in the Atlantic or Pacific was as far away as ever, in spite of the brilliant victories that had been won in the east.[81]

The final offensive

In the spring of 1918, as the annexationist agitation of the Fatherland Party reached its climax, the Supreme Command was also laying the foundations for its last great offensive on the western front. The aim was to achieve a decisive breakthrough before the arrival of large numbers of American troops, i.e. before the balance of power moved irreversibly in favour of the Entente powers. Had this offensive succeeded, there can be little doubt that Germany would have implemented the war aims programme laid down in 1914 for western and central Europe, including the establishment of permanent control over Belgium and parts of north and north-eastern France. Many optimists in Germany also continued to believe that the defeat of Britain and America was close at hand, and that soon the whole world would be forced to recognise the new power position gained by the Reich as a result of its territorial conquests. One important figure in the military section of the Foreign

Office, for instance, who had previously been a passionate advocate of a compromise peace settlement in the west, returned from a visit to the front near Amiens with the words: 'Ach, seien Sie ruhig! Wer das erlebt hat! . . . Die Weltherrschaft!' ('Stop worrying! Just imagine the experience! . . . World domination!')[82]

The victories which had been won in the east and which were now confidently expected in the west also determined the behaviour of the majority parties in the Reichstag. The change of mood since the summer of 1917 was most apparent among the National Liberals, the party which had felt least comfortable with the overall shift towards the left and towards majority parliamentary rule in the aftermath of the Reichstag Peace Resolution. As early as December 1917, for instance, when the negotiations at Brest Litovsk were just beginning, one of their deputies in the Prussian House of Deputies, Ludwig Scheffer, gave his interpretation of what was meant by the German promise of a 'peace without annexations and indemnities':

If the British consent to a referendum in India, we will allow the population of Vilna and Grodno to have the same. If they consent to self-determination for Ireland and Egypt, we will do the same for the Baltic provinces.[83]

A few weeks later, the party used the involvement of Social Democratic leaders in the Berlin strike movement as an excuse to stage a walk-out from the Reichstag Inter-Party Parliamentary Committee. At the same time, the National Liberal leader Stresemann welcomed the government's decision to go for all-out victory on the western front with the words: 'Never has our policy been more favourable than at present. We are poised to strike the first blow.'[84]

Although the Progressives, the Centre Party and the Majority Social Democrats, who even without the National Liberals formed a majority in the Reichstag, continued to pay lip-service to the principles behind the Peace Resolution, in practice they too were under pressure to abandon their anti-annexationist stand. Speakers from both the Progressive and the Centre parties, for instance, pointed out quite regularly that, because the enemy had refused to accept their peace offer in July 1917, Germany was now free to make whatever peace settlement it desired.[85] This applied as much to Germany's war aims in the west as it did to its territorial objectives in the east. Indeed, as early as 9 February 1918, Catholic Reichstag deputy Trimborn made this clear when he told a sitting of the Inter-Party Parliamentary Committee that his party was on the verge of dissociating itself completely from the Peace Resolution: 'On the issue of the west we are ready to defect at any moment. We will have to fight our corner in the [parliamentary] *Fraktion* if necessary.'[86] The majority parties therefore made their own position on the war aims question dependent on the changing military situation and were clearly prepared, in the event of a substantial German victory, to move even closer to the Conservative and National Liberal standpoint. Only the handful of Independent Socialists maintained their anti-annexationist stand by voting against the Treaty of Brest Litovsk in the Reichstag. On the other hand, the Majority Social Democrats merely abstained during this debate, and even voted in favour of the Treaty of Bucharest with Romania.

As a result of the illusory military victories of the spring of 1918, the right-wing and extreme anglophobe groups were once again able to seize the political initiative and reverse the barely perceptible trend towards responsible government and a negotiated peace which had taken hold in the summer of 1917. As in the years 1914–16, the extremists could rely on the support of substantial sections of middle- and upper-middle-class opinion, which, in spite of the terrible suffering caused by the war and a growing feeling of 'war-weariness', remained overwhelmingly hostile towards any kind of settlement which fell short of total victory over the '*Hauptfeind*' England. This can be seen quite clearly from the detailed reports on civilian morale which continued to be collected by the police and military authorities in Berlin. On 22 April 1918, for instance, Police President Heinrich von Oppen was able to record with evident satisfaction: 'The mood is one of jubilation. People are following the victorious advance on French and Belgian territory with the greatest and most confident expectations. The final bloody reckoning with the English is seen here as the order of the day.'[87] Similar views were expressed by the Prussian Ministry of War in its monthly assessment of domestic conditions in Germany in April 1918. In north Germany, for instance, the acting commander of the 9th Prussian army corps spoke of the joy which many people in Schleswig-Holstein and Mecklenburg felt at being able to take part in the 'revenge against the hated English'.[88] Likewise in Silesia the local military authorities claimed that the news of 'our magnificent victories against England' had been met with 'general satisfaction' and had strengthened the resolve to fight on 'until the end'.[89] And in May 1918 the acting army commander in Magdeburg reported that: 'The demand for a peace of understanding without annexations or reparations is being pushed into the background even by elements within the Social Democratic Party.'[90]

The reactionary mood was further underlined on 2 May, when the two main Conservative parties in the Prussian House of Deputies, possessing a majority by virtue of the three-class franchise, defeated a government bill to introduce equal male suffrage for Prussian state elections. Approximately half the National Liberal deputies and a minority from the Centre party also voted against this measure. Instead, an alternative proposal to maintain the most important elements of the plural franchise was passed by a large majority, representing a humiliating defeat for the government's efforts to maintain a semblance of harmony and tranquillity on the home front. In order to restore his own authority, the Chancellor, Count Hertling, was forced to reassure public opinion that equal suffrage would still be delivered in Prussia, even if this meant taking drastic measures to reduce the power of the anti-reform parties.[91]

The Kaiser, who in theory had backed 'his' government's reform bill when it was first officially announced in November 1917, now came out unambiguously in favour of the annexationists and the cause of political reaction at home. At the end of March 1918, no doubt buoyed up by news of the initial successes achieved by the German offensive on the western front, he declared at Imperial Headquarters: 'If a British parliamentarian comes to sue for peace, he must first kneel before the imperial standard, for this is a victory of monarchy over democracy.'[92] Less than three months later, on 15 June, he used the occasion of a speech marking the thirtieth anniversary of his accession to the throne to re-affirm his personal commitment to the much-quoted 'ideas of 1914':

At the beginning of the war the German people were still unclear about what this war actually means . . . But I knew exactly what it was about, since England's intervention meant a world war, whether we wanted one or not. It is not a question of one strategic campaign, but a question of a struggle between two *Weltanschauungen*. Either the Prussian-German-Germanic *Weltanschauung* – justice, freedom, honour and morals – will maintain its self-distinction or the Anglo-Saxon – that means: idolisation of money . . . These two *Weltanschauungen* are fighting against one another, and one of them must be completely overcome . . . The victory of the German *Weltanschauung*, that is what we are fighting for [*den gilt es!*].[93]

The weekly report drawn up by the War Press Office recorded widespread agreement with the Kaiser's interpretation of the war within the Conservative and right-wing press. The nationalist *Kölnische Zeitung*, for instance, argued that the battle between the two different world philosophies could best be seen on a personal level as a battle between the 'unpretentious, duty-driven Hindenburg' and the 'business leader' (*Geschäftsführer*) Lloyd George. Similarly, Heinrich Claß, writing in the Pan-German *Deutsche Zeitung*, welcomed the Kaiser's statement as a fresh stimulus to those who 'right from the very beginning have viewed and waged the war against England as a struggle between two *Weltanschauungen*, [one] in which there can be no compromises'.[94]

Not surprisingly, the left-liberal and Social Democratic press took a much more sceptical line, seeing no end to the war other than via a peace of understanding which would put an end to conflict and mistrust between different nations. The SPD's central organ *Vorwärts* even took a big risk by deciding to compare the views contained in the Kaiser's speech with an article which had appeared in the racist

Politisch-Anthropologische Monatsschrift at the beginning of June. In the latter case, the journal's anti-Semitic editor, Dr Schmidt-Giebiechenfels, had written:

It is quite possible that future generations will call it the 'Jews' war' [*Judenkrieg*], since the war in its ultimate, deepest sense revolves around the question of whether the heroic or the commercial [*die heldische oder die händlerische*], the Pan-German or Pan-British/Pan-Jewish *Weltanschauung* or view of life will in future dominate the world.[95]

No doubt mindful of the censor, *Vorwärts* was anxious to point out that 'the words used by Dr Schmidt reveal a motive which is lacking in the Kaiser's speech'. Whichever way these ideas were formulated, however, they still serve as a chilling reminder of the central underlying continuity between the war aims of the Kaiser's Germany and those of the Third Reich some twenty years later.

The annexationist triumph was almost complete, but it was also short lived. In the second half of June the Italians repulsed the Austrian attack across the Piave and in July the German offensive on the western front was halted and thrown back. The submarine warfare against England and its allies was also growing less and less effective, particularly as it failed to prevent the arrival of more and more American troops from across the Atlantic. At a meeting of the Crown Council at Spa in mid-August, presided over by the Kaiser, Hindenburg reported that his armies could no longer hope to break the will of the Allies by military operations, and advocated a wearing down of the enemy by a 'strategic defensive'.[96] Events moved rapidly, and in September it was Ludendorff who called for immediate peace negotiations in order to deflect blame for the defeat from the military onto the civilian authorities at home.

Even now, however, in the last few weeks of the war, hopes of victory were still being expressed by leading political and military figures. At the beginning of September, for instance, the Crown Prince of Prussia gave an interview to a Viennese journal in which he claimed that England would have intervened in the war 'even if we had not swept through Belgium' and continued: 'Germany and its allies must go on waging war until our enemies realise that we cannot be defeated and that they themselves will not profit if they continue the war.'[97] Similarly, in the Bavarian Landtag the Bavarian Minister of War spoke angrily of the 'wild and extravagant rumours' engineered by enemy propaganda, and the *Berliner Lokalanzeiger* complained that German morale was being shattered by 'shameful and impudent lies'.[98] Perhaps most interesting of all was an article in the arch-conservative and traditionally pro-Tsarist *Kreuzzeitung*, which accused England of being behind a new conspiracy to overthrow the Soviet government in Moscow and murder its leaders, Lenin and Trotsky.

England entered the war from [motives of] commercial jealousy . . . All the talk about the struggle for Belgium, for freedom, etc. is sheer humbug. And it is not by chance that the dishonesty of English policy, which always claims to promote the finest ideals, should be shown up in all its colours through the exposure of the conspiracy against the Soviet government in Moscow. When we see how England's official representatives are at work there with bribery, falsified documents, violence and even murder – for we cannot describe the planned assassination of Lenin and Trotsky in any other way – then we are obliged to conclude that the present English state is an amoral being, to which we do no injustice when we credit it with being willing to commit any crime if [that crime] appears to be in the interests of English policy.[99]

Once the new government of Prince Max von Baden had made an official request for an armistice on 4–5 October, appealing to President Wilson on the basis of his fourteen points, any hopes for a continuation of the war against England and its allies vanished once and for all. The Pan-German leader Heinrich Claß made one last desperate appeal for a 'spirited national party' which would make the 'struggle against Jewry' its primary post-war concern.[100] It was now only a matter of weeks before the decisive military defeat at the front was followed by an equally dramatic revolution at home, leading to the enforced abdication of the Kaiser and the collapse of the old order in Germany.

Epilogue

> It is a misfortune of the nation that it has never drawn a line under its militaristic past, never come to terms with the old, never begun a new kind of politics. The concrete forces and intellectual currents which held sway in Germany in 1914 still determine the shape of the nation today.
>
> Heinrich Ströbel, 1924[1]

We have now come to the end of the First World War and of our study of German anglophobia. The conclusion of hostilities left Germany faced with the gigantic problems of political turmoil and large-scale famine, while the victorious Allies continued their economic blockade of Germany throughout the seven-month period of the armistice (November 1918 to June 1919).[2] This was followed by the Treaty of Versailles, whereby the new Weimar government was forced not only to accept the war aims of Germany's erstwhile enemies, but also to shoulder the entire moral and financial responsibility for the misery and destruction which the war had caused. As a final humiliation, the victor powers also demanded the extradition of 'war criminals' to face trial before an international tribunal. This latter requirement was successfully evaded, however.[3]

Not surprisingly, it was during the armistice period that feelings against England were at their most virulent, whereas later it was France that was identified as the chief proponent of a punitive peace settlement. In April 1919, for instance, the *Berliner Lokalanzeiger* carried a report by Julius Schwalbe, Professor of Medicine at the University of Berlin, who argued that the English were aiming at the 'racial destruction' of the Germans by means of a systematic policy of starvation.

I am convinced that not only tens of thousands of as yet unborn Germans are destined for a life of physical inferiority, but that further thousands, who have not even been conceived yet, will also fall victim to the same fate. The 'English disease' ['*englische Krankheit*'] will be the affliction which one most often meets in unfit Germans in the time after the war.[4]

As a reaction to the continuing blockade and to their country's devastating military defeat, a growing number of German political economists also began looking towards expansion in the east as the best means of securing Germany's long-term economic and biological needs. This *Drang nach Osten* had first arisen during the Kaiserreich and reached its height in the Treaty of Brest Litovsk, only to re-emerge in a more radical guise in the aftermath of the events of 1918–19.[5] Similarly, many nationalist writers remained adamantly opposed to the re-establishment of trading relations with either Britain or the United States on the grounds that this would further expose the country to the dangers of international capitalism and the free market society. Germany's economic fate, it was now argued, should never again be the sole prerogative of foreign, especially western (or 'Jewish') powers.[6]

But it was not only the extreme right who held such views; many of Weimar Germany's more mainstream politicians and statesmen also continued to maintain a distrust of England and its policies until well beyond 1919. It was only in the aftermath of the Franco-Belgian occupation of the Ruhr in 1923, for instance, that the former nationalist turned moderate republican Gustav Stresemann felt brave enough to argue in public that 'in certain respects the Treaty of Versailles, in comparison with the policy of force practised [by France], protects German interests'.[7] For this he was subject to the most bitter attacks from the right, including former members of the now dissolved National Liberal Party. A speaker for the nationalist Deutschnationale Volkspartei (DNVP) in the summer of 1925, for instance, declared:

Our programme must be: down with Stresemann! Down with the war guilt lie! Revision of the Treaty of Versailles! . . . Only when we have regained our place in the sun can we do away with hatred. Only then can come the day of international reconciliation. And not before![8]

After 1923 the notion that a republican and democratic Germany, inspired by British principles of constitutional government and French concepts of political liberty, could cooperate with the west in a new partnership continued to be an ideal to which a significant number of German liberals and Social Democrats aspired. It found brief success when Germany was re-admitted to the League of Nations in 1926 and when it signed up to the Kellogg–Briand pact renouncing war in 1928. But in practice there were too many obstacles, both national and international, in the way of the long-term realisation of this ideal. The former leftist Konrad Haenisch perhaps gave the most concrete expression to these views when he wrote in 1919, shortly after the Treaty of Versailles:

This termination of the war, this peace of shame . . . which represents the temporary victory of Entente capitalism over German socialism is not yet the last word . . . In the end the 'ideas of 1914' . . . will yet triumph over the military and political successes of the western powers and over the 'ideas of 1789', which are now seemingly victorious . . . The peace of Versailles will ultimately mean nothing more than a 'scrap of paper'.[9]

In the meantime, the realisation of these anti-western and revisionist trends in post-war German society came only after the Nazi seizure of power in 1933. Hitler, as we shall see in more detail below, managed to mobilise the various forms of nationalist discontent in Germany far more effectively than his predecessors, mainly by incorporating them within the framework of his overall foreign policy programme. This programme culminated in an image of the Second World War as a struggle not only against the 'culture-destroying [menace of] Judaeo-Bolshevism' in the east, but also against the 'dying bourgeois capitalist order' in the west. Shortly after the fall of France in 1940, for instance, one of the leading SS ideologists, Franz Six, wrote:

The beliefs put forward by the representatives of the new *Weltanschauung* in the struggle for power and German racial unity have been known to Europe and the entire world since 1933: National Socialism in all its postulates constitutes itself as the antithesis of the west.[10]

On a more general level, too, historians of ideas have often pointed to the structural similarities between National Socialism and the anti-English traditions in German racist thinking.[11] In addition to the *Lebensraum* ideology, for instance, the Nazis adopted much of the programme of the *Drang nach Westen*, including the use of anti-English ideas as means of popularising and legitimising imperialist war aims.[12] Furthermore, in combating 'liberal individualist tendencies' on the home front during the Second World War, the Nazi regime also saw itself as being in the forefront of the battle against the continuing invasion of the German 'national community' by Anglo-Saxon cultural forms and lifestyles. One party newspaper, for instance, commented in 1942 on the appearance of jazz-loving 'Swing Youth' gangs in Hamburg:

We don't want them. With their umbrellas, *'ready-rolled'*, and their hats, *made by Bloody*, and their jackets, the latest *city* fashion – and all the bits and pieces of being a *gentleman* . . . The details needn't bother us. Anyone who needs an umbrella should carry one. A hat is a hat and a jacket a jacket. That's not the point. It's the fact that people imitate the 'English style', the stupid, phoney magic, the yid-glamour typical of the island, which upsets us . . . we are not prepared to put up with these yid-Eton style girls and boys behaving as if there wasn't a war on.[13]

In fact, concerns about this threat to the German war effort even reached the very top of the Nazi hierarchy, as can be seen in the following letter from Heinrich Himmler to Reinhard Heydrich, dated 26 January 1942:

All the leaders and that means both male and female and those teachers who are hostile and support the Swing Youth are to be sent to a concentration camp

. . . Only if we act brutally will we be able to avoid a dangerous spreading of these anglophile tendencies at a time when Germany is fighting for its existence. Please send me further reports.[14]

Given the evidence outlined above, it would therefore seem appropriate to conclude this study with a detailed analysis of the anti-English elements within National Socialist ideology, how they affected Hitler's foreign policy programme and how they can be squared with his obsessive pursuit of an alliance with Britain between 1933 and 1941. The intention here is not to repeat the incessant anti-British slogans which Nazi propaganda broadcast on a daily basis between 1939 and 1945, but rather to demonstrate the way in which these slogans were based on themes that had already taken root in Germany during the First World War and the post-war period. For the Nazi period itself I am grateful to be able to draw on the work of previous experts in the field, and especially the excellent studies produced over the years by Norman Rich, Gerhard Weinberg, Andreas Hillgruber, Klaus Hildebrand, Eberhard Jäckel, Dietrich Aigner and Woodruff D. Smith.[15]

Nazi ideology

Most experts on Nazism are agreed that it constituted a unique combination of a wide variety of conflicting ideas and interests, few of them original and none of them entirely compatible with one another. Especially before 1924, Nazi policies at home and abroad – including the stance of the party towards England – are therefore difficult to pin down in concrete terms.[16] Early Nazi economic thought, for instance, favoured the anti-capitalist line handed down from Sombart and Spengler. It also developed strong connections with the pro-Boer view that linked British imperialism with Jewish power and the rule of Mammon and found its ultimate expression in Hans Grimm's famous post-war novel of colonial intrigue, *Volk ohne Raum* (1926).[17] And yet alongside this radical anti-Jewish and anti-capitalist critique of Britain there was also much respect and admiration for the 'determined British will for power' which had allegedly held this nation together during the war.[18] The unrelenting nature of its propaganda, the cohesiveness of its society and above all its strong political leadership were all qualities which the Germans allegedly lacked and which Hitler and the Nazis wished them to develop in order to be a match for the British in the future.

In terms of its historical origins, Nazism was, in fact, a peculiar blend of the different ideological positions described in chapter 2 of this book, albeit taken to their extremes and without the limitations previously prescribed by religion or *Realpolitik*. From the point of view of the need to attract a mass following, the eclectic nature of the Nazi political programme was also clearly related to the desire to popularise its message without alienating hard-core anti-Semitic supporters. In this the Nazis differed little from other right-wing political parties during the Weimar era, including the equally racist DNVP, which campaigned alongside the Nazis against German acceptance of the Dawes Plan (1924) and the Young Plan (1929) and developed an extensive propaganda organisation of its own.[19] There were, however, two fundamental differences between National Socialism and the revisionist nationalism of the DNVP. The first was the concept of the nation as a biological phenomenon, which led Hitler to regard race itself as the guide to his foreign and domestic policies. And the second was Hitler's ruthless ambition to succeed in his quest to rid Germany of 'undesirable' racial elements and to conquer and enslave large parts of eastern Europe.[20] Several factors need to be considered in explaining how such an intolerant and violent set of beliefs could generate widespread support inside Germany before 1933. I shall leave the question of its precise relationship to the traditions of German anglophobia until later.

In the first instance, of course, the Nazi movement was able to grow in the soil that had already been prepared by the anti-Versailles propaganda of the 1920s and the failure of the republican regime to carry through a proper investigation of the causes of the war. As the left-wing pacifist Hellmut von Gerlach wrote in an article published shortly after the Nazi electoral successes in the Reichstag elections of July 1932:

Hitler would never be the power factor he is today if the republic had made a decisive break with the past in 1918 . . . However, the rulers of the German republic chose to draw a line not between themselves and those responsible for 1914, but only between themselves and the few Germans who after 1914 dared to oppose the war and the policies of the empire. Instead of spreading the truth about the war among the broadest sections of the population, they allowed the anti-Versailles campaign [*Unschuldskampagne*] of the nationalists to poison the minds of the masses. They failed to sow the seeds of truth. And for this reason Hitler is now reaping the fruits of falsehood.[21]

Similar views were put forward by another prominent anti-war campaigner, the biologist Friedrich Wilhelm Foerster, in August 1932:

The Hitler movement [*Das Hitlertum*] thrives on that interpretation of the war and the post-war era which was spread among the German people by the admirable efforts of the Prussian nationalist propaganda machine; Hitler is equally just an echo of these Prussian operations which have had such damaging effects on the German soul.[22]

But more important, perhaps, than this survival of militaristic beliefs was the psychological impact of the war and of defeat in 1918. The sense of shock and national humiliation was indeed all the greater because until the very last days of the war the military authorities had encouraged the people to believe in ultimate victory or at worst an honourable settlement on the basis of Wilson's fourteen points.[23] Even before the guns had fallen silent, prominent officers and right-wing political leaders had begun a press campaign aimed at deflecting the blame for defeat onto Marxist and Jewish politicians at home. The Nazis themselves were able to transform this 'stab-in-the-back' myth into a propaganda frenzy aimed at undermining the legitimacy of the Versailles settlement and the new republican regime at home. Their nationalist zeal appealed to those who had suffered as a result of the war and the Allied economic blockade, and gained extra credence through the fact that Hitler himself and many of his party colleagues were veterans of the conflict. Indeed, in one of his earliest recorded speeches, delivered in Munich in December 1919, Hitler showed his concern to harness the wartime resentments against England as Germany's enemy number one in order to win popularity and support for his new party.

In earlier times English diplomacy has understood how to estrange all the nations from one another in order to secure advantages for herself. The removal of our colonies represents an irreparable loss for us. We are compelled to secure our raw materials from the Allies and at such an expense that we will be excluded from the world market as effective competitors.[24]

Over the next five years, Hitler gradually moved away from this conventional revisionist position to develop his own, more radical foreign policy programme as enshrined in *Mein Kampf*. The opposition of the British government to the French action in the Ruhr in 1923 also led him to place greater emphasis on Germany's eternal enmity with France when writing this book from his prison cell in Landsberg.[25] Nonetheless, elements of the old hatred for England did appear in more subtle guises in many of Hitler's speeches and writings after 1924. Once again, this was usually directed at specific audiences – particularly the radical conservative opponents of modernity and 'Jewish materialism' – and was designed to recall slogans that were current during the war.[26] At other times, though, Hitler deliberately distanced himself from anglophobe extremists in order to appeal to more 'moderate' elements of the business community and government establishment who were anxious to improve trading links with Britain and the west. In general it can be assumed that Hitler's open quest for an alliance with Britain in the 1930s was popular in these same circles.[27]

The final factor of great significance in the rise of Nazism, and undoubtedly the most controversial one, was the seemingly widespread acceptance of racial ideology and anti-Semitic stereotypes among the German middle class.[28] Whether or not they were willing to go along with the ultimate horrors of the 'Final Solution', vast numbers of Germans were prepared to accept the basic premise that the Jews were an unassimilable minority who had somehow been responsible for Germany's defeat in 1918. It is significant, for instance, that in a country in which education and scientific research were held in high esteem, very few German professors were willing to raise their voice in protest when their Jewish colleagues were removed from their positions in the universities after 1933.[29] And even among more progressive sections of society, such as the SPD or the women's movement, there was a basic lack of sympathy or understanding for specific Jewish interests and concerns. As one expert has written:

More common and widespread than outright hatred or sympathy for the Jews was . . . moderate anti-Semitism, that vague sense of unease about the Jews that stopped far short of wanting to harm them but that may have helped to neutralise whatever aversion Germans might otherwise have felt for the Nazis.[30]

After the Second World War, of course, many of those Germans who had supported Hitler claimed that they had been tricked by him or had hoped that his extreme ideas could be harnessed to their own more moderate goals of national regeneration. Nonetheless, on a number of occasions before 1933 the Nazis had made clear to the German people and to the world in general what the ultimate intentions of their anti-Jewish policies were. In one of the best-known passages of the first volume of *Mein Kampf*, for instance, Hitler wrote:

Kaiser Wilhelm II was the first German Emperor to hold out a conciliatory hand to the leaders of Marxism, without suspecting that scoundrels have no honour . . . With the Jews, there can be no bargaining, but only the hard either–or.[31]

And in August 1932, after five stormtroopers were sentenced to death for the murder of a pro-Communist worker in Silesia, Joseph Goebbels also declared in the party journal *Der Angriff*:

The Jews are guilty, the punishment is coming . . . The hour will strike when the state prosecutor will have other tasks to fulfil than to protect the traitors to the people from the anger of the people. Forget it never, comrades! Tell it to yourself a hundred times a day, so that it may follow you in your deepest dreams: the Jews are guilty! And they will not escape the punishment they deserve.[32]

From this we can see that Nazism, from the early 1920s onwards, was first and foremost an ideology of racial hatred, that racism was the driving force behind Hitler's foreign and domestic political programme as formulated in the years before 1933, and that it was this that distinguished the Nazi movement from any previous political organisation in Germany.[33] It was also, of course, one of the reasons for the ultimate defeat of Hitler's Third Reich in the Second World War, when vast amounts of human and material resources were diverted from the war effort to help implement the 'Final Solution' to the Jewish question in Europe.

Hitler and German anglophobia

How, then, did England fit into the National Socialist concept of race, and what did the Nazis make of the traditional link between anti-Semitism and anglophobia in German nationalist ideology? Furthermore, how can this link be squared with Hitler's well-known pursuit of an alliance with England before the outbreak of the Second World War? One answer to this question was provided by Hermann Rauschning, the former party leader in Danzig who broke with Hitler and the Nazi movement in 1938 and became an important conservative critic of the regime. In his book *Die Revolution des Nihilismus*, which was published in Zurich at the end of 1938 and appeared in English translation a few months later, Rauschning wrote:

One of the essential features of National Socialist relations with England is the fact that, alongside a certain sense of racial kinship and the desire for an alliance, there exists a very plain dislike of England . . . [This] German dislike of England is derived directly from the ideas of anti-Semitism. The Englishman in his Puritanism, saturated with the spirit of the Old Testament, has become the chief representative of the capitalism which, in the eyes of National Socialists, is the principal Jewish achievement; thus, the British empire is a Jewish empire, an empire in which the typically Jewish way of thinking, guidance by economic considerations, the spirit of profit-making dominates.[34]

On the other hand, Nazi propaganda against England was intended not only to revive the old wartime slogans of the German right, but also to transcend their limitations. In *Mein Kampf* Hitler openly expressed his regard for the individual bravery of the 'tommies' he had encountered in Flanders, and put this down more generally to England's 'determination for victory, [its] tenacity and ruthless pursuit of the struggle'.[35] He was also highly critical of Germany's rulers for the amateur nature of their 'enlightenment' campaign against England during the war, and more especially for their 'criminal folly' in failing to conclude an alliance with England before 1914. 'To gain England's favour, no sacrifice should have been too great . . . Consequently . . . we should have renounced colonies and sea power, and spared English industry our competition.'[36] In the more immediate context of the post-war world, too, Hitler felt that ideological differences between British parliamentarism and the revolutionary, anti-democratic claims of the Nazi movement were – at least in the short term – less important than questions of pure power politics. In fact, from an early stage in his career, Hitler had envisaged England as Germany's 'natural ally'; and in keeping with this idea he made substantial efforts of his own to court an alliance with Britain in the 1930s.[37] He was even willing to abandon many of the traditional aims of German *Weltpolitik*, including the demand for a substantial colonial empire and a larger share in world trade, if only England would recognise

Germany's own claim to hegemony in Europe. At other times, his admiration for England seemed to go beyond questions of foreign policy to address basic issues of race and racial purity as well. The English upper class, he believed, owed their survival and political success to their adherence to the principles of selective breeding. Furthermore, their harsh methods of rule in India could provide a possible model for German expansion and colonisation in the east, where the subjugation and enslavement of subject peoples was also seen as a 'biological necessity'.[38]

The explanations given by most historians for Hitler's avid pursuit of an alliance with England are twofold. First, by the time of the Ruhr crisis in 1923 Hitler had become convinced that French policies in Europe were aimed at the permanent dismemberment of Germany. Britain, on the other hand, was bound to oppose the French claim to continental hegemony, not only because it threatened the principle of the balance of power in Europe but because, ultimately, it also threatened Britain's imperial position in the outside world.[39] The idea of an alliance between Germany and Britain against France therefore seemed to him to be a distinct possibility, and perhaps even a necessity if Germany was to recover its freedom of action in European affairs. In the event of a war, he would be able to 'destroy' France, or at least neutralise it, by relying on Britain's support. This in turn would enable him to concentrate on his more immediate objectives in the east (the destruction of Poland and Czechoslovakia, autarky for the Greater German Reich, preparations for an invasion of the Soviet Union, etc.), none of which directly clashed with Britain's interests overseas.[40]

Secondly, historians of the 'programme school', such as Klaus Hildebrand and Andreas Hillgruber, believe that in the long run Hitler was banking on a conflict of interest between England and the United States, the country which most threatened England's overseas markets and spheres of influence in Asia, Africa and the Middle East. In other words, he was convinced that in the final showdown between the great world powers, which would follow Germany's defeat of the Soviet Union, England would see that its true interests lay with Germany against America.[41] The one essential precondition for the realisation of this *Stufenplan* (plan in stages) was that the Jews in 'democratic' England should not succeed in gaining a dominant position in affairs of state, as they previously had done in France and America. In *Mein Kampf* Hitler therefore identified what was for him the biggest conundrum of his foreign policy programme: 'Can the forces of traditional British statesmanship . . . break the devastating Jewish influence or not?'[42]

It was not until his so-called 'Second Book', however, written in 1928 but never published in his lifetime, that Hitler managed to resolve another contradiction in his plans for an alliance with England: why should England's statesmen allow German hegemony on the continent if they had traditionally pursued a policy of the balance of power? Would they not in this scenario align with the United States against Germany?[43] The answer which Hitler now gave was a rather unconvincing one. On the one hand he foresaw a situation in which, somewhere in the distant future, Germany's desire for economic expansion overseas might make a breach with England possible. On the other hand he also stuck to his original view that in the short term England would not oppose his plans to dominate Europe so long as Germany did not appear to threaten England's extra-European interests. As proof of this theory he cited Prussia's successful efforts to avoid British enmity during the eighteenth century and contrasted this with the mistakes committed in earlier times by the Dutch and the French, and, more recently, by the Kaiser's Germany. This historical analogy in turn led him to conclude that, 'if Germany adopts a fundamentally new political orientation that no longer clashes with England's naval and commercial interests, instead concentrating on Europe, then England would have no grounds for hostility [against us]'.[44]

In the end, of course, Hitler was wrong in his predictions about British foreign policy, in much the same way as his predecessors had been wrong in 1914. After coming to power in 1933, he developed a set of highly risky policies – the re-militarisation of the Rhineland, the annexation of Austria and the Sudetenland, the repeated demands for the return of Germany's pre-war colonies – which were designed, among other things, to demonstrate to the British what might happen if they refused to come to terms with the rising power on the continent. This assessment of the international situation was in turn based on a series of faulty assumptions about Britain's likely response to such a challenge, assumptions that had ended in disaster for Germany in 1914 – and would do so again between 1939 and 1945.[45] Significantly, the continuity of error between regimes had already been noticed by Hermann Rauschning, the former Gauleiter of Danzig, who announced to world opinion in 1938:

It has long been the foremost axiom of National Socialist foreign policy that England can no longer venture on a war, and that she may therefore be offered any affront with impunity. Von Bethmann Hollweg used to say as Chancellor that he regarded his highest task as that of 'appeasement' [kalmieren]. This, it is considered by the party leaders, is today the only maxim left for England. And there seems to be good reason for supposing that the policy of 'appeasement' will be equally ineffectual in this case.[46]

Such warnings, however, were ignored by Hitler and the other leaders of the Nazi regime. In fact, even after the outbreak of war with

Britain and France over Poland in September 1939, Hitler continued to hope that Britain would come to terms with Germany so long as it could do so without losing its empire. At the end of June 1940, for instance, in the aftermath of the Wehrmacht's victory over France, he spoke to his generals of his deep regret that England seemed determined to continue with the war: 'The reason [he gave] is that if we crush England's military power the British Empire will collapse. This is of no use to Germany. German blood would be shed to accomplish something that would benefit only Japan, America and others.'[47]

Likewise, in a conversation with the Bulgarian Foreign Minister, Popoff, in November 1941, he once more asserted the belief 'that the present war would not be fought out between any of the European states but that ultimately England would have to fight America . . . Some day it must dawn upon the English that only Europe could have an interest in keeping England and the Empire intact. America can only wish to dismember and then inherit the British Empire.'[48]

Ultimately, however, Hitler was forced to recognise the fact that, contrary to his own expectations, England was determined to continue fighting against Germany to the bitter end – even if this did mean losing an empire in the process. The inner contradictions in his race ideology and Social Darwinist thinking slowly began to unravel as it became clear that England had decided to cooperate with 'Jew-ridden America' against the healthier instincts of its 'Aryan' population. Increasingly England itself was portrayed in Nazi propaganda as being infested with 'Jewish elements of decomposition' and as becoming more and more decadent as the war continued.[49] In this situation the dominance of the traditional 'Germanic' element in England seemed to offer the only hope of salvation, although this hope was vanishing with every day of the war and was all but extinguished after Rudolf Hess's doomed flight to Scotland in June 1941. In the summer of 1940 Hitler had made one of his last efforts to flatter the English people and undermine their support for the Churchill government when he declared in an interview for an American journal:

One thing and one thing only will have been annihilated as a result of this war – the capitalist bloc which set itself to cause the death of millions of men for its private and ignoble interests. I am convinced, however, that not we but the English themselves will be the instrument by which the destruction of this plutocratic group is brought about.[50]

But by the end of 1944 he had changed his mind about the British and their supposed commitment to racial purity. Now he admitted, in a conversation with Martin Bormann on 4 February 1945, that 'I myself . . . underestimated one factor. Namely, the extent to which Churchill's Englishmen were influenced by the Jews'.[51] The course of history had thus come full circle and Hitler had returned to the anti-English views that he, like many other anti-Semitic Germans, had held in 1919. England, so it seemed, was Germany's eternal enemy, because, like the Jews, it had stabbed Germany in the back in the final moment of victory.

Conclusion

Obviously it would be wrong to argue from this that all of the disastrous decisions made by the Nazi regime and everything that went wrong for Germany in the period 1914–45 can be attributed directly to the ideology of anglophobia. Other factors would also have to be taken into account, especially the strong elements of anti-French and anti-Polish feeling which characterised German imperialist thought from the time of Bismarck onwards and were used to such violent effect during the two world wars. Anglophobia shared many features with these other forms of hatred, whilst developing a number of distinct characteristics of its own. To some extent it was also superseded by Hitler's own obsession with race and racial purity, which at times led him to praise England more highly than the Germans themselves.

Not much has been said, either, about the actual extent of anti-English feeling in Germany during the First World War. The reports of the Berlin Police President and the monthly assessments of domestic conditions commissioned by the Prussian and Bavarian Ministries of War do shed some light here on the swings in public opinion and the mood 'on the streets' during the years 1914–18. But recent research into the impact of the First World War on other parts of the Reich, particularly in rural areas, has revealed a less enthusiastic reception for government propaganda and a greater indifference on the part of the local population towards the 'August experience' of 1914.[52] Moreover, in addition to anti-English feelings there is also no doubt that pro-English feelings continued to be very strong, especially among left-liberals such as Theodor Wolff and Social Democrats such as Eduard Bernstein. The explanation for the continuation of these traditions in the 1920s and 1930s belongs, however, to another chapter of German history and cannot be dealt with here.

In spite of these various qualifications, there are a number of theoretical and practical conclusions which can be made on the basis of the evidence offered in this study. In the first instance, it is clearly no longer acceptable to regard German anglophobia as a spontaneous outburst of patriotic anger caused by England's declaration of war in August 1914. Rather, it was the product of intense imperialist rivalries and competition for world power which even before 1914 had managed to impose a radical and intolerant stamp on German right-wing politics. Anti-English feeling, for instance, had already made itself felt at the time of the Boer war and, later, in the aftermath of the Daily Telegraph affair of 1908/9. It was further encouraged by the government's own distorted view of international relations and its tendency to exaggerate the extent of the external threat facing Germany in order to justify its continued expenditure on armaments. To mention just one example, in December 1904 the German ambassador in London, Count Paul Wolff-Metternich, reported to Berlin:

England does not want war. It wants peace [*Es will Ruhe haben*] . . . Most people in England would simply not understand if they were told that we credited them with war-like intentions against Germany. Rather, many English people believe in reverse that we are planning a war against England, and that we are building our fleet for this very purpose.[53]

Such reports did not, however, deter the then Chancellor Bernhard von Bülow from sending the following instructions to the Foreign Office on 12 October 1905, at the height of the first Moroccan crisis: 'The German people must be made to realise for all future eventualities that our policy has always been a loyal and peaceful one, but that we could be attacked and invaded if we are not strong on land and water. This must not be said in a single article in some review, but must proceed as the keynote through a series of articles in the daily papers.' Three days later, he set out the aims of propaganda activity against England in greater detail: 'It is all the more important to awaken the impression, everywhere and especially in the German people, that England wants to incite and push the French forward and unleash a world war, whereas Germany has never intended to attack France, or even to use force to draw it over to its side, or to play it off against England.'[54]

This situation was almost identical to that in 1914, when the German press asserted first, that England would never fight Germany, on account of its domestic difficulties and its opposition to Russia, and then that it had deliberately instigated the war in order to crush Germany and reap the economic reward. The only difference now was that the government fed selective information to the leaders of the SPD justifying the war as a defence of Germany's borders against Tsarist aggression. Even so, public opinion immediately swung round to an anti-English position in the first days after 4 August 1914. It is here too that we can find the ultimate confirmation of Fritz Fischer's view that Germany had begun the war with the conscious intention of grasping for world power, at the expense not only of Russia and France, but also of Britain and the British empire.

During the war itself, anglophobia became an integral part both of the war aims movement and of the 'national opposition' to the Chancellor, Bethmann Hollweg. Anti-English and pro-submarine agitation was conducted by the Pan-Germans, the Rhineland industrialists, the Prussian Junkers, anti-Prussian and nationalistic elements in Bavaria, a significant number of German academics, and, in the Reichstag, by all the political parties except the SPD. It was even supported by a number of prominent former liberals, including the editor of the *Vossische Zeitung*, Georg Bernhard. The latter in particular emerged as a strong advocate of a future alliance between Germany and Russia against the Anglo-Saxon powers. Similar views were also held by reactionary elements within the civilian and military leadership, including such influential figures as the Prussian Minister of the Interior, Friedrich Wilhelm von Loebell, and the Commander-in-Chief in the Marches, General von Kessel.

Once again, however, this anti-English orientation cannot be understood in isolation from broader trends in German history. It was closely linked, for instance, to the rise of 'organised capitalism' in Germany from the 1890s onwards and its opposition – in alliance with the organs of state power and the ruling aristocratic Junker class – to 'Manchesterism' and the English laissez-faire economic system.[55] Moving forward to the beginning of the twentieth century it also formed part of an internal critique of cosmopolitan modernity and liberal ideas which found favour with the Pan-German League and other radical right-wing groups that were close to, but so far excluded from, the reins of political influence. Some of the latter's fiercest criticisms, especially during the war years, were directed towards the Kaiser and his leading ministers, whom they accused of being too weak-kneed and liberal, too tolerant of left-wing subversives within Germany and too conciliatory towards Germany's enemies abroad. But their chief aim remained one and the same: defence of the existing authoritarian order in Germany and resistance to the rise of Social Democracy. Or, to put it in another way, what they feared most of all was the contrasting political system in England, which, if transported to Germany, would (in their view) be the equivalent of handing over power to the SPD and its left-liberal allies.[56]

Having said this, it would also be wrong to see anglophobia as entirely a creature of the Pan-German League or the reactionary Junker class or both. Other factors besides extreme nationalist agitation included the social and economic dislocations brought about by the war itself and in particular the devastating impact of the Allied economic blockade on the living standards of most ordinary middle- and working-class Germans. In this sense it was no coincidence that Bavaria became the centre of anti-English feeling, since it was this part of Germany, with its large number of small businesses and relative absence of heavy industry, which was hardest hit by the economic consequences of the war. Evidence for this can be seen in the bitter protest sent by Crown Prince Rupprecht of Bavaria to the Reich authorities in Berlin in 1917:

Heavy industry is now supreme in Germany . . . the Berlin business people have managed . . . to bring the entire economic life of Germany under their control . . . and the consequence will be that . . . the middle class . . . will disappear and a trustification worse than America's will set in. For Bavaria . . . this will be catastrophic.[57]

Added to these economic and regional factors was the more general feeling of bitterness towards England which stemmed from fears regarding Germany's inability to find its 'place in the sun', as the quote from Heinrich Mann at the beginning of this book suggests. Particularly revealing in this sense is the emphasis placed on the notion of English 'cant' or moral hypocrisy, England's ability to put itself forward as the 'guardian of international law' and the 'protector of the rights of smaller nations' while at the same time managing to build an empire covering over one quarter of the earth's surface.[58] It is here too that the ambivalent love–hate relationship with England came subliminally into play, with hate replacing love as the dominant element in the equation after 1914. Indeed, as Wolfgang Mommsen has argued in a recent essay, it is in the secret desire of many German statesmen for an agreement with England on colonial questions before 1914 – with Germany as junior partner to the British empire – that we can find the true sociopsychological roots of German anglophobia, including the heartfelt accusation of perfidy.[59] How else, for instance, can we explain Wilhelm II's famous marginal comment of 30 July 1914: 'if we must bleed to death [on the continent], then at least England shall lose India.'[60]

German historians – like their counterparts across the Channel – also undoubtedly played an important part in transmitting the disappointments and frustrations of one generation to feed the irrational needs and expectations of the next.[61] At times, this mutual hostility and distrust were the product of a genuine conflict of interest, as was the case in the rise of Anglo-German antagonism before 1914. At other times, the memory of such conflicts and the animosities they had generated were revived by interested parties with a particular axe to grind. Instances where historians made an original contribution to the debate are extremely hard to find, however, at least before 1945. Rather, for the most part German scholars tended to present 'the facts' about England as they saw them or as they met the political needs of the day. The only possible exception here would be Eckart Kehr's challenge to traditional state-supporting historiography in his essays on the domestic causes of *Englandhass* in the 1920s. Even here, though, Kehr's ideas were considered to be 'beyond the pale' by most German historians until well into the 1960s.[62]

Apart from historiography, religion too was a factor here, especially given the large number of clerics from both sides of the confessional divide who became involved in propaganda on behalf of the German war effort.[63] As recent sociological works have demonstrated, however, religion is associated with war only when it becomes fused with other, secular institutions, such as the nation or the state, which are concerned with gaining monopoly control over the use of propaganda and violence. Religion then becomes just one more aspect of group identity to be mobilised in the event of international conflicts.[64] In 1925 the conservative historian Gerhard Ritter made this clear in his celebrated biography of Martin Luther, when he declared:

In recent years it has been much disputed whether Luther belonged to the Middle Ages or 'the modern world'. To me the far more important question seems to be whether we ourselves belong to the modern world – or want to belong to it – if by that term one means primarily the spirit of Anglo-Saxon and Romance culture.[65]

Finally, the evidence offered in this study bears out the conclusions of previous works on the role of collective memory in the social construction and reconstruction of national *Feindbilder*.[66] Such hostile images are important historical facts in their own right, and cannot be dismissed by post-modernists as mere 'cultural constructs'.[67] The accumulated resentments of past conflicts and the nationalist phobias they give rise to can be overcome only through the patient efforts of our own and future generations. In this field, governments, educators and historians might play a more constructive role than they have done in the past.

Notes

Introduction

1 Heinrich Mann, 'Ihr ordinärer Antisemitismus', in Mann, *Der Haß. Deutsche Zeitgeschichte*, 2nd ed. (Amsterdam, 1933), pp. 125–6.

2 Hans-Albert Walter, 'Heinrich Mann im französischen Exil', in Heinz Ludwig Arnold (ed.), *Heinrich Mann* (Munich, 1971), pp. 115–40.

3 Jörg Bernhard Bilke, 'Heinrich Mann in der DDR', in Klaus Matthias (ed.), *Heinrich Mann, 1871/1971. Bestandaufnahme und Untersuchung* (Munich, 1973), pp. 367–84. It should nonetheless be pointed out that Mann had an abiding dislike for Walter Ulbricht and other Communist Party functionaries which went back to their first meeting in Paris in 1937 (ibid., pp. 369–70).

4 See e.g. Charles E. McClelland, *The German Historians and England. A Study in Nineteenth Century Views* (Cambridge, 1971), esp. pp. 168–90; Peter Winzen, 'Treitschke's Influence on the Rise of anti-British Nationalism in Germany', in Paul Kennedy and Anthony Nicholls (eds.), *Nationalist and Racialist Movements in Britain and Germany before 1914* (Oxford, 1981), pp. 154–70; Pauline Anderson, *The Background of Anti-English Feeling in Germany, 1890–1902*, Reprint (Washington D.C., 1964); Harald Rosenbach, *Das deutsche Reich, Großbritannien und der Transvaal. Anfänge deutsch-britischer Entfremdung* (Göttingen, 1993).

5 Mann, 'Ihr ordinärer Antisemitismus', pp. 126–7.

6 The literature on this issue has now grown to enormous proportions. For a summary of recent trends see Jürgen Kocka, 'German History before Hitler. The Debate on the German *Sonderweg*', *Journal of Contemporary History* 23 (1988), pp. 3–16. Also George Steinmetz, 'German Exceptionalism and the Origins of Nazism. The Career of a Concept', in Ian Kershaw and Moshe Lewin (eds.), *Stalinism and Nazism. Dictatorships in Comparison* (Cambridge, 1997), pp. 251–84.

7 An overview, containing a useful if somewhat outdated bibliography, is provided by Wolfgang J. Mommsen, *Two Centuries of Anglo-German Relations. A Reappraisal* (London, 1984).

8 Fritz Fischer, *Griff nach der Weltmacht. Die Kriegszielpolitik des kaiserlichen Deutschland, 1914/1918,* 2nd ed. (Düsseldorf, 1962). On the controversy sparked off by this book and by Fischer's second major study, *Krieg der Illusionen*, 2nd ed. (Düsseldorf, 1970), see John A. Moses, *The Politics of Illusion. The Fischer Controversy in German Historiography* (London, 1975).

9 See e.g. Wolfgang J. Mommsen, 'Zur Entwicklung des Englandbildes der Deutschen seit dem Ende des 18. Jahrhunderts', in Lothar Kettenacker, Manfred Schlenke and Hellmut Seier (eds.), *Studien zur Geschichte Englands und der deutsch-britischen Beziehungen. Festschrift für Paul Klucke*, (Munich, 1981), pp. 375–97; and Rolf Peter Sieferle, 'Der deutsch-englische Gegensatz und die "Ideen von 1914"', in Gottfried Niedhart (ed.), *Das kontinentale Europa und die britischen Inseln. Wahrnehmungsmuster und Wechselwirkungen seit der Antika* (Mannheim, 1993), pp. 139–60, both of which deal with German wartime anglophobia exclusively in terms of the history of ideas. A broader perspective, encompassing a consideration of popular as well as elitist forms of anti-English feeling, is taken by Christoph Jahr, '"Das Krämervolk der eitlen Briten". Das deutsche Englandfeindbild im Ersten Weltkreig', in Christoph Jahr, Uwe Mai and Kathrin Roller (eds.), *Feindbilder in der deutschen Geschichte. Studien zur Vorurteilsgeschichte im 19. und 20. Jahrhundert* (Berlin, 1994), pp. 115–42.

10 For a classic East German account see Fritz Klein et al., *Deutschland im Ersten Weltkrieg*, 3 vols. (East Berlin, 1968–9).

11 See esp. Eckart Kehr's influential essay, 'Englandhass und Weltpolitik', first published in *Zeitschrift für Politik* 7 (1928), pp. 500–27, and reproduced in Kehr, *Der Primat der Innenpolitik*, edited by Hans-Ulrich Wehler (West Berlin, 1965), pp. 149–75. For recent versions of the Kehrite thesis see also Lothar Wieland, 'Der deutsche Englandhaß im Ersten Weltkrieg und seine Vorgeschichte', in: Wilhelm Alff (ed.), *Deutschlands Sonderung von Europa, 1862–1945* (Frankfurt am Main, 1984), pp. 317–53; and Gerhard Schmidt, 'Der deutsch-englische Gegensatz im Zeitalter des Imperialismus', in Henning Kohler (ed.), *Deutschland und der Westen. Vorträge und Diskussionsbeiträge des Symposions zu Ehren von Gordon Craig* (West Berlin, 1984), pp. 59–81.

12 See David Blackbourn and Geoff Eley, *Mythen deutscher Geschichtsschreibung. Die gescheiterte bürgerliche Revolution von 1848* (Frankfurt am Main, 1980), and the English language version, *The Peculiarities of German History. Bourgeois Society and Politics in Nineteenth Century Germany* (Oxford, 1984).

13 For some wide-ranging interpretations of these questions see (among other works) Ludwig Dehio, *Germany and World Politics in the Twentieth Century* (New York, 1959); David Calleo, *The German Problem Reconsidered* (Cambridge, 1978); Andreas Hillgruber, *Germany and the Two World Wars* (London, 1981); Klaus Hildebrand, *German Foreign Policy from Bismarck to Adenauer. The Limits of Statecraft* (London, 1989); Gerhard Weinberg, *Germany, Hitler and World War II* (Cambridge, 1995); Wolfgang J. Mommsen (ed.), *Die ungleichen Partner. Deutsch-Britische Beziehungen im 19. und 20. Jahrhundert* (Stuttgart, 1999).

14 Paul Kennedy, *The Rise of Anglo-German Antagonism, 1860–1914* (London, 1980). See also the reference to this book in Woodruff D. Smith, *The Ideological Origins of Nazi Imperialism* (Oxford, 1986), p. 11.

15 See e.g. Donald Cameron Watt's comments in *The Sunday Times*, 19 January 1992, Books, p. 3, review of Robert K. Massie's *Dreadnought. Britain, Germany and the Coming of the Great War* (London, 1992). Also the more

recent studies by Holger Herwig, *The First World War. Germany and Austria-Hungary, 1914–1918* (London, 1997), p. 7; and Niall Ferguson, *The Pity of War* (London, 1998), pp. 83–7.

16 Kennedy, *The Rise of Anglo-German Antagonism*, pp. 205–88, 410–31.

17 Ibid., pp. 334–5, 451–63.

18 Werner Sombart, *Händler und Helden. Patriotische Besinnungen* (Munich, 1915).

19 Cf. Klaus Schwabe, 'Anti-Americanism within the German Right', *Jahrbuch für Amerikastudien* 21 (1976), pp. 89–107. Chapter 2 of this book owes much to the different categories of anti-American feeling suggested by Schwabe in this essay.

20 On this theme see Raffael Scheck, *Alfred von Tirpitz and German Right-Wing Politics, 1914–1930* (Atlantic Highlands, 1998), esp. pp. 35–64.

21 Heinz Hagenlücke's very well-received study of the Fatherland Party, *Deutsche Vaterlandspartei. Die nationale Rechte am Ende des Kaiserreiches* (Düsseldorf, 1997), mentions this committee in passing (pp. 231–2), but does not go into any detail.

22 Werner T. Angress, 'The German Army's "Judenzählung" of 1916. Genesis – Consequences – Significance', *Year Book of the Leo Baeck Institute* 23 (1978), pp. 117–37.

23 On the stab-in-the-back myth, the best study available is still Joachim Petzold, *Die Dolchstoßlegende. Eine Geschichtsfälschung im Dienste des deutschen Imperialismus und Militarismus* (East Berlin, 1963). See also John A. Moses, 'Die Wirkung der Dolchstoßlegende im Deutschen Geschichtsbewußtsein', in Bernd Hüppauf (ed.), *Ansichten vom Krieg. Vergleichende Studien zum Ersten Weltkrieg in Literatur und Gesellschaft* (Königstein, 1984), pp. 240–56.

24 On the Kaiser's anti-English views see John C.G. Röhl, 'Der Kaiser und England', in Wilfried Rogasch (ed.), *Victoria & Albert, Vicky & the Kaiser. Ein Kapitel deutsch-englischer Familiengeschichte* (Berlin, 1997), pp. 165–84. On the connection with his anti-Semitic and conspiracist thinking more generally see also Röhl, 'Kaiser Wilhelm II and German anti-Semitism', in Röhl, *The Kaiser and His Court. Wilhelm II and the Government of Germany* (Cambridge, 1994), pp. 190–212.

25 Cf. Wilhelm Deist, 'The German Army, the Authoritarian Nation-State and Total War', in John Horne (ed.), *State, Society and Mobilization in Europe during the First World War* (Cambridge, 1997), p. 169.

26 Jeffrey T. Verhey, 'Some Lessons of the War. The Discourse on Propaganda and Public Opinion in Germany in the 1920s', in Bernd Hüppauf (ed.), *War, Violence and the Modern Condition* (Berlin and New York, 1997), pp. 99–117.

27 Adolf Hitler, *Mein Kampf*, translated by Ralph Manheim (London, 1969), pp. 161–9.

28 Norman Rich, *Hitler's War Aims. Ideology, the Nazi State and the Course of Expansion*, 2 vols. (London, 1973–4), vol. 1, p. 97.

29 Ibid., pp. 157–64. Cf. Andreas Hillgruber, *Hitlers Strategie. Politik und Kriegführung, 1940/1* (Frankfurt am Main, 1965), pp. 144–91; Gerhard Weinberg, 'Hitler and England, 1933–1945. Pretense and Reality', in Weinberg, *Germany, Hitler and World War II*, pp. 85–94.

30 See here the important essay by H.D. Schmidt, 'Anti-Western and Anti-Jewish Tradition in German Historical Thought', *Year Book of the Leo Baeck Institute* 4 (1959), pp. 37–60. On German anti-Semitism more generally the best study is still Peter Pulzer's *The Rise of Political Anti-Semitism in Germany and Austria*, 2nd ed. (London, 1988).

31 Fischer, *Krieg der Illusionen*, pp. 740–4, 766.

32 See e.g. K. Joy Melhuish, 'Deutschland und der deutsche Feind in den Augen der Briten und Franzosen, 1914–1916', in Hüppauf (ed.), *Ansichten vom Krieg*, pp. 155–76; Stuart Wallace, *War and the Image of Germany. British Academics, 1914–1918* (Edinburgh, 1988); and Panikos Panayai, *The Enemy in Our Midst. Germans in Britain during the First World War* (Oxford, 1988).

33 See e.g. H.D. Schmidt, 'The Idea and Slogan of "Perfidious Albion"', *Journal of Historical Ideas* 14 (1953), pp. 604–16. Also Norman Hampson, *The Perfidy of Albion. French Perceptions of England during the French Revolution* (London, 1998).

34 Examples can be found in the anthology of anti-English quotations edited by Karl Strecker, *England im Spiegel der Kulturmenschheit* (Munich, 1915).

35 Eckart Kehr, *Schlachtflottenbau und Parteipolitik, 1894–1901* (Berlin, 1930), p. 360.

36 See e.g. Gerhard von Schulze-Gaevernitz, *Britischer Imperialismus und englischer Freihandel zu Beginn des zwanzigsten Jahrhunderts* (Leipzig, 1906); and Schulze-Gaevernitz, *England und Deutschland*, 3rd ed. (Berlin, 1911).

37 Ibid.

38 See e.g. Hans-Dietrich Kluge, *Irland in der deutschen Geschichtswissenschaft. Politik und Propaganda vor 1914 und im Ersten Weltkrieg* (Frankfurt am Main, 1985); and Gerhard Loh, *Irland in der Berichterstattung deutscher Tageszeitungen, 1914–1918*, 2 vols. (Frankfurt am Main, 1987).

1 *Unser gehasstester Feind*. German anglophobia and the 'spirit of 1914'

1 *August 1914. Ein Volk zieht in den Krieg*, edited by the Berliner Geschichtswerkstatt (West Berlin, 1989). On the weakness of the German peace movement before 1914 see also Roger Chickering, *Imperial Germany and a World without War. The Peace Movement and German Society, 1892–1914* (Princeton, N.J., 1975).

2 See Volker Berghahn, *Germany and the Approach of War in 1914*, 2nd ed. (London, 1993); and Berghahn, *Rüstung und Machtpolitik. Zur Anatomie des Kalten Krieges vor 1914* (Düsseldorf, 1973).

3 Wolfgang J. Mommsen, 'Domestic Factors in German Foreign Policy before 1914', *Central European History* 6 (1973), pp. 3–43.

4 On the Pan-German League see Roger Chickering, *We Men Who Feel Most German. A Cultural Study of the Pan-German League, 1886–1914* (London, 1984). On the Navy League see Geoff Eley, 'The German Navy League in German Politics, 1898–1914', D.Phil. thesis (University of Sussex, 1974).

5 Paul Lensch, *Drei Jahre Weltrevolution* (Berlin, 1917).

6 Wolfgang J. Mommsen, 'The Spirit of 1914 and the Ideology of a German "Sonderweg"', in *Imperial Germany, 1867–1918. Politics, Culture and Society*

in an Authoritarian State (London, 1995), pp. 205–16. See also Klaus Schwabe, *Wissenschaft und Kriegsmoral. Die deutschen Hochschullehrer und die politischen Grundfragen des Ersten Weltkrieges* (Göttingen, 1969).

7 'Deutschlands Befreiungskrieg', anonymous article in *Bayerische Staatszeitung*, 9 August 1914.

8 See e.g. Michael Jeismann, *Das Vaterland der Feinde. Studien zum nationalen Feindbegriff und Selbstverständnis in Deutschland und Frankreich, 1792–1918* (Stuttgart, 1992).

9 Friedrich Thimme (ed.), *Bethmann Hollwegs Kriegsreden* (Stuttgart and Berlin, 1919), pp. 3–6.

10 On the Kaiser see Walther Görlitz (ed.), *The Kaiser and His Court. The Diaries, Note Books and Letters of Admiral Georg Alexander von Müller, Chief of the Naval Cabinet, 1914–1918* (London, 1961); on Falkenhayn see the biography by Holger Afflerbach, *Falkenhayn. Politisches Denken und Handeln im Kaiserreich* (Munich, 1994); on Tirpitz see his *Erinnerungen* (Leipzig, 1919); on Riezler see Karl Dietrich Erdmann (ed.), *Kurt Riezler: Tagebücher, Aufsätze, Dokumente* (Göttingen, 1972); on Rathenau see Hartmut Pogge von Strandmann, *Walther Rathenau. Notes and Diaries, 1907–1922* (Oxford, 1985); on Ballin see Alfred von Tirpitz, *Deutsche Ohnmachtspolitik im Weltkriege* (Hamburg and Berlin, 1926); also the study by Lamar Cecil, *Albert Ballin. Business and Politics in Imperial Germany, 1888–1918* (Princeton, N.J., 1967).

11 Fischer, *Griff nach der Weltmacht*, p. 353.

12 Werner Sombart, 'Unsere Feinde', *Berliner Tageblatt*, 2 November 1914.

13 Julius Schiller, 'Der deutsche Haß', *Vossische Zeitung*, 20 January 1915.

14 Pourtalès to Jagow, 30 July 1914, in Imanuel Geiss (ed.), *Julikrise und Kriegsausbruch, 1914*, 2 vols. (Hanover, 1963–4), vol. II, no. 698, pp. 291–3.

15 On the *Kölnische Zeitung* see Berghahn, *Germany and the Approach of War*, pp. 179–80.

16 See e.g. ibid., and Fischer, *Krieg der Illusionen*, p. 547–8.

17 'Ein Wort an England', anonymous article in *Welt am Montag*, 3 August 1914.

18 The information had been passed on to the German Foreign Office by a spy in the Russian embassy in London, which in turn leaked details to the newspaper editor Theodor Wolff. Wolff published an article in the *Berliner Tageblatt* on 22 May 1914, without, however, revealing his source. For further details see Johannes Lepsius et al. (eds.), *Die Große Politik der europäischen Kabinette, 1871–1914*, 40 vols. (Berlin, 1922–7), vol. 39, pp. 617–8.

19 'Krieg mit England', anonymous article in *Frankfurter Zeitung*, 4 August 1914.

20 *Alldeutsche Blätter*, no. 32, 8 August 1914, p. 290. Cf. ibid., Sondernummer, 3 August 1914, pp. 287–8.

21 'Deutschland und England', anonymous article in *Germania*, 9 August 1914.

22 'E.R.' (i.e. Ernst zu Reventlow), 'Fürst Lichnowsky', *Deutsche Tageszeitung*, 8 August 1914.

23 See Harry F. Young, *Prince Lichnowsky and the Great War* (Athens, Ga., 1977), pp. 131–2.

24 See Kurt Koszyk, *Deutsche Pressepolitik im Ersten Weltkrieg* (Düsseldorf, 1968), p. 116.
25 Johannes Haller, 'Britannia delenda!', *Süddeutsche Zeitung*, 16 September 1914.
26 'Wider die englische Tyrannei', anonymous article in *Kölnische Zeitung*, 29 September 1914.
27 Wieland, 'Der deutsche Englandhaß im Ersten Weltkrieg', p. 318.
28 *Frankfurter Zeitung*, 5 August 1914, quoted in ibid., pp. 318–19.
29 Professor A. Brandl, 'Das englische Rätsel', *Vossische Zeitung*, 6 September 1914.
30 *Leipziger Neueste Nachrichten*, 18 September 1914.
31 Hellmut von Gerlach, *Die große Zeit der Lüge. Der Erste Weltkrieg und die deutsche Mentalität, 1871–1921* [1921/26], ed. Helmat Donat and Adolf Wild (Bremen, 1994), p. 107.
32 Cf. Eberhard Demm, 'Les thèmes de la propagande allemande en 1914', *Guerres mondiales et conflits contemporains* 150 (1988), pp. 3–17. Also Karl Alexander von Müller, 'Deutschland und Frankreich', *Süddeutsche Monatshefte* 12/1 (March 1915), pp. 315–29. Here Müller notes that 'many among us, living in the midst of the chaos and entangled conflicts which are ripping Europe apart, find this war against the old motherland of occidental culture particularly painful'.
33 Quoted in Gerlach, *Große Zeit*, pp. 108–9.
34 Traugott von Jagow, '10. Stimmungsbericht', 5 October 1914; in Ingo Materna and Hans-Joachim Schrenkenbach (eds.), *Berichte des Berliner Polizeipräsidenten zur Stimmung und Lage der Bevölkerung in Berlin, 1914–1918* (Weimar, 1987), pp. 14–15, emphasis in the original.
35 Jagow, '14. Stimmungsbericht', 2 November 1914; in ibid., pp. 22–3.
36 Jagow, '15. Stimmungsbericht', 9 November 1914; in ibid., p. 23.
37 Gerlach, *Große Zeit*, p. 111.
38 Traugott von Jagow, '27. Stimmungsbericht', 30 January 1915; in Materna and Schrenkenbach (eds.), *Berichte des Berliner Polizeipräsidenten*, p. 40.
39 John Williams, *The Home Fronts. Britain, France and Germany, 1914–1918* (London, 1972), pp. 32 and 94.
40 Gerlach, *Große Zeit*, p. 112.
41 Quoted in A.J. Hoover, *God, Germany and Britain in the Great War. A Study in Clerical Nationalism* (New York, 1989), p. 57.
42 For translations of captions and wider commentary on figures 1, 2, 3, 4, 5, 8, and 9, I have used William A. Coupe, *German Political Satires from the Reformation to the Second World War*, Part II, 1849–1918 (New York, 1987). I am grateful to Professor Coupe for his assistance in this matter.
43 Gerlach, *Große Zeit*, p. 109.
44 Ibid., p. 110.
45 Ernst Lissauer, 'Haßgesang gegen England', in Robert Gersbach, *Kriegsgedichte von 1914* (Berlin, 1915), p. 24.
46 Material on this organisation is available in PA-AA Bonn, R 22415: Presse und Journalisten, vol. 4 (October–December 1914). See especially the brochure 'England's Perfidy Exposed by the Americans', produced by the American Truth Society, Munich, 12 October 1914.

47 Gerlach, *Große Zeit*, p. 113.
48 Quoted in J.C.G. Röhl, 'Admiral von Müller and the Approach of War, 1911–1914', *Historical Journal* 12 (1969), p. 669.
49 Ibid., p. 670.
50 J.C.G. Röhl, 'Vorsätzlicher Krieg? Die Ziele der deutschen Politik im Juli 1914', in Wolfgang Michalka (ed.), *Der Erste Weltkrieg. Wirkung, Wahrnehmung, Analyse* (Munich, 1994), pp. 193–215.
51 Röhl, 'Admiral von Müller and the Approach of War', pp. 661–2.
52 See also J.C.G. Röhl, 'An der Schwelle zum Weltkrieg. Eine Dokumentation über den "Kriegsrat" vom 8. Dezember 1912', *Militärgeschichtliche Mitteilungen* 26 (1977), p. 100. For the debate on the significance of the 'war council' more generally, see Fischer, *Krieg der Illusionen*, pp. 232–41; Moses, *The Politics of Illusion*, pp. 73–94; and Röhl, 'Die Generalprobe. Zur Geschichte und Bedeutung des "Kriegsrats" vom 8. Dezember 1912', in Wilhelm Alff (ed.), *Deutschlands Sonderung von Europa, 1862–1945* (Frankfurt am Main, 1984), pp. 149–224.
53 The documents were first published in the *Norddeutsche Allgemeine Zeitung* on 13 October and 25 November 1914, and later appeared in one of the German government's 'white books' on the origins of the war. For further details see the relevant archival material in PA-AA Bonn, R 22378: England (October–December 1914).
54 *Vorwärts*, 17 September 1914.
55 *Berliner Tageblatt*, 13 October 1914.
56 For a detailed account of how the law on the state of siege operated in practice see Wilhelm Deist (ed.), *Militär und Innenpolitik im Weltkrieg 1914–1918* (Düsseldorf, 1970), esp. pp. xxxi–li.
57 Quoted in Werner Thönessen, *The Emancipation of Women. The Rise and Decline of the Women's Movement in German Social Democracy, 1863–1933* (London, 1973), p. 79.
58 Quoted in Annemarie Lange, *Das Wilhelminische Berlin. Zwischen Jahrhundertwende und Novemberrevolution* (East Berlin, 1984), p. 685.
59 Theodor Wolff, *Tagebücher, 1914–1919. Der Erste Weltkrieg und die Entstehung der Weimarer Republik in Tagebüchern, Leitartikeln und Briefen des Chefredakteurs am "Berliner Tageblatt" und Mitbegründers der "Deutschen Demokratischen Partei"*, ed. Bernd Sösemann, 2 vols. (Boppard am Rhein, 1984), vol. I, pp. 108–10 (diary entries for 12 and 17 October 1914).
60 Dr Friedrich Freund, 'Wehe Dir, England', *Vossische Zeitung*, 23 September 1914. Freund also sent a copy of the article to Bethmann Hollweg and received a reply on 24 September. According to Bethmann the article contained 'much which is true, but unfortunately the English newspapers will refuse to print it' – copies of both letters in BA Potsdam, Reichskanzlei, no. 2465.
61 See also Georg Bernhard, 'Gegenwart oder Zukunft', *Vossische Zeitung*, 5 May 1919.
62 Quoted in Geiss (ed.), *Julikrise und Kriegsausbruch*, vol. II, no. 678, pp. 277–80.
63 BA Potsdam, Reichskanzlei, no. 2437/3. Cf. Koszyk, *Deutsche Pressepolitik*, pp. 121–2.

64 Friedrich Wilhelm von Loebell, 'Gedanken über den Friedensschluß', 4 November 1914. Copy in BA Koblenz, Nachlaß Loebell, no. 5.

65 'Bericht des Oberkommandos in den Marken an Kaiser Wilhelm II.', 3 December 1914; in Materna and Schrenkenbach (eds.), *Berichte des Berliner Polizeipräsidenten*, pp. 30–1.

66 See e.g. Wilhelm Deist, 'Censorship and Propaganda in Germany during the First World War', in Jean-Jacques Becker and Stéphane Audoin-Rouzeau (eds.), *Les sociétés européennes et la guerre de 1914–1918* (Paris-Nanterre, 1990), p. 202.

67 Ernst zu Reventlow, *England der Feind* (Stuttgart and Berlin, 1914), p. 10.

68 Ibid., pp. 34–5.

69 Alexander von Peez, *England und der Kontinent*, 8th ed. (Vienna, 1915).

70 Peez, *England und der Kontinent*, quoted from 3rd ed. (Vienna, 1909), p. 44.

71 Ibid., p. 45.

72 Gerhard von Schulze-Gaevernitz, *Freie Meere!* (Stuttgart and Berlin, 1915), p. 20.

73 Cf. Theodor Wolff, *The Eve of 1914* (London, 1935), p. 80.

74 Ernst Haeckel, 'Englands Blutschuld am Krieg', *Vossische Zeitung*, 14 August 1914.

75 Copy of statement in BA Potsdam, Reichskanzlei, no. 2465.

76 Hermann Oncken, 'Deutschland und England', *Süddeutsche Monatshefte* 11/2 (September 1914), pp. 804–5.

77 Ibid., p. 803.

78 Ibid., p. 804.

79 Ibid., p. 810.

80 Copy of both letters in BA Potsdam, Reichskanzlei, no. 2465.

81 *Norddeutsche Allgemeine Zeitung*, 5 September 1914.

82 Quoted in Fischer, *Griff nach der Weltmacht*, p. 130.

83 Thimme (ed.), *Bethmann Hollwegs Kriegsreden*, pp. 15–16. Cf. Bethmann's *Betrachtungen zum Weltkriege*, 2 vols. (Berlin, 1919), vol. I, pp. 174–5.

84 Schmidt, 'The Idea and Slogan of "Perfidious Albion"', passim.

85 Johannes Lepsius, 'John Bull. Eine politische Komödie in fünf Aufsätzen', *Der Panther. Eine deutsche Monatsschrift für Politik und Volkstum*, ed. Axel Ripke, 3/4 (April 1915), pp. 457–512.

86 Ibid., p. 464.

87 Ibid., p. 465.

88 Ibid., p. 482.

89 Ibid., p. 465: 'For me, war justifies itself.'

90 Ibid., p. 474.

91 Ibid., p. 483–4.

92 Walter Unus, *England als Henker Frankreichs. Ein Kampf um die Weltherrschaft und sein Ende* (Braunschweig, 1915), pp. 45–6.

93 Eduard Meyer, *Nordamerika und Deutschland* (Berlin, 1915), p. 195.

94 Friedrich Weidig, *An Albion!* (Munich, 1914); Copy in BA Koblenz, Zsg. 2/58 (13).

95 Otto Ernst, *Deutschland an England. Kriegsgedichte* (Hamburg, 1914); Ernst, *Gewittersegen. Ein Kriegsbuch* (Leipzig, 1915).

96 Ernst, *Deutschland an England*, p. 3.

97 Ibid., pp. 6–7.
98 Cf. J. Knight-Bostock, *Some Well-Known German War Novels, 1914–1930* (Oxford, 1931), p. 14.
99 *Schulthess' Europäischer Geschichtskalender*, Neue Folge (Munich, 1917), vol. 30, p. 397.
100 Thimme (ed.), *Bethmann Hollwegs Kriegsreden*, p. 18.
101 Woldemar Schütze, *Englands Blutschuld gegen die weiße Rasse* (Berlin, 1914).
102 Ibid., pp. 5–6.
103 Ibid., pp. 20–1.
104 Ibid., pp. 21–2.
105 Ibid., pp. 17–18.
106 Ibid., p. 11.
107 *Verzeichnis von Kriegschriften* (Berlin, 1916). Copy in ABBAW, Nachlaß Dietrich Schäfer, no. 4 / II.
108 Quoted in Röhl, 'Kaiser Wilhelm II and German Anti-Semitism', p. 211.
109 See Williams, *The Home Fronts*, p. 93.
110 Quoted in Douglas H. Robinson, *The Zeppelin in Combat. A History of the German Naval Airship Division, 1912–1918* (London, 1962), p. 64.
111 See Karl-Ludwig Ay, *Die Entstehung einer Revolution. Die Volksstimmung in Bayern während des ersten Weltkrieges* (West Berlin, 1968), p. 79.
112 On *Kladderadatsch* and *Simplicissimus* see Ann Taylor Allen, *Satire and Society in Wilhelmine Germany. Kladderadatsch and Simplicissimus, 1890–1914* (Lexington, Ky., 1984).
113 Simplicissimus, *Gott strafe England!* (Munich, 1915); Kladderadatsch, *Am Pranger. England-Album des Kladderadatsch von der Zeit des Burenkrieges bis zur Gegenwart* (Berlin, 1915).
114 Eberhard Demm, 'Propaganda and Caricature in the First World War', *Journal of Contemporary History* 28 (1993), p. 166. See also the relevant correspondence in BA Potsdam, Bestand Auswärtiges Amt, vol. 35: Zentralstelle für Auslandsdienst, 1914–1921, no. 103.
115 Quoted in Allen, *Satire and Society*, p. 135.
116 Dum-dum bullets were bullets which had been blunted in order that they wobbled in flight and therefore had a much more devastating and painful effect on impact with human flesh. Their alleged use by British and French soldiers on the western front was a constant cause for complaint by the German government and its spokesmen, although little hard evidence was ever produced. On 4 September 1914 the Kaiser even addressed an open letter of protest to American President Woodrow Wilson on this issue, claiming that Britain and France were breaking the recognised principles of international law. See also the pamphlet *Dumdum-Geschosse und Lugenkrieg*, produced on behalf of the German Foreign Office in September 1914. Copies of both documents in PA-AA Bonn, R 22413: Presse und Journalisten, September 1914.
117 Harold Dwight Lasswell, *Propaganda Technique in the World War* (London, 1927), p. 82.

2 The cultural war. German intellectuals and England

1 See e.g. Wolfgang Kruse, *Krieg und nationale Integration. Eine Neuinterpretation des sozialdemokratischen Burgfriedenschlusses, 1914/1915* (Essen, 1993); Michael Stöcker, *Augusterlebnis in Darmstadt. Legende und Wirklichkeit* (Darmstadt, 1994); Benjamin Ziemann, *Front und Heimat. Kriegserfahrungen im südlichen Bayern, 1914–1923* (Essen, 1997); Christian Geinitz and Uta Hinz, 'Das Augusterlebnis in Südbaden: Ambivalente Reaktionen der deutschen Öffentlichkeit auf den Kriegsbeginn 1914', in Gerhard Hirschfeld et al. (eds.), *Kriegserfahrungen. Studien zur Sozial- und Mentalitätsgeschichte des Ersten Weltkriegs* (Essen, 1997), pp. 20–35.

2 See also Jeffrey T. Verhey, *The Spirit of 1914. Militarism, Myth and Mobilization in Germany* (Cambridge, 2000).

3 Johann Plenge, *Der Krieg und die Volkswirtschaft* (Münster, 1915), p. 187.

4 Cf. Wolfgang J. Mommsen, 'German Artists, Intellectuals and the Meaning of the War, 1914–1918', in John Horne (ed.), *State, Society and Mobilization in Europe during the First World War* (Cambridge, 1997), pp. 21–38.

5 Thomas Mann, *Betrachtungen eines Unpolitischen* (Berlin, 1918).

6 Friedrich Meinecke, *Die deutsche Erhebung von 1914* (Stuttgart and Berlin, 1915).

7 Ernst Troeltsch, *Der Kulturkrieg* (Berlin, 1915).

8 Rudolf Eucken, *Die weltgeschichtliche Bedeutung des deutschen Geistes* (Stuttgart and Berlin, 1915).

9 Sombart, *Händler und Helden*.

10 Max Scheler, *Der Genius des Krieges und der deutsche Krieg* (Leipzig, 1915).

11 Alfred Weber, *Gedanken zur deutschen Sendung* (Berlin, 1915).

12 Rudolf Kjellén, 'Die Ideen von 1914. Eine weltgeschichtliche Perspektive', in *Zwischen Krieg und Frieden* (Leipzig, 1916).

13 On German atrocities in Belgium and France in 1914 see Lothar Wieland, *Belgien 1914. Die Frage des belgischen 'Franktireurkrieges' und die deutsche öffentliche Meinung, 1914 bis 1936* (Frankfurt am Main, 1984); Alan Kramer, '"Greueltaten". Zum Problem der deutschen Kriegsverbrechen in Belgien und Frankreich, 1914', in Gerhard Hirschfeld and Gerd Krumeich (eds.), *Keiner fühlt sich hier als Mensch . . . Erlebnis und Wirkung des Ersten Weltkriegs* (Essen, 1993), pp. 85–114; and, most recently, Helen McPhail, *The Long Silence. Civilian Life under the German Occupation of Northern France, 1914–1918* (London, 1999).

14 Quoted from the improved English translation in ABBAW, Nachlaß Eduard Meyer, no. 327. On the origins of this appeal see also Jürgen von Ungern-Sternberg von Pürkel and Wolfgang von Ungern-Sternberg, *Der Aufruf an die Kulturwelt: Das Manifest der 93 und die Anfänge der Kriegspropaganda im Ersten Weltkrieg* (Stuttgart, 1996); and Bernhard vom Brocke, '"Wissenschaft und Militarismus". Der Aufruf der 93 "An die Kulturwelt!" und der Zusammenbruch der internationalen Gelehrtenpolitik im Ersten Weltkrieg', in W.M. Calder III et al. (eds.), *Wilamowitz nach 50 Jahren* (Darmstadt, 1985), pp. 649–719.

15 Text of the 'Aufruf an die Europäer' in Georg Friedrich Nicolai, *Die Biologie des Krieges*, 2nd ed. (Zurich, 1919), pp. 12–14.
16 Reproduced in Hermann Kellermann, *Der Krieg der Geister. Eine Auslese deutscher und ausländischer Stimmen zum Weltkriege 1914* (Weimar, 1915), pp. 28–9.
17 Wolff, *Tagebücher*, vol. I, p. 107.
18 Paul Rohrbach, *Warum es der Deutsche Krieg ist!* (Stuttgart and Bonn, 1915).
19 Wolff, *Tagebücher*, vol. I, pp. 103–4 (diary entry for 8 October 1914).
20 For further examples see Kellermann, *Der Krieg der Geister*, pp. 86–99.
21 Quoted in Ay, *Die Entstehung einer Revolution*, pp. 44–5.
22 George Mosse, *Towards the Final Solution. A History of European Racism* (Madison, Wis., 1978), p. 55.
23 On the Bayreuth circle see also Geoffrey G. Field, *Evangelist of Race. The Germanic Vision of Houston Stewart Chamberlain* (New York, 1981); and Hartmut Zelinsky, *Richard Wagner. Ein deutsches Thema*, 3rd ed. (West Berlin and Vienna, 1983).
24 See Chamberlain's letter to the Kaiser of 15 November 1901 and the Kaiser's reply of 31 December 1901 in Houston Stewart Chamberlain, *Briefe, 1882–1924*, 2 vols. (Munich, 1928), vol. II, pp. 137–40.
25 Chamberlain, *Politische Ideale*, 2nd ed. (Munich, 1915), p. 39.
26 Field, *Evangelist of Race*, pp. 352–95.
27 Geoffrey G. Field, 'Antisemitism and *Weltpolitik*', *Year Book of the Leo Baeck Institute* 18 (1973), p. 91.
28 Schwabe, *Wissenschaft und Kriegsmoral*, p. 53.
29 Fischer, *Krieg der Illusionen*, p. 748.
30 Karl Lamprecht, *Zur neuen Lage* (Leipzig, 1914), pp. 10–11.
31 Ibid., p. 91.
32 Ibid., pp. 14–15.
33 Kellermann, *Der Krieg der Geister*, pp. 98–9.
34 Fischer, *Krieg der Illusionen*, p. 561.
35 Dr Matthias Schwann, 'Die englischen Vettern', *Frankfurter Zeitung*, 3 November 1914.
36 Professor Albrecht Haupt, 'Unsere englischen Vettern', *Tag*, 4 November 1914.
37 Heinrich Spies, *Deutschlands Feind! England und die Vorgeschichte des Weltkrieges* (Berlin, 1915), pp. 8–9.
38 Ibid., p. 94.
39 See Chamberlain to Wilhelm II, 26 November 1914; in Chamberlain, *Briefe*, vol. II, p. 245.
40 Houston Stewart Chamberlain, *The Ravings of a Renegade*, translated by Charles H. Clarke, with an introduction by Lewis Melville (London, 1916).
41 Ibid., pp. 114–15.
42 Ibid., pp. 61–2.
43 Cf. Chamberlain, *Politische Ideale*, pp. 36–7.
44 Chamberlain, *Ravings of a Renegade*, p. 53.
45 Field, *Evangelist of Race*, p. 352.
46 Chamberlain, *Ravings of a Renegade*, p. 113.

47 Chamberlain, *Politische Ideale*, p. 36.
48 Wilhelm II to Chamberlain, 25 November 1914; in Chamberlain, *Briefe*, vol. II, pp. 244–5.
49 See e.g. *Reichsbote*, 5 March 1915, which carried a review of Chamberlain's *Kriegsaufsätze* under the title 'Houston Stewart Chamberlain über England und Deutschland'.
50 Cf. Schwabe, *Wissenschaft und Kriegsmoral*, p. 34.
51 See Dehio, *Germany and World Politics in the Twentieth Century*, esp. pp. 38–71.
52 *Deutsche Reden in schwerer Zeit*, ed. Zentralstelle für Volkswohlfahrt und dem Verein für volkstümliche Kurse von Berliner Hochschullehrern (Berlin, 1914).
53 Ulrich von Wilamowitz-Moellendorff, 'Krieges Anfang', in *Deutsche Reden in schwerer Zeit*, p. 6.
54 Ibid., p. 8.
55 Gustav Roethe, 'Wir Deutschen und der Krieg', in *Deutsche Reden in schwerer Zeit*, p. 20.
56 Hans Delbrück, 'Über den kriegerischen Charakter des deutschen Volkes', in: ibid., pp. 66 and 72–3. Cf. Annelise Thimme, *Hans Delbrück als Kritiker der Wilhelminischen Epoche* (Düsseldorf, 1955).
57 Wilhelm Dibelius, *England und wir* (Hamburg, 1914), p. 3.
58 Ibid., p. 10.
59 Ibid., p. 8.
60 Ibid., pp. 26–7.
61 See e.g. Spies, *Deutschlands Feind!*, p. 103 and n. 9.
62 Quoted in Schwabe, *Wissenschaft und Kriegsmoral*, p. 48.
63 The historical and philosophical justifications for this demand were first discussed in depth by Ferdinand Jakob Schmidt, 'Das Ethos des politischen Gleichgewichtsgedankens', *Preussische Jahrbücher* 158 (Oct.–Dec. 1914), pp. 1–15. See also the editor's (Hans Delbrück's) comments in the same volume, pp. 182–92.
64 Schwabe, *Wissenschaft und Kriegsmoral*, p. 47 and n. 16. The target here was the pamphlet written by a group of Oxford historians in October 1914 with the title *Why We Are at War* (Oxford, 1914).
65 Schulze-Gaevernitz, *Freie Meere!*, p. 23.
66 Ibid., p. 28.
67 Otto Hintze et al., *Deutschland und der Weltkrieg* (Berlin, 1915). For further details on the origins of this volume see Christoph Cornelißen, 'Politische Historiker und deutsche Kultur. Die Schriften und Reden von Georg von Below, Hermann Oncken und Gerhard Ritter im Ersten Weltkrieg', in Wolfgang J. Mommsen (ed.), *Kultur und Krieg. Die Rolle der Intellektuellen, Künstler und Schriftsteller im Ersten Weltkrieg*, (Munich, 1996), pp. 119–42.
68 Ernst Troeltsch, 'Der Geist der deutschen Kultur', in Hintze et al., *Deutschland und der Weltkrieg*, pp. 52–76.
69 Otto Hintze, 'Der Sinn des Krieges', in: ibid., p. 681.
70 Ibid., p. 678.
71 Ibid., p. 679.

72 Ibid., pp. 681–2.
73 Hermann Oncken, 'Deutschland und England', *Süddeutsche Monatshefte*, 11/2 (September 1914), p. 810.
74 Erich Marcks, 'Die Machtpolitik Englands', in Hintze et al., *Deutschland und der Weltkrieg*, p. 322. Also quoted in Wolfgang J. Mommsen, *Bürgerliche Kultur und künstlerische Avantgarde. Kultur und Politik im deutschen Kaiserreich, 1870–1918* (Frankfurt am Main and Berlin, 1994), p. 123.
75 Hans Delbrück, 'Das deutsche Militärsystem', in Hintze et al., *Deutschland und der Weltkrieg*, p. 180.
76 Friedrich Meinecke, 'Kultur, Machtpolitik und Militarismus', in Hintze et al., *Deutschland und der Weltkrieg*, pp. 620–1.
77 Ibid., p. 643. Also quoted in Dehio, *Germany and World Politics*, pp. 58–9.
78 Schwabe, *Wissenschaft und Kriegsmoral*, p. 52.
79 Cornelißen, 'Politische Historiker und deutsche Kultur', p. 129.
80 Schwabe, *Wissenschaft und Kriegsmoral*, p. 213 n. 42.
81 Otto von Gierke, 'Krieg und Kultur', in *Deutsche Reden in schwerer Zeit*, pp. 96–7.
82 Eduard Meyer, *England. Seine staatliche und politische Entwicklung und der Krieg gegen Deutschland* (Stuttgart and Berlin, 1915), p. 202.
83 Martin Spahn, *Im Kampf um unsere Zukunft* (Mönchen-Gladbach, 1915), p. 58.
84 Cf. Fischer, *Griff nach der Weltmacht*, pp. 217–18 and Fischer, *From Kaiserreich to Third Reich*. translated by Roger Fletcher (London, 1986), p. 66; also chapter 3 below.
85 Otto Hoetzsch, 'Gedanken über die politischen Ziele des Krieges', December 1914, pp. 2–3; copy in BA Potsdam, Reichskanzlei, no. 2476.
86 Hermann Schumacher, 'Unsere Kriegsziele, insbesondere im Westen', 20 June 1915; copy in ABBAW, Nachlaß Dietrich Schäfer, no. 4 / II.
87 Quoted in Cecil, *Albert Ballin. Business and Politics*, pp. 264–5.
88 See e.g. Schäfer's brochure 'Deutschland und der Osten', n.d. [1915]; copy in ABBAW, Nachlaß Dietrich Schäfer, no. 4 / I.
89 Johannes Haller, 'Britannia Delenda!', *Süddeutsche Zeitung*, 16 September 1914.
90 Oswald Spengler, *Briefe, 1913–1936*, ed. Anton M. Koktanek (Munich, 1963), p. 32.
91 Ibid., p. 33. Zama was the place where Hannibal's army was wiped out by the Romans at the end of the Second Punic War.
92 Cf. Spengler, *Preußentum und Sozialismus* (Munich, 1920).
93 Spengler, *Briefe*, p. 29.
94 Max von Gruber, *Krieg, Frieden und Biologie* (Berlin, 1915), p. 9.
95 Ibid., p. 12.
96 Ibid., p. 20.
97 Ibid., pp. 25–6.
98 Ibid., p. 22.
99 Max von Gruber, 'Die Mobilisierung des Ernährungswesens', *Süddeutsche Monatshefte* 11/2 (September 1914), p. 860.
100 Roger Chickering, *Karl Lamprecht. A German Academic Life, 1856–1915* (Atlantic Highlands, 1993), p. 435.

101 Wolfgang J. Mommsen, *Max Weber and German Politics, 1890–1920* (London, 1984), p. 208.

102 Stefan Kestler, *Die deutsche Auslandsaufklärung und das Bild der Ententemächte im Spiegel zeitgenössischer Propagandaveröffentlichungen während des Ersten Weltkrieges* (Frankfurt am Main, 1994).

103 Quoted in Jürgen von Ungern-Sternberg, 'Eduard Meyer und die deutsche Propaganda zu Beginn des Ersten Weltkrieges', *Wissenschaftliche Zeitschrift der Humboldt-Universität zu Berlin, Reihe Geistes- und Sozialwissenschaften* 40 (1991), pp. 38–9.

104 Meinecke, *Die deutsche Erhebung von 1914*, p. 51.

105 Ibid., pp. 34–5.

106 Otto Hintze, 'Deutschland und das Weltstaatensystem', in Hintze et al., *Deutschland und der Weltkrieg*, p. 4.

107 Alfred Lasson, 'Deutsche Art und Deutsche Bildung', in *Deutsche Reden in schwerer Zeit*, p. 116.

108 Thomas Mann, 'Gedanken im Kriege' (November 1914); reproduced in Thomas Mann, *Essays Band I: Frühlingssturm, 1893–1918*, ed. Hermann Kurzke and Stephan Stachorski (Frankfurt am Main, 1993), p. 188.

109 Ibid., p. 204–5.

110 Ibid., p. 197.

111 See Mann's famous short novel *Death in Venice* [1911] (Penguin edition, 1955) , p. 17.

112 Hans Kohn, *The Mind of Germany. The Education of a Nation* (New York, 1961), p. 254.

113 Cf. Peter Gay, *Weimar Culture. The Outsider as Insider* (Penguin edition, 1968), p. 83.

114 Sombart, *Händler und Helden*, p. 5.

115 Ibid., p. 64.

116 Ibid., p. 108.

117 Ibid., p. 48.

118 Ibid., pp. 144–5.

119 Friedrich Lenger, 'Werner Sombart als Propagandist eines deutschen Sieges', in Mommsen (ed.), *Kultur und Krieg*, p. 69. See also Lenger, *Werner Sombart, 1863–1941. Eine Biographie* (Munich, 1994), esp. pp. 219–52.

120 Scheler, *Der Genius des Krieges*, p. 413.

121 Cf. Dehio, *Germany and World Politics*, pp. 96–7.

122 Scheler, *Der Genius des Krieges*, pp. 53–4.

123 Ibid., p. 388.

124 Ibid., p. 38.

125 Cf. Kohn, *The Mind of Germany*, p. 301.

126 The Marxist–Hegelian contribution to the 'ideas of 1914' can best be seen through an examination of articles published in *Die Glocke*, the left-wing periodical edited by the Russian Revolutionary Alexander Helphand ('Parvus') between 1915 and 1919. See also Robert Sigel, 'Die Lensch–Cunow–Haenisch Gruppe. Ihr Einfluss auf die Ideologie der deutschen Sozialdemokratie im Ersten Weltkrieg', *Internationale wissenschaftliche Korrespondenz zur Geschichte der deutschen Arbeiterbewegung* 11 (1975), pp. 421–36.

127 Friedrich Naumann, *Mitteleuropa* (Berlin, 1915), pp. 142–3.
128 Schulze-Gaevernitz, *Freie Meere!*, p. 30.

3 German war aims and propaganda against England

1 Kruse, *Krieg und nationale Integration*, passim.
2 Such views were also common among right-wing Social Democrats such as Eduard David. As early as November 1914, in response to an article by Eduard Bernstein in the *Leipziger Volkszeitung* which was critical of the war, David wrote in the *Mainzer Volkszeitung*: 'Just as it is self-evident to us Social Democrats that we should see a rotten peace with Russia as a grave political error, so it must become self-evident that we will also show our teeth against the English war machine with its white and coloured allies.' Quoted in the *Deutsche Tageszeitung*, 21 November 1914.
3 Apart from Fritz Fischer's major study of war aims, this chapter is heavily indebted to two earlier studies: Hans Gatzke's *Germany's Drive to the West (Drang nach Westen). A Study of Germany's Western War Aims during the First World War* (Baltimore, Md., 1950); and Klaus Epstein's *Matthias Erzberger and the Dilemma of German Democracy* (Princeton, N.J., 1959). For more recent accounts see also Torsten Oppelland, *Reichstag und Aussenpolitik im Ersten Weltkrieg. Die deutschen Parteien und die Politik der USA, 1914–1918* (Düsseldorf, 1995); and Roger Chickering, *Imperial Germany and the Great War, 1914–1918* (Cambridge, 1998).
4 Cf. Volker Berghahn, *Der Tirpitz-Plan. Genesis und Verfall einer innenpolitischen Krisenstrategie unter Wilhelm II.* (Düsseldorf, 1971); Jonathan Steinberg, *Yesterday's Deterrent. Tirpitz and the Birth of the German Battle Fleet* (London, 1965); Holger Herwig, *'Luxury' Fleet. The Imperial German Navy, 1888–1918* (Atlantic Highlands, 1991).
5 Werner Rahn, 'The German Naval War, 1914–1918. Strategy and Experience', in Hugh Cecil and Peter H. Liddle (eds.), *Facing Armageddon. The First World War Experienced* (London, 1996), pp. 121–33.
6 Cf. Berghahn, *Germany and the Approach of War in 1914*, pp. 125–44.
7 Fischer, *Griff nach der Weltmacht*, pp. 41–6.
8 Görlitz (ed.), *The Kaiser and His Court*, pp. 15–16.
9 Fischer, *From Kaiserreich to Third Reich*, pp. 61–2; Scheck, *Alfred von Tirpitz*, p. 23.
10 Cf. Volker Berghahn and Wilhelm Deist, 'Kaiserliche Marine und Kriegsausbruch 1914. Neue Dokumente zur Julikrise', *Militärgeschichtliche Mitteilungen* 7 (1970), pp. 37–58.
11 Tirpitz, *Erinnerungen*, p. 395.
12 Ibid., pp. 395–6.
13 Fischer, *From Kaiserreich to Third Reich*, p. 62.
14 See e.g. Riezler's diary entry of 1 August 1916, which defined the 'threefold purpose' of the war, from the German point of view, as 'defence against present-day France, preventive war against the Russia of the future (as such, too late), struggle with Britain for world domination'. Quoted in Fischer, *From Kaiserreich to Third Reich*, pp. 54–5.

15 Ballin to Tirpitz, 1 October 1914; in Tirpitz, *Deutsche Ohnmachtspolitik*, pp. 131–3.

16 Hugo von Pohl, *Aus Aufzeichnungen und Briefen während der Kriegszeit* (Berlin, 1920), pp. 40–1.

17 Quoted in Fischer, *Griff nach der Weltmacht*, p. 218.

18 See Holger H. Herwig, 'Admirals *versus* Generals. The War Aims of the Imperial German Navy, 1914–1918', *Central European History* 5 (1972), pp. 208–33.

19 Moltke to Wilhelm II, 15 January 1915; in Helmuth von Moltke, *Erinnerungen, Briefe, Dokumente* (Stuttgart, 1922), p. 411.

20 Ibid., p. 412, emphasis added.

21 Herwig, 'Admirals *versus* Generals', pp. 212–13.

22 Afflerbach, *Falkenhayn*, pp. 321–5. Tirpitz had a fairly low opinion of Falkenhayn anyway, describing him once as an 'Armee- und persönlicher Egoist' – see Tirpitz to Capelle, 6 September 1914; in Tirpitz, *Deutsche Ohnmachtspolitik*, p. 95.

23 Tirpitz to Wilhelm II, 6 August 1914; in Tirpitz, *Deutsche Ohnmachtspolitik*, p. 42.

24 Tirpitz to Prince Heinrich von Preußen, 10 September 1914; in ibid., p. 102.

25 Tirpitz, *Erinnerungen*, p. 408.

26 See e.g. Tirpitz, *Deutsche Ohnmachtspolitik*, pp. 58–9, 65, 144–5, 179. Also Tirpitz, *Erinnerungen*, pp. 421–2, 440; and Gatzke, *Germany's Drive*, p. 11.

27 Cf. Cecil, *Ballin*, pp. 269–70.

28 Herwig, 'Admirals *versus* Generals', p. 213.

29 Ibid., p. 232.

30 Pohl to Behncke, 6 September 1914; in BA-MA Freiburg, Nachlaß Behncke, no. 2.

31 Ibid.

32 Egmont Zechlin, 'Deutschland zwischen Kabinettskrieg und Wirtschaftskrieg. Politik und Kriegsführung in den ersten Monaten des Weltkrieges 1914', *Historische Zeitschrift* 199 (1964), pp. 392–4.

33 Pohl, *Aus Aufzeichnungen und Briefen*, p. 40.

34 Cf. Tirpitz to Admiral v. Capelle, 6 September 1914, Tirpitz, *Deutsche Ohnmachtspolitik*, p. 95.

35 Tirpitz, *Erinnerungen*, p. 399.

36 Ibid., p. 398.

37 Herwig, 'Admirals *versus* Generals', p. 213.

38 'Die Bedeutung Belgiens und seiner Häfen für unsere Seegeltung', October 1915, p. 3. Copy in BA-MA Freiburg, Nachlaß Tirpitz, N 253/231.

39 Ibid., p. 8.

40 For examples see Scheck, *Alfred von Tirpitz*, pp. 68–9.

41 On this theme see also Scheck, 'Der Kampf des Tirpitz-Kreises um den uneingeschränkten U-Boot-Krieg und einen politischen Kurswechsel im deutschen Kaiserreich, 1916–1917', *Militärgeschichtliche Mitteilungen* 55 (1996), pp. 66–91.

42 Roesicke to Wangenheim, 17 March 1915, in BA Koblenz, Kl. Erw. 230 (Gustav Roesicke), no. 1.

43 On Reventlow's life and ideas see Horst Boog, 'Graf Ernst zu Reventlow (1869–1943). Eine Studie zur Krise der deutschen Geschichte seit dem Ende des 19. Jahrhunderts', Ph.D. thesis (University of Heidelberg, 1965). Also see the highly critical account by the naval correspondent of the *Berliner Tageblatt* during the war, Lothar Persius, published as *Graf Ernst zu Reventlow* (Berlin, 1918).

44 Cf. Heinrich Claß, *Wider den Strom. Vom Werden und Wachsen der nationalen Opposition im alten Reich* (Leipzig, 1932), pp. 129–30.

45 *Neue Preußische (Kreuz-)Zeitung*, 2 September 1914.

46 Ernst zu Reventlow, 'Wieder Verständigung?', *Deutsche Tageszeitung*, 3 September 1914.

47 Klaus Meyer, *Theodor Schiemann als politischer Publizist* (Frankfurt am Main and Hamburg, 1956), pp. 194–200.

48 See e.g. Hoetzsch to Westarp, 21 January 1915; in BA Potsdam, Nachlaß Westarp, no. 5.

49 'Die zwei imperialistischen Strömungen in Deutschland', anonymous article in *New Yorker Vorwärts*, 8 May 1915; cited in Eduard Bernstein, *Die Wahrheit über die Einkreisung Deutschlands* (Berlin, 1920), pp. 9–10.

50 Quoted in Koszyk, *Deutsche Pressepolitik*, p. 161.

51 Roesicke to Wangeheim, 13 October 1915; in BA Potsdam, Nachlaß Wangenheim, no. 10. Cf. Kuno Graf von Westarp, *Konservative Politik im letzten Jahrzehnt des Kaiserreiches*, 2 vols. (Berlin, 1935), vol. II, p. 181. The ban on the *Deutsche Tageszeitung* was officially lifted on the same evening.

52 See Bethmann Hollweg's marginal comments on a telegram from Jagow on 8 October 1915; in PA-AA Bonn, R 22416: Presse und Journalisten, vol. 5.

53 In September 1915 a 12-foot-high wooden statue of Hindenburg was erected in the middle of the Königsplatz. Visitors were encouraged to hammer nails into the statue as a means of raising funds for German war widows, thus turning it into an 'iron Hindenburg'. For further details see Peter Fritzsche, *Germans into Nazis* (London, 1998), p. 50.

54 'Kundgebung am Eisernen Hindenburg', *Deutsche Tageszeitung*, 3 October 1915.

55 On the domestic political impact of the Lusitania and Arabic affairs in Germany see also Oppelland, *Reichstag und Aussenpolitik*, pp. 60–93.

56 Wilhelm II's marginal comments on a telegram from Police President von Jagow to Valentini, 5 October 1915; in GStA Berlin-Dahlem, Ministerium des Innern, Rep. 77, Tit. 863a, no. 6.

57 See also Police President von Jagow's report to Loebell, 12 October 1915; in ibid. Here Jagow describes Reventlow as 'a person who is no doubt somewhat partisan in his approach to journalism, but nonetheless places the Fatherland above politics, and whose services to the Fatherland before the war were duly recognised through the award of an order'.

58 Ernst zu Reventlow, *Der Vampir des Festlandes. Eine Darstellung der englischen Politik nach ihren Triebkräften, Mitteln und Wirkungen* (Berlin, 1915); quoted from the abridged American translation by George Chatterton-Hill, *The Vampire of the Continent* (New York, 1916), pp. 2–3.

59 Ibid., pp. 17–18.

60 See the introduction to the third German edition, (Berlin, 1915), p. 1.

61 See e.g. Zimmermann to Jagow, 22 October 1914; in PA-AA Bonn, R 22414: Presse und Journalisten (September–October 1914): 'Reventlow is working, according to confidential information, in the rooms of the Reich Naval Office; on whose behalf we are still trying to find out.'

62 See Tirpitz, *Deutsche Ohnmachtspolitik*, pp. 628–33; also see the declaration by Reventlow of 9 March 1916 in ibid., p. 497.

63 Ernst zu Reventlow, 'Land und See', *Das Größere Deutschland*, no. 6, 5 February 1916, p. 169.

64 Ernst zu Reventlow, *Indien. Seine Bedeutung für Großbritannien, Deutschland und die Zukunft der Welt* (Berlin, 1917), pp. 24–5.

65 Ibid., p. 23.

66 Ibid., p. 25.

67 Westarp to Bethmann Hollweg, 17 April 1915; in BA Potsdam, Nachlaß Westarp, no. 6.

68 Quoted in Gatzke, *Germany's Drive*, p. 15.

69 On Stinnes' war aims programme see Claß, *Wider den Strom*, pp. 327–9; Gatzke, *Germany's Drive*, pp. 34–7; Fischer, *Griff nach der Weltmacht*, p. 115.

70 Quoted in Fischer, *Griff nach der Weltmacht*, p. 198.

71 For a useful overview of recent literature on this subject see Martin Kröger, 'Revolution als Programm. Ziele und Realität deutscher Orientpolitik im Ersten Weltkrieg', in Michalka (ed.), *Der Erste Weltkrieg*, pp. 366–91.

72 Max Freiherr von Oppenheim, 'Denkschrift betreffend die Revolutionierung der islamischen Gebiete unserer Feinde', October 1914; copy in PA-AA Bonn, R 20938: Unternehmungen und Aufwiegelungen gegen unsere Feinde (1915).

73 Theodor Springmann, *Deutschland und der Orient* (Hagen in Westfalen, 1915), pp. 22–3.

74 Konrad von Winterstetter (i.e. Dr Albert Ritter), *Nordkap–Bagdad. Das politische Programm des Krieges* (Frankfurt am Main, 1915), pp. 32–3.

75 Significant exceptions here included, as we saw in the previous chapter, the German intellectuals Oswald Spengler and Werner Sombart, both of whom argued that the military occupation of Britain was a realisable German war aim.

76 Stresemann to Riesser, 17 November 1914; in PA-AA Bonn, Nachlaß Stresemann, no. 139.

77 Jakob Riesser, *England und Wir. Finanzielle und wirtschaftliche Kriegswirkungen in England und Deutschland*, 2nd ed. (Leipzig, 1915), pp. 112–13.

78 Cf. Berghahn, *Germany and the Approach of War*, pp. 160–1.

79 Verein Deutscher Eisen- und Stahlindustrieller, 'Beschlussantrag zum Kampf gegen England', 17 February 1915; copy in PA-AA Bonn, Nachlaß Stresemann, no. 145.

80 Cf. Gatzke, *Germany's Drive*, pp. 37–8.

81 For further details see Gary D. Stark, *Entrepreneurs of Ideology. Neoconservative Publishers in Germany, 1890–1933* (Chapel Hill, N.C., 1981), pp. 126–7.

82 Gustav Stresemann, 'Aufzeichnungen über die Sitzung des Unterausschusses des Kriegsausschusses der deutschen Industrie am 7. November 1914'; in PA-AA Bonn, Nachlaß Stresemann, no. 139.
83 Cf. Fischer, *Griff nach der Weltmacht*, pp. 191–2.
84 Text of the May 1915 petition in Salomon Grumbach, *Das annexionistische Deutschland. Eine Sammlung von Dokumenten* (Lausanne, 1917), pp. 123–32.
85 Further details in Gatzke, *Germany's Drive*, pp. 38–44.
86 Cf. Roesicke to Wangenheim, 20 September 1914; in BA Potsdam, Nachlaß Wangenheim, no. 9
87 Wangenheim to Roesicke, 9 September 1914; in ibid.
88 Gatzke, *Germany's Drive*, p. 40; Claß, *Wider den Strom*, pp. 354–5.
89 Wangenheim to Roesicke, 21 December 1914; in BA Potsdam, Nachlaß Wangenheim, no. 9.
90 See e.g. *Die Auskunftstelle Vereinigter Verbände und ihre Ausgaben*, n.d. (1915); copy in BA Koblenz, Nachlaß Traub, no. 43.
91 Cf. Gatzke, *Germany's Drive*, p. 169.
92 Auskunftstelle Vereinigter Verbände (ed.), *Gedanke und Wünsche deutscher Vereine und Verbände zur Gestaltung des Friedens*, various editions (Berlin, 1915–18); J. Neumann, *Die Zerschmetterung Deutschlands. Die Kriegsziele unserer Feinde im Spiegel ihrer eigenen Äußerungen* (Berlin, 1915); Paul Fleischer, *Welche Gefahr droht Deutschland und seine Arbeiter von einem unbesiegten England?* (Berlin, 1916); Oskar Poensgen, *Was haben die Engländer gegen uns?* (Berlin, 1917). For further examples see BA Koblenz, ZSg. 2/26.
93 On the Independent Committee, apart from the extensive archival sources, see Karl-Heinrich Schädlich, 'Der "Unabhängige Ausschuß für einen deutschen Frieden" als ein Zentrum der Annexionspropaganda des deutschen Imperialismus im Ersten Weltkrieg', in: Fritz Klein et al. (eds.), *Politik im Krieg. Studien zur Politik der deutschen herrschenden Klassen im Ersten Weltkrieg* (East Berlin, 1964), pp. 50–65. Also see Dirk Stegmann, *Die Erben Bismarcks. Parteien und Verbände in der Spätphase des Wilhelminischen Deutschlands. Sammlungspolitik, 1897–1918* (Cologne and West Berlin, 1970), pp. 465–72.
94 Cf. Dietrich Schäfer, *Mein Leben* (Berlin, 1926), p. 172.
95 Traugott von Jagow to Loebell, 23 March 1916; in GStA Berlin-Dahlem, Ministerium des Innern, Rep. 77, Tit. 863a, no. 6.
96 Cf. Hartmut Thieme, *Nationalliberalismus in der Krise. Die nationalliberale Fraktion des Preußischen Abgeordnetenhauses, 1914–1918* (Boppard am Rhein, 1963), pp. 53–4. Also see Gustav Stresemann, *Deutsches Ringen und Deutsches Hoffen* (Berlin, 1914); Stresemann, *Englands Wirtschaftskrieg gegen Deutschland* (Stuttgart, 1915); Stresemann, *Das deutsche Wirtschaftsleben im Kriege* (Leipzig, 1915). Since Stresemann's views on England and English economic rivalry have already been discussed in detail elsewhere – e.g. in Marvin L. Edwards, *Gustav Stresemann and the Greater Germany, 1914–1918* (New York, 1963), and more recently in Constanze Baumgart, *Stresemann und England* (Cologne, Weimar and Vienna, 1996) – I have decided to focus more on other National Liberal leaders in this section. Stresemann's views were in any case far from untypical for members of his party.

97 Quoted in Grumbach, *Das annexionistische Deutschland*, pp. 71–2.
98 Ibid., p. 74.
99 Karl-Peter Reiß (ed.), *Von Bassermann zu Stresemann. Die Sitzungen des nationalliberalen Zentralvorstandes, 1912–1917* (Düsseldorf, 1967), p. 203.
100 Grumbach, *Das annexionistische Deutschland*, p. 76.
101 Thieme, *Nationalliberalismus in der Krise*, p. 53.
102 Grumbach, *Das annexionistische Deutschland*, p. 37.
103 Ibid., pp. 45, 53–6.
104 Adolf Grabowsky, 'Die Weltmacht', *Das Neue Deutschland*, no. 4, 28 October 1914, p. 3; quoted in Grumbach, *Das annexionistische Deutschland*, p. 213.
105 Cf. Hoetzsch to Westarp, 21 January 1915; in BA Potsdam, Nachlaß Westarp, no. 5.
106 Grumbach, *Das annexionistische Deutschland*, p. 40.
107 Quoted in Abraham J. Peck, *Radicals and Reactionaries. The Crisis of Conservatism in Wilhelmine Germany* (Cincinnati, Ohio, 1978), p. 189.
108 On the Army League see Marilyn Shevin Coetzee, *The German Army League. Popular Nationalism in Wilhelmine Germany* (Oxford, 1990).
109 'Denkschrift des Deutschen Wehrvereins über Belgien', November 1914; copy in BA Potsdam, Reichskanzlei, no. 1415.
110 Kurt von Strantz, 'Englands irische Gefahr', *Die Wehr* 11/12, (1914); quoted in Coetzee, *The German Army League*, p. 110. For further examples of Army League speeches and propaganda see Grumbach, *Das annexionistische Deutschland*, pp. 151–5.
111 Großadmiral von Koester, 'Der Deutsche Flotten-Verein und die Kriegsziele', June 1916; copy in BA Koblenz, Nachlaß Haller, no. 2.
112 'Gott strafe England', *Alldeutsche Blätter*, no. 50, 12 December 1914, pp. 436–7.
113 Grumme-Douglas to Westarp, 12 December 1914; in BA Potsdam, Nachlaß Westarp, no. 4.
114 Roesicke to Westarp, 17 December 1914; in ibid.
115 Gebsattel to Cetto, 14 January 1915; quoted in Peck, *Radicals and Reactionaries*, p. 168.
116 Quoted in Stark, *Entrepreneurs of Ideology*, p. 128. On Lehmann see also Melanie Lehmann (ed.), *Verleger J.F. Lehmann. Ein Leben im Kampf für Deutschland* (Munich, 1935).
117 Gebsattel to Westarp, 3 December 1914; in BA Potsdam, Nachlaß Westarp, no. 4.
118 Gebsattel to Theodor, 16 July 1915; in BA Potsdam, Nachlaß Gebsattel, no. 2.
119 Wangenheim to Roesicke, 8 April 1915; in BA Potsdam, Nachlaß Wangenheim, no. 10.
120 Konstantin von Gebsattel, 'Forderungen zum Kriegsziel', May 1915; copy in BA Potsdam, Reichskanzlei, no. 1415.
121 On the genesis of the 'Petition of the Intellectuals' see Gatzke, *Germany's Drive*, pp. 117–20; and Klaus Schwabe, 'Zur politischen Haltung der deutschen Professoren im Ersten Weltkrieg', *Historische Zeitschrift* 192 (1961), pp. 601–34.
122 Quoted in Gatzke, *Germany's Drive*, p. 120.

123 Schwabe, 'Zur politischen Haltung der deutschen Professoren', p. 616.
124 See e.g. below, p. 127.
125 Fischer, *Griff nach der Weltmacht*, pp. 217–18.
126 Hoetzsch to Westarp, 21 January 1915; in BA Potsdam, Nachlaß Westarp, no. 5.
127 Görlitz (ed.), *The Kaiser and His Court*, p. 105 (Müller's diary entry for 9 September 1915).
128 Ibid., pp. 100–1 (Müller's diary entry for 17 August 1915). See also Scheck, 'Der Kampf des Tirpitz Kreises', p. 75; Scheck, *Alfred von Tirpitz*, pp. 48–9.
129 Cf. Westarp, *Konservative Politik*, vol. II, p. 303: 'One final hindrance in the campaign for Bethmann's overthrow was the question of who his successor should be. The decision here was not in our hands, and the choice was very limited.'

4 'U-boat demagogy' and the crisis of Bethmann Hollweg's chancellorship

1 Cf. Rahn, 'The German Naval War', passim.
2 On the neutrality period and America's entry into the war in 1917 see in particular E.R. May, *The World War and American Isolation, 1914–1917* (Cambridge, Mass., 1959). A useful overview is also provided in David Stevenson, *The First World War and International Politics* (Oxford, 1988), pp. 64–86.
3 Görlitz (ed.), *The Kaiser and His Court*, pp. 126–7 (Müller's diary entry for 15 January 1916).
4 Ibid., p. 153 (Müller's diary entry for 30 April 1916).
5 Cf. Isabel Hull, *The Entourage of Kaiser Wilhelm II. 1888–1918* (Cambridge, 1982), pp. 279–81; Scheck, *Alfred von Tirpitz*, pp. 28–9.
6 Görlitz (ed.), *The Kaiser and His Court*, pp. 126 and 129 (Müller's diary entries for 15 and 24 January 1916). See also Holtzendorff's confidential memorandum of 12 February, 'Die englische Wirtschaft und der U-Bootkrieg', which put forward the same arguments in greater detail; copy in BA Potsdam, Reichskanzlei, no. 2410.
7 Görlitz (ed.), *The Kaiser and His Court*, pp. 133–4 (Müller's diary entry for 9 February 1916).
8 Matthias Erzberger, *Erlebnisse im Weltkrieg* (Berlin, 1920), p. 213.
9 Conrad Haußmann, *Schlaglichter. Reichstagsbriefe und Aufzeichnungen*, ed. Ulrich Zeller (Frankfurt am Main, 1924), esp. pp. 60–1.
10 Count Johann Heinrich Bernstorff, *Deutschland und Amerika. Erinnerungen aus dem fünfjährigen Kriege* (Berlin, 1920), pp. 240–50.
11 For the Kaiser's earlier 'humane' standpoint see Görlitz (ed.), *The Kaiser and His Court*, p. 126 (Müller's diary entry for 15 January 1916). For Erzberger's views see his *Erlebnisse im Weltkrieg*, pp. 208–28, and Epstein, *Matthias Erzberger*, pp. 153–63.
12 Görlitz (ed.), *The Kaiser and His Court*, p. 153 (Müller's diary entry for 30 April 1916).
13 See e.g. Haase's Reichstag speech on 24 March 1916 calling for an immedi-

ate peace 'without victors or vanquished'; in Sten. Ber./Reichstag, vol. 307, pp. 842–4.

14 For further details on the debate on press censorship led by Freiherr von Zedlitz und Neukirch on 22 and 23 February see GStA Berlin-Dahlem, Ministerium des Innern, Rep. 77, Tit. 885, no. 4. Also Sten. Ber./Pr. Abg. Haus, 22nd legislative period 1916/17, vol. 1, pp. 778–840 and 842–923.

15 See e.g. Wolff, *Tagebücher*, vol. I, p. 352 (diary entry for 25 February 1916). In the above-mentioned debate in the Prussian House of Deputies, the National Liberal Walter Bacmeister had declared: 'In spite of Liebknecht and Theodor Wolff, these are wonderful times' (p. 901).

16 Bodelschwingh to Ullstein press, 3 December 1914; copy in BA Potsdam, Reichskanzlei, no. 1415.

17 See e.g. the Cologne incident of July 1915, when National Liberal leaders, invited to address a joint meeting of the National Liberal steering committees for the Rhineland and Westphalia, made speeches attacking the Chancellor's 'weak' policies and criticising the government's censorship regulations. Further details in BA Potsdam, Reichskanzlei, no. 2447/3.

18 Haußmann, *Schlaglichter*, p. 57.

19 Hopp to Weilnböck, 22 March 1916; in BA Koblenz, Nachlaß Weilnböck, no. 27b.

20 Traugott von Jagow, '61. Stimmungsbericht', 18 March 1916; in Materna and Schrenkenbach (eds.), *Berichte des Berliner Polizeipräsidenten*, p. 116.

21 Ibid.

22 Sten. Ber./Reichstag, vol. 307, pp. 1257–78 and 1334–59. See also the Conservative Party pamphlet, *Die Zensur im Reichstag. Aus der Sitzungen vom 25. und 30. Mai 1916 nach den stenographischen Berichten* (Berlin, 1916); copy in GStA Berlin-Dahlem, Rep. 92, Nachlaß Wolfgang Kapp, no. 424.

23 Erzberger, *Erlebnisse*, p. 216.

24 Copies of two of these letters (2 April and 6 July 1916) were illegally distributed in pamphlet form under the title 'Zeppelin und der Reichskanzler' (Als Handschrift gedruckt), with a contribution from an anonymous writer suggesting that Zeppelin had become increasingly disillusioned with the Chancellor's weak stance towards England and his refusal to take advice from experts. For further details see, e.g., BHStA IV Munich, Akten des stellvertretenden Generalkommandos des I. bayerischen Armeekorps, no. 1938.

25 See e.g. Traugott von Jagow, '26. Stimmungsbericht', 23 January 1915, in Materna and Schrenkenbach (eds.), *Berichte des Berliner Polizeipräsidenten*, p. 38: 'The air raids on England's east coast have been received with undisguised satisfaction as the beginning of the long-awaited reckoning.'

26 Haußmann, *Schlaglichter*, p. 56.

27 See the report sent by Wilhelm von Stumm to Bethmann Hollweg, 22 March 1916; in BA Potsdam, Reichskanzlei, no. 2448/2.

28 Haußmann, *Schlaglichter*, pp. 58–9. In the summer of 1916 Zeppelin came under increased pressure to distance himself publicly from right-wing attacks on the Chancellor and to deny his own involvement in these attacks. He finally did so in a letter to Bethmann on 5 September, which was

published a few days later in the official government newspaper, the *Norddeutsche Allgemeine Zeitung*. For further details see BA Potsdam, Reichskanzlei, no. 2448/2.

29 Hans von Liebig, *Die Politik Bethmann Hollwegs* (Munich, 1919), pp. 39–75.

30 Peck, *Radicals and Reactionaries*, p. 177.

31 Liebig, *Die Politik Bethmann Hollwegs*, pp. 278–9.

32 See e.g. Gebsattel to Claß, 12 November 1915; in BA Potsdam, Reichskanzlei, no. 1418, concerning the planned distribution of Liebig's book; and Gebsattel to Lehmann, 24 November 1915, in: ibid., Nachlaß Gebsattel, no. 2, containing list of people to whom Liebig's book was to be sent.

33 Stark, *Entrepreneurs of Ideology*, pp. 129–30.

34 Quoted in Konrad Jarausch, *The Enigmatic Chancellor. Bethmann Hollweg and the Hubris of Imperial Germany* (New Haven and London, 1973), p. 360 and n. 19.

35 Stark, *Entrepreneurs of Ideology*, p. 128.

36 Cf. Lehmann an die Mitarbeiter im Felde, 8 July 1916; in Lehmann, *Lebenslauf und Briefe*, p. 136.

37 See copy of report sent by the Polizeiamt der Stadt Leipzig to the Saxon Ministry of the Interior, 24 July 1917; in BA Potsdam, Reichskanzlei, no. 1420.

38 See e.g. Deutscher Volksrat to Bethmann Hollweg, 30 June 1917; in ibid.

39 Copy of Pudor's 'Anklageschrift gegen den Reichskanzler' in BA Potsdam, Reichskanzlei, no. 2410. According to a letter in the same file from the Reich Justice Office to Bethmann, dated 31 July 1916, the Berlin state prosecutor had already informed Pudor of his decision not to proceed with his complaint.

40 Pudor, 'Anklageschrift gegen den Reichskanzler', pp. 28–39.

41 Copy in BA Koblenz, Nachlaß Loebell, no. 19.

42 Sten. Ber./Reichstag, vol. 307, pp. 1510–11. Also quoted in Gatzke, *Germany's Drive*, p. 130.

43 See e.g. BA Koblenz, Kl. Erw. 341, Nachlaßpapiere Rudolf von Valentini, no. 2, Auszug aus einem Schreiben Kaiser Wilhelm II. an Generalfeldmarschall von Hindenburg betr. Hetzschreiben gegen den Kanzler Bethmann Hollweg, 28 June 1916. Also the various press reactions to Bethmann's Reichstag speech of 5 June 1916 cited in Thimme (ed.), *Bethmann Hollwegs Kriegsreden*, pp. 128–9.

44 Wolff, *Tagebücher*, vol. I, p. 387 (diary entry for 4 June 1916).

45 Erich Matthias and Susanne Miller (eds.), *Das Kriegstagebuch des Reichstagsabgeordneten Eduard David* (Düsseldorf, 1966), p. 193.

46 On the middle-class German peace movement during the war see e.g. James D. Shand, 'Doves among the Eagles. German Pacifists and Their Government during World War I', *Journal of Contemporary History* 10/1 (1975), pp. 95–108; Ludwig Quidde, *Der deutsche Pazifismus während des Ersten Weltkrieges, 1914–1918*, ed. Karl Holl (Boppard am Rhein, 1979); and Wilfried Eisenbeiss, *Die bürgerliche Friedensbewegung in Deutschland während des Ersten Weltkrieges: Organisation, Selbstverständnis und politische Praxis, 1913/14–1919* (Frankfurt am Main, 1980).

47 This was also the main idea put forward by Bethmann Hollweg in a con-

versation with Bülow on 8 August 1914. See Fischer, *From Kaiserreich to Third Reich*, p. 61, n. 56.

48 Cf. Hans Delbrück, *Bismarcks Erbe* (Berlin and Vienna, 1915), p. 202: 'The first and most important of all our demands, which we must raise in any future peace negotiations, must be [the acquisition of] a very large colonial empire, a German India.'

49 Cf. Fischer, *Griff nach der Weltmacht*, pp. 117–31.

50 Quoted in Gatzke, *Germany's Drive*, p. 57.

51 Daniel Frymann (i.e. Heinrich Claß), *Wenn ich der Kaiser wär'* (Leipzig, 1912).

52 Otto Hammann, *Bilder aus der letzten Kaiserzeit* (Berlin, 1922), pp. 113–14.

53 For interviews with Bethmann Hollweg see Wolff, *Tagebücher*, vol. I, pp. 153–64 (diary entry for 19 February 1915); pp. 263–5 (diary entry for 30 July 1915); pp. 318–23 (diary entry for 9 December 1915).

54 See e.g. Anton von Monts, 'Die Kriegsziele unserer Gegner', *Berliner Tageblatt*, 14 April 1915.

55 Monts to Wolff, 30 April 1915; in Wolff, *Tagebücher*, vol. II, pp. 886–7.

56 Ibid.

57 Wolff, *Tagebücher*, vol. I, p. 206 (diary entry for 19 April 1915); p. 186 (diary entry for 18 March 1915); p. 195 (diary entry for 30 March 1915).

58 Ibid., p. 178 (diary entry for 7 March 1915); p. 197 (diary entry for 5 April 1915).

59 Ibid., p. 207 (diary entry for 20 April 1915).

60 See Wolff's account in Wolff, *Tagebücher*, vol. I, pp. 251–3 (diary entry for 9 July 1915).

61 Text of declaration in Grumbach, *Das annexionistische Deutschland*, pp. 409–11. Cf. Gatzke, *Germany's Drive*, pp. 132–3; Mommsen, *Max Weber and German Politics*, pp. 197–8.

62 Schwabe, 'Zur politischen Haltung der deutschen Professoren', p. 616.

63 Cf. Gatzke, *Germany's Drive*, p. 133.

64 Ballin to Wolff, 13 July 1915; in Wolff, *Tagebücher*, vol. II, p. 890.

65 Cecil, *Ballin*, pp. 267–8. Also Conrad Haußmann to Ballin, 25 October 1915, and Ballin to Haußmann, 28 October 1915; in PA-AA Bonn, Nachlaß Stresemann, no. 149.

66 The following is based on the account in Wolff, *Tagebücher*, vol. I, pp. 247–51 (diary entry for 7 July 1915).

67 Hans Delbrück, 'Der diplomatische Werkzeug – die Wilson'sche Friedens-Rede', *Preussische Jahrbücher* 167 (January–March 1917), pp. 345–6.

68 Gatzke, *Germany's Drive*, pp. 134–7; Schwabe, *Wissenschaft und Kriegsmoral*, pp. 117–20; Mommsen, *Max Weber and German Politics*, pp. 235–40.

69 Quoted in *Vorwärts*, 20 July 1916.

70 Cf. Gatzke, *Germany's Drive*, p. 135; Stegmann, *Die Erben Bismarcks*, pp. 472–3.

71 Quoted in Mommsen, *Max Weber and German Politics*, p. 204.

72 Mumm to Hammann, 30 August 1915; in BA Potsdam, Nachlaß Hammann, no. 31.

73 Hammann, *Bilder aus der letzten Kaiserzeit*, p. 114.

74 Schoen to Bethmann Hollweg, 5 March 1916; in PA-AA Bonn, R 2560: Alldeutscher Verband, vol. 7.

75 Eisendecher to Bethmann Hollweg, 4 May 1917; in ibid.
76 Wolff, *Tagebücher*, vol. I, p. 446 (diary entry for 16 October 1916). Cf. Röhl, 'Vorsätzlicher Krieg?', pp. 200–1.
77 Wedel to Bethmann Hollweg, 11 May 1917; in PA-AA Bonn, R 2560: Alldeutscher Verband, vol. 7.
78 This and the following passages, unless otherwise indicated, are cited from a report in *Vorwärts*, 3 August 1916.
79 Cf. Rohrbach's article 'Unser Kolonialbesitz', *Das Größere Deutschland*, no. 37, 11 September 1915. Here Rohrbach writes: 'The day on which England sees her position in Egypt and the rest of the world vanishing before its eyes will also mark the birth of the new overseas Germany.'
80 Gwinner to Admiral von Capelle, 22 August 1914; in Tirpitz, *Deutsche Ohnmachtspolitik*, p. 67.
81 Fischer, *Griff nach der Weltmacht*, p. 109.
82 See pp. 131–2 below.
83 Pogge von Strandmann (ed.), *Walther Rathenau*, pp. 183–91. Cf. Zechlin, 'Deutschland zwischen Kabinettskrieg und Wirtschaftskrieg', pp. 397–405.
84 Rathenau to Mutius, 16 October 1914; in BA Potsdam, Reichskanzlei, no. 2465.
85 Cf. Gatzke, *Germany's Drive*, p. 59.
86 The entire article is reproduced in Epstein, *Matthias Erzberger*, pp. 410–12.
87 Fischer, *Griff nach der Weltmacht*, p. 355, n. 6.
88 On the divisions of the German left during the war, which first began to emerge in the spring of 1915, see also Susanne Miller, *Burgfriede und Klassenkampf. Die deutsche Sozialdemokratie im Ersten Weltkrieg* (Düsseldorf, 1974).
89 Wolff, *Tagebücher*, vol. I, p. 163 (diary entry for 9 February 1915).
90 Fischer, *Griff nach der Weltmacht*, pp. 192–3.
91 For further details see ibid., pp. 107–13.
92 Wolff, *Tagebücher*, vol. I, p. 229 (diary entry for 30 May 1915).
93 Ibid., pp. 209–10.
94 Westarp, *Konservative Politik*, vol. II, pp. 51–2.
95 Thimme (ed.), *Bethmann Hollwegs Kriegsreden*, pp. 57–8.
96 Ibid., pp. 60–1.
97 Fischer, *Griff nach der Weltmacht*, p. 261.
98 See e.g. BA-MA Freiburg, Nachlaß Schulze-Gaevernitz, no. 2, Schulze-Gaevernitz über die allgemeine Lage, 5 December 1914.
99 Fischer, *Griff nach der Weltmacht*, pp. 361–2.

5 The submarine crisis deepens

1 On Hindenburg and Ludendorff see Martin Kitchen, *The Silent Dictatorship. The Politics of the High Command under Hindenburg and Ludendorff, 1916–1918* (London, 1976).
2 Both the above quotations in Baldur Kaulisch, 'Die Auseinandersetzung über den uneingeschränkten U-Bootkrieg innerhalb der herrschenden Klassen im zweiten Halbjahr 1916 und seine Eröffnung im Februar 1917', in Fritz Klein et al. (eds.), *Politik im Krieg*, p. 91.

3 Reinhard Scheer, *Deutschlands Hochseeflotte im Weltkrieg* (Berlin, 1919), pp. 245–6.
4 The committee itself was a largely non-Prussian affair. Its three permanent members were the kingdoms of Bavaria, Saxony and Württemberg and its two other members were elected annually by the Bundesrat itself. In the 1914–18 period it met only five times and failed to exercise any real control over the direction of foreign policy. For further details see Ernst Deuerlein, *Der Bundesratsausschuß für auswärtige Angelegenheiten, 1870–1918* (Regensburg, 1955).
5 Kaulisch, 'Die Auseinandersetzung über den uneingeschränkten U-Boot-Krieg', p. 104.
6 Copy of petition in BA Potsdam, Reichskanzlei, no. 1417/1.
7 See Karl Alexander von Müller, *Mars und Venus. Erinnerungen, 1914–1919* (Stuttgart, 1954), pp. 125–6; and Schwabe, *Wissenschaft und Kriegsmoral*, p. 120.
8 Cf. Schäfer, *Mein Leben*, p. 185.
9 Copy of the Committee's founding appeal in BA Potsdam, Reichskanzlei, no. 1418.
10 Gebsattel to Lezius, 16 July 1915; in BA Potsdam, Nachlaß Gebsattel, no. 2.
11 Gatzke, *Germany's Drive*, p. 78.
12 Willy Albrecht, *Landtag und Regierung in Bayern am Vorabend der Revolution von 1918* (West Berlin, 1968), p. 155.
13 Thomsen to Gebsattel, 22 June 1915; in BA Potsdam, Nachlaß Gebsattel, no. 2.
14 Gebsattel to Dandl, 28 June 1915, and Dandl to Gebsattel, 20 July 1915; in ibid.
15 Karl-Heinrich Janßen, *Macht und Verblendung. Kriegszielpolitik der deutschen Bundesstaaten 1914/18* (Göttingen, 1963), pp. 67–9.
16 Gebsattel to Schäfer, 29 August 1915; in BA Potsdam, Nachlaß Gebsattel, no. 2.
17 Cf. Fischer, *Griff nach der Weltmacht*, pp. 223–35.
18 Ay, *Die Entstehung einer Revolution*, pp. 26–31.
19 Cf. Haußmann, *Schlaglichter*, pp. 62–3.
20 Quoted in Albrecht, *Landtag und Regierung*, p. 167.
21 Ibid., p. 168.
22 See the police report on this meeting in BHStA IV Munich, Akten des stellvertretenden Generalkommandos des I. bayerischen Armeekorps, no. 1710.
23 'Die deutsche Landwirtschaft und der Krieg gegen England!', anonymous article in *Deutsche Tageszeitung*, 19 July 1916.
24 According to a secret police report in BHStA IV Munich, Akten des Kriegsministerium, MKr. 11521. Cf. Albrecht, *Landtag und Regierung*, p. 170; Müller, *Mars und Venus*, pp. 128–9.
25 Full report on Reventlow's speech, entitled 'England, der Feind', *Münchner Neueste Nachrichten*, 30 July 1916.
26 See e.g. Meyer's memorandum on U-boat warfare, sent out to members of the Bundesrat, the Chief of General Staff and the Chief of Admiralty Staff on 16 March 1916; copy in BA Potsdam, Reichskanzlei, no. 2410.

27 'Konferenz des Ausschusses für einen dauernden Frieden in München am 30. Juli 1916 im Hotel Union, Barstrasse', anonymous report containing confidential details of proceedings at the meeting; in BA Potsdam, Reichskanzlei, no. 1417/2.

28 Ibid.

29 Copy of petition in Ernst Deuerlein (ed.), *Briefwechsel Hertling-Lerchenfeld, 1912–1917. Dienstliche Privatkorrespondenz zwischen dem bayerischen Ministerpräsidenten Georg Graf von Hertling und dem bayerischen Gesandten in Berlin, Hugo Graf von und zu Lerchenfeld*, 2 vols. (Boppard am Rhein, 1973), vol. II, pp. 660–7.

30 See *Bayerische Staatszeitung*, 6 August 1916; reproduced in Deuerlein (ed.), *Briefwechsel Hertling-Lerchenfeld*, vol. II, p. 659, n. 2.

31 See e.g. Lerchenfeld to Hertling, 2 August 1916; in ibid., pp. 654–6.

32 Albrecht, *Landtag und Regierung*, p. 166.

33 Bayerisches Kriegsministerium to Traub, 1 August 1916; in BA Koblenz, Nachlaß Traub, no. 44.

34 'Schreiben des bayerischen Kriegsministeriums an die bayerischen stellv. kommandierenden Generale', 5 August 1916; in Deist (ed.), *Militär und Innenpolitik*, vol. I, pp. 406–14.

35 Archival material on these police raids is available in BHStA IV Munich, Akten des stellvertretenden Generalkommandos des I. bayerischen Armeekorps, no. 1710.

36 Claß to Gebsattel, 12 August 1916; in BA Potsdam, Nachlaß Gebsattel, no. 2.

37 Gebsattel to Preysing, 29 August 1916; in ibid., emphasis in the original.

38 Hertling to Lerchenfeld, 4 August 1916; copy in BA Potsdam, Reichskanzlei, no. 1417/1.

39 Copy of report in BA Potsdam, Reichskanzlei, no. 1417/1.

40 Günther to Bethmann Hollweg, 13 August 1916; in BA Potsdam, Reichskanzlei, no. 1417/2.

41 Schäfer, *Mein Leben*, p. 190.

42 Ibid., pp. 191–2.

43 Copy of petition, which was signed by Beckh and Löwenstein on behalf of the Bavarian campaigners and by Schäfer and Prince Otto Salm-Horstmar on behalf of the Independent Committee, in ABBAW, Nachlaß Schäfer, no. 1 / I.

44 Haußmann, *Schlaglichter*, p. 69. See also the transcripts of this meeting which were passed on to the Chancellor by Matthias Erzberger on 17 October; in BA Potsdam, Reichskanzlei, no. 1422.

45 Full report published in the *Kölnische Zeitung*, 20 September 1916.

46 *Neue Preußische (Kreuz-)Zeitung*, 16 September 1916.

47 *Deutsche Tageszeitung*, 26 September 1916.

48 See the lengthy report in the *München-Augsburger Zeitung*, 19 September 1916.

49 See e.g. Schwabe, *Wissenschaft und Kriegsmoral*, p. 120; Albrecht, *Landtag und Regierung*, pp. 163–72; Stegmann, *Die Erben Bismarcks*, p. 468, n. 131; Scheck, 'Der Kampf des Tirpitz Kreises', p. 78; Hagenlücke, *Deutsche Vaterlandspartei*, pp. 231–2; Dieter Albrecht, 'Bayern im Ersten Weltkrieg,

1914–1918', in Max Spindler (ed.), *Handbuch der Bayerischen Geschichte. Vierter Band/I. Das neue Bayern, 1800–1970* (Munich, 1974), pp. 369–70; Wolfgang Zorn, *Bayerns Geschichte im 20. Jahrhundert* (Munich, 1986), pp. 94–5; Paul Hoser, *Die politischen, wirtschaftlichen und sozialen Hintergründe der Münchner Tagespresse zwischen 1914 und 1934. Teil 1: Methoden der Pressebeeinflussung* (Frankfurt am Main, 1990), pp. 43–9.

50 This chest of documents is mentioned in the memoirs of the historian Karl Alexander von Müller, himself a prominent member of the committee, who writes: 'Gruber later once showed me an entire chest full of letters and records pertaining to this committee, whose first chairman he was. If they have survived, they would almost certainly contain a rich source on the internal political history of those years, not least regarding the question of how the many different nationalist groups which established themselves in Germany were related to one another and the extent to which the Pan-German League and the associations closely linked to it were able to act as their secret sponsors' (Müller, *Mars und Venus*, p. 125). Unfortunately, correspondence between myself and various archives in Munich, as well as with German scholars who have worked either on Gruber himself or on Bavaria during the First World War, failed to reveal the whereabouts of this chest, which probably went missing at some point towards the end of the Second World War.

51 Volksausschuß für die rasche Niederkämpfung Englands. Mitgliederliste für Bayern (September 1917); copy in GStA Berlin-Dahlem, Rep. 92, Nachlaß Kapp, no. 665.

52 Müller, *Mars und Venus*, p. 126. For further evidence of these links see e.g. Salm to Claß, 30 August 1916; in BA Potsdam, Akten des Alldeutschen Verbandes, no. 453; Max von Gruber to Eduard Meyer, 4 October 1916; in ABBAW, Nachlaß Meyer, no. 321; Schäfer to Max Bauer, 30 January 1917; in BA Koblenz, Nachlaß Bauer, no. 11.

53 *Vorwärts*, 19 September 1916.

54 Wenng to Beckh, 9 January 1917; copy in BA Koblenz, Nachlaß Weilnböck, no. 28b.

55 Cf. Stegmann, *Die Erben Bismarcks*, p. 468; Hagenlücke, *Deutsche Vaterlandspartei*, p. 231.

56 Membership figures for Army League and Navy League taken from Coetzee, *The German Army League*, p. 99. Membership of the Pan-German League itself had fluctuated between 15,000 and 25,000 before the war, but by 1917 had increased considerably to 34,000, with an indirect following (via subsidiary organisations) of over 100,000. Cf. Gatzke, *Germany's Drive*, p. 25.

57 Cf. Gruber to Martin Spahn, 22 March 1917; in BA Koblenz, Nachlaß Spahn, no. 29.

58 See e.g. *Münchener Mitteilungen*, edited by the Münchener Volksausschuß für die rasche Niederkämpfung Englands, no. 2, 8 November 1916, containing article 'Was haben wir zu erwarten wenn wir England nicht besiegen?' Copy in BA Potsdam, Pressearchiv des Reichslandbundes, no. 8274, vol. 17. Unfortunately I have not been able to discover how many further issues of this publication were produced, or when it ceased to appear.

59 For Cossman's involvement see Müller, *Mars und Venus*, p. 250. For the involvement of J.F. Lehmann and Houston Stewart Chamberlain see Chamberlain to Lehmann, 12 August 1916; copy in BHStA IV Munich, Akten des stellvertretenden Generalkommandos des I. bayerischen Armeekorps, no. 1938.

60 Zorn, *Bayerns Geschichte*, p. 95. Cf. Franz Meffert, *Englands Verbrechen am katholischen Irland. Eine apologetische Studie* (Mönchen-Gladbach, 1917).

61 Albrecht, *Landtag und Regierung*, pp. 171–2. Even the archbishop of Munich, Cardinal Bettinger, was a supporter of unrestricted submarine warfare and it was only with considerable difficulty that Count Hertling finally persuaded him on 14 August to issue instructions to his clergy to desist from agitation against the Chancellor. Bettinger insisted, however, that he would first have to consult with other German bishops in order to produce a joint declaration on the issue.

62 Volksausschuß für die rasche Niederkämpfung Englands. Mitgliederliste für Bayern (see note 51 above).

63 For further evidence of anti-Prussian feeling in wartime Bavaria see David Clay Lodge, *Where Ghosts Walked. Munich's Road to the Third Reich* (London, 1997), pp. 59–65.

64 Cf. Franz von Bodelschwingh, *Innere Hemmungen kraftvoller Aussenpolitik* (Hanover, 1918), pp. 22–3. This speech, made to the local branch of the Pan-German League on 8 June 1918, contained a direct appeal to particularist Hanoverian sentiment. The Hanoverians had never felt themselves to be Prussians but were nonetheless 'proud to be citizens of the German Reich' and as such were entitled to feel ashamed of the 'weak' policies pursued by successive wartime governments in Berlin.

65 Biographical details in Karl Bosl, *Bosls Bayerische Biographie. 8000 Persönlichkeiten aus 15 Jahrhunderten* (Regensburg, 1983), p. 279.

66 Max von Gruber and Ernst Rüdin (eds.), *Fortpflanzung, Vererbung, Rassenhygiene. Illustrierter Führer durch die Gruppe Rassenhygiene der internationalen Hygiene-Ausstellung 1911 in Dresden* (Munich: J.F. Lehmann Verlag, 1911).

67 See e.g. Max von Gruber, 'Rassenhygiene als die wichtigste Aufgabe völkischer Innenpolitik', *Deutschlands Erneuerung* 2/1 (January 1918), pp. 17–32. Also Houston Stewart Chamberlain, 'Rasse und Nation', *Deutschlands Erneuerung*, 2/7 (July 1918), pp. 449–58.

68 See Hans Peter Bleuel, *Strength through Joy. Sex and Society in Nazi Germany* (London, 1973), pp. 39–42. For a highly subjective but not altogether uncritical view of Gruber and his academic career see also Karl Alexander von Müller, *Im Wandel einer Zeit. Erinnerungen, 1919–1932*, ed. Otto Alexander von Müller (Munich, 1966), pp. 245–8.

69 The following account of Gruber's political views is based on his article 'Völkische Außenpolitik', *Deutschlands Erneuerung* 1/1 (April 1917), pp. 74–87.

70 Full text of manifesto printed in *München-Augsburger Zeitung*, 19 September 1916.

71 Gruber to Traub, 9 September 1916; in BA Koblenz, Nachlaß Traub, no. 44.

72 Gruber to Spahn, 17 March 1917; in BA Koblenz, Nachlaß Spahn, no. 29.

73 Substance of Gruber's speech as reported in *Münchner Neueste Nachrichten*, 29 March 1917.
74 According to Karl Alexander von Müller (*Mars und Venus*, p. 125) the Volksausschuß included among its members 'Socialists aligned to David and Lensch', but he does not give any names. This is contradicted by Emil Kraepelin (*Lebenserinnerungen*, ed. H. Hippins, G. Peters and D. Ploog, West Berlin and Heidelberg, 1983, p. 192) who writes: 'Our efforts to draw in representatives of the Social Democratic Party remained, unfortunately, without result.' Certainly there is no mention of the Volksausschuß in David's wartime diaries, although they do contain a lot of adverse criticism of the nationalist opponents of Bethmann Hollweg, suggesting that David would not have been well disposed to the committee's aims. The idea of Lensch's involvement is more plausible, particularly because of his increasingly right-wing opinions and his willingness to engage in a radical defence of the Prusso-German state. Once again, however, there is no conclusive evidence.
75 See e.g. Max Cohen-Reuß, 'England und Rußland', *Die Glocke* 2/2 (October 1916), pp. 5–9. Also Wolff, *Tagebücher*, vol. I, p. 505 (diary entry for 13 June 1917). In Wolff's view there was little doubt that Cohen-Reuß was working on behalf of the pro-submarine lobby.
76 Paul Lensch, 'Friedensvermittlung?' *Tag*, 25 November 1916.
77 Westarp to the Volksausschuß für die rasche Niederkämpfung Englands, 19 September 1916; in BA Potsdam, Nachlaß Westarp, no. 16.
78 Oktavio Freiherr von Zedlitz und Neukirch, 'Unser Hauptfeind und seine Bekämpfung', *Post*, 21 September 1916.
79 'Dr Stresemann über die politische Lage', report in *Deutsche Tageszeitung*, 25 October 1916.
80 Ibid.
81 Roesicke to Westarp, 23 September 1916; copy in BA Koblenz, Nachlaß Weilnböck, no. 27a.
82 Bund der Landwirte, Königreich Bayern, no. 39, 24 September 1916; copy in ibid.
83 Gerlich to Traub, 5 October 1916; in BA Koblenz, Nachlaß Traub, no. 44.
84 Treutler to Bethmann Hollweg, 4 January 1917; in PA-AA Bonn, R 2560: Alldeutscher Verband, vol. 7.
85 Wenng to Beckh, 9 January 1917; copy in BA Koblenz, Nachlaß Weilnböck, no. 28b.
86 Cf. Zorn, *Bayerns Geschichte*, pp. 103–4.
87 Wenng to Weilnböck, 11 January 1917; in BA Koblenz, Nachlaß Weilnböck, no. 28b.
88 Ibid.
89 *Leipziger Volkszeitung*, 20 September 1916.
90 Ibid.
91 On the SPD's meeting in Munich on 4 September 1916, at which the Bavarian Landtag deputy Adolf Müller was the main speaker, see the police report in BHStA IV Munich, Akten des Kriegsministerium, MKr. 11522.
92 Copies of flysheet in BA Potsdam, Reichskanzlei, no. 1418, and BHStA IV

Munich, Akten des stellvertretenden Generalkommandos des I. bayerischen Armeekorps, no. 1938.

93 Angress, 'The German Army's "Judenzählung" of 1916', passim.

94 See e.g. Westarp, *Konservative Politik*, vol. II, p. 36; Schäfer, *Mein Leben*, p. 192.

95 Paul Rohrbach, 'Unmassgebliche Bemerkungen über den Zweifrontenkrieg', 29 September 1916; copy in BA Koblenz, Nachlaß Loebell, no. 19.

96 Rohrbach in *Die Hilfe*, no. 44, 2 November 1916; quoted in Kaulisch, 'Die Auseinandersetzung über den uneingeschränkten U-Boot-Krieg', p. 100.

97 Carl Peters, 'Die Niederringung Englands', *Süddeutsche Zeitung*, 4 January 1917.

98 Quoted in Kaulisch, 'Die Auseinandersetzung über den uneingeschränkten U-Boot-Krieg', p. 102.

99 Vize-admiral Kirchhoff, 'Zur Niederringung Englands', *Tägliche Rundschau*, 9 January 1917.

100 Fischer, *Griff nach der Weltmacht*, p. 369.

101 Bethmann Hollweg to Professor Wach, 10 October 1916; in BA Potsdam, Reichskanzlei, no. 1418, emphasis in the original.

102 Gatzke, *Germany's Drive*, p. 146.

103 Fischer, *Griff nach der Weltmacht*, pp. 370–1.

104 'Erklärung über die Stellung der Fortschrittlichen Volkspartei zur auswärtigen Politik', 10 November 1916; copy in BA Koblenz, Nachlaß Traub, no. 44.

105 Ibid.

106 Both the above quoted in Mommsen, *Max Weber and German Politics*, p. 241.

107 Wenng to Weilnböck, 15 December 1916; in BA Koblenz, Nachlaß Weilnböck, no. 27a.

108 On the German Peace Note see also Stevenson, *The First World War*, pp. 103–6.

109 The minutes of the meeting at Schloss Pless are reproduced in Helmut Otto and Karl Schmiedel (eds.), *Der Erste Weltkrieg. Dokumente* (East Berlin, 1977), pp. 222–4.

110 Görlitz (ed.), *The Kaiser and His Court*, p. 231 (Müller's diary entry for 9 January 1917). According to Müller, Bethmann's reaction was 'not so much approval as acceptance of the facts'.

111 Figures in John Keegan, *The First World War* (London, 1998), p. 401.

6 The Anglo-American powers and the collapse of the German empire

1 Fischer, *Griff nach der Weltmacht*, p. 822.

2 On Deutelmoser's conflict with the OHL see in particular Dirk Stegmann, 'Die Deutsche Inlandspropaganda, 1917/18. Zum innenpolitischen Machtkampf zwischen OHL und ziviler Reichsleitung in der Endphase des Kaiserreiches', *Militärgeschichtliche Mitteilungen* 12 (1972), pp. 75–103. Also Kitchen, *The Silent Dictatorship*, pp. 56–7.

3 Deist (ed.), *Militär und Innenpolitik*, vol. I, pp. 451–6.

4 See e.g. 'Denkschrift des Chefs des Kriegspresseamts über die Vor- und Nachteile einer öffentlichen Erörterung der Kriegsziele', 5 November 1916; reproduced in ibid., vol. I, pp. 431–40.

5 'Bericht der Abteilung VII an den Polizeipräsidenten Berlin', 14 March 1917; in Materna and Schrenkenbach (eds.), *Berichte des Berliner Polizeipräsidenten*, p. 178.

6 Cf. Ruth Glatzer, *Das Wilhelminische Berlin. Panorama einer Metropole, 1890–1918* (Berlin, 1997), p. 405.

7 Deist (ed.), *Militär und Innenpolitik*, vol. II, pp. 744–6.

8 Fischer, *Griff nach der Weltmacht*, p. 464.

9 Quoted in Wolfgang J. Mommsen, 'Die deutsche öffentliche Meinung und der Zusammenbruch des Regierungssystems Bethmann Hollweg im Juli 1917', in Mommsen, *Der autoritäre Nationalstaat. Verfassung, Gesellschaft und Kultur im deutschen Kaiserreich* (Frankfurt am Main, 1990), pp. 429.

10 For the relevant documentary evidence see PA-AA Bonn, R 22332: Sozialistenkonferenz in Stockholm, April 1917 – March 1918.

11 Mommsen, 'Die deutsche öffentliche Meinung', p. 428.

12 Ibid., p. 435.

13 Ibid., p. 436.

14 Deist (ed.), *Militär und Innenpolitik*, vol. II, pp. 688–9.

15 Mommsen, 'Die deutsche öffentliche Meinung', p. 433.

16 *Die Deutsche Freiheit. Fünf Vorträge*, edited by the Bund deutscher Gelehrte und Künstler (Gotha, 1917).

17 Adolf von Harnack, 'Wilsons Botschaft und die deutsche Freiheit'; in ibid., pp. 3–4.

18 Ibid., p. 5.

19 Friedrich Meinecke, 'Die deutsche Freiheit'; in ibid., p. 35.

20 Max Sering, 'Staat- und Gesellschaftsverfassung bei den Westmächten und in Deutschland'; in ibid., p. 40.

21 Ernst Troeltsch, 'Der Ansturm der westlichen Demokratie'; in ibid., pp. 110–11. For a further discussion see also Schwabe, *Wissenschaft und Kriegsmoral*, pp. 103–5; Mommsen, *Bürgerliche Kultur und künstlerische Avantgarde*, pp. 160–2.

22 For further details see BA Potsdam, Bestand Auswärtiges Amt, vol. 35: Zentralstelle für Auslandsdienst, 1914–1921, no. 276.

23 Otto Hintze, 'Imperialismus und deutsche Weltpolitik'; in *Die Deutsche Freiheit*, p. 157.

24 Ibid., p. 163.

25 Ibid., p. 164.

26 Eduard Meyer, 'Der Eintritt Amerikas in den Weltkrieg', *Berliner Neueste Nachrichten*, 9 May 1917.

27 Ibid; a typescript copy of this article can be found in ABBAW, Nachlaß Meyer, no. 326.

28 Ernst zu Reventlow, 'Die amerikanisch-deutschen Beziehungen während des Krieges', *Süddeutsche Monatshefte* 13/2 (June 1916), p. 385. Also quoted in Schwabe, 'Anti-Americanism within the German Right', p. 92.

29 See e.g. *Dresdner Nachrichten*, 14 April 1917.

30 Quoted in Klein et al., *Deutschland im Ersten Weltkrieg*, vol. 2, p. 203.
31 Robert Schmölder, 'Lloyd George und Wilson als Fallensteller', *Kölnische Zeitung*, 14 September 1917.
32 Ibid.
33 The list of publications on the July 1917 crisis in Germany and the Reichstag Peace Resolution is immense. Still the best accounts are to be found in Fischer, *Griff nach der Weltmacht*, pp. 506–23; and Epstein, *Matthias Erzberger*, pp. 182–213.
34 'Englands letzter Kriegsmittel', anonymous article in *Deutsche Kurier*, 5 April 1917.
35 'Arbeiterpolitik und Arbeiterunruhen im Kriege', Denkschrift des Vereins deutscher Eisen- und Stahlindustrieller, August 1917. Reproduced in Gunther Mai, *Das Ende des Kaiserreichs. Politik und Kriegführung im Ersten Weltkrieg* (Munich, 1987), p. 196.
36 Ibid., p. 194.
37 Ibid., p. 197.
38 Cf. the pamphlet by Friedrich Otto Engelhardt, *Die verbrecherischen Methoden des englischen kapitalistischen Imperialismus bei der Durchführung seiner Weltherrschaftspläne* (Düsseldorf, 1917); copy in BA Koblenz, ZSg. 2 /26.
39 Quoted in Matthew Stibbe, 'Kaiser Wilhelm II. The Hohenzollerns at War', in Matthew Hughes and Matthew Seligmann (eds.), *Leadership in Conflict, 1914–1918* (London, 2000), pp. 275–6.
40 Quoted in Röhl, 'Kaiser Wilhelm II and German Anti-Semitism', p. 208.
41 Grünau to the AA, 13 May 1917; reproduced in André Scherer and Jacques Grunewald (eds.), *L'Allemagne et les problèmes de la paix pendant la Première Guerre Mondiale*, 4 vols. (Paris, 1966–78), vol. II, pp. 194–5.
42 Röhl, 'Kaiser Wilhelm II and German Anti-Semitism', p. 208.
43 Kaiser's marginal comments on a telegram from Stumm to Grünau, 15 June 1917; copy in PA-AA Bonn, R 22172, England: Allgemeines, 1915–1919.
44 Zimmermann to Grünau, 29 June 1917; copy in ibid.
45 Zimmermann to Grünau, 4 July 1917; copy in ibid.
46 Quoted in Herwig, 'Admirals *versus* Generals', p. 218.
47 Ibid., p. 221.
48 Quoted in Willibald Gutsche, *Wilhelm II. Der letzte Kaiser des deutschen Reiches. Eine Biographie* (Berlin, 1991), p. 183.
49 Cf. Richard von Kühlmann, *Erinnerungen* (Heidelberg, 1948).
50 Deist, 'Censorship and Propaganda', pp. 205–6.
51 Kriegspresseamt, *Richtlinien für die Aufklärungsarbeit* (Berlin, 1917).
52 Cf. Kitchen, *The Silent Dictatorship*, p. 59.
53 Kriegspresseamt, *Richtlinien für die Aufklärungsarbeit*, p. 9.
54 Ibid., pp. 15–16.
55 Ibid., p. 10.
56 See Gerald Feldman, *Army, Industry and Labor in Germany, 1914–1918* (Princeton, N.J., 1966), esp. pp. 197–249.
57 Mommsen, *Max Weber and German Politics*, pp. 157–9.
58 Martin Lezius, 'Hindenburgs Vorgänger und seine freisinnige Kritiker', *Deutsche Tagezeitung*, 19 July 1917.

59 Copy of declaration in ABBAW, Nachlaß Schäfer, no. 1 / II.

60 August Eigenbrot, *Berliner Tageblatt und Frankfurter Zeitung in ihrem Verhalten zu den nationalen Fragen, 1887–1914. Ein geschichtlicher Rückblick* (Berlin, 1917).

61 Schäfer to Max Bauer, 21 January 1918; in BA Koblenz, Nachlaß Bauer, no. 12.

62 Quoted in Koszyk, *Deutsche Pressepolitik*, p. 150. The War Ministry replied that a ban could not be justified at the moment. The responsible military governors were nonetheless to be instructed to make clear to the editorship of the three named newspapers that a ban would follow if they brought out further articles aimed at having an unfavourable influence on the mood in the army.

63 Fischer, *Griff nach der Weltmacht*, p. 834.

64 On the Fatherland Party see the study by Heinz Hagenlücke, *Deutsche Vaterlandspartei. Die nationale Rechte am Ende des Kaiserreiches* (Düsseldorf, 1997).

65 Quoted in Fischer, *Griff nach der Weltmacht*, pp. 560–1.

66 Richard Fester, *Die Politik der Reichstagsmehrheit* (Halle, 1917), p. 24.

67 Quoted in Karl Wortmann, *Geschichte der Deutschen Vaterlandspartei, 1917–1918* (Halle, 1926), p. 47.

68 Text of speech printed in *Mitteilungen der Deutschen Vaterlandspartei*, no. 3, 10 January 1918.

69 *Los vom 19. Juli! Wider den Klein- und Aberglauben unserer Verzichtler* (Dresden, n.d.).

70 Quoted in Gatzke, *Germany's Drive*, p. 248.

71 Quoted in Volker Ullrich, *Kriegsalltag. Hamburg im Ersten Weltkrieg* (Cologne, 1982), p. 125.

72 *Deutschlands Kampf auf Leben und Tod. Zwei Kriegs-Vorträge von Dr. Karl Alexander von Müller und Wilhelm Seitz* (Munich, 1917), pp. 10–11.

73 Ibid., p. 15.

74 Hagenlücke, *Deutsche Vaterlandspartei*, p. 212.

75 Ibid., p. 213.

76 Alfred von Tirpitz, 'Deutschland und die belgische Frage', *Süddeutsche Monatshefte* 15 / 1 (February 1918), p. 419.

77 Herwig, 'Admirals *versus* Generals', p. 231.

78 Hagenlücke, *Deutsche Vaterlandspartei*, pp. 212–13.

79 Ibid., p. 213.

80 Rechtsanwalt Dr. jur. Eggers (Bremen), 'Grundsätzliches zu den Kriegszielen', *Alldeutsche Blätter*, no. 2, 12 January 1918, pp. 11–12. The possibility of a conflict between the Pan-German League and moderates within the Fatherland Party over the question of territorial expansion in the East is also discussed in Scheck, *Alfred von Tirpitz*, p. 71.

81 On the dispute over war aims between the army General Staff and the naval leadership in the summer of 1918 compare Herwig, 'Admirals *versus* Generals', pp. 225–7 with Michael Epkenhans, 'Die kaiserliche Marine im Ersten Weltkrieg: Weltmacht oder Untergang?', in Michalka (ed.), *Der Erste Weltkrieg*, pp. 331–3.

82 Max, Prinz von Baden, *Erinnerungen und Dokumente* (Stuttgart and Berlin, 1927), p. 265.

83 Quoted in David Shub, *Lenin. A Political Biography*, unabridged ed. (London, 1966), p. 331.
84 Quoted in Fischer, *From Kaiserreich to Third Reich*, p. 70.
85 Cf. Gatzke, *Germany's Drive*, pp. 272–3.
86 Quoted in Erich Matthias and Rudolf Morsey (eds.), *Der Interfraktionelle Ausschuß*, 2 vols. (Düsseldorf, 1959), vol. I, p. 219.
87 Heinrich von Oppen, '96. Stimmungsbericht', 22 April 1918; in Materna and Schrenkenbach (eds.), *Berichte des Berliner Polizeipräsidenten*, p. 273.
88 Zusammenstellung aus der Monats-Berichte der stellvertretenden Generalkommandos, Berlin, 15 April 1918, p. 5; copy in BHStA IV Munich, Akten des Kriegsministeriums, MKr. 12852.
89 Ibid., p. 7.
90 Zusammenstellung aus der Monats-Berichte der stellvertretenden Generalkommandos, Berlin, 15 May 1918, p. 6; copy in BHStA IV Munich, Akten des Kriegsministeriums, MKr. 12852.
91 On the question of Prussian electoral reform see in particular Hellmuth Weber, 'Zum Problem der Wahlrechtsreform in Preußen während der Jahre 1917–1918', in Klein et al. (eds.), *Politik im Krieg*, pp. 189–203.
92 Fischer, *Griff nach der Weltmacht*, p. 831.
93 *Schulthess' Europäischer Geschichtskalender*, vol. 34, pp. 197–8.
94 Wochenbericht vom Kriegspresseamt, no. 132, n.d. [June 1918]; copy in BA Potsdam, Bestand Auswärtiges Amt, vol. 34: Nachrichten- und Presseabteilung, no. 54604.
95 Quoted in *Vorwärts*, 25 June 1918.
96 Fischer, *Griff nach der Weltmacht*, p. 844.
97 As quoted in the *Berliner Morgenpost*, 4 September 1918.
98 Quoted in Williams, *The Home Fronts*, p. 283.
99 *Neue Preußische (Kreuz-)Zeitung*, 4 September 1918.
100 Cf. Fischer, *From Kaiserreich to Third Reich*, p. 72.

Epilogue

1 Heinrich Ströbel, 'Nichts gelernt und nichts vergessen', *Der Pazifist*, no. 25, 13 July 1924; quoted in Wieland, *Belgien 1914*, p. 413.
2 C. Paul Vincent, *The Politics of Hunger. The Allied Blockade of Germany, 1915–1919* (Athens, Ohio, and London, 1985), esp. pp. 124–51.
3 Cf. Harald Wiggenhorn, 'Eine Schuld fast ohne Sühne', *Die Zeit*, 16 August 1996, pp. 9–11.
4 Julius Schwalbe, 'Die englische Krankheit', *Berliner Lokalanzeiger*, 19 April 1919.
5 Vincent, *The Politics of Hunger*, p. 150 and n. 116. See also Michael Burleigh, *Germany Turns Eastwards. A Study of Ostforschung in the Third Reich* (London, 1988).
6 This view was put forward most forcefully by Max von Gruber in his article 'Völkische Außenpolitik'. See also Alfred Schmidt, 'Der Kampf gegen die Goldwährung', *Deutschlands Erneuerung* 2/3 (March 1918), pp. 188–98; Erich Jung, 'Die Einheitsfront der Geldmächte', *Deutschlands Erneuerung* 2/5 (May 1918), pp. 305–17; and Cornelius Jacobs,

'Verzichtfriede und Welthandel', *Alldeutsche Blätter*, no. 4, 26 January 1918, pp. 25–6.

7 Quoted in Baumgart, *Stresemann und England*, p. 142.

8 Quoted in Manfred Dörr, 'Die Deutschnationale Volkspartei, 1924–1928', unpublished dissertation (University of Marburg, 1964), pp. 512–13.

9 Konrad Haenisch, *Die deutsche Sozialdemokratie in und nach dem Weltkrieg* (Berlin, 1919), p. 6.

10 Quoted in Dietrich Aigner, *Das Ringen um England. Die öffentliche Meinung, 1933–1939. Tragödie zweier Völker* (Munich and Eßlingen, 1969), p. 74.

11 The first writer to do this was Franz Neumann in his famous wartime essay *Behemoth. The Structure and Practice of National Socialism*, Left Book Club Edition (London, 1942), pp. 153–80.

12 Cf. Kehr, 'Englandhass und Weltpolitik', passim.

13 Quoted in Jeremy Noakes (ed.), *Nazism, 1919–1945. A Documentary Reader, Vol. 4: The German Home Front in World War II* (Exeter, 1998), p. 459.

14 Himmler to Reinhard Heydrich, 26 January 1942; in ibid., p. 460.

15 Norman Rich, *Hitler's War Aims*; Gerhard Weinberg, *The Foreign Policy of Hitler's Germany*, 2 vols. (Chicago and London, 1970–80); Andreas Hillgruber, 'England's Place in Hitler's Plans for World Dominion', *Journal of Contemporary History* 9 (1974), pp. 5–22; Klaus Hildebrand, *The Foreign Policy of the Third Reich, 1933–1945* (London, 1973); Eberhard Jäckel, *Hitler's World View. A Blueprint for Power* (London, 1972); Dietrich Aigner, *Das Ringen um England. Die öffentliche Meinung, 1933–1939. Tragödie zweier Völker* (Munich and Eßlingen, 1969); Woodruff D. Smith, *Ideological Origins of Nazi Imperialism*.

16 The following pages owe much to the final chapter in Woodruff D. Smith's *Ideological Origins* (pp. 231–58). On Nazi ideology see also Barbara Miller Lane and Leila J. Rupp, *Nazi Ideology before 1933. A Documentation* (London, 1978).

17 Hans Grimm, *Volk ohne Raum*, 2 vols. (Munich, 1926). For a discussion of this novel and its impact on Nazi ideology see Smith, *Ideological Origins*, pp. 224-30.

18 Cf. Verhey, 'Some Lessons of War', passim.

19 On the DNVP see also Annelise Thimme, *Flucht in den Mythos. Die deutschnationale Volkspartei und die Niederlage von 1918* (Göttingen, 1969); and John A. Leopold, *Alfred Hugenberg. The Radical Nationalist Campaign against the Weimar Republic* (New Haven and London, 1977).

20 Rich, *Hitler's War Aims*, vol. 1, p. xlii; Jäckel, *Hitler's World View*, pp. 34–5.

21 Quoted in Wieland, *Belgien 1914*, p. 404.

22 Ibid., p. 561.

23 Cf. Chickering, *Imperial Germany and the Great War*, p. 204.

24 Quoted in Jeremy Noakes and G. Pridham (eds.), *Nazism, 1919–1945. A Documentary Reader, Vol. 3: Foreign Policy, War and Racial Extermination* (Exeter, 1988), p. 610. In fact two versions of this speech were recorded by different police spies in Munich. This quotation comes from the second version, whereas the first version also had Hitler speaking of England and America as Germany's 'absolute opponents'.

25 Adolf Hitler, *Mein Kampf*, p. 565.

26 For further evidence see Weinberg, *The Foreign Policy of Hitler's Germany*, vol. 1, pp. 14–18.

27 Smith, *Ideological Origins*, p. 246.

28 See e.g. Daniel Jonah Goldhagen, *Hitler's Willing Executioners. Ordinary Germans and the Holocaust* (London and New York, 1996), which has attracted much criticism for overstating its case. For a more nuanced view, which recognises that only a minority of Germans actually approved of violence, see Saul Friedländer, *Nazi Germany and the Jews. Vol. 1: The Years of Persecution, 1933–1939* (London, 1997).

29 Friedländer, *Nazi Germany and the Jews*, pp. 49–59.

30 Donald L. Niewyk, *The Jews in Weimar Germany* (London, 1980), p. 80. Also quoted in Friedländer, *Nazi Germany and the Jews*, p. 110.

31 Hitler, *Mein Kampf*, p. 187.

32 Friedländer, *Nazi Germany and the Jews*, p. 111.

33 Jäckel, *Hitler's World View*, p. 53.

34 Hermann Rauschning, *Germany's Revolution of Destruction* (London, 1939), pp. 204–5.

35 Hitler, *Mein Kampf*, p. 132.

36 Ibid., p. 129. Cf. Jäckel, *Hitler's World View*, p. 35.

37 Hildebrand, *The Foreign Policy of the Third Reich*, pp. 38–50.

38 Cf. Weinberg, *The Foreign Policy of Hitler's Germany*, vol. 1, p. 15.

39 Hitler, *Mein Kampf*, pp. 559–64.

40 Cf. Hildebrand, *The Foreign Policy of the Third Reich*, p. 20; Smith, *Ideological Origins*, p. 246.

41 Hillgruber, 'England's Place', p. 12.

42 Hitler, *Mein Kampf*, p. 581. Cf. Jäckel, *Hitler's World View*, p. 55.

43 Gerhard Weinberg (ed.), *Hitlers Zweites Buch. Ein Dokument aus dem Jahr 1928* (Stuttgart, 1961).

44 Ibid., p. 173. Also quoted in Hillgruber, 'England's Place', p. 9.

45 Cf. Smith, *Ideological Origins*, p. 247; Jäckel, *Hitler's World View*, p. 46.

46 Rauschning, *Germany's Revolution of Destruction*, p. 204.

47 Extract from the war diaries of General Halder, Chief of the General Staff; reproduced in Noakes and Pridham (eds.), *Nazism, 1919–1945*, vol. 3, p. 783.

48 Hillgruber, 'England's Place', p. 19.

49 See e.g. the evidence cited in Thomas Grosser, 'Perzeptionssteuerung durch Propaganda. England in der nationalsozialistischen Karikatur', in Gottfried Niedhart (ed.), *Das kontinentale Europa und die britischen Inseln*, (Mannheim, 1993), pp. 178–204.

50 From the New York journal *American*, 14 June 1940; quoted in Rich, *Hitler's War Aims*, p. 158.

51 Hillgruber, 'England's Place', p. 21.

52 See the books and articles mentioned in chapter 2, notes 1 and 2.

53 *Große Politik*, vol. 19/1, no. 6140, Aufzeichnungen Metternichs, 18 December 1904; quoted in Wieland, 'Der deutsche Englandhaß', p. 333. For further evidence see also Prince Lichnowsky's *Meine Londoner Mission, 1912–1914* (Berlin, 1919).

54 Bülow to AA, 12 October 1905, *Große Politik*, vol. 20/2, no. 6875, and Bülow

to AA, 15 October 1905, in ibid., no. 6878; also quoted in Wieland, 'Der deutsche Englandhaß', p. 333.

55 Cf. Hans Ulrich-Wehler, *The German Empire, 1871–1918* (Leamington Spa, 1985), esp. pp. 40–51.

56 For a classic restatement of this position see Count Ernst zu Reventlow, *Von Potsdam nach Doorn*, 5th ed. (Berlin, 1940).

57 Quoted in Feldman, *Army, Industry and Labor*, p. 422.

58 On English 'cant' see esp. Scheler, *Der Genius des Krieges*, p. 388.

59 Wolfgang J. Mommsen, 'Vom Kriegsgegner zum Partner', in Mommsen (ed.), *Die ungleichen Partner*, p. 186.

60 Quoted in Fischer, *Griff nach der Weltmacht*, p. 134.

61 See e.g. Bernd Faulenbach, *Ideologie des deutschen Weges. Die deutsche Geschichte in der Historiographie zwischen Kaiserreich und Nationalsozialismus* (Munich, 1980). Also my essay 'German Historians' Views of England during the First World War', in Stefan Berger, Peter Lambert and Peter Schumann (eds.), *A Dialogue of the Deaf? Historiographical Connections between Britain and Germany, c. 1750–2000* (Göttingen, forthcoming).

62 See Hans-Ulrich Wehler's introduction to Kehr's *Der Primat der Innenpolitik*.

63 Cf. Fritz Fischer, 'Die Kirchen in Deutschland und die beiden Weltkriege', in: Fischer, *Hitler war kein Betriebsunfall. Aufsätze* (Munich, 1992), pp. 182–214.

64 David Martin, *Does Christianity Cause War?* (Oxford, 1998).

65 Gerhard Ritter, *Luther. Gestalt und Symbol* (Munich, 1925), p. 154; quoted in Fritz Stern, *The Failure of Illiberalism. Essays on the Political Culture of Modern Germany* (New York, 1972), p. 22.

66 See e.g. Franz Bosbach (ed.), *Feindbilder. Die Darstellung der politischen Publizistik des Mittelalters und der Neuzeit* (Cologne, Weimar and Vienna, 1992), especially the contributions by Peter Segl and Michael Wolter.

67 See, for example, the discussion in Bosbach, *Feindbilder*, pp. 235–42.

Bibliography

Unpublished sources

Politisches Archiv des Auswärtigen Amtes, Bonn

(a) Akten des Auswärtigen Amtes, R 2558–61, R 20936–39, R 22172–75, R 22215–16, R 22252, R 22332, R 22377–81, R 22412–16
(b) Nachlaß Gustav Stresemann

Bundesarchiv, Koblenz

(a) Zeitgeschichtliche Sammlungen (ZSg. 2), nos. 22–26, 53, 58
(b) Nachlässe:
    Nachlaß Max Bauer
    Nachlaß Hans Delbrück
    Nachlaß Matthias Erzberger
    Nachlaß Richard Fester
    Nachlaß Johannes Haller
    Nachlaß Georg von Hertling
    Nachlaß Friedrich Wilhelm von Loebell
    Nachlaß Wilhelm Solf
    Nachlaß Martin Spahn
    Nachlaß Gottfried Traub
    Nachlaß Luitpold Weilnböck
(c) Kleine Erwerbungen:
    Kl. Erw. 342 (Theobald von Bethmann Hollweg)
    Kl. Erw. 230 (Gustav Roesicke)
    Kl. Erw. 353 (Paul Rohrbach)
    Kl. Erw. 341 (Rudolf von Valentini)

Bundesarchiv, Abteilung Potsdam (now Bundesarchiv Berlin-Lichterfelde)

(a) Bestand Auswärtiges Amt, vols. 34 and 35
(b) Akten der Reichskanzlei, nos. 15, 1415–1420, 1422, 1422/1, 1422/2, 1422/4, 2398, 2398/1, 2410, 2437/3–2439/3, 2440, 2447/3, 2448/2, 2463, 2465, 2476, 2477
(c) Akten des Alldeutschen Verbandes, nos. 198–204, 356, 453, 455, 638

(d) Pressearchiv des Reichslandbundes/Bund der Landwirte, nos. 8270–8277
(e) Nachlässe:
   Nachlaß Konstantin von Gebsattel
   Nachlaß Otto Hammann
   Nachlaß Conrad von Wangenheim
   Nachlaß Kuno Graf von Westarp

Bundesarchiv-Militärarchiv, Freiburg i. Br.

Nachlaß Paul Behncke
Nachlaß Helmuth von Moltke (the younger)
Nachlaß Gerhard von Schulze-Gaevernitz
Nachlaß Alfred von Tirpitz

Geheimes Staatsarchiv Preußischer Kulturbesitz, Berlin-Dahlem

(a) Preußisches Ministerium des Innern, Rep. 77, Tit. 863a, no. 6, and Tit. 885, no. 4
(b) Zeitungsausschnitte, Rep. 77 CB S, nos. 970h, 970i, 970l, 970n, 974, 980, 987
(c) Nachlässe, Rep. 92:
   Nachlaß Wolfgang Kapp
   Nachlaß Rudolf von Valentini

Archiv der Berlin-Brandenburgischen Akademie der Wissenschaften, Berlin

Nachlaß Eduard Meyer
Nachlaß Dietrich Schäfer

Bayerisches Hauptstaatsarchiv, Munich

Abteilung IV: Kriegsarchiv
Akten des Stellvertretenden Generalkommandos des I. bayerischen Armeekorps, nos. 1705, 1710, 1714, 1938, 2414
Akten des Königlich Bayerischen Kriegsministerium, MKr. 11521–24, 12842–50, 12851–53, 13915, 13940

Published sources

Newspapers and periodicals

Newspapers
Bayerische Staatszeitung
Berliner Lokalanzeiger
Berliner Tageblatt
Deutsche Kurier
Deutsche Tageszeitung
Deutsche Zeitung
Frankfurter Zeitung

Münchner Post
Neue Preußische (Kreuz-) Zeitung
Norddeutsche Allgemeine Zeitung
Post
Reichsbote
Rheinisch-Westfälische Zeitung
Schwäbische Tagwacht (Stuttgart)

Bibliography

Germania
Kölnische Volkszeitung
Kölnische Zeitung
Leipziger Neueste Nachrichten
Leipziger Volkszeitung
Münchner Neueste Nachrichten

Straßburger Post
Süddeutsche Zeitung (Stuttgart)
Tag
Tägliche Rundschau
Vorwärts
Vossische Zeitung
Welt am Montag

Periodicals
Alldeutsche Blätter (1914/18)
Deutschlands Erneuerung (1917/18)
Die Glocke (1915/18)
Das Größere Deutschland (1914/18)
Der Panther (1915/18)
Preussische Jahrbücher (1914/18)
Süddeutsche Monatshefte (1914/18)

Books, articles and dissertations

Afflerbach, Holger, Falkenhayn. Politisches Denken und Handeln im Kaiserreich (Munich, 1994).

Aigner, Dietrich, Das Ringen um England. Die öffentliche Meinung, 1933–1939. Tragödie zweier Völker (Munich and Eßlingen, 1969).

Albrecht, Dieter, 'Bayern im Ersten Weltkrieg' 1914–1918', in: Max Spindler (ed.), Handbuch der Bayerischen Geschichte. Vierter Band/I. Das neue Bayern, 1800–1970 (Munich, 1974), pp. 364–86.

Albrecht, Willy, Landtag und Regierung in Bayern am Vorabend der Revolution von 1918 (West Berlin, 1968).

Allen, Ann Taylor, Satire and Society in Wilhelmine Germany. Kladderadatsch and Simplicissimus, 1890–1914 (Lexington, Ky., 1984).

Anderson, Pauline, The Background of Anti-English Feeling in Germany, 1890–1902, Reprint (Washington D.C., 1964).

Angress, Werner T., 'The German Army's "Judenzählung" of 1916. Genesis – Consequences – Significance', Year Book of the Leo Baeck Institute 23 (1978), pp. 117–37.

August 1914. Ein Volk zieht in den Krieg, edited by the Berliner Geschichtswerkstatt (West Berlin, 1989).

Ay, Karl-Ludwig, Die Entstehung einer Revolution. Die Volksstimmung in Bayern während des Ersten Weltkrieges (West Berlin, 1968).

Baumgart, Constanze, Stresemann und England (Cologne, Weimar and Vienna, 1996).

Berghahn, Volker, Der Tirpitz-Plan. Genesis und Verfall einer innenpolitischen Krisenstrategie unter Wilhelm II. (Düsseldorf, 1971).

Rüstung und Machtpolitik. Zur Anatomie des Kalten Krieges vor 1914 (Düsseldorf, 1973).

Germany and the Approach of War in 1914, 2nd ed. (London, 1993).

Berghahn, Volker, and Wilhelm Deist, 'Kaiserliche Marine und Kriegsausbruch

1914. Neue Dokumente zur Julikrise', *Militärgeschichtliche Mitteilungen* 7 (1970), pp. 37–58.

Bernstein, Eduard, *Die Wahrheit über die Einkreisung Deutschlands* (Berlin, 1920).

Bernstorff, Count Johann Heinrich, *Deutschland und Amerika. Erinnerungen aus dem fünfjährigen Kriege* (Berlin, 1920).

Bethmann Hollweg, Theobald von, *Betrachtungen zum Weltkriege*, 2 vols. (Berlin, 1919).

Birnbaum, Karl E., *Peace Moves and U-Boat Warfare. A Study of Imperial German Policy towards the United States, 18 April, 1916 – 9 January, 1917* (Stockholm, 1958).

Blackbourn, David, and Geoff Eley, *Mythen deutscher Geschichtsschreibung. Die gescheiterte bürgerliche Revolution von 1848* (Frankfurt am Main, 1980).

The Peculiarities of German History. Bourgeois Society and Politics in Nineteenth Century Germany (Oxford, 1984).

Bodelschwingh, Franz von, *Innere Hemmungen kraftvoller Aussenpolitik* (Hanover, 1918).

Boog, Horst, 'Graf Ernst zu Reventlow (1869–1943). Eine Studie zur Krise der deutschen Geschichte seit dem Ende des 19. Jahrhunderts', Ph.D. thesis (University of Heidelberg, 1965).

Bosbach, Franz (ed.), *Feindbilder. Die Darstellung der politischen Publizistik des Mittelalters und der Neuzeit* (Cologne, Weimar and Vienna, 1992).

Brocke, Bernhard vom, '"Wissenschaft und Militarismus": Der Aufruf der 93 "An die Kulturwelt!" und der Zusammenbruch der internationalen Gelehrtenpolitik im Ersten Weltkrieg', in: W.M. Calder III et al. (eds.), *Wilamowitz nach 50 Jahren* (Darmstadt, 1985), pp. 649–719.

Bund deutscher Gelehrte und Künstler (ed.), *Die Deutsche Freiheit. Fünf Vorträge* (Gotha, 1917).

Cecil, Lamar, *Albert Ballin. Business and Politics in Imperial Germany, 1888–1918* (Princeton, N.J., 1967).

Chamberlain, Houston Stewart, *The Ravings of a Renegade* (London, 1916).

Kriegsaufsätze (Munich, 1915).

Politische Ideale, 2nd ed. (Munich, 1915).

Briefe, 1882–1924, 2 vols. (Munich, 1928).

Chickering, Roger, *Imperial Germany and a World without War. The Peace Movement and German Society, 1892–1914* (Princeton, N.J., 1975).

We Men Who Feel Most German. A Cultural Study of the Pan-German League, 1886–1914 (London, 1984).

Karl Lamprecht. A German Academic Life, 1856–1915 (Atlantic Highlands, 1993).

Imperial Germany and the Great War, 1914–1918 (Cambridge, 1998).

Claß, Heinrich [published under the pseudonym Daniel Frymann], *Wenn ich der Kaiser wär'* (Leipzig, 1912).

Wider den Strom. Vom Werden und Wachsen der nationalen Opposition im alten Reich (Leipzig, 1932).

Coetzee, Marilyn Shevin, *The German Army League. Popular Nationalism in Wilhelmine Germany* (Oxford, 1990).

Cohen-Reuß, Max, 'England und Rußland', *Die Glocke* 2/2 (October 1916), pp. 5–9.

Coupe, William A., *German Political Satires from the Reformation to the Second World War*, Part II, 1849–1918 (New York, 1987).

David, Eduard, *Die deutsche Sozialdemokratie im Weltkrieg* (Berlin, 1915).
Wer trägt die Schuld am Kriege? (Berlin, 1917).
Dehio, Ludwig, *Germany and World Politics in the Twentieth Century* (New York, 1959).
Deist, Wilhelm (ed.), *Militär und Innenpolitik im Weltkrieg, 1914–1918*, 2 vols. (Düsseldorf, 1970).
'Censorship and Propaganda in Germany during the First World War', in: Jean-Jacques Becker and Stéphane Audoin-Rouzeau (eds.), *Les sociétés européennes et la guerre de 1914–1918* (Paris-Nanterre, 1990), pp. 199–210.
'The German Army, the Authoritarian Nation-State and Total War', in: John Horne (ed.), *State, Society and Mobilization in Europe during the First World War* (Cambridge, 1997), pp. 160–71.
Delbrück, Hans, *Bismarcks Erbe* (Berlin and Vienna, 1915).
Demm, Eberhard, *Der erste Weltkrieg in der internationalen Karikatur* (Hanover, 1988).
'Les thèmes de la propagande allemande en 1914', *Guerres mondiales et conflits contemporains* 150 (1988), pp. 3–17.
'Propaganda and Caricature in the First World War', *Journal of Contemporary History* 28 (1993), pp. 163–92.
Deuerlein, Ernst, *Der Bundesratsausschuß für auswärtige Angelegenheiten, 1870–1918* (Regensburg, 1955).
(ed.), *Briefwechsel Hertling–Lerchenfeld, 1912–1917. Dienstliche Privatkorrespondenz zwischen dem bayerischen Ministerpräsidenten Georg Graf von Hertling und dem bayerischen Gesandten in Berlin, Hugo Graf von und zu Lerchenfeld*, 2 vols. (Boppard am Rhein, 1973).
Dibelius, Wilhelm, *England und wir* (Hamburg, 1914).
England, 2 vols. (Leipzig, 1922).

Edwards, Marvin L., *Gustav Stresemann and the Greater Germany, 1914–1918* (New York, 1963).
Eigenbrot, August, *Berliner Tageblatt und Frankfurter Zeitung in ihrem Verhältnis zu den nationalen Fragen, 1887–1914. Ein geschichtlicher Rückblick* (Berlin, 1917).
Eisenbeiss, Wilfried, *Die bürgerliche Friedensbewegung in Deutschland während des Ersten Weltkrieges: Organisation, Selbstverständnis und politische Praxis, 1913/14–1919* (Frankfurt am Main, 1980).
Eley, Geoff, 'The German Navy League in German Politics, 1898–1914', D.Phil. thesis (University of Sussex, 1974).
Reshaping the German Right. Radical Nationalism and Political Change after Bismarck (New Haven, Conn., 1980).
From Unification to Nazism. Reinterpreting the German Past (London, 1986).
Epstein, Klaus, *Matthias Erzberger and the Dilemma of German Democracy* (Princeton, N.J., 1959).
Erdmann, Karl Dietrich (ed.), *Kurt Riezler. Tagebücher, Aufsätze, Dokumente* (Göttingen, 1972).

Ernst, Otto, *Deutschland an England. Kriegsgedichte* (Hamburg, 1914)
  Gewittersegen. Ein Kriegsbuch (Leipzig, 1915).
Erzberger, Matthias, *Erlebnisse im Weltkrieg* (Berlin, 1920).
Eucken, Rudolf, *Die weltgeschichtliche Bedeutung des deutschen Geistes* (Stuttgart
  and Berlin, 1915).

Faulenbach, Bernd, *Ideologie des deutschen Weges. Die deutsche Geschichte in der
  Historiographie zwischen Kaiserreich und Nationalsozialismus* (Munich, 1980).
Feldman, Gerald D., *Army, Industry and Labor in Germany, 1914–1918* (Princeton,
  N.J., 1966).
Fester, Richard, *Die Politik der Reichstagsmehrheit* (Halle, 1917).
Field, Geoffrey G., 'Antisemitism and *Weltpolitik*', *Year Book of the Leo Baeck
  Institute* 18 (1973), pp. 65–91.
  Evangelist of Race. The Germanic Vision of Houston Stewart Chamberlain (New
  York, 1981).
Fischer, Fritz, *Griff nach der Weltmacht. Die Kriegszielpolitik des kaiserlichen
  Deutschland, 1914/1918*, 2nd ed. (Düsseldorf, 1962).
  Krieg der Illusionen. Die deutsche Politik, 1911–1914, 2nd ed. (Düsseldorf, 1970).
  *From Kaiserreich to Third Reich. Elements of Continuity in German History,
  1871–1945*, translated by Roger Fletcher (London, 1986).
  Hitler war kein Betriebsunfall. Aufsätze (Munich, 1992).
Fleïscher, Paul, *Welche Gefahr droht Deutschland und seine Arbeiter von einem
  unbesiegten England?* (Berlin, 1916).
Fritzsche, Peter, *Germans into Nazis* (London, 1998).

Gatzke, Hans, *Germany's Drive to the West (Drang nach Westen). A Study of
  Germany's Western War Aims during the First World War* (Baltimore, Md.,
  1950).
Gay, Peter, *Weimar Culture. The Outsider as Insider* (Pengiun edition, 1968).
Geiss, Imanuel (ed.), *Julikrise und Kriegsausbruch 1914*, 2 vols. (Hanover, 1963–4).
Gerlach, Hellmut von, *Die große Zeit der Lüge. Der Erste Weltkrieg und die deutsche
  Mentalität, 1871–1921* [1921/26], edited by Helmat Donat and Adolf Wild
  (Bremen, 1994).
Gersbach, Robert, *Kriegsgedichte von 1914* (Berlin, 1915).
Glatzer, Ruth, *Das Wilhelminische Berlin. Panorama einer Metropole, 1890–1918*
  (Berlin, 1997)
Görlitz, Walther (ed.), *The Kaiser and His Court. The Diaries, Note Books and Letters
  of Admiral Georg Alexander von Müller, Chief of the Naval Cabinet, 1914–1918*
  (London, 1961).
Grosser, Thomas, 'Perzeptionssteuerung durch Propaganda. England in der
  nationalsozialistischen Karikatur', in: Gottfried Niedhart (ed.), *Das konti-
  nentale Europa und die britischen Inseln. Wahrnehmungsmuster und
  Wechselwirkungen seit der Antike* (Mannheim, 1993), pp. 178–204.
Gruber, Max von, 'Die Mobilisierung des Ernährungswesen', *Süddeutsche
  Monatshefte* 11/2 (September 1914), pp. 860–76.
  Krieg, Frieden und Biologie (Berlin, 1915).
  'Völkische Außenpolitik', *Deutschlands Erneuerung* 1/1 (April 1917), pp.
  74–87.

'Rassenhygiene als die wichtigste Aufgabe völkischer Innenpolitik', *Deutschlands Erneuerung* 2/1 (January 1918), pp. 17–32.

Grumbach, Salomon, *Das annexionistische Deutschland. Eine Sammlung von Dokumenten, die seit dem 4. August 1914 in Deutschland öffentlich oder geheim verbreitet wurden* (Lausanne, 1917).

Gutsche, Willibald, *Wilhelm II. Der letzte Kaiser des deutschen Reiches. Eine Biographie* (Berlin, 1991).

Haenisch, Konrad, *Die deutsche Sozialdemokratie in und nach dem Weltkrieg* (Berlin, 1916) and new edition (Berlin, 1919).

Hagenlücke, Heinz, *Deutsche Vaterlandspartei. Die nationale Rechte am Ende des Kaiserreiches* (Düsseldorf, 1997).

Hammann, Otto, *Bilder aus der letzten Kaiserzeit* (Berlin, 1922).

Hampson, Norman, *The Perfidy of Albion. French Perceptions of England during the French Revolution* (London, 1998).

Haußmann, Conrad, *Schlaglichter. Reichstagsbriefe und Aufzeichnungen*, edited by Ulrich Zeller (Frankfurt am Main, 1924).

Heinemann, Ulrich, *Verdrängte Niederlage. Politische Öffentlichkeit und Kriegsschuldfrage in der Weimarer Republik* (Göttingen, 1983).

Herwig, Holger H., 'Admirals *versus* Generals. The War Aims of the Imperial German Navy, 1914–1918', *Central European History* 5 (1972), pp. 208–33.

'Luxury' Fleet. The Imperial German Navy, 1888–1918 (Atlantic Highlands, 1991).

The First World War. Germany and Austria-Hungary, 1914–1918 (London, 1997).

Hildebrand, Klaus, *The Foreign Policy of the Third Reich, 1933–1945* (London, 1973).

German Foreign Policy from Bismarck to Adenauer. The Limits of Statecraft (London, 1989).

Hillgruber, Andreas, *Hitlers Strategie. Politik und Kriegführung, 1940/41* (Frankfurt am Main, 1965).

'England's Place in Hitler's Plans for World Dominion', *Journal of Contemporary History* 9 (1974), pp. 5–22.

Germany and the Two World Wars (London, 1981).

Hintze, Otto et al., *Deutschland und der Weltkrieg* (Berlin, 1915).

Hirschfeld, Gerhard et al. (eds.), *Kriegserfahrungen. Studien zur Sozial- und Mentalitätsgeschichte des Ersten Weltkriegs* (Essen, 1997).

Hitler, Adolf, *Mein Kampf.* Translated by Ralph Manheim with an introduction by Donald Cameron Watt (London, 1969).

Hoover, A.J., *God, Germany and Britain in the Great War. A Study in Clerical Nationalism* (New York, 1989).

Hoser, Paul, *Die politischen, wirtschaftlichen und sozialen Hintergründe der Münchner Tagespresse zwischen 1914 und 1934* (Frankfurt am Main, 1990).

Howard, Michael, 'Die deutsch-britischen Beziehungen im 20. Jahrhundert. Eine Haßliebe', in: Wolfgang J. Mommsen (ed.), *Die ungleichen Partner. Deutsch-Britische Beziehungen im 19. und 20. Jahrhundert* (Stuttgart, 1999), pp. 125–39.

Hull, Isabel, *The Entourage of Kaiser Wilhelm II, 1888–1918* (Cambridge, 1982).

Hüppauf, Bernd (ed.), *Ansichten vom Krieg. Vergleichende Studien zum Ersten Weltkrieg in Literatur und Gesellschaft* (Königstein, 1984).

Jahr, Christoph, '"Das Krämervolk der eitlen Briten". Das deutsche Englandfeindbild im Ersten Weltkrieg', in: Christoph Jahr, Uwe Mai and Kathrin Roller (eds.), *Feindbilder in der deutschen Geschichte. Studien zur Vorurteilsgeschichte im 19. und 20. Jahrhundert* (Berlin, 1994), pp. 115–42.

Janßen, Karl-Heinrich, *Macht und Verblendung. Kriegszielpolitik der deutschen Bundesstaaten, 1914/18* (Göttingen, 1963).

Jarausch, Konrad, *The Enigmatic Chancellor. Bethmann Hollweg and the Hubris of Imperial Germany* (New Haven and London, 1973).

'Die Alldeutschen und die Regierung Bethmann Hollwegs. Eine Denkschrift Kurt Riezlers vom Herbst 1916', *Vierteljahrshefte für Zeitgeschichte* 21 (1973), pp. 435–68.

Jeismann, Michael, *Das Vaterland der Feinde. Studien zum nationalen Feindbegriff und Selbstverständnis in Deutschland und Frankreich, 1792–1918* (Stuttgart, 1992).

Kaulisch, Baldur, 'Die Auseinandersetzung über den uneingeschränkten U-Boot-Krieg innerhalb der herrschenden Klassen im zweiten Halbjahr 1916 und seine Eröffnung im Februar 1917', in: Fritz Klein et al. (eds.), *Politik im Krieg, 1914–1918. Studien zur Politik der deutschen herrschenden Klassen im Ersten Weltkrieg* (East Berlin, 1964), pp. 90–117.

Alfred von Tirpitz und die imperialistische deutsche Flottenrüstung (East Berlin, 1982).

Kehr, Eckart, *Schlachtflottenbau und Parteipolitik, 1894–1901* (Berlin, 1930).

Der Primat der Innenpolitik. Gesammelte Aufsätze zur preußisch-deutschen Sozialgeschichte im 19. und 20. Jahrhundert, edited by Hans-Ulrich Wehler (West Berlin, 1965).

Kellermann, Hermann, *Der Krieg der Geister. Eine Auslese deutscher und ausländischer Stimmen zum Weltkriege 1914* (Weimar, 1915).

Kennedy, Paul, *The Rise of Anglo-German Antagonism, 1860–1914* (London, 1980).

Kestler, Stefan, *Die deutsche Auslandsaufklärung und das Bild der Ententemächte im Spiegel zeitgenössischer Propagandaveröffentlichungen während des Ersten Weltkrieges* (Frankfurt am Main, 1994).

Kitchen, Martin, *The Silent Dictatorship. The Politics of the High Command under Hindenburg and Ludendorff, 1916–1918* (London, 1976).

Kjellén, Rudolf, 'Die Ideen von 1914. Eine weltgeschichtliche Perspektive', in: *Zwischen Krieg und Frieden* (Leipzig, 1916).

Kladderadatsch, *Am Pranger! England-Album des Kladderadatsch von der Zeit des Burenkrieges bis zur Gegenwart* (Berlin, 1915).

Klein, Fritz et al. (eds.), *Politik im Krieg, 1914–1918. Studien zur Politik der deutschen herrschenden Klassen im Ersten Weltkrieg* (East Berlin, 1964)

Deutschland im Ersten Weltkrieg, 3 vols. (East Berlin, 1968–9).

Knight-Bostock, J., *Some Well-Known German War Novels, 1914–1930* (Oxford, 1931).

Kohn, Hans, *The Mind of Germany. The Education of a Nation* (New York, 1961).

Koszyk, Kurt, *Deutsche Pressepolitik im Ersten Weltkrieg* (Düsseldorf, 1968).

Kraepelin, Emil, *Lebenserinnerungen*, edited by H. Hippius, G. Peters and D. Ploog (West Berlin and Heidelberg, 1983).

Kramer, Alan, '"Greueltaten". Zum Problem der deutschen Kriegsverbrechen in Belgien und Frankreich, 1914', in: Gerhard Hirschfeld and Gerd Krumeich (eds.), *Keiner fühlt sich hier als Mensch . . . Erlebnis und Wirkung des Ersten Weltkrieges* (Essen, 1993), pp. 85–114.

Kriegspresseamt, *Richtlinien für die Aufklärungsarbeit* (Berlin, 1917).

Kruse, Wolfgang, *Krieg und nationale Integration. Eine Neuinterpretation des sozialdemokratischen Burgfriedensschlusses, 1914/15* (Essen, 1993).

Kühlmann, Richard von, *Erinnerungen* (Heidelberg, 1948).

Lamprecht, Karl, *Zur neuen Lage* (Leipzig, 1914).

Large, David Clay, *Where Ghosts Walked. Munich's Road to the Third Reich* (London, 1997).

Lasswell, Harold Dwight, *Propaganda Technique in the World War* (London, 1927)

Lehmann, Melanie (ed.), *Verleger J.F. Lehmann. Ein Leben im Kampf für Deutschland. Lebenslauf und Briefe* (Munich, 1935).

Lenger, Friedrich, *Werner Sombart, 1863–1941. Eine Biographie* (Munich, 1994).

Lensch, Paul, *Die deutsche Sozialdemokratie und der Weltkrieg* (Berlin, 1915).

Drei Jahre Weltrevolution (Berlin, 1917).

Lepsius, Johannes, 'John Bull. Eine politische Komödie in fünf Aufsätzen', *Der Panther. Eine deutsche Monatsschrift für Politik und Volkstum*, edited by Axel Ripke, 3/4 (April 1915), pp. 457–512.

Lepsius, Johannes, et al. (eds.), *Die Große Politik der europäischen Kabinette, 1871–1914*, 40 vols. (Berlin, 1922–7).

Liebig, Hans von, *Die Politik Bethmann Hollwegs* (Munich, 1919).

McClelland, Charles E., *The German Historians and England. A Study in Nineteenth Century Views* (Cambridge, 1971).

Mai, Günther, '"Aufklärung der Bevölkerung" und "Vaterländischer Unterricht" in Württemberg 1914–1918', *Zeitschrift für Württembergische Landesgeschichte* 36 (1977), pp. 199–235.

Das Ende des Kaiserreichs. Politik und Kriegführung im Ersten Weltkrieg (Munich, 1987).

Mann, Heinrich, *Der Haß. Deutsche Zeitgeschichte*, 2nd ed. (Amsterdam, 1933).

Mann, Thomas, *Death in Venice* [1911] (Penguin edition, 1955).

Betrachtungen eines Unpolitischen (Berlin, 1918).

Essays Band I: Frühlingssturm, 1893–1918, edited by Hermann Kurzke and Stephan Stachorski (Frankfurt am Main, 1993).

Massie, Robert, *Dreadnought. Britain, Germany and the Coming of the Great War* (London, 1992).

Materna, Ingo, and Hans-Joachim Schrenkenbach (eds.), *Berichte des Berliner Polizeipräsidenten zur Stimmung und Lage der Bevölkerung in Berlin, 1914–1918* (Weimar, 1987).

Matthias, Erich, and Rudolf Morsey (eds.), *Der Interfraktionelle Ausschuß, 1917/18*, 2 vols. (Düsseldorf, 1959).

Matthias, Erich, and Susanne Miller (eds.), *Das Kriegstagebuch des Reichstagsabgeordneten Eduard David* (Düsseldorf, 1966).

May, E.R., *The World War and American Isolation, 1914–1917* (Cambridge, Mass., 1959).

Max, Prinz von Baden, *Erinnerungen und Dokumente* (Stuttgart and Berlin, 1927).

Meinecke, Friedrich, *Die deutsche Erhebung von 1914. Vorträge und Aufsätze* (Stuttgart and Berlin, 1915).

Meyer, Eduard, *England. Seine staatliche und politische Entwicklung und der Krieg gegen Deutschland* (Stuttgart and Berlin, 1915).

Nordamerika und Deutschland (Berlin, 1915).

Weltgeschichte und Weltkrieg. Gesammelte Aufsätze (Berlin, 1916).

Meyer, Klaus, *Theodor Schiemann als politischer Publizist* (Frankfurt am Main and Hamburg, 1956).

Michalka, Wolfgang (ed.), *Der Erste Weltkrieg. Wirkung, Wahrnehmung, Analyse* (Munich, 1994).

Miller, Susanne, *Burgfriede und Klassenkampf. Die deutsche Sozialdemokratie im Ersten Weltkrieg* (Düsseldorf, 1974).

Moltke, Helmuth von, *Erinnerungen, Briefe, Dokumente* (Stuttgart, 1922).

Mommsen, Wolfgang J., 'Domestic Factors in German Foreign Policy before 1914', *Central European History* 6 (1973), pp. 3–43.

'Zur Entwicklung des Englandbildes der Deutschen seit dem Ende des 18. Jahrhunderts', in: Lothar Kettenacker, Manfred Schlenke and Hellmut Seier (eds.), *Studien zur Geschichte Englands und der deutsch-britischen Beziehungen. Festschrift für Paul Kluke* (Munich, 1981), pp. 375–97.

Max Weber and German Politics, 1890–1920, translated by Michael S. Steinberg (Chicago and London, 1984).

Two Centuries of Anglo-German Relations. A Reappraisal (London, 1984).

'Die deutsche öffentliche Meinung und der Zusammenbruch des Regierungssystems Bethmann Hollweg im Juli 1917', in: Mommsen, *Der autoritäre Nationalstaat. Verfassung, Gesellschaft und Kultur im deutschen Kaiserreich* (Frankfurt am Main, 1990), pp. 422–40.

Bürgerliche Kultur und künstlerische Avantgarde. Kultur und Politik im deutschen Kaiserreich, 1870–1918 (Frankfurt am Main and Berlin, 1994).

Imperial Germany, 1867–1918. Politics, Culture and Society in an Authoritarian State (London, 1995).

(ed.), *Kultur und Krieg. Die Rolle der Intellektuellen, Künstler und Schriftsteller im Ersten Weltkrieg* (Munich, 1996).

'German Artists, Intellectuals and the Meaning of the War, 1914–1918', in: John Horne (ed.), *State, Society and Mobilization in Europe during the First World War* (Cambridge, 1997), pp. 21–38.

(ed.), *Die ungleichen Partner. Deutsch-Britische Beziehungen im 19. und 20. Jahrhundert* (Stuttgart, 1999).

Moses, John A., *The Politics of Illusion. The Fischer Controversy in German Historiography* (London, 1975).

Mosse, George L., *Towards the Final Solution. A History of European Racism* (Madison, Wis., 1978).

Fallen Soliders. Reshaping the Memory of the World Wars (Oxford, 1990).

Müller, Karl Alexander von, 'Deutschland und Frankreich', *Süddeutsche Monatshefte* 12/1 (March 1915), pp. 315–29.
  Deutschlands Kampf auf Leben und Tod. Zwei Kriegs-Vorträge von Dr. Karl Alexander von Müller und Wilhelm Seitz (Munich, 1917).
  Mars und Venus. Erinnerungen, 1914–1919 (Stuttgart, 1954).
  Im Wandel einer Zeit. Erinnerungen, 1919–1932, edited by Otto Alexander von Müller (Munich, 1966).

Naumann, Friedrich, *Mitteleuropa* (Berlin, 1915).
Nicolai, Walter, *Nachrichtendienst und Volksstimmung im Weltkrieg* (Berlin, 1920).

Oncken, Hermann, 'Deutschland und England', *Süddeutsche Monatshefte* 11/2 (September 1914), pp. 801–25.
Oppelland, Torsten, *Reichstag und Aussenpolitik im Ersten Weltkrieg. Die deutschen Parteien und die Politik der USA, 1914–1918* (Düsseldorf, 1995).
Otto, Helmut, and Karl Schmiedel (eds.), *Der Erste Weltkrieg. Dokumente* (East Berlin, 1977).

Peck, Abraham J., *Radicals and Reactionaries. The Crisis of Conservatism in Wilhelmine Germany* (Cincinnati, Ohio, 1978).
Peez, Alexander von, *England und der Kontinent*, 3rd ed. (Vienna, 1909) and 8th ed. (Vienna, 1915).
Plenge, Johann, *Der Krieg und die Volkswirtschaft* (Münster, 1915).
  1789 und 1914. Die symbolischen Jahre in der Geschichte des deutschen Geistes (Berlin, 1916).
Poensgen, Oskar, *Was haben die Engländer gegen uns?* (Berlin, 1917).
Pogge von Strandmann, Hartmut (ed.), *Walther Rathenau. Notes and Diaries, 1907–1922* (Oxford, 1985).
Pohl, Hugo von, *Aus Aufzeichnungen und Briefen während der Kriegszeit* (Berlin, 1920).

Quidde, Ludwig, *Der deutsche Pazifismus während des Ersten Weltkrieges, 1914–1918*, edited by Karl Holl (Boppard am Rhein, 1979).

Rauschning, Hermann, *Germany's Revolution of Destruction* (London, 1939).
Reiß, Karl-Peter (ed.), *Von Bassermann zu Stresemann. Die Sitzungen des national-liberalen Zentralvorstandes, 1912–1917* (Düsseldorf, 1967).
Rettallack, James N., *Notables of the Right. The Conservative Party and Political Mobilization in Germany, 1876–1918* (London and Boston, 1988).
Reventlow, Count Ernst zu, *England der Feind* (Stuttgart and Berlin, 1914).
  Der Vampir des Festlandes. Eine Darstellung der englischen Politik nach ihren Triebkräften, Mitteln und Wirkungen, 3rd ed. (Berlin, 1915).
  Vampire of the Continent (New York, 1916).
  Indien. Seine Bedeutung für Großbritannien, Deutschland und die Zukunft der Welt (Berlin, 1917).
  Brauchen wir die flandrische Küste? (Berlin, 1917).
  Von Potsdam nach Doorn, 5th ed. (Berlin, 1940).

Rich, Norman, *Hitler's War Aims. Ideology, the Nazi State and the Course of Expansion*, 2 vols. (London, 1973–4).

Riesser, Jakob, *England und Wir. Finanzielle und wirtschaftliche Kriegswirkungen in England und Deutschland*, 2nd ed. (Leipzig, 1915).

Ritter, Gerhard, *The Sword and the Scepter. The Problem of Militarism in Germany*, translated by Heinz Norden, 4 vols. (Coral Gables, Fla., 1969–73).

Röhl, John C.G., 'Admiral von Müller and the Approach of War, 1911–1914', *Historical Journal* 12 (1969), pp. 651–78.

'An der Schwelle zum Weltkrieg. Eine Dokumentation über den "Kriegsrat" vom 8 Dezember 1912', *Militärgeschichtliche Mitteilungen* 26 (1977), pp. 77–134.

'Die Generalprobe. Zur Geschichte und Bedeutung des "Kriegsrats" vom 8. Dezember 1912', in: Wilhelm Alff (ed.), *Deutschlands Sonderung von Europa, 1862–1945* (Frankfurt am Main, 1984), pp. 149–224.

'Kaiser Wilhelm II and German Anti-Semitism', in: Röhl, *The Kaiser and His Court. Wilhelm II and the Government of Germany* (Cambridge, 1994), pp. 190–212.

'Der Kaiser und England', in: Wilfried Rogasch (ed.), *Victoria & Albert, Vicky & the Kaiser. Ein Kapitel deutsch-englischer Familiengeschichte* (Berlin, 1997), pp. 165–84.

Rohrbach, Paul, *Warum es der deutsche Krieg ist!* (Stuttgart and Bonn, 1915).

Rosenbach, Harald, *Das deutsche Reich, Großbritannien und der Transvaal. Anfänge deutsch-britischer Entfremdung* (Göttingen, 1993).

Rürup, Reinhard, '"Der Geist von 1914" in Deutschland. Kriegsbegeisterung und Ideologisierung des Krieges im Ersten Weltkrieg', in: Bernd Hüppauf (ed.), *Ansichten vom Krieg. Vergleichende Studien zum Ersten Weltkrieg in Literatur und Gesellschaft* (Königstein, 1984), pp. 1–30.

Schädlich, Karl-Heinz, 'Der "Unabhängige Ausschuß für einen deutschen Frieden" als Zentrum der Annexionspropaganda im Ersten Weltkrieg', in: Fritz Klein et al. (eds.), *Politik im Krieg. Studien zur Politik der deutschen herrschenden Klassen im Ersten Weltkrieg* (East Berlin, 1964), pp. 50–65.

Schäfer, Dietrich, *Mein Leben* (Berlin and Leipzig, 1926).

Shand, James D., 'Doves among the Eagles. German Pacifists and Their Government during World War I', *Journal of Contemporary History* 10/1 (1975), pp. 95–108.

Scheck, Raffael, 'Der Kampf des Tirpitz Kreises um den uneingeschränkten U-Boot-Krieg und einen politischen Kurswechsel im deutschen Kaiserreich, 1916–1917', *Militärgeschichtliche Mitteilungen* 55 (1996), pp. 66–91.

Alfred von Tirpitz and German Right-Wing Politics, 1914–1930 (Atlantic Highlands, 1998).

Scheler, Max, *Der Genius des Krieges und der deutsche Krieg* (Leipzig, 1915).

Scherer, André and Jacques Grunewald (eds.), *L'Allemagne et les problèmes de la paix pendant la Première Guerre Mondiale. Documents extraits des archives de l'office allemand des affaires étrangères*, 4 vols. (Paris, 1966–78).

Schmidt, Gerhard, 'Der deutsch-englische Gegensatz im Zeitalter des Imperialismus', in: Henning Kohler (ed.), *Deutschland und der Westen* (West Berlin, 1984), pp. 59–81.

Schmidt, H.D., 'The Idea and Slogan of "Perfidious Albion"', *Journal of Historical Ideas* 14 (1953), pp. 604–16.

'Anti-Western and Anti-Jewish Tradition in German Historical Thought', *Year Book of the Leo Baeck Institute* 4 (1959), pp. 37–60.

Schulthess' Europäischer Geschichtskalender, Neue Folge, vols. 30–34, 1914–1918 (Munich, 1917–20).

Schulze-Gaevernitz, Gerhard von, *Britischer Imperialismus und englischer Freihandel zu Beginn des zwanzigsten Jahrhunderts* (Leipzig, 1906).

England und Deutschland, 3rd ed. (Berlin, 1911).

Freie Meere! (Stuttgart and Berlin, 1915).

Schütze, Woldemar, *Englands Blutschuld gegen die weiße Rasse* (Berlin, 1914).

Schwabe, Klaus, 'Zur politischen Haltung der deutschen Professoren im Ersten Weltkrieg', *Historische Zeitschrift* 192 (1961), pp. 601–34.

Wissenschaft und Kriegsmoral. Die deutschen Hochschullehrer und die politischen Grundfragen des Ersten Weltkrieges (Göttingen, 1969).

'Anti-Americanism within the German Right', *Jahrbuch für Amerikastudien* 21 (1976), pp. 89–107.

Selig, Wolfram, *Paul Nikolaus Cossmann und die süddeutschen Monatshefte von 1914–1918. Ein Beitrag zur Geschichte der nationalen Publizistik im Ersten Weltkrieg* (Osnabrück, 1967).

Sieferle, Rolf Peter, 'Der deutsch-englische Gegensatz und die "Ideen von 1914"', in: Gottfried Niedhart (ed.), *Das kontinentale Europa und die britischen Inseln. Wahrnehmungsmuster und Wechselwirkungen seit der Antika* (Mannheim, 1993), pp. 139–60.

Sigel, Robert, 'Die Lensch–Cunow–Haenisch Gruppe. Ihr Einfluss auf die Ideologie der deutschen Sozialdemokratie im Ersten Weltkrieg', *Internationale wissenschaftliche Korrespondenz zur Geschichte der deutschen Arbeiterbewegung* 11 (1975), pp. 421–36.

Simplicissimus, *Gott strafe England!* (Munich, 1915).

Smith, Woodruff D., *The Ideological Origins of Nazi Imperialism* (Oxford, 1986).

Sombart, Werner, *Händler und Helden. Patriotische Besinnungen* (Munich, 1915).

Spahn, Martin, *Im Kampf um unsere Zukunft* (Mönchen-Gladbach, 1915).

Spengler, Oswald, *Der Untergang des Abendlandes*, 2 vols. (Munich, 1918–21).

Preußentum und Sozialismus (Munich, 1920).

Briefe, 1913–1936, edited by Anton M. Koktanek (Munich, 1963).

Spies, Heinrich, *Deutschlands Feind! England und die Vorgeschichte des Weltkrieges* (Berlin, 1915).

Springmann, Theodor, *Deutschland und der Orient* (Hagen in Westfalen, 1915).

Stark, Gary D., *Entrepreneurs of Ideology. Neoconservative Publishers in Germany, 1890–1933* (Chapel Hill, N.C., 1981).

Staude, John Raphael, *Max Scheler, 1874–1928. An Intellectual Portrait* (New York, 1967).

Stegmann, Dirk, *Die Erben Bismarcks. Parteien und Verbände in der Spätphase des Wilhelminischen Deutschlands. Sammlungspolitik, 1897–1918* (Cologne and West Berlin, 1970).

'Die deutsche Inlandspropaganda 1917/18. Zum innenpolitischen Machtkampf zwischen OHL und ziviler Reichsleitung in der Endphase des Kaiserreiches', *Militärgeschichtliche Mitteilungen* 12 (1972), pp. 75–103.

Steinberg, Jonathan, *Yesterday's Deterrent. Tirpitz and the Birth of the German Battle Fleet* (London, 1965).

Steiner, Zara, *Britain and the Origins of the First World War* (London, 1977).

Stern, Fritz, *The Politics of Cultural Despair. A Study in the Rise of the Germanic Ideology* (Berkeley, Calif., 1961).

Stevenson, David, *The First World War and International Politics* (Oxford, 1988).

Stibbe, Matthew, 'Vampire of the Continent. German Anglophobia during the First World War, 1914–1918', D.Phil. thesis (University of Sussex, 1997).

'Kaiser Wilhelm II. The Hohenzollerns at War', in: Matthew Hughes and Matthew Seligmann (eds.), *Leadership in Conflict, 1914–1918* (London, 2000), pp. 265–83.

'German Historians' Views of England during the First World War', in: Stefan Berger, Peter Lambert and Peter Schumann (eds.), *A Dialogue of the Deaf? Historiographical Connections between Britain and Germany, c. 1750–2000*, (Göttingen, forthcoming).

Strecker, Karl, *England im Spiegel der Kulturmenschheit* (Munich, 1915).

Stresemann, Gustav, *Deutsches Ringen und Deutsches Hoffen* (Berlin, 1914).

Englands Wirtschaftskrieg gegen Deutschland (Stuttgart, 1915).

Das deutsche Wirtschaftsleben im Kriege (Leipzig, 1915).

Thieme, Hartmut, *Nationalliberalismus in der Krise. Die nationalliberale Fraktion des Preußischen Abgeordnetenhauses, 1914–1918* (Boppard am Rhein, 1963).

Thimme, Annelise, *Hans Delbrück als Kritiker der Wilhelminischen Epoche* (Düsseldorf, 1955).

Thimme, Friedrich (ed.), *Bethmann Hollwegs Kriegsreden* (Stuttgart and Berlin, 1919).

Tirpitz, Alfred von, *Erinnerungen* (Leipzig, 1919).

Deutsche Ohnmachtspolitik im Weltkriege (Hamburg and Berlin, 1926).

Troeltsch, Ernst, *Der Kulturkrieg* (Berlin, 1915).

Ullrich, Volker, *Kriegsalltag. Hamburg im Ersten Weltkrieg* (Cologne, 1982).

Ungern-Sternberg, Jürgen von, 'Eduard Meyer und die deutsche Propaganda zu Beginn des Ersten Weltkrieges', *Wissenschaftliche Zeitschrift der Humboldt-Universität zu Berlin, Reihe Geistes- und Sozialwissenschaften* 40 (1991), pp. 37–43.

Ungern-Sternberg, Jürgen von and Wolfgang von Ungern-Sternberg, *Der Aufruf an die Kulturwelt. Das Manifest der 93 und die Anfänge der Kriegspropaganda im Ersten Weltkrieg* (Stuttgart, 1996).

Unus, Walter, *England als Henker Frankreichs. Ein Kampf um die Weltherrschaft und sein Ende* (Braunschweig, 1915).

Verhey, Jeffrey T., 'Some Lessons of the War. The Discourse on Propaganda and Public Opinion in Germany in the 1920s', in: Bernd Hüppauf (ed.), *War, Violence and the Modern Condition* (Berlin and New York, 1997), pp. 99–117.

The Spirit of 1914. Militarism, Myth and Mobilization in Germany (Cambridge, 2000).

Vincent, C. Paul, *The Politics of Hunger. The Allied Blockade of Germany, 1915–1919* (Athens, Ohio, and London, 1985).

Weidig, Friedrich, *An Albion!* (Munich, 1914).

Weinberg, Gerhard, *The Foreign Policy of Hitler's Germany*, 2 vols. (Chicago, 1970–1980).

'Hitler and England, 1933–1945. Pretense and Reality', in: *Germany, Hitler and World War II* (Cambridge, 1995), pp. 85–94.

Westarp, Kuno von, *Konservative Politik im letzten Jahrzehnt des Kaiserreiches*, 2 vols. (Berlin, 1935).

Wieland, Lothar, *Belgien 1914. Die Frage des belgischen 'Franktireurkrieges' und die deutsche öffentliche Meinung von 1914 bis 1936* (Frankfurt am Main, 1984).

'Der deutsche Englandhaß im Ersten Weltkrieg und seine Vorgeschichte', in: Wilhelm Alff (ed.), *Deutschlands Sonderung von Europa, 1862–1945* (Frankfurt am Main, 1984), pp. 317–53.

Williams, John, *The Home Fronts. Britain, France and Germany, 1914–1918* (London, 1972).

Winzen, Peter, 'Treitschke's Influence on the Rise of anti-British Nationalism in Germany', in: Paul Kennedy and Anthony Nicholls (eds.), *Nationalist and Racialist Movements in Britain and Germany before 1914* (Oxford, 1981), pp. 154–70.

Woerden, A.V.N. van, 'Hitler, Duitsland en de Engelse Wereldmacht', *Tijdschrift voor Geschiedenis* 77 (1964), pp. 403–38.

Wolff, Theodor, *The Eve of 1914* (London, 1935).

Tagebücher, 1914–1919. Der Erste Weltkrieg und die Entstehung der Weimarer Republik in Tagebüchern, Leitartikeln und Briefen des Chefredakteurs am "Berliner Tageblatt" und Mitbegründers der "Deutschen Demokratischen Partei", edited by Bernd Sösemann, 2 vols. (Boppard am Rhein, 1984).

Wortmann, Karl, *Geschichte der Deutschen Vaterlandspartei, 1917–1918* (Halle, 1926).

Young, Harry F., *Prince Lichnowsky and the Great War* (Athens, Ga., 1977).

Zechlin, Egmont, 'Deutschland zwischen Kabinettskrieg und Wirtschaftskrieg', *Historische Zeitschrift* 199 (1964), pp. 347–458.

Zelinsky, Hartmut, *Richard Wagner. Ein deutsches Thema*, 3rd ed. (West Berlin and Vienna, 1983).

Sieg oder Untergang. Sieg und Untergang. Kaiser Wilhelm II., die Werk-Idee Richard Wagners und der Weltkampf (Munich, 1990).

Zentralstelle für Volkswohlfahrt (ed.), *Deutsche Reden in schwerer Zeit* (Berlin, 1914).

Zorn, Wolfgang, *Bayerns Geschichte im 20. Jahrhundert* (Munich, 1986).

Index

Index

Studies in the Social and Cultural History of Modern Warfare

Titles in the series:

10 *The Spirit of 1914: Militarism, Myth and Mobilization in Germany*
    Jeffrey Verhey
    ISBN 0 521 77137 4

11 *German Anglophobia and the Great War, 1914–1918*
    Matthew Stibbe
    ISBN 0 521 78296 1